Planning for PKI

**Best Practices Guide
for Deploying
Public Key Infrastructure**

Planning for PKI

**Best Practices Guide
for Deploying
Public Key Infrastructure**

Russ Housley
Tim Polk

Wiley Computer Publishing

John Wiley & Sons, Inc.

NEW YORK · CHICHESTER · WEINHEIM · BRISBANE · SINGAPORE · TORONTO

Publisher: Robert Ipsen
Editor: Carol A. Long
Assistant Editor: Adaobi Obi
Managing Editor: Gerry Fahey
Text Design & Composition: Publishers' Design and Production Services, Inc.

Designations used by companies to distinguish their products are often claimed as trademarks. In all instances where John Wiley & Sons, Inc., is aware of a claim, the product names appear in initial capital or ALL CAPITAL LETTERS. Readers, however, should contact the appropriate companies for more complete information regarding trademarks and registration.

This book is printed on acid-free paper. ∞

Published by John Wiley & Sons, Inc.

Published simultaneously in Canada.

This publication is designed to provide accurate and authoritative information in regard to the subject matter covered. It is sold with the understanding that the publisher is not engaged in professional services. If professional advice or other expert assistance is required, the services of a competent professional person should be sought.

Printed in the United States of America.

10 9 8 7 6 5 4 3 2 1

Wiley Networking Council Series

Series Editors:

Scott Bradner
Senior Technical Consultant, Havard University
Vinton Cerf
Senior Vice President, MCIWorldCom
Lyman Chapin
Chief Scientist, BBN/GTE

Books in series:

- *WAN Survival Guide: Strategies for VPNs and Multiserivce Networks*
  Howard C. Berkowitz
  ISBN: 0-471-38428-3
- *ISP Survival Guide: Strategies for Running a Competitive ISP*
  Geoff Huston
  ISBN: 0-471-31499-4
- *Implementing IPsec: Making Security Work on VPN's, Intranets, and Extranets*
  Elizabeth Kaufman, Andrew Newman
  ISBN 0-471-34467-2
- *Internet Performance Survival Guide: QoS Strategies for Multiservice Networks*
  Geoff Huston
  ISBN: 0-471-37808-9
- *ISP Liability Survival Guide: Strategies for Managing Copyright, Spam, Cache, and Privacy Regulations*
  Tim Casey
  ISBN 0-471-37748-1
- *VPN Applications Guide: Real Solutions for Enterprise Networks*
  Dave McDysan
  ISBN: 0-471-37175-0
- *Converged Networks and Services: Internetworking IP and the PSTN*
  Igor Faynberg, Hui-Lan Lu, and Lawrence Gabuzda
  ISBN 0-471-35644-1

Contents

Networking Council Foreword

The Networking Council Series was created in 1998 within Wiley's Computer Publishing group to fill an important gap in networking literature. Many current technical books are long on details but short on understanding. They do not give the reader a sense of where, in the universe of practical and theoretical knowledge, the technology might be useful in a particular organization. The Networking Council Series is concerned more with how to think clearly about networking issues than with promoting the virtues of a particular technology—how to relate new information to the rest of what the reader knows and needs, so the reader can develop a customized strategy for vendor and product selection, outsourcing, and design.

In *Planning for PKI: Best Practices Guide for Deploying Public Key Infrastructure* by Russ Housley and Tim Polk, you'll see the hallmarks of Networking Council books— examination of the advantages and disadvantages, strengths and weaknesses of market-ready technology, useful ways to think about options pragmatically, and direct links to business practices and needs. Disclosure of pertinent background issues needed to understand who supports a technology and how it was developed is another goal of all Networking Council books.

The Networking Council Series is aimed at satisfying the need for perspective in an evolving data and telecommunications world filled with hyperbole, speculation, and unearned optimism. In *Planning for PKB: Best Practices Guide for Deploying Public Key Infrastructure*, you'll get clear information from experienced practitioners.

We hope you enjoy the read. Let us know what you think. Feel free to visit the Networking Council web site at www.wiley.com/networkingcouncil.

Scott Bradner
Senior Technical Consultant, Harvard University

Vinton Cerf
Senior Vice President, MCIWorldCom

Lyman Chapin
Chief Scientist, BBN/GTE

Acknowledgments

All mistakes and incorrect predictions are ours. Numerous people have contributed to this book, directly or indirectly. Most notably, we could never have completed the book without the patience and support of our wives and families. We need to recognize the following people. Some provided review, and others provided technical input. Thank you for the help: Al Arsenault, Tom Berson, David Cooper, Leslie DeAnda, Steve Dougherty, Yuriy Dzambasow, Trevor Freeman, Rich Guida, Peter Gutmann, Nelson Hastings, Carl Hauser, Burt Kaliski, Joe Mettle, Aldo Nevarez, Karen Randall, Randy Sabett, Alice Sturgeon, Marianne Swanson, Wunna Tun, and Clark Wagner. We would also like to thank Carol Long and Scott Bradner for their guidance and encouragement.

Finally, researchers, standards developers, and application developers have been developing this technology for the last 25 years. We hope that we have provided the appropriate credit to all of those who came before us.

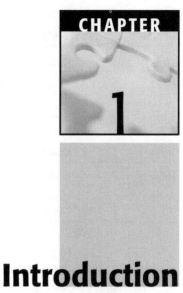

CHAPTER 1

Introduction

In the early days of the Internet, no one worried about security. Those days are long gone. Today, everyone is concerned about protecting electronic information. The question is not whether security is necessary, but how to implement it. Public key infrastructure (PKI) is a particularly powerful information protection tool for systems and services on the Internet. PKI has captured the imagination of security advocates over the past few years, but it has been in development for over a quarter of a century.

While we were still in high school, some very smart gentlemen invented public key cryptography. Public key cryptography provides the basis for digital signatures and management of symmetric cryptographic keys. Public key cryptography remained a research topic for years. Table 1.1 shows a few milestones in the development of public key cryptography. Application developers were not ready to use public key cryptography, and a standard mechanism for distributing public keys was needed.

Early works discuss a bulletin board system that distributed public keys. Unfortunately, it was difficult to figure out which posted public key belonged to which user. Certificates were invented to solve this problem. They bind an identity and a public key. Table 1.2 shows a few milestones in the development of public key certificates. Application developers were still not satisfied, though. They needed an infrastructure to support certificate generation, distribution, and revocation.

Applications and widely available PKI are needed to fully leverage public key cryptography. Unfortunately, PKI-enabled applications cannot flourish without a widely available PKI, and a widely available PKI will not be developed without applications

Table 1.1   A Brief History of Public Key Cryptography

YEAR	EVENT
1976	Diffie, Hellman, and Merkle invent public key cryptography
1977	Rivest, Shamir, and Adleman invent the RSA algorithm
1985	Kiblitz and Miller propose elliptic curves for cryptography
1993	RSA Labs publish PKCS #1
1994	DSA Federal Standard (FIPS PUB 186)
1995	DSA Banking Standard (ANSI X9.30)
2000	D-H, RSA, and ECDH will complete key management standards (ANSI X9.42, X9.44, X9.63)

Table 1.2   A Brief History of Certificates

YEAR	EVENT
1978	Lohnfelder invents the certificate (BS EE Thesis at MIT)
1988	X.509—Version 1 Certificates
1993	X.509—Version 2 Certificates
1996	X.509—Version 3 Certificates
1996	ABA Digital Signature Guidelines
1999	Internet PKI Certificate and CRL Profile (RFC 2459)
1999	Internet PKI Certificate Policy and Certification Practices Framework (RFC 2527)

that need it. This chicken-and-egg situation has slowly been resolved, as incremental improvements have occurred in both areas.

Today, you do not need to be an expert in public key cryptography to realize its benefits. Products are available. This book provides the information needed to select wisely from these offerings, and then successfully deploy them. The case studies at the end of the book allow you to emulate the successes and avoid the potholes found by the early adopters.

How This Book Is Organized

We organized this book into six sections. The later sections build on material presented in the earlier ones. A person familiar with public key cryptography may be able to skip the early parts, but most readers will want to read the book from front to back.

We start by introducing the technology. We present the rationale for implementing a PKI, not every detail of the technology. Building on this foundation, we present many of the technology details. We tried to avoid delving into nit-picky implementation details, but we present enough detail to be conversant with any PKI expert. In security, technology and policy always go hand in hand. The next section discusses PKI-specific policy issues. The goal of any PKI is to support security in applications, so we discuss standard PKI-enabled applications. Next, we present three case studies. Lessons learned from these pioneers will prove invaluable when deploying your own PKI. Finally, we provide our crystal ball view of the future. Only time will tell if our crystal ball was cloudy or not.

Part One: PKI Background

Part One includes three chapters, and establishes the foundation for the remainder of the book. Chapter 2, "Cryptography Primer," introduces the basics of cryptography. Chapter 3, "PKI Basics," introduces fundamental building blocks of PKI, such as certificates and certificate revocation lists (CRLs). Chapter 4, "Authentication Mechanisms," describes the evolution of authentication mechanisms. This discussion shows the value of public key cryptography and PKI. Of course, public key cryptography and PKI may be used to implement other security services. We chose authentication as an example. A similar evolution could be presented for each security service.

Part Two: PKI Details

Part Two includes seven chapters. In these chapters, we provide the information needed to select the PKI components that best fit your requirements. We also provide the information needed to design a PKI topology that best fits your network environment. Chapter 5, "PKI Components and Users," describes the various players in a PKI system. Chapter 6, "PKI Architectures," describes the many ways in which the various PKI components can be interconnected. Chapter 7, "X.509 Public Key Certificates," describes the X.509 certificate format. Chapter 8, "Certificate Revocation Lists," describes the X.509 certificate revocation list (CRL) format. Chapter 9, "Repository Protocols," discusses the various methods for distributing certificates and CRLs. Chapter 10, "Building and Validating Certification Paths," describes whether a particular certificate can be trusted. Chapter 11, "PKI Management Protocols," describes protocols for issuing and revoking certificates.

Part Three: Policy Issues

Part Three contains a single chapter. Chapter 12, "Policies, Procedures, and PKI," provides the information needed to develop certificate policies (CPs) and certification practices statements (CPSes). These documents must be developed for any PKI deployment.

Part Four: The Standard Applications

Part Four also contains a single chapter. Chapter 13, "PKI-Enabled Applications," discusses the most common applications that employ public key cryptography and X.509 certificates: S/MIME, TLS, and IPsec.

Part Five: PKI Case Studies

Part Five contains three chapters, one for each case study. Chapter 14, "Defense Message System 1.0," describes the biggest deployment of X.509 version 1 certificates. Chapter 15, "California Independent Service Operator," describes a successful deployment for the security of the California electric power grid. Chapter 16, "The Federal Bridge CA Project," describes a method that allows several independently deployed PKIs to interoperate. We hope that the lessons learned from these deployments will prove invaluable in deploying your own PKI.

Part Six: Adding Value
to PKI in the Future

Part Six contains a single chapter. Chapter 17, "Future Developments," has a structure that parallels Parts One through Four. We offer our predictions for developments in each of these areas.

Appendices

We provide supplemental information in two appendices. Appendix A, "ASN.1 Primer," provides an introduction to *Abstract Syntax Notation One*. We provide sufficient detail to read and understand the structures used in this book, not a complete coverage of the topic. Appendix B, "Object Identifiers," provides several ways to obtain object identifiers. Most new PKI deployments require at least one object identifier assignment.

Who Should Read This Book

This book is intended for the Chief Technology Officer (CTO) or the person who the CTO assigns to implement a PKI. It is a pragmatic guide for the planning, deployment, operation, and maintenance of a successful PKI. It is not a guide for developers. We recommend that developers refer to the IETF standards for details of the syntax and semantics of PKI-related protocols.

While there are many pitfalls to PKI, we believe that the benefits grossly outweigh the aggravation. It is our hope that this book will help you achieve the benefits and avoid the hazards.

Cryptography Primer

This book is not about cryptography; however, the reader must have a fundamental understanding of cryptography to fully understand public key infrastructure (PKI). For this reason, we include this primer. For a more complete coverage of cryptography, we suggest [KAHN67], [MENE97], and [SCHN96]. Kahn provides a remarkably complete history of cryptography from its origins to the middle of the twentieth century. Menezes, van Oorschot, and Vanstone provide an encyclopedia of known techniques with an emphasis on the secure and the practical. Schneier provides a complete discussion of the applications of cryptography with a focus on engineers and computer programmers.

The word *cryptography* means hidden or secret writing. Cryptography is generally thought of as the scrambling, and the unscrambling, of private messages. A message is scrambled to keep it private or to protect its *confidentiality*. Modern cryptographic techniques are also used to determine whether a message has been changed since it was created and to identify the message sender. An unaltered message has *integrity*. Knowledge of message origin is *authentication*.

A cryptographic algorithm defines the series of steps that a sender takes to scramble a private message and the series of steps that a receiver takes to unscramble it. Most cryptographic algorithms use two inputs to scramble the message, protect its integrity, or authenticate its source. The first input is the message content, and the second is a secret value known as a *key*. There are several different types of cryptographic algorithms that are differentiated by the security services that they provide and the type of keys that they employ.

Symmetric Cryptography

In symmetric cryptography, both the sender and the receiver use the same key value. As a result, symmetric key systems are sometimes called *shared secret* key systems. When Alice wants to send a private message to Bob, she selects an encryption algorithm and a key that Bob knows. Alice encrypts the plaintext message using the encryption algorithm and the key, obtaining ciphertext. Alice sends the ciphertext to Bob. Bob uses the decryption algorithm and key to recover the plaintext from the ciphertext (Figure 2.1).

For an attacker, Charlie, to obtain the plaintext, he must guess or intercept the key. The most difficult keys to guess are random bit strings. Charlie may use a computer to try all possible key values. Such a brute-force attack will take centuries on many cooperating fast computers if the key is long. To make it difficult for Charlie to intercept the key during distribution, it must be encrypted during transmission. Secure key distribution of shared secret keys is a difficult task, and some of the tools needed to do it are discussed later in this chapter.

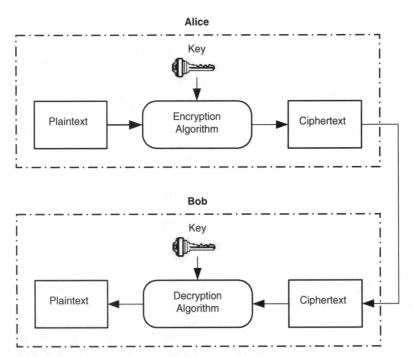

Figure 2.1   Symmetric encryption and decryption.

There are two primary symmetric encryption algorithm types: *stream ciphers* and *block ciphers*. Stream ciphers operate on the plaintext one bit at a time. (A few stream algorithms operate an octet at a time, but they are not the normal case.) RC4 is a well-known stream cipher. Block ciphers operate on a group of bits called a *block*.

The Data Encryption Standard (DES), also known as the Data Encryption Algorithm (DEA), is the most well-known symmetric block cipher. The U.S. Government made DES a standard in 1977, and many people adopted DES because the U.S. Government was standing behind it. DES is published as FIPS PUB 46 [FIPS46] and ANSI X3.92 [X392]. It uses a 56-bit key, and encrypts a 64-bit block with each operation. Many cryptographers are concerned about the DES key length; they believe that a longer key is needed to provide security. Computing power has increased many fold since DES became a standard in 1977, and a 56-bit random key is no longer sufficient to protect against a brute-force attack [EFF98].

Using the DES encryption multiple times can increase the effective key size [TUCH79, X952] and thus its strength. Triple-DES involves the encryption with one key, followed by the decryption of the resulting ciphertext with a second key, followed by the encryption of the result with a third key. This is called *Three-Key Triple-DES*. If the same key value is used for the first and third keys, the algorithm is called *Two-Key Triple-DES*. Both Two-Key Triple-DES and Three-Key Triple-DES are significantly stronger than DES.

The National Institute of Standards and Technology (NIST) is in the process of defining a replacement for DES. The replacement algorithm, called *Advanced Encryption Standard* (AES), will be much stronger than DES and much more efficient than Triple-DES. AES will support three key sizes: 128, 192, and 256 bits. The AES block size will be 128 bits.

In order to encrypt arbitrary messages with a block cipher, the blocks must be processed one after another. The handling of the blocks is called the *mode of operation*. [FIPS81] defines four common modes of operation:

- Electronic Codebook (ECB)

- Cipher Block Chaining (CBC)

- Cipher Feedback (CFB)

- Output Feedback (OFB)

CBC is by far the most common. CBC encryption works as follows. The message is broken into a sequence of blocks, and the last block is padded to create a complete block if necessary. A random block, called the *initialization vector* (IV), is generated. Each block is XORed (that is, bitwise exclusive OR) with the ciphertext from the previous block before it is encrypted. The IV serves as the previous ciphertext block for the first plaintext block. The IV need not be kept secret. If one block obtains an error in transmission, the decryption will synchronize after two garbled blocks. When the message is decrypted, only the block that contains the transmission error and the block that follows will be garbled (Figure 2.2).

Alice

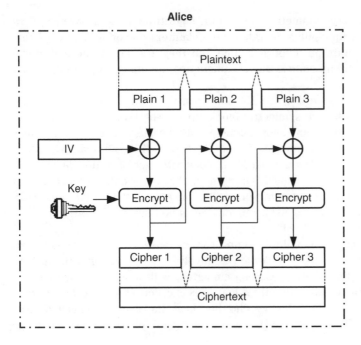

Bob

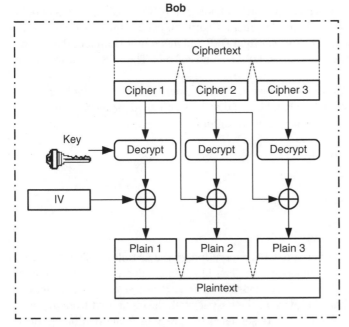

Figure 2.2   Cipher Block Chaining (CBC) mode.

Symmetric Integrity Functions

A value that is carried with the message and used to ensure that the message sent by Alice is the message received by Bob is called an *Integrity Check Value* (ICV), a *Message Integrity Check* (MIC), or a *Message Authentication Code* (MAC). Unfortunately, all of these terms are in common use.

DES MAC uses DES encryption in CBC mode to provide integrity. An IV of all zero bits is used, which is the same as having no IV at all. Instead of transmitting the ciphertext blocks, all except the last one are discarded. Alice transmits the last block, or a portion of it, along with her message to Bob. Bob performs the same encryption on the received message. If the received MAC and the locally computed one match, then Bob can be sure that the received message was not altered (Figure 2.3).

If Alice wants to provide confidentiality by encrypting with DES, and authentication and integrity by computing a DES MAC, independent keys must be used for the two operations. Furthermore, it is best to compute the MAC, and then encrypt the message as well as the MAC.

Since both Alice and Bob have access to the key, either party can compute a MAC. The MAC ensures that Charlie, the attacker, cannot alter the message without Bob detecting it. However, the MAC is not helpful in resolving disputes between Alice and Bob. Using the key, either Alice or Bob can generate an altered message and an associated valid MAC. Alice and Bob can each provide a different message to a judge, and both messages will have a valid MAC. In addition, the symmetric key must be provided to the judge for him or her to validate the MAC. This disclosure permits the judge to generate another altered message with a valid MAC.

One-way hash functions may also be used to provide integrity. One-way hash functions operate on an arbitrary-length-input message and produce a fixed-length output. Many functions have this property, but a one-way hash function must also have two additional properties:

- It is computationally infeasible to recreate the input message from the hash value.

- It is computationally infeasible to construct two different input messages that produce the same output hash value.

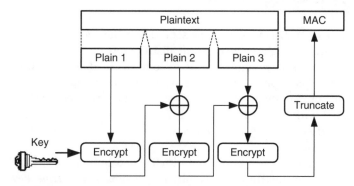

Figure 2.3   Message Authentication Code (MAC).

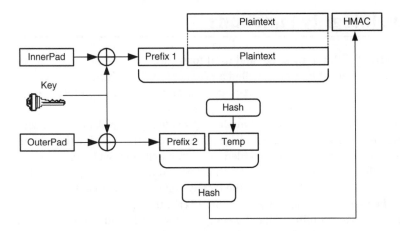

HMAC = Hash ((Key XOR OuterPad) || Hash ((Key XOR InnerPad) || Plaintext))

Figure 2.4   Keyed Hashing for Message Authentication (HMAC).

Any weakness in these properties may result in weakness in the integrity and authentication mechanisms that depend on the one-way hash function.

The Secure Hash Algorithm 1 (SHA-1) is the most well-known one-way hash function. It is published as FIPS PUB 180-1 [FIPS180] and ANSI X9.30-2 [X9302]. It produces a 160-bit output.

NIST is in the process of defining three additional one-way hash functions: SHA-256, SHA-384, and SHA-512. The new algorithms will provide longer hash values to offer integrity and authentication functions that are of comparable strength to the new AES encryption algorithm.

The hash-based message authentication code (HMAC) [KRAW97] function is the most common method of using a shared secret, or key, with a one-way hash function to create an integrity check value (Figure 2.4). This method applies the one-way hash function twice.

Asymmetric Key Management

When Alice wants to encrypt or MAC a message being sent to Bob, the two parties must first share the same symmetric key value. The creation, distribution, use, archive, and destruction of that key is called *key management*. If Alice needs to share keys with Bob, Bruce, Burt, Barney, Brad, and Bill, then she will need to store six separate keys. The storage technique must protect the keys from disclosure, and it must ensure that the keys remain associated with the correct party. If Bill's key and Bob's key are swapped in Alice's protected key storage, then Bill may be able to decrypt messages that Alice intended only for Bob.

You can avoid many of the complexities associated with the distribution and storage of symmetric keys by using asymmetric cryptography to provide *just-in-time* key establishment.

Asymmetric cryptography is also called *public key cryptography* because there are two distinct keys, one that must be kept private and one that can be made public. The two keys are complementary, but the value of the private key cannot be determined from the public key. Public key cryptography greatly simplifies the management of symmetric keys used for encryption or integrity by significantly reducing the number of keys that need to be stored for an extended period. Generally, the symmetric keys are used for a short period of time and are then discarded. Only the private key must be protected for an extended period. Further, public keys can be distributed openly since they do not need to be kept secret.

Public key cryptography is not generally used to encrypt user data. Public key algorithms require significantly more computational power than comparable symmetric encryption algorithms. Thus, the expensive public key operations are performed infrequently for the establishment of symmetric keys; then the efficient symmetric algorithm is used to encrypt the bulk of the data.

There are two key management public key algorithm types:

Key agreement. With key agreement algorithms, Alice and Bob exchange public keys, and then combine their own private key with the public key of the other party to compute a symmetric key that is known only to the two parties. The Diffie-Hellman algorithm [DIFF76] (Figure 2.5) is the most well-known key agreement algorithm.

Key transport. With key transport algorithms, Alice creates a symmetric key and encrypts it with Bob's public key, and then Bob uses his own private key to decrypt the value and recover the symmetric key. The RSA algorithm [RIVE78] (Figure 2.6) is the most well-known key transport algorithm.

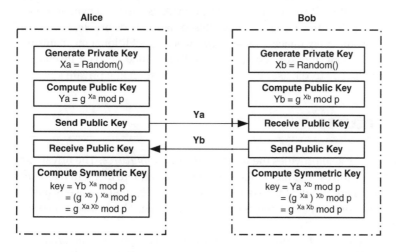

Alice and Bob have prior agreement on the generator, g, and the prime modulus, p.
Alice and Bob compute the same symmetric key, $g^{Xa\,Xb}$ mod p.
An eavesdropper cannot derive the key value from Ya and Yb.

Figure 2.5 Diffie-Hellman key agreement.

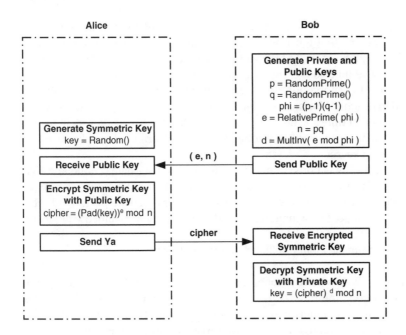

The symmetric key generated by Alice is securely transferred to Bob.
An eavesdropper cannot derive the key value from e, n, and cipher.

Figure 2.6 RSA key transport.

Authentication of the public key is needed with both key agreement and key transport algorithms. Alice must know that the public key she is using corresponds to the private key known only to Bob. If this is not the case, then Alice shares a symmetric key with an unknown party. In a few circumstances, this situation is desirable, but in general, this situation is completely unacceptable. Alice needs an additional mechanism to complement key agreement and key transport algorithms. Alice needs a mechanism that connects the public key to the user who holds the corresponding private key.

Digital Signatures

Public key cryptography also provides the basis for *digital signatures*. The private key is used to generate signatures, and the public key is used to validate them. In real-world applications, messages are not digitally signed directly. Rather, the message is hashed using a one-way hash function, and the resulting hash value, also called a *message digest*, is signed.

Unlike symmetric integrity functions, digital signatures can provide important evidence in a dispute. If Alice uses her private key to sign a message, Bob can validate it with her public key. Since Bob does not need Alice's private key to validate the signature, he does not have the information he needs to generate a valid signature on an altered message. Furthermore, the judge can use Alice's public key to validate the signed message.

There are two digital signature public key algorithm types:

Digital signature with message recovery. With these algorithms, Alice signs by encrypting the message digest with her own private key. Bob validates the signature by comparing a message digest that he computes locally with one that is obtained by decrypting the signature value with Alice's public key. If the two message digest values match exactly, then the digital signature is valid. The RSA algorithm [RIVE78] (Figure 2.7) is the most well-known digital signature with message recovery algorithm.

Digital signature without message recovery. With these algorithms, Alice uses her private key and the message digest to generate the signature value. Alice may also need to provide additional parameters, such as a unique random value.

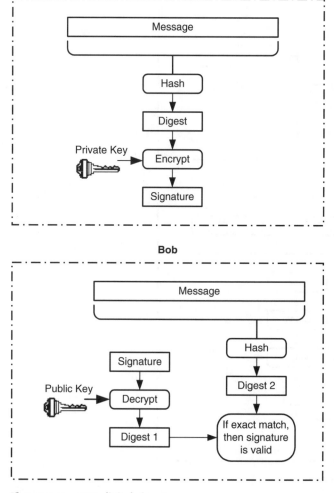

Figure 2.7   RSA digital signature.

Bob validates the the signature value with Alice's public key and a locally computed message digest to the verify function. The verify function returns a result of either valid or invalid, rather than the message digest. The Digital Signature Algorithm (DSA) [FIPS186] (Figure 2.8) is the most well-known digital signature algorithm that does not provide message recovery.

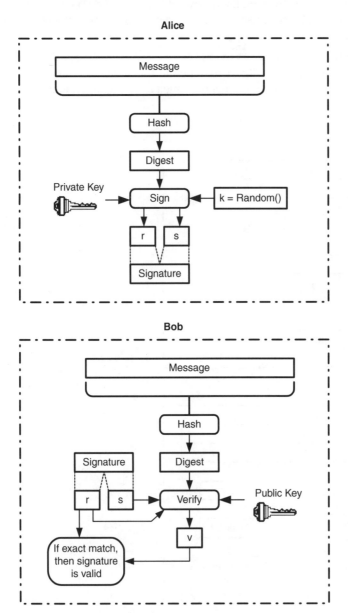

Figure 2.8 DSA digital signature.

Authentication of the public key is needed with all digital signature algorithms. Bob must know that the public key he is using corresponds to the private key known only to Alice. If this is not the case, then Bob has no proof regarding the origin of the message. Bob has evidence that the message has not been modified since the signer signed it, but he does not know who signed it. As with key management, Bob needs an additional mechanism to complement digital signature algorithms. He needs a mechanism that connects the public key to the user who holds the corresponding private key.

Public key certificates are the solution. As we will see in Chapter 3, certificates are used to bind an identity to the public key. By using certificates, Bob can be sure that he is using Alice's public key, and therefore, that Alice signed the message.

CHAPTER 3

PKI Basics

Chapter 2, "Cryptography Primer," left us with the promise of public key cryptography and some unresolved problems. First and foremost, before Alice can use a public key, she needs to know *who* has the corresponding private key. When Alice verifies a signature, she is confirming (or denying) that Bob signed the message. If someone else has the corresponding private key, he or she sent the message, not Bob. When Alice encrypts her response to Bob, she needs to be sure that only Bob can read it. If Bob does not have the corresponding private key, he will not be able to decrypt the response.

Alice also needs to know *what* applications are appropriate for Bob's key. Perhaps Bob's key should only be used to sign or encrypt electronic mail, but not to sign contracts. Finally, she needs a solution that will be *scalable*. That is, the solution must continue to work for Alice if she communicates with hundreds of people instead of just Bob.

This chapter introduces the basic tools of a PKI in a rather abstract fashion. There are two basic tools used in a PKI to determine *who* has a private key: the *public key certificate* and the *certificate revocation list*. The former will establish who, and the latter will ensure the information is up to date. The basic PKI tool that answers the question *what* the key can be used for is the *certificate policy*. The basic PKI tool for scalability—the tool that lets Alice communicate with hundreds of people—is the *certification path*.

In *Part Two*, *PKI Details*, we will revisit each of these topics in detail, devoting a chapter or more to each.

Simple Certificates

As described in Chapter 2, the basic problem with public key cryptography is determining *who* holds the corresponding private key. To answer this question, a PKI relies upon the concept of a *public key certificate*, or simply *certificate*. A certificate is the most basic element of a PKI. Each certificate contains a public key and identifies the user with the corresponding private key. For example, if Alice has a certificate with Bob's public key, she will know that Bob has the private key.

Certificates are not really a new concept to us. They will resemble a couple of everyday objects in important ways. Those everyday objects are the credit card and the business card. The features of these objects are insufficient, but we will build the "ideal certificate" from their features. Finally, we will describe real public key certificates and contrast them with the ideal certificate.

The Business Card

The business card is inescapable. It is almost impossible to return from a meeting or conference without a handful of these little paper cards. Each card identifies a particular person and provides some additional information about him or her. In general, that information will include the person's employer, telephone number, mailing address, and electronic mail address. Some people print their public key on the card as well, making this the most rudimentary form of a certificate.

Bob can distribute his business card to everyone he meets. By printing his public key on the back of his business card, Bob is declaring that he holds the corresponding private key. (Bob's card is shown in Figure 3.1.) If Alice has Bob's card, she has the public key, and she knows Bob has the private key because his name is on the front of the card. She trusts the information because she obtained it directly from Bob.

There are a number of drawbacks to this type of certificate. The user must receive the business card in person, or the user will have no basis on which to trust it. This is very limiting; all participants must have met face to face. What if Bob and Alice need to work together, but they have never met? Twenty years ago, this may not have been a realistic question, but it is a real problem today. Frequently, project teams are formed that cross geographical and organizational boundaries. There may not be a single person who has personally met every member of the team.

In addition, the information on the business card is all self-proclaimed. Bob has proclaimed that he works for Fox Consulting and that he is the Chief Technical Officer. If all of that information is true, Bob may be the ideal recipient of Alice's wonderful project idea. Of course, "Bob" may have a reason to lie, and anyone with a personal computer can generate business cards! How well does Alice know Bob? Without additional information, Alice can only be sure that the man in the gray suit introduced himself as Mr. Burton and handed her the card.

Alice also can't tell if the card is a forgery or has been altered since she received it. Anyone with a computer and a printer can create a business card. Is it real? People commonly update the information on their cards by hand. Is that Bob's handwriting with the new e-mail address? In most cases, Alice can't be sure.

Figure 3.1 Bob's business card.

It is also impossible to retrieve or correct those business cards once they are distributed. This is a problem, since the information on the card may have been true when the card was distributed, but is now false. If Bob loses his private key, it will be very difficult to contact everyone he gave a card to tell them. If the card identifies an organization, the same dilemma emerges at every job change.

Last, but not least, before Alice can use Bob's public key, she needs to type it in. That is no small feat for a 1024-bit key, much less a 2048-bit key!

A business card meets the most basic requirement for a public key certificate—it can contain the public key and identify the user with the corresponding private key. However, Alice should be nervous about implementing security with a certificate that is so easy to forge or alter. In addition, any tool that requires face-to-face meetings and retyping keys is hardly scalable.

The Credit Card

Almost everyone is familiar with the credit card. In general, a credit card does not contain a public key, so it really isn't a certificate at all. However, the basic problem is very similar. In this arena, Alice wants to determine *who* is associated with an account number. The techniques used to determine *who* provide an excellent counterpoint to the model of the business card.

The credit card certainly shares some features with the business card; it includes the name of the cardholder and the account number. If this is a corporate card, it names the company or organization as well. It is missing the contact information (for example, the telephone number and mailing address). However, it has several important features that the business card lacks. The credit card includes the logo of the issuer (for example, VISA, MasterCard, American Express, or Discover). A credit card includes an expiration date. Sometimes it includes a holographic image, and most of the information is in raised letters. Finally, the cardholder has signed it on the back. These features provide some very different properties from those we found in the business card certificates.

First, credit card use is not restricted to parties who have met. Credit cards can be used to purchase items over the Internet or by telephone. The basis for trusting credit cards does not involve the cardholders, so it doesn't matter if they have met. The credit card issuer is proclaiming this information to be true, not the cardholder. People accept the card explicitly because they trust the issuer, not because they trust the cardholder.

There are a number of features to help Alice decide if Bob's credit card issued by Trusty Cards Corporation (Figure 3.2) is genuine for *card present* transactions. People can generally tell if a credit card seems legitimate by the look and feel. If the card includes a recognizable hologram, that distinguishing characteristic makes the card more difficult to forge. The cardholder's name, account number, and expiration date are all in raised letters. It would be difficult to change that information once a card has been issued. Alice can look at the signature stripe on the back of the card. The signature is difficult to erase, so a thief would have to duplicate Bob's signature.

The Trusty Cards credit card company cannot retrieve Bob's credit card when the information becomes out of date (for example, when Bob quits paying the bill) anymore than Bob can retrieve his out-of-date business cards. However, the credit card's expiration date limits this problem. Issuers recognize up front that the information may not be good forever, so they include an expiration date. After that date, Alice knows not to accept the card. This is not a complete solution, though. Bob may quit paying the bill long before the card expires.

Finally, the credit card includes that magnetic stripe. Instead of typing the information into a computer or sales register, Alice swipes the card through a magnetic stripe reader. All the information she needs is transferred automatically into the system. This is a great improvement over typing the public key that was printed on the business card.

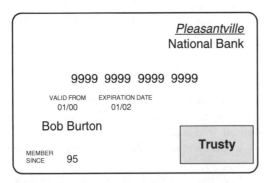

Figure 3.2   Bob's credit card.

The Ideal Certificate

The ideal certificate would combine all the features found in the business card and credit cards, but with several important additions. The ideal certificate would have the following nine properties:

1. It would be a purely digital object, so it could be distributed over the Internet and processed automatically.

2. It would contain the name of the user who holds the private key, identify the user's company or organization, and include contact information.

3. It would be easy to determine if the certificate was issued recently.

4. It would be created by a trusted party rather than the user who holds the private key.

5. Since the trusted party might create a lot of certificates, even for the same user, it should be easy to tell them apart.

6. It would be easy to determine if the ideal certificate were genuine or forged.

7. It would be tamper-proof so no one could change its contents.

8. We could immediately determine if the information on our ideal certificate is no longer current.

9. We could determine from the certificate the applications to which it applies .

Public Key Certificates

An approximation of this ideal certificate exists today. It is called a *public key certificate.*[1] A public key certificate is a purely digital object. Alice can process the certificates with her computer and she will never have to type a public key again. The public key certificate contains fields for Bob's name and his public key. Bob's certificate can indicate his company or organization along with his name, and it may include his contact information as well (especially his electronic mail address). The certificate also includes two date fields that specify an activation date and an expiration date. The certificates also contain the name of the trusted party who created the certificate. (We refer to this party as the *issuer.*) The issuer includes a unique serial number in every certificate that they create to clearly identify each certificate.

Finally, the entire contents of the certificate are protected by the issuer's digital signature. The issuer treats the certificate contents as a message and generates a digital signature.

Figure 3.3 depicts Bob's public key certificate. It was issued by the Awfully Big Certificate (ABC) company. The certificate was activated on January 10, 2000, and will expire

---

[1] There are several types of public key certificates. The information in this section assumes a certificate based on the [X.509] specification, as does the bulk of this book. Some public key certificates may omit certain fields that appear in [X.509] certificates, but they are all similar.

```
Serial Number:      48
Certificate for:    Bob Burton
Company:            Fox Consulting
Issued By:          Awfully Big Certificate Co.
Email Address:      bsmith@pleasantville.ca.us
Activation:         Jan. 10, 2000
Expiration:         Jan. 10, 2002


Public Key:         24219743597430832a2187b
                    6219a75430d843e432f21e09
                    bc080da43509843


ABC's Digital Signature

        0a213fe67de49ac8e9602046fa7de22
        39316ab233dec70095762121aef4fg6
        6854392ab02c4
```

Figure 3.3   Bob's public key certificate.

January 10, 2002. This certificate has serial number 48. It includes Bob's name, e-mail address, and says he works for Fox Consulting. It includes his public key, and includes a digital signature generated by ABC. By generating the certificate, ABC is asserting that Bob has the corresponding private key.

Alice has received a signed request for 100 widgets from Bob. She is supposed to ship them to a warehouse, not directly to Fox Consulting. She needs to decide if this is a legitimate request, and a key factor will be the digital signature. Alice can use Bob's certificate to verify his signature, as shown in Figure 3.4, if two criteria are met. First, Alice

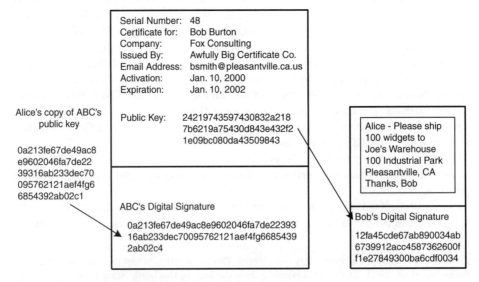

Figure 3.4   Using a certificate to verify Bob's signature.

has to trust the issuer. Second, Alice needs to have a copy of the issuer's public key. Alice can use the issuer's public key to verify that the certificate in her possession was really generated by the issuer, and that the contents have not been changed. If that succeeds, she can use the public key in the certificate to verify Bob's signature.

So, how does this stack up against our ideal certificate? The public key certificate is a digital object, and includes all the necessary information about the user. The activation and expiration dates satisfy our need to determine if the certificate is current. The issuer's name and signature support our concept of a trusted issuer, and the issuer's signature can be used to verify its authenticity. Together, the issuer name and serial number uniquely describe a particular certificate. These features satisfy the first six properties of the ideal certificate very nicely.

The seventh property is a bit more problematic. How can we make the certificate tamper-proof? We can't, but the issuer's signature provides the next best thing. The signature makes the certificate *tamper-evident*. If anyone changes the contents of Bob's certificate, Alice can detect it by treating the certificate contents as a message and verifying the digital signature. If the digital signature does not verify, the contents have been changed or the certificate is a fake. Either way, Alice knows she can't trust it.

The eighth property is even more problematic. How can Alice tell from the certificate if it should not be trusted because the contents are no longer valid? Can Alice tell from the certificate if Bob dies, quits his job, or is fired? No. She can't tell if Bob's certificate is no longer valid, anymore than she can tell if Bob's credit card has been revoked. Alice needs to supplement Bob's unexpired certificate with an additional tool to tell her if the certificate is still trustworthy. We haven't addressed the ninth property yet, either. How can Alice decide if a certificate is good for a particular application?

The public key certificate appears to be a rather nice tool, but it hasn't resolved problems 8 and 9. It has introduced a new problem as well—now we have to place our trust in an issuer rather than a user. Who is going to be that trusted party? How do we decide if we trust them? How do we get their public key? If Alice isn't familiar with the issuer, she will have to obtain enough information to determine whether those certificates are trustworthy. Every time Alice receives a certificate from a new issuer, she will have some work to do. (Of course, Alice will be able to trust any additional certificates she encounters from that issuer in the future.)

The following sections introduce the rest of our PKI tools. These tools mitigate these three shortcomings.

Certificate Revocation List

Let's deal next with the eighth feature of our ideal certificate: determining if the certificate contents are current. Consider Bob, who changed jobs soon after obtaining a public key certificate. The contact information has changed, and he may have a new public key as well. Bob would like to be sure that Alice, and the rest of the world, get rid of his old certificate. Unfortunately, it won't expire for a long time. What should Bob do?

Public key certificates have one important feature in common with business cards. Once they are distributed, it is practically impossible to get them all back. In fact, the problem is worse for certificates. Since they are digital objects, they can be easily replicated and redistributed. Bob cannot retrieve and destroy all his certificates after he changes jobs because he can't determine how many copies exist or who has them!

The issuer's job is to link a public key with a user's identity in a trustworthy fashion. Bob notifies the issuer that the certificate is no longer correct. The issuer needs to get that information to Alice or anyone else who will use Bob's certificate. Unfortunately, the issuer cannot predict who will attempt to use Bob's certificate. Alice will need to get the information about Bob's certificate from the issuer when she needs it.

Credit card issuers face a similar problem. When they revoke a credit card, they cannot predict where it will be used next. The merchant has to check the credit card's status at the time it is used. The traditional mechanism for credit card status was the combined warning bulletin, which was sometimes called the *hot list*. The hot list was a paper booklet listing all the unexpired credit cards that had been stolen or revoked. The credit card issuer distributed this list to all the merchants, and they could check the list whenever a credit card was used. The hot list had the date it was issued printed on the cover, so the merchants could be sure they had up-to-date information.

The basic PKI tool to distribute status information about public key certificates is the *certificate revocation list* (CRL). The CRL borrows some features from the credit card hot list and the certificate itself. The CRL contains a list of serial numbers from unexpired certificates that should not be trusted. The CRL is a digital object, so the issuer can distribute and Alice can process it electronically, just like the certificate. The CRL is tamper-evident because the issuer signs it, just like the certificate. Rather than mailing the CRL to Alice, and every other possible user, the issuer generates a CRL frequently and posts it on the Internet for anyone to obtain. The issuer includes the issuance date in the CRL, and perhaps an expiration date as well, so Alice can be sure she has current information.

Alice would like to determine the status of Bob's certificate (the certificate depicted in Figure 3.3), so she obtains a CRL issued by Awfully Big Certificates. Figure 3.5 graphically describes the contents of the CRL. The CRL was issued by the ABC, and it includes

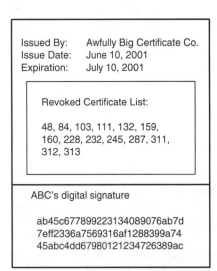

Figure 3.5   Awfully Big Certificates' CRL.

an expiration date and a list of certificate serial numbers. This is the list of unexpired certificates that cannot be trusted (we will call such a certificate *revoked*). Finally, the CRL includes the digital signature. Alice checks the signature and determines that ABC did issue the CRL, it has not expired, and it has not been modified. Now she looks through the list of revoked certificates. The serial number of Bob's certificate is on the list, since Bob changed jobs, so she cannot trust it.

The CRL is a reasonable implementation of the eighth feature on our wish list. Alice cannot tell if the certificate contents are current from the certificate itself, but she can obtain status information anytime she needs it.

Certificate Policies

Now it is time to address the ninth feature of our ideal certificate: How can we determine for what purpose this certificate can be used ? How can Alice decide if Bob's certificate is appropriate for her intended application? For example, should she trust it to verify a signature on a contract?

Well, this is a matter of *policy*. In computer security, policy is all about what should be done and who should do it. Certificate issuers have policies as well, and these policies impact how much we can trust the certificates they issue.

Credit card issuers only issue credit cards to people who are likely to pay their bills. They determine if an applicant is likely to pay by checking his or her job status, income level, and credit history. The more confident the issuer can be, the higher the credit limit they award. The issuer indicates that confidence level by providing a color-coded credit card. The "silver," "gold," "platinum," or even "titanium" credit cards signify increasing levels of confidence from the issuer.

Alice would like to know the level of confidence associated with Bob's key. Certificates can convey this information in a similar fashion to the credit card. In public key certificates, we will call this information *certificate policy*. An issuer can describe how the decision was made to issue a particular certificate in the policy. Alice can use this policy to decide if Bob's signature on the contract should be trusted.

Credit card issuers may address other notions of policy besides confidence of payment. For example, some credit cards can only be used at certain stores or can only be used to buy particular types of goods and services. Credit cards issued by chains of stores are only good for purchases in that company's stores. Credit cards issued by gasoline companies may be used to purchase gasoline and automotive repair services, but are not useful if you need new sneakers. A department store credit card is perfect for those sneakers, but it can't be used to buy gasoline.

Alice would also like to know what applications she can perform with Bob's key. Certificates can convey this information in the certificate policy as well. An issuer can describe the applications that may be implemented with a particular certificate. For example, the certificate could specify *signing e-mail* or *signing contracts*. Alice can review this information to decide if Bob's signature on the contract is meaningful.

In Figure 3.6, we have another certificate for Bob. This time, he obtained a certificate from the Little Shop of Certificates (LSC), and LSC has added some policy information. Bob has a gold certificate, which means that LSC has a lot of confidence, but not enough

```
Serial Number: 96
Certificate for:  Bob Burton
Company:          Burton Consulting
Issued By:        Little Shop of Certificates
Email Address:    bsmith@pleasantville.ca.us
Activation:       June 21, 2000
Expiration:       June 21, 2003
Policy:           Gold, contract signing
Public Key:       24219743597430832a2187
                  b6219a75430d843e432f21e
                  09bc080da43509843
────────────────────────────────────────────
LSC's digital signature

  4765adef0012784c59a930276534a8dfa7
  de2239316ab233dec70095762121aef4fg
  66854392ab02c4
```

Figure 3.6   Policy information in Bob's certificate.

to award the platinum certificate! LSC also specified that Bob's certificate is intended for contract signing. Alice has to decide if a gold certificate for contract signing from LSC is good enough to verify a signature on a contract for 100 widgets.

The certificate policy is a reasonable implementation of our ninth requirement. The certificate policy information allows the issuer to express a level of confidence and specify an appropriate set of applications for a public key in the certificate.

Certification Paths

At this point, we have addressed every feature of our ideal certificate. However, we haven't resolved one of the basic requirements stated at the beginning of this chapter. We said we need a solution that can scale. Our solution needs to work for Alice even if she communicates with dozens or even hundreds of different users.

By adopting the concept of a trusted party issuing certificates, Alice can establish trust with users she has not met. Unfortunately, she needs to determine which certificate issuers she can trust. If she can select a single issuer, her life will be simple, but this may not be realistic. Each user with whom she communicates may have obtained his or her certificate from a different issuer! If Alice wants to transact business, she has to determine if she can trust those other issuers.

To complicate matters, Alice may wish to perform a wide range of applications. She may want to protect her e-mail, verify signatures on contracts, and control equipment on her factory floor. Alice may reasonably determine that different issuers are appropriate for each application. The certificates that protect e-mail are probably less important than the certificates used to recalibrate or reprogram her robotic widget-maker.

Alice can, of course, choose to trust more than one issuer for a particular application, but this solution does not scale. Evaluating each new issuer is time consuming.

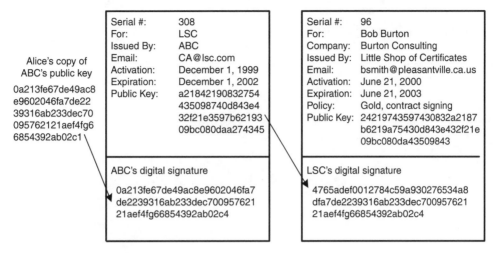

Figure 3.7 A certificate chain.

Alice needs an automatic process to determine whether a new issuer is trustworthy. One solution is to expand the role of the trusted certificate issuer. Alice has already decided that ABC can vouch for the user of a public key by issuing a certificate. Perhaps ABC could vouch for other certificate issuers by issuing certificates to them as well. Alice can develop a chain of certificates and automatically decide if certificates from another issuer are okay. This simplifies her world!

In Figure 3.7, Alice has constructed a chain of certificates. ABC has issued a certificate to LSC, and LSC has issued a gold certificate to Bob. Alice only trusts issuer ABC, but she can still accept a certificate issued to Bob from LSC based on this certificate chain. By delegating the responsibility for evaluating new issuers to ABC, Alice has created a scalable solution.

Summary

In this chapter, we described the basic tools of a PKI: certificates, CRLs, certificate policies, and certification paths. By leveraging public key cryptography, we have devised mechanisms we can trust to determine several attributes of a public key: *who* has the corresponding private key and *what* applications are appropriate for the key. Through certification paths, we have made the mechanisms *scalable*. While we will add more detail in later chapters, these basic mechanisms will be used throughout the book.

Authentication Mechanisms

No one implements a public key infrastructure (PKI) for its own sake. Rather, one implements a PKI to support security in other applications. There are, of course, other security mechanisms that do not employ public key cryptography, much less PKI. However, PKI not only offers a more comprehensive solution, it also mitigates many of the problems found in the more traditional security mechanisms.

In this chapter, we review several authentication mechanisms. PKI offers one means of providing authentication; there are many others. Each authentication mechanism has different benefits and drawbacks. Authentication mechanisms have evolved over time, building on the features of their predecessors. PKI-based authentication is a logical step in this evolution, providing improvements in security, usability, scalability, and survivability.

All of the authentication mechanisms described in this chapter can be used to authenticate a user to a remote server over a network. Some of the mechanisms require no additional administrative effort to enable authentication for more than one remote server. All of the authentication mechanisms provide *unilateral authentication*, authenticating the user to the remote server. Only a few of the authentication mechanisms provide *mutual authentication*, authenticating the user to the remote server and authenticating the remote server to user. PKI-based authentication can provide either unilateral authentication or mutual authentication, depending on the environment in which it is used.

This study of authentication mechanisms demonstrates the power of PKI. Yet, authentication is just one of the security services supported by PKI. In later chapters, we will see PKI applied to support other security services as well.

Passwords

Almost every computer system requires users to identify themselves at the beginning of a session. Usually, the user is prompted for a name and password. The password is a secret shared by the user and the remote server. The user remembers the secret, and the server stores either a copy of the secret or a value computed from the secret. Authentication involves verification of the password presented by the user and the stored value. Password-based authentication is the most common form of user authentication. It is easy to implement and easy to use. It is also the weakest form of user authentication. If an eavesdropper obtains the secret password, he or she can masquerade as the user. Once Charlie is able to masquerade as Alice, there is nothing that the server can do to prevent Charlie from doing anything that Alice is authorized to do.

In Figure 4.1, Alice provides her name and password to a server over a network. Anyone who can observe the transmission medium can steal Alice's password. Once Charlie, the attacker, knows that Alice's password is "Sailboat," he can pretend to be Alice until she changes her password—and that could be a long time! This is the reason why many corporate computing environments require Alice to change her password regularly.

There are several ways in which Charlie can observe the secret password on the network. He could install a *sniffer* program. Sniffer programs are readily available on the Internet, and they allow anyone to capture network traffic sent from one computer to another on the same local area network, such as the office baseband Ethernet. By employing a sniffer, Charlie does not need to be in the room with Alice, and he does not need access to her computer. Charlie only needs a network connection on the same local area network. These programs make eavesdropping so simple that password stealing is often called a *sniffer attack*. If Alice changes her password, Charlie simply runs his sniffer program to obtain her new one. If Charlie is constantly running his sniffer program, he will obtain Alice's new password at the time Alice selects it.

Some local area network technologies are more susceptible to sniffer attack than others. Those that employ a broadcast medium, like baseband Ethernet, are the most vulnerable. Those that employ a hub, like switched Ethernet, are not susceptible. The hub only transmits the traffic on the wires connecting the communicating computers. In this case, Charlie faces the more difficult task of installing a sniffer program on Alice's computer to obtain the same data.

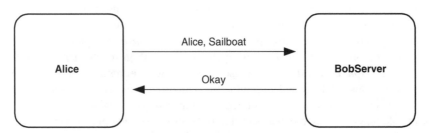

Figure 4.1   Password-based authentication.

Sniffer attacks highlight the two biggest problems with password-based authentication. First, for Alice to authenticate, she must transmit her password, the shared secret. In doing so, Alice may disclose it. Second, Alice's shared secret is long-lived. Charlie only needs to observe the password once, and then he can masquerade until Alice changes her password. These weaknesses make sniffer attacks highly successful.

Password-based authentication is not well suited to multiserver environments. Suppose that Alice regularly uses a half-dozen remote servers. She could use the same password on all the servers or she can use a different password on each. If Alice uses the same password on each system, then a successful sniffer attack will gain Charlie access to all of her accounts, even those for which he was unable to observe a login attempt. Further, depending on the password implementation, one of the six server administrators may be able to get her password and masquerade on the other five servers. If Alice uses different passwords for each server, a successful sniffer attack will gain Charlie access to a single server. Unfortunately, Alice must remember six different passwords. To do so, she will probably write down her passwords, thereby leading to other vulnerabilities.

Password-based authentication does not readily provide mutual authentication. Alice's password authenticates her to the server. For the server to authenticate to her, a second shared secret is needed. The server will need a second shared secret for each user. This secret will have to be different for each user to prevent one user from masquerading as the server to another user. Each user would have to remember the server password, as well as his or her password.

Further, the lack of mutual authentication gives Charlie another means with which to obtain Alice's password. Charlie can put up a fake server. When users try to access the server, Charlie can collect user names and their associated passwords.

The evolution of authentication mechanisms begins by addressing the sniffer attack. The obvious protection against the sniffer attack might appear to be encryption. If Alice's transmission is encrypted, then Charlie cannot unscramble the password. Password disclosure is prevented, but what encryption key should Alice use? If all of the users use the same key, then any of the server users can perform the sniffer attack and decrypt Alice's password in the same manner as the server. If each user has a different key, then the management of these keys provides a stronger basis for authentication than passwords. We will discuss several of these approaches.

Alice is also protected if her password can only be used one time. A successful sniffer attack will gain Charlie a stale password. Of course, Alice needs a new password for each authentication attempt. While this might seem difficult, several authentication mechanisms do just that.

One-Time Authentication Values

One-time authentication values counter the sniffer attack by using a different secret for each authentication attempt. Therefore, when Charlie eavesdrops on Alice's transmission, the information he obtains cannot be used to masquerade as Alice. Challenge/response authentication protocols provide the most common one-time authentication values. Three different one-time authentication mechanisms are presented in the following sections: challenge-response, implicit challenge, and hash-based authentication.

Challenge/Response Authentication

As shown in Figure 4.2, the server generates a random challenge and sends it to Alice. Instead of responding with a password, Alice encrypts the challenge with a key known only to Alice and the server. Alice sends her name and the ciphertext to the server. The server performs the same encryption, and then compares the ciphertext sent by Alice and the locally generated ciphertext. If the two match, then authentication succeeds; otherwise, authentication fails.

This simple protocol provides several improvements over simple password authentication. Since the challenge is randomly generated, Charlie cannot reuse the ciphertext generated by Alice to masquerade. The value she sent will only authenticate her identity one time. Alice's name is transmitted in plaintext, and there is no reason to keep her name a secret. Eavesdropping is no longer a threat. Alice can authenticate her identity to the remote server over an open network.

This mechanism can be difficult to use when Alice needs to authenticate to many different remote servers. Like passwords, Alice needs a different challenge-encrypting key for each server. If she uses the same key for more than one server, then those servers with the same key can masquerade as Alice. Also, securely storing a different key for each remote server can be difficult.

For this mechanism to be used for mutual authentication, a second challenge and response are needed. Alice can provide the second challenge along with the encrypted first challenge, and the server can provide the encrypted response along with the indication that Alice's challenge correctly verified. In this manner, this mechanism can be extended to provide mutual authentication without a second shared challenge-encrypting key.

In some environments, challenge/response authentication protocols cannot be used because the server has no means to present the challenge to Alice. This is especially true when trying to modify a system that was originally designed for simple passwords. In this case, an implicit challenge is needed. Time is the most common implicit challenge, and we discuss this mechanism next.

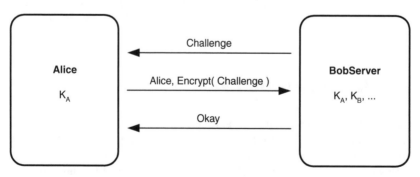

Figure 4.2   Challenge/response authentication.

Time-Based Implicit Challenge

Figure 4.3 illustrates time-based authentication. Alice reads her computer clock, encrypts the time value, and sends her name and the ciphertext to the server. The server decrypts the value provided by Alice. If the time is close enough to the server computer clock, then authentication succeeds; otherwise, authentication fails. Since Alice's computer clock and the server computer clock are not synchronized and the transmission will take some time, the server must allow for more than one time value. However, if the server allows too many time values, then Charlie will be able to capture the value generated by Alice and send it to the server, successfully authenticating as Alice. This attack is called a *replay attack*. Charlie does not know Alice's secret time-encrypting key, but by quickly replaying her transmission to the server, he fools the server into believing that Alice is starting a second session.

This mechanism is not a great improvement over the challenge/response protocols. It works when the server has no means to present the challenge to Alice, but it is vulnerable to replay attack. Like challenge/response authentication mechanisms, this mechanism does not readily support authentication to multiple servers, and it can be extended to support mutual authentication. Mutual authentication is not usually implemented because additional values must be exchanged. Time-based challenges are most often used when additional exchanges and additional fields within exchanges are unavailable. As we will see, using a one-way hash function can provide the best features of these two mechanisms.

Using One-Way Hash Functions

Leslie Lamport proposed one technique to solve the problems associated with implicit challenges [LAMP81]. One implementation of these ideas is the S/KEY One-Time Password System [HALL95].

S/KEY generates a sequence of one-time passwords by successively applying a one-way hash function. The initial hash value is computed by hashing the user's secret passphrase concatenated with a non-secret seed value. The secret passphrase should be at least eight characters long, but longer is better. The hash value resulting from the first

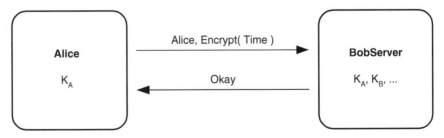

Figure 4.3   Time-based challenge authentication.

application of the hash function becomes the input to the second application of the hash function, and so on. The hash function is applied between 500 and 1000 times. The first one-time password is the final hash value. The second one-time password is the second-to-last hash value, and so on. When Charlie monitors the transmission of a one-time password, he will not be able to generate any succeeding password. To do so requires inverting the one-way hash function.

A preparatory step is needed to initialize the server. In this step, Alice's initial password (the final hash value in the sequence), a sequence number, and a seed are transmitted to the server. The server must know that these values come from Alice, but they do not have to be kept secret. The non-secret seed allows Alice to use the same secret passphrase with multiple servers, each server using a different seed. Alice can also safely recycle secret passphrases by changing the seed.

The server may issue an S/KEY challenge, consisting of the sequence number and seed. Using the sequence number and seed in conjunction with her secret passphrase, Alice can compute (or look up) the one-time password. The server can omit the challenge if Alice stores the sequence number and seed after each successful authentication. Portable tokens like smartcards or even personal data assistants (PDAs) could be used to conveniently store these values. Finally, Alice passes the one-time password to the server for verification.

For each user, the server stores the one-time password from the most recent successful login. The first one-time password of the sequence is stored in the initialization step. To verify an authentication attempt, the server hashes the transmitted one-time password, and if the resulting hash value matches the stored previous one-time password, then the authentication is successful and the accepted one-time password is stored for future use.

Because the one-way hash function is applied one less time for each successive authentication, at some point the user must reinitialize the system or be unable to authenticate again. Reinitialization is accomplished by changing the sequence number and the seed. One can increment the trailing digits of the seed and reset the sequence number, usually to something in the range of 500 to 1000.

The requirement to reinitialize the server after 500 to 1000 successful authentication attempts can be a significant burden. To authenticate to multiple remote servers, Alice would need a different secret passphrase, sequence number, and seed for each remote server. Further, mutual authentication is not provided, and S/KEY cannot be readily extended to provide it.

None of the authentication mechanisms discussed so far supports confidentiality. That is, the authentication mechanisms do not enable the encryption of communications between the user and the server after a successful authentication. A solution that provides mutual authentication while distributing an encryption key for encryption is desirable.

Kerberos

Roger Needham and Michael Schroeder first described a mechanism for authentication that was based on encryption [NEED78]. This mechanism had freshness problems, and it did not provide the same guarantees to both parties. Two solutions to these problems were devised, and both were implemented. Ken Bauer, Tom Berson, and Rich Feiertag employed counters (they called them *event markers*) to solve these problems [BAUE82, BAUE83]. This improved authentication mechanism was first implemented in the Sytek Secure LocalNet in 1981. Dorothy Denning and Giovanni Sacco devised another solution using timestamps [DENN81]. This improved authentication mechanism was first implemented in the Xerox Network System [ISRA82, XNS82, XNS84] in 1982. The most popular implementation was done at the Massachusetts Institute of Technology (MIT) beginning in 1985 [STEI88, NEUM94]. This implementation uses timestamps to overcome the problems with the original Needham-Schroeder mechanism, and it adds a *Ticket Granting Service* to the original design. MIT named its implementation *Kerberos*, after the three-headed dog in Greek mythology that guards the entrance to Hades.

The three-headed dog is appropriate because authentication involves three parties: Alice, the server to which she is authenticating, and the Authentication Server or Key Distribution Center (KDC). A session begins by Alice obtaining a Ticket-Granting Ticket (TGT) from the KDC. When Alice wants to access a server, she sends the TGT to the KDC along with a request for a ticket to the server. The TGT contains information about Alice's login session, and it allows the KDC to operate without maintaining state information about each user login session. In response to her request, Alice receives an encrypted session key and a ticket to the server. The session key is encrypted in a master key known only to Alice and the KDC. The server ticket contains the same session key; however, it is encrypted in a master key known only to the server and the KDC. Authentication results when Alice and the server prove that they both know the session key. Alice encrypts a timestamp and sends it to the server. The server decrypts it, increments it, encrypts it again, and sends the ciphertext to Alice. Alice decrypts the response. If the plaintext is the incremented original timestamp, then authentication succeeds; otherwise, authentication fails. After authentication, the session key can be used to encrypt communications between Alice and the server.

It is clear that all parties must trust the KDC because it holds copies of all master keys. The KDC must be trusted to keep them secret, and it must not use them inappropriately.

With the preceding high-level overview as background, let's examine each step in the Kerberos authentication process in a bit more detail. The whole process is illustrated in Figure 4.4.

Obtaining a Ticket-Granting Ticket

Alice uses the Kerberos Authentication Service (AS) exchange at the start of a login session to obtain credentials for a KDC, which will subsequently be used to obtain credentials for other servers. Alice's master key is used for encryption, but this exchange does not by itself provide any identity assurance.

The exchange consists of two messages: KRB_AS_REQ from Alice to the KDC, and KRB_AS_REP in reply. The KRB_AS_REQ request consists of Alice's name. The KRB_AS_REP response contains KDC credentials encrypted in Alice's master key, K_A. Usually, K_A is derived from Alice's password. This allows Alice to use Kerberos from any workstation, and she does not need to remember a binary symmetric key. The credentials contain a login session key, S_A, and a TGT. The TGT contains S_A, Alice's name,

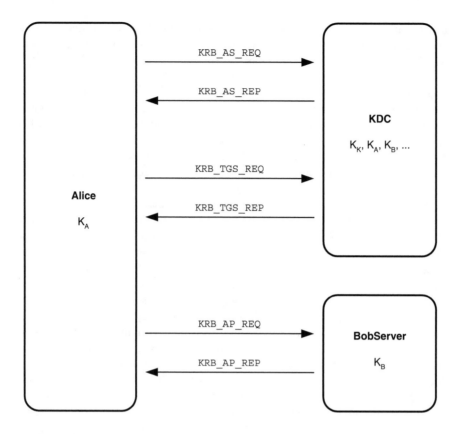

Legend

`KRB_AS_REQ`: "Alice"

`KRB_AS_REP`: $K_A[\ S_A,$ TGT$: K_K[$ "Alice", S_A, ExpireTime]]

`KRB_TGS_REQ`: "Alice", "BobServer", TGT$: K_K[$ "Alice", S_A, ExpireTime]$,S_A[$ Time]

`KRB_TGS_REP`: $S_A[$ "BobServer", K_{AB}, TICKET$: K_B[$ "Alice", K_{AB}, ExpireTime]]

`KRB_AP_REQ`: TICKET$: K_B[$ "Alice", K_{AB}, ExpireTime], $K_{AB}[$ Time]

`KRB_AP_REP`: $K_{AB}[$ Time+1]

K_A: Alice's master key; known by Alice and KDC

K_B: BobServer's master key; known by BobServer and KDC

K_{AB}:   Session key for Alice and BobServer; known by Alice, BobServer, and KDC

K_K: KDC's master key; known ony by KDC

S_A: Alice's login session key; known by Alice and KDC

Figure 4.4   Kerberos authentication.

and an expiration time, all encrypted with the KDC's master key, K_K. Again, the TGT allows the KDC to operate without maintaining state about each user login session. It also permits the KDC to more easily recover from a crash without impacting clients.

At this point, Alice's master key, originally derived from her password, can be discarded. The login session key, S_A, will be used instead of K_A for the remainder of the login session when the KDC wants to encrypt messages for Alice.

Authenticating to a Server

When Alice accesses a server, she sends to the KDC the TGT, a request for a ticket for the server, and an *authenticator*. This message is called the KRB_TGS_REQ request. The authenticator proves to the KDC that Alice knows the login session key, S_A. The authenticator is the current date and time encrypted with the session key. Encryption prevents the attacker, Charlie, from sniffing the TGT from the KRB_AS_REP response.

The use of the current date and time in the authenticator requires that Alice's clock and the KDC clock be synchronized. The KDC can permit some skew (usually five minutes). In practice, a time synchronization protocol such as the Simple Network Time Protocol (SNTP) [MILL96] is needed to keep clocks adequately synchronized.

The KDC receives the KRB_TGS_REQ request from Alice and responds with the KRB_TGS_REP reply. Using K_K, the KDC decrypts the TGT from the KRB_TGS_REQ request; recovers the login session key, S_A; and checks the expiration time of the TGT. If the TGT is valid, then the KDC generates a key for Alice and the server to share, K_{AB}, and constructs a *ticket*. The ticket is encrypted in the server's master key, K_B, and it contains K_{AB}, Alice's name, and an expiration time. The KRB_TGS_REP reply contains the server's name, the ticket for the server, and K_{AB}, all encrypted in the login session key, S_A.

When Alice receives the KRB_TGS_REP reply, she decrypts it with the login session key, S_A. She sends the server a KRB_AP_REQ request consisting of the ticket from the KRB_TGS_REP reply and an authenticator, which is the current date and time encrypted with K_{AB}.

Again, the use of the current date and time in the authenticator requires clock synchronization. In this case, Alice's clock and the server clock must be synchronized. The same mechanism should be used throughout the system to keep all clocks adequately synchronized.

The server receives the KRB_AP_REQ request from Alice and responds with the KRB_AP_REP reply. The server decrypts the ticket with its master key, K_B, discovering K_{AB}, Alice's name, and the expiration time. The server trusts the KDC to have shared K_{AB} only with the party named in the ticket, in this case, Alice. If decryption of the authenticator with K_{AB} results in a date and time value close to the current time, say within five minutes, then only Alice could have performed the encryption. Thus, Alice is authenticated to the server.

To ensure that Charlie cannot replay the legitimate KRB_AP_REQ request from Alice, the server should check that the same user name does not present the same authenticator more than once. To do this, the server should keep track of the authenticators that it has processed in the time window defined by the acceptable clock skew.

To provide authentication from the server to Alice, the server increments the time value from the KRB_AP_REQ request and reencrypts it with K_{AB}. This single ciphertext value is the KRB_AP_REP reply.

Alice receives the KRB_AP_REP reply from the server, and decrypts it with K_{AB}. Alice trusts the KDC to have shared K_{AB} only with the server for which she requested a ticket. If decryption of the KRB_AP_REP reply with K_{AB} results in the original date and time value plus one, then only the server could have performed the encryption. Thus, the server is authenticated to Alice.

With mutual authentication complete, the session key, K_{AB}, can be used to provide confidentiality or integrity of the communications between Alice and the server.

Kerberos is a powerful mechanism. Alice can authenticate her identity across an open network. Kerberos readily supports authentication to multiple remote servers. Kerberos supports mutual authentication. Alice verifies the identity of the remote server with the same mechanism that is used to establish her own identity. Yet, the Kerberos KDC presents a very attractive target for attack.

If Charlie is successful in attacking the KDC, the result is a catastrophic problem. If Charlie obtains the master key held by the KDC, he will be able to masquerade as any user. When the system administrators discover that Charlie has broken into the KDC, they must change all of the master keys—a monumental task. The system administrators can easily change the master keys associated with servers since they know where all of them are located, and they do not move around. Human users, on the other hand, are quite mobile. Locating each user to issue a new password (from which the master key is derived) can require significant effort. Public key cryptography offers a solution.

Kerberos Public Key Initialization

Kerberos Public Key Initialization (PKINIT) [TUNG00] replaces the initial exchange with the KDC, but all other exchanges remain unchanged. In the request, Alice provides her signature certificate and a signed public key. Alice's signature certificate includes her name and the public key used to validate digital signatures generated by Alice. The public key will be used for key management; it may be either a key transport key (an RSA public key) or a key agreement public key (an ephemeral Diffie-Hellman public key). The KDC verifies the digital signature to ensure that the key management public key originated with Alice. Once verified, the KDC makes use of the key management public key to return S_A. The format of the KDC reply depends on the type of key management key provided by Alice. If Alice provided an ephemeral Diffie-Hellman public key, then the KDC returns its signed ephemeral Diffie-Hellman public key. Alice validates the digital signature to ensure that the reply originated with the KDC. Alice and the KDC each compute the same symmetric key using the Diffie-Hellman algorithm, and the resulting symmetric key is used as S_A. Alternatively, if Alice provided an RSA public key, then the KDC generates a temporary symmetric key and encrypts it with Alice's RSA public key. The KDC generates and digitally signs a second symmetric key that will be used as S_A. The signed S_A value is then encrypted with the temporary key. The KDC returns the temporary key encrypted in Alice's RSA public key and the encrypted and signed S_A. Alice is able to retrieve S_A by decrypting the temporary key with her RSA private key, and then using the temporary key to decrypt the signed S_A. Validating the signature ensures that the S_A originated with the KDC.

Without a certificate, the KDC would need another authentication mechanism for Alice's public key. The binding of Alice's name with Alice's signature public key allows the KDC to authenticate the request. The KDC relies on the certification authority (CA) to confirm that Alice has the private key that corresponds to the public key before issuing the certificate.

Kerberos with public key initialization continues to satisfy authentication requirements. Introducing public key cryptography reduces the number of secrets stored by the KDC, significantly reducing risk. In this environment, if Charlie is successful in attacking the KDC, the result is much less severe because only the servers need new master keys. The KDC no longer holds master keys for users, so the damage caused by a break-in is significantly easier to repair.

Certificate-Based Authentication

Once Alice has a certificate, the reliance on the KDC can be removed. This does not remove the need to trust any third parties; rather, the CA becomes the trusted third party. However, the CA is not involved in any protocol exchanges. Unlike the KDC, if the CA is unavailable, authentication can still be accomplished.

Several popular protocols provide authentication based on certificates. Secure Socket Layer (SSL) [FREI96] is probably the most widely known and deployed. It is included in nearly every Web browser. Others include Transport Layer Security (TLS) [DIER99], Internet Key Exchange (IKE) [HARK98], S/MIME [RAMS99b], PGP [ATKI96, ELKI96], and OpenPGP [CALL98].

Each of these protocols uses certificates in a slightly different manner, yet the basic principles are the same. Figure 4.5 illustrates a typical certificate-based authentication exchange using digital signatures. This one is adapted from Federal Information Processing Standard Publication 196, *Standard for Entity Authentication Using Public Key Cryptography* [FIPS196].

In many protocol environments, the client requests the server to initiate the authentication exchange. This technique ensures that both Alice and BobServer support the same authentication option. The authentication and encryption extensions to the Internet File Transfer Protocol [HORO97] use this approach; some other protocol environments do not require this preparatory step.

If BobServer supports the authentication approach requested by Alice, then the authentication exchange begins. The TokenID indicates that mutual authentication will be performed, the version number of the protocol, and the protocol unit identifier. While this identifier is optional, it greatly simplifies implementation, so it is usually included. At this point in the exchange, Alice is expecting a TokenBA1 from BobServer. The protocol unit identifier within TokenID allows Alice to quickly confirm that BobServer is providing the expected data. TokenBA1 consists solely of a random number, ranB. This is a challenge. The correct response will be a signature that covers ranB.

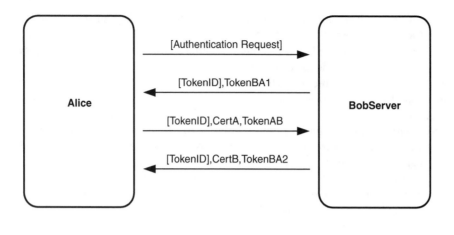

Legend

[Authentication Request]: Optional. Alice asks the server to start authentication.

[TokenID]: Optional. Identifies authentication type (e.g., mutual), protocol version, and protocol unit.

CertA: Alice's certificate; binds Alice's name and her signature public key (used to verify Alice's signature).

CertB: BobServer's certificate; binds server's name and its signature public key (used to verify server's signature).

TokenBA1: **ranB**, a random number generated by BobServer.

TokenAB: **ranA**, **ranB**, and **nameB**, all *signed* by Alice. ranA is a random number generated by Alice; ranB is repeated from TokenBA1; and nameB is the server's name.

TokenBA2: **ranA**, **ranB**, and **nameA**, all *signed* by BobServer. ranA is repeated from TokenAB; ranB is repeated from TokenAB and TokenBA1; and nameA is the Alice's name.

Figure 4.5 Certificate-based mutual authentication using digital signatures.

Alice's response is signed. She provides her certificate so that BobServer has the public key needed to validate the signature. Alice signs a sequence of three values: ranA, ranB, and nameB. The ranA value is a challenge to BobServer, but it also ensures that Alice is not signing an arbitrary message composed by BobServer (or someone masquerading as BobServer). The ranB value is the BobServer's challenge. The nameB value is the name of the server, BobServer.

Upon receipt of Alice's response, BobServer confirms that the ranB value is the same value supplied in TokenBA1, and confirms that Alice intends to authenticate to BobServer by checking the nameB value. If either check fails, then authentication fails. Next, BobServer validates Alice's certificate and her signature. If they are valid, then Alice is authenticated to BobServer. The response from BobServer to Alice will complete the mutual authentication.

BobServer's response is a signed sequence of three values: ranA, ranB, and nameA. The ranA value is the challenge generated by Alice. The ranB value is the BobServer's original challenge, but it also ensures that BobServer is not signing an arbitrary message composed by Alice. The nameA value is the name of the client, Alice.

Upon receipt of BobServer's response, Alice confirms that the ranA value is the same value supplied in TokenAB, and confirms that BobServer intends to authenticate to her by checking the nameA value. If either check fails, then authentication fails. Next, Alice validates BobServer's certificate and its signature. If they are valid, then BobServer is authenticated to Alice, completing mutual authentication.

Certificate-based mechanisms offer some desirable properties. Since no secrets are transmitted, Alice can readily authenticate her identity to a remote server across an open network without worrying about eavesdroppers. These mechanisms support authentication to multiple remote servers, since Alice and the servers do not share any long-term secrets. Mutual authentication is provided; Alice verifies the identity of the remote server with the same mechanism that is used to establish her own identity. Unlike Kerberos, certificate-based authentication protocols do not require the active participation of third parties. Only the user and the server need to be available for successful authentication.

Certificate-based mechanisms leverage public key cryptography to meet the requirements for authentication in a distributed environment. They build on many of the features of their predecessors, and add new features. Of course, authentication is only one of the desirable security services. Many applications also require confidentiality, integrity, and non-repudiation. Certificate-based mechanisms can also provide these services.

CHAPTER 5

PKI Components and Users

As described in Chapter 3, a public key infrastructure (PKI) is designed to facilitate the use of public key cryptography. A PKI meets this goal through the creation and distribution of public key certificates and certificate revocation lists (CRLs). In Chapter 3, PKIs are constructed from a single component called the *issuer* that performed all these functions. Users, such as Alice and Bob, could use public key cryptography in their applications by obtaining and processing the certificates and CRLs.

It is difficult to build a single component that can securely create and distribute certificates and CRLs. PKIs are built from a variety of components, each designed to perform a few tasks particularly well. This chapter reviews the tasks facing an issuer, groups similar tasks, and assigns these groups to the four basic functional components of a PKI:

- The certification authority
- The registration authority
- The repository
- The archive

In Chapters 3 and 4, Alice and Bob played various user roles. At the simplest level, there are always two distinct users in any PKI-enabled transaction. The first user has a private key and is the subject of a certificate containing the corresponding public key.

This user is called the *subscriber* or *certificate holder*, and will participate in the transaction using the private key. The second user obtains the certificate and uses the corresponding public key to participate in the transaction. The second user is called the *relying party* or *certificate user*.

Infrastructure Components

In this section, we introduce the four components of the PKI and describe their functionality. The functionality described for these components must be present in any PKI. However, specific implementations may divide this functionality differently. Functions may be combined into a single component or may be assigned to multiple components. For example, the certification authority and registration authority are sometimes combined into a single component. This does not affect *what* functions must be performed, just *where* those functions are performed.

Certification Authority

The certification authority (CA) is the basic building block of the PKI. The CA is a collection of computer hardware, software, and the people who operate it. The CA is known by two attributes: its name and its public key. The CA performs four basic PKI functions:

- Issues certificates (that is, creates and signs them).
- Maintains certificate status information and issues CRLs.
- Publishes its current (unexpired) certificates and CRLs, so users can obtain the information they need to implement security services.
- Maintains archives of status information about the expired or revoked certificates that it issued.

We examine each of these functions and identify responsibilities and requirements they impose on the CA. These requirements may be difficult to satisfy simultaneously. To fulfill these requirements, the CA may delegate certain functions to the other components of the infrastructure.

Issuing Certificates

A CA may issue certificates to users, to other CAs, or to both. When a CA issues a certificate, it is asserting that the subject (the entity named in the certificate) has the private key that corresponds to the public key contained in the certificate. If the CA includes additional information in the certificate, the CA is asserting that information corresponds to the subject as well. This additional information might be contact information (for example, an e-mail address) or policy information (for example, the types of applications that can be performed with this public key). When the subject of the certificate is another CA, the issuer is asserting that the certificates issued by the other CA are trustworthy.

The CA inserts its name in every certificate and CRL it generates, and signs them with its private key. Once users establish that they trust a CA (directly or through a certification path), they can trust certificates issued by that CA. Users can easily identify certificates issued by that CA by comparing its name. To ensure that the certificate is genuine, they verify the signature using the CA's public key.

The CA's name is generally public information, and the CA's signature is the actual basis of trust for these certificates. If an attacker obtains the CA's private key, users will trust the certificates the attacker generates as if the CA itself generated them. *The first and primary responsibility of a CA is to protect its private key from disclosure.*

To protect the private key, a CA must protect the private key when in use and in storage. To meet this requirement, the CA relies on a cryptographic module. Cryptographic modules generate keys, protect private keys, and implement cryptographic algorithms. They may be implemented in hardware, software, or a combination of hardware and software. Software cryptographic modules are programs that run on the computer system. Hardware cryptographic modules, such as smart cards and PCMCIA cards, perform cryptographic operations on an external processor. Hardware cryptographic modules keep the private key out of the host system memory, so their security is less dependent on the operating system.

Cryptographic modules may also offer varying levels of protection due to flaws in their design or implementation. The National Institute of Standards and Technology (NIST) developed FIPS 140, *Security Requirements for Cryptographic Modules*, which specifies four increasing security levels for cryptographic modules [FIPS140]. NIST and the Canadian Communications Security Establishment (CSE) accredit third-party laboratories to perform validation testing of cryptographic modules against the FIPS 140 standard.

A CA's private key is at risk when stored in host memory or on an unvalidated cryptographic module. A CA should always use a validated hardware cryptographic module to generate its signing key and to protect it during storage and use. At a minimum, the module must be validated as meeting FIPS 140 Level 2. Higher levels of assurance may be required if the CA is located on a site where physical security is weak.

Of course, the contents of the certificates must be correct to be useful. The information in the certificate (for example, the public key, policy information, and contact information) must all correspond to the subject named in the certificate. *The second responsibility of a CA is to verify the information in a certificate before it is issued.*

Verifying a user's identity, personal information, and policy information are quite different from protecting the CA's private key. Performing this verification is inherently an external matter; it relies on information provided by parties outside the CA operational staff.

The CA can verify some of the certificate contents based on technical mechanisms, though. In particular, the CA can use the digital signature mechanism to ensure that a user actually has the private key corresponding to the public key in the certificate. This verification process is often called *proof of possession*. Proof of possession may be achieved by examining the request itself, rather than examining external data.

In addition to correctness, the contents of the certificates and CRLs must also reflect the CA's certificate profile. A CA specifies the types of information that it will include in certificates. Assume the Little Shop of Certificates CA has stated that it will only issue certificates for e-mail. It cannot issue Bob a certificate for contract signing, even if he has that authority. *The third responsibility of a CA is to ensure that all certificates and CRLs it issues conform to its profile.*

To ensure that a CA issues certificates and CRLs that conform to its profile, a CA has to perform two actions: it must protect the integrity of the profile, and it must verify that each and every certificate and CRL it generates conforms to the profile. To ensure that certificates and CRLs conform, the CA must examine them and compare them to the profile before signing them.

To protect the integrity of the profile, the CA restricts access to the CA components. These restrictions may be physical restrictions (for example, locked and guarded rooms or keycard access), logical restrictions (such as network firewalls), or procedural restrictions. Procedural restrictions might include two-person control (for example, requiring two CA staff members to modify the system) or separation of duty (for example, preventing system operators from approving the audit logs).

Maintaining Status Information and Issuing CRLs

As with certificates, the contents of the CRLs must be correct to be useful. The information in the CRL (for example, the list of revoked certificates, the date the certificate was revoked, and the reason why the certificate was revoked) must be complete and correct. Errors of omission may cause a user to accept an untrustworthy certificate, resulting in a loss of security. Listing trustworthy certificates, or incorrect revocation dates, may cause a user to reject a trustworthy certificate, resulting in denial of service. *The fourth responsibility of a CA is to accurately maintain the list of certificates that should no longer be trusted.*

Protecting the certificate status information is similar to protecting the profile. However, the decision to modify the status of a certificate relies on information provided by parties outside the CA operational staff. This is similar to verifying identity and other attributes of the certificate subject.

Publishing Certificates and CRLs

A CA is only useful if the certificates and CRLs that it generates are available to the users. If Alice and Bob cannot obtain the certificates and CRLs they need, they will not be able to implement the security services they want. Of course, Alice and Bob can always exchange their own personal certificates and their CRLs. However, each may need additional CA certificates to establish a certification path. *The fifth responsibility of a CA is to distribute its certificates and CRLs.*

When a CA serves an unrestricted user community, distribution of certificates and CRLs is all about availability and performance, not security. There is no requirement to restrict access to certificates and CRLs, since they need not be secret. An attacker could deny service to Alice and Bob by deleting or modifying information, but the attacker cannot make them trust the altered information without obtaining the CA's private key.

A CA may restrict its services to a closed user community, though. In this case, the CA may wish to deny the attacker access to the certificates. To achieve these goals, the

CA may wish to secure the distribution of certificates and CRLs. The integrity of the certificates and CRLs is not at risk, but the CA may not wish to disclose the information they contain. For example, if a company's certificates implicitly identify its R&D personnel, this could be exploited by a competitor. The competitor could determine the types of R&D by their backgrounds or simply try to hire the engineers away.

Maintaining Archives

Finally, the CA needs to maintain information to identify the signer of an old document based on an expired certificate. To support this goal, the archive must identify the actual person or system named in a certificate, establish that they requested the certificate, and show that the certificate was valid at the time the document was signed.[1] The archive must also include any information regarding the revocation of this certificate. *The sixth responsibility of a CA is the maintenance of sufficient archival information to establish the validity of certificates after they have expired.*

CAs are well suited to the generation of archive information, but not to its maintenance. A CA can create a detailed audit trail, with sufficient information to describe why it generated a certificate or revoked it. This is a common attribute of computer systems. However, maintaining that information for long periods of time is not a common function.

Delegating Responsibility

As stated earlier, these requirements may be difficult to satisfy simultaneously. A CA may choose to fulfill its highest-priority requirements, and delegate the remaining functions to other components. The primary responsibility of a CA is to protect the private key or keys used to sign certificates and CRLs. To satisfy this requirement, a CA must construct a security perimeter with physical, procedural, and technical controls. Having achieved this, the CA can also satisfy the third and fourth responsibilities. The same security perimeter may be used to protect the integrity of the CA certificate profile that is used to protect the integrity of certificate status information.

However, that same security perimeter may impede fulfillment of the remaining responsibilities. The three remaining infrastructure components are designed to accept those responsibilities on behalf of the CA, separating these requirements from the CA's security-focused tasks.

An entity that verifies certificate contents (especially identifying the user) is called a *registration authority* (RA). An RA may also assume some of the responsibility for certificate revocation decisions. An entity that distributes certificates and CRLs is called a *repository*. A repository may be designed to maximize performance and availability. The entity that provides long-term secure storage for the archival information is called an *archive*. An archive does not require the performance of a repository, but must be designed for secure storage.

---

[1] This may require additional information, such as a cryptographic timestamp. Chapter 17 presents a PKI-based protocol for obtaining cryptographic timestamps from a timestamp server. Additional information on cryptographic timestamps may be found in [SCHN96].

A CA is not restricted to a single RA, repository, or archive. In practice, a CA is likely to have multiple RAs; different entities may be needed for different groups of users. Repositories are often duplicated to maximize availability, increase performance, and add redundancy. There is no requirement for multiple archives.

Registration Authority

As stated previously, an RA is designed to verify certificate contents for the CA. Certificate contents may reflect information presented by the entity requesting the certificate, such as a driver's license or recent pay stub. They may also reflect information provided by a third party. For example, the credit limit assigned to a credit card reflects information obtained from credit bureaus. A certificate may reflect data from the company's Human Resources department or a letter from a designated company official. For example, Bob's certificate could indicate that he has signature authority for small contracts. The RA aggregates these inputs and provides this information to the CA.

Like the CA, the RA is a collection of computer hardware, software, and the person or people who operate it. Unlike a CA, a single person often operates an RA. Each CA will maintain a list of accredited RAs; that is, a list of RAs determined to be trustworthy. Each RA is known to the CA by a name and a public key. By verifying the RA's signature on a message, the CA can be sure that an accredited RA provided the information, and it can be trusted. Therefore, it is important that the RA provide adequate protection for its own private key. RAs should always use hardware cryptographic modules that have been validated against FIPS 140.

There are two basic models for RA verification of certificate contents. In the first model, the RA collects and verifies the necessary information for the requesting entity before a request for a certificate is submitted to the CA. The CA trusts the information in the request because the RA already verified it. In the second model, the CA provides the RA with information regarding a certificate request it has already received. The RA reviews the contents and determines if the information accurately describes the user. The RA provides the CA with a "yes" or "no" answer.

The first model is used when a user appears physically at the RA. When a user appears physically at the RA, identity can be established based on standard forms of identification (for example, driver's license or company identification card). If the user has already generated his or her key pair, the RA requests a certificate with the appropriate information from the CA. Alternatively, the RA may provide the user with a secret value for a one-time authentication. The user generates his or her key pair, requests his or her own certificate, and authenticates the request with the secret value.

This model may also be used when the RA possesses the user's hardware cryptographic module. In general, it is preferable for users to generate their own keys. However, key generation, depending on the public key algorithm employed, can be a particularly demanding cryptographic task. To limit the cost of a cryptographic module, it may be desirable to generate key pairs using special-purpose hardware and load the private keys onto the user's module at the RA. In this case, the RA generates a key pair and creates a certificate request with the public key, user name, and personal information. After obtaining the certificate from the CA, the RA conveys the cryptographic module to the user through out-of-band means, or the user appears at the RA to obtain the cryptographic module.

The second model is used when the user cannot be identified beforehand, and the user generates the certificate request. In this case, the user requests that a certificate be created containing certain information. The CA can determine that the user holds both the private and public keys, but may not know if other information is correct. For example, a user may assert ownership of a particular e-mail address. The CA would pass this request to the RA, which would validate (or disprove) the information and provide the result to the CA.

Repository

A repository distributes certificates and CRLs. A repository accepts certificates and CRLs from one or more CAs and makes them available to parties that need them to implement security services.

A *repository* is a system, and is known by its address and access protocol. It provides certificates and CRLs upon request. Requests could be based on the name of a user or CA or other information. Repositories are not trusted entities; the user accepts the certificates and CRLs because the CA signed them. The source of the information does not affect its trustworthiness. Since the data itself establishes its integrity, a repository may be designed to maximize availability and performance (for example, network throughput or query response time).

Of course, repositories need to restrict the set of users who can update the information. If an attacker replaces the correct certificates with garbage, or simply inserts an expired CRL, he or she can achieve a denial-of-service (DoS) attack. Users of the PKI would not be fooled into accepting the out-of-date information, but may be denied the security services they need.

There are two basic models for repositories. In the most common model, a repository will provide information upon request without authenticating the requester. In this case, the repository is supported through overhead costs for an organization. This implies a business model in which the cost of the PKI is underwritten by an organization, or the costs are based on a fee for each certificate issued. An alternative model exists, where the repository identifies and authenticates each request. This model is designed to support a cost-recovery business model based on pay per use. This model moves the cost from the subject of the certificate to the users of the certificate.

Archive

An archive accepts the responsibility for long-term storage of archival information on behalf of the CA. An archive asserts that the information was good at the time it was received, and has not been modified while in the archive. The information provided by the CA to the repository must be sufficient to determine if a certificate was actually issued by the CA as specified in the certificate, and was valid at that time. The archive protects that information through technical mechanisms and appropriate procedures while in its care. If a dispute arises at a later date, the information can be used to verify that the private key associated with the certificate was used to sign a document. This permits the verification of signatures on old documents (such as wills) at a later date.

Infrastructure Users

In this section, we introduces the two types of users supported by a PKI and describe their functionality. The two types of PKI users are certificate holders and relying parties. Certificate holders are the subject of a certificate and hold the corresponding private key. Relying parties use the public key in a certificate to verify signatures, encrypt data (key transport), or perform key agreement.

In theory, it is possible to design systems where the certificate holders are not relying parties and vice versa. They are described separately for completeness.

In practice, most entities hold both roles, and certificate holders behave as relying parties when they exchange messages with a CA or RA. In addition, the CA and RA are generally PKI users themselves. They generate and verify signatures and perform key agreement or key transport between themselves and with users.

Certificate Holders

Certificate holders obtain certificates from the infrastructure and use their private keys to implement security services. They generate digital signatures, decrypt data (for example, recover symmetric keys encrypted with their public key), and use their private key to establish symmetric keys through key agreement.

To meet these goals, a certificate holder must perform the following:

- Identify a CA to issue the certificate(s).
- Request a certificate directly from the CA or through the RA.
- Include the certificate in transactions as appropriate.

Certificate holders may need to interact with the repository to obtain their own certificate, but do not regularly interact with the repository.

Relying Party

Relying parties use the PKI to implement security services by employing the public key in another user's certificate. They can verify digital signatures, encrypt data (for example, encrypt a symmetric key), and use the public key in another party's certificate to establish a symmetric key through key agreement. Relying parties may include CAs, RAs, persons, and computing systems such as routers and firewalls.

To implement these security services, a relying party must perform the following:

- Identify a CA as its initial trust point.
- Verify signatures on certificates and CRLs.
- Obtain certificates and CRLs from a repository.
- Construct and validate certification paths.

A relying party interacts with the repositories on a day-to-day basis. Its interactions with CAs are limited to selection of an initial trust point. Relying parties have no interactions with RAs.

Build It or Buy It?

When an organization decides to deploy a PKI, it must determine whether to operate the infrastructure itself, outsource the operation, or some combination thereof. Any of the four infrastructure components may be outsourced. To determine which components, if any, can be appropriately outsourced, an organization must review its requirements and its abilities.

The CA must be operated in a secure manner. Some organizations are used to operating secure facilities and have the physical security in place. Organizations that do not have security expertise may find this more difficult, and may consider outsourcing.

The RA is designed to check the user's identity, personal information, policy information, privileges, and authorizations. This may be the most difficult component to outsource. In general, an organization knows its members best, and can most easily perform these functions.

The repository and archive can most easily be outsourced. Repositories are evaluated on performance and availability, not security issues. However, many organizations already maintain repositories that can be used to support a PKI with minimal incremental cost. Archives play a minor role in daily operations of a PKI, but demand strict technical and procedural controls. If an organization has not already established an archive, it may be cost effective to outsource this component.

CHAPTER 6

PKI Architectures

In Chapter 3, scalability was identified as one of Alice's basic PKI requirements. It is easy for Alice to accept and validate Bob's certificate when they both use the same certification authority (CA). However, Alice needs to communicate with hundreds of people, and some of them will choose another CA. In fact, Alice may need to process certificates from many different CAs. This introduces a problem. How can Alice determine if a trustworthy CA issued Bob's certificate?

There are two basic solutions to this problem. First, Alice can maintain a list of the CAs she deems trustworthy. This may be reasonable for a small number of CAs, but places the burden squarely on Alice. Alternatively, the CAs can establish trust relationships between themselves. Alice can combine these trust relationships to form a certification path. Then, Alice can examine the trust relationships in the path and determine whether Bob's certificate is trustworthy. This shifts the burden from Alice to the infrastructure, but it introduces additional complexity in the certificates that CAs issue to each other. Certificates issued to CAs may contain information that describes or limits CA trust relationships. Such information is not required in user certificates.

The architecture of a PKI describes the organization of its CAs and their trust relationships. PKI architectures are differentiated by the answers to several key questions:

- How many CAs are directly trusted?
- What types of trust relationships exist between the CAs?
- How easily can new CAs be added to the PKI?

- How complex is the construction of certification paths? Once built, how complex is verification?

- What is the impact if a CA is compromised? Is the impact the same for all CAs?

Each architecture has different strengths and weaknesses. This chapter begins by examining the attributes of the single CA and CA list architectures. These simple PKI architectures offer a complete solution for small PKI deployments and define the basis for evaluating other architectures.

To satisfy the needs of a larger *enterprise*, such as a large company or government agency, more complex enterprise PKI architectures are required. We will define two enterprise PKI architectures:

- Hierarchical PKI

- Mesh PKI

These architectures include multiple CAs that are connected by trust relationships. The two architectures employ different trust relationships, resulting in very different attributes.

Of course, Alice may need to communicate with users from different enterprises, and these enterprises may use different PKI architectures. For example, Alice and Bob may be users in a single CA PKI, Carol in a hierarchical PKI, and Doug in a mesh PKI. Alice still needs to communicate securely with each of them. We will describe three hybrid PKI architectures that can satisfy Alice's requirements:

- Extended CA List model

- Cross-certified enterprise PKIs

- Bridged PKI

Each of the architectures described in this chapter has strengths and weaknesses. Each is appropriate for some environments and inappropriate for others. This chapter will conclude by considering common environments and identifying appropriate PKI architectures.

Simple PKI Architectures

Where users have simple requirements, the PKI architecture may also be very simple. The two architectures presented in this section are the single CA and the CA Trust List. These architectures are sufficient when Alice only communicates with users from the CA that issued her certificate or a very small number of CAs. In these architectures, CAs need not establish trust relationships with other CAs. That is, the CAs only issue certificates to users.

Single CA

The most basic PKI architecture is a single CA that provides all the certificates and CRLs for a community of users. In this configuration, all users trust the CA that issued their own certificate. By definition, new CAs cannot be added to the PKI. Since there is only one CA, there are no CA trust relationships. The users accept only certificates and CRLs issued by their CA. As a result, certification paths can be constructed with a single certificate and a single CRL. Since all certificates are user certificates, path analysis will not include information that describes or limits CA trust relationships. Path construction and analysis can't get any easier than that!

Figure 6.1 depicts a single CA, the Fox Consulting CA, that issues certificates to the employees of the Fox Consulting company. Alice and Bob are two of those employees. Alice trusts the Fox CA, so she can easily construct and validate Bob's certification path.

While the simplest to implement, this architecture does not scale easily to support very large or diverse user communities. As Alice and Bob expand their set of secure applications, they may need to communicate with Carol at Hawk Data. The Fox CA only offers services to Fox Consulting employees, so Carol must get her certificate from another CA. Alice and Bob need an architecture that incorporates additional CAs to communicate with Carol.

The single CA PKI presents a single point of failure. Compromise of the CA invalidates the trust point information and all certificates that have been issued in this PKI. Every user in the PKI must be informed about the compromise immediately, or they may establish security based on unreliable information. To reestablish the CA, all certificates must be reissued and the new trust point information must be distributed to all the users.

Basic Trust Lists

The *trust list* is the most straightforward enhancement to the single CA architecture. In this architecture, more than one CA provides PKI services, but there are no trust relationships between CAs. In this model, Alice maintains a list of CAs that she trusts.

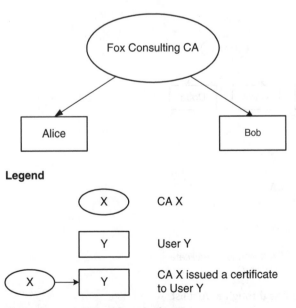

Figure 6.1   A PKI with a single CA.

She trusts valid certificates issued by any of them. New CAs can be added to the PKI by modifying the trust list. As with a single CA, there are no CA trust relationships. The users accept only certificates and CRLs issued by a CA in their trust list. As a result, one certificate and one CRL are all that is needed for any user. However, this is complicated slightly by the increase in the number of trust points. Once again, there are no CA certificates, so complex certificate extensions do not appear. Path construction and analysis are very easy.

In Figure 6.2, Carol has obtained certificates from the Hawk Data company CA. There is no trust relationship between the Fox CA and the Hawk CA. Alice wants to communicate with Carol securely, but there is no certification path beginning with Fox CA (whom Alice trusts most) that ends with Carol's certificate. Alice needs to add a new CA to her trust list. Once the Hawk CA is added to her trust list, Alice can verify Carol's certificate.

The primary advantage of this architecture is simplicity. There are no certification paths, just single certificates. In addition, the mechanics of adding a new CA to the PKI are very straightforward—Alice simply adds one more CA to her list of trusted CAs.

There are important disadvantages, however. Alice added the new CA to her trust list out of expediency because she wanted to communicate with Carol. However, Alice really should have investigated the Hawk CA before she added it to her trust list. In addition, Alice should maintain critical information about every CA that she trusts. As this number grows, it will be very difficult for her to keep this information up to date.

CA compromise is very difficult to handle with trust lists. If the Hawk CA private key is compromised, it will probably notify all its users immediately. However, the Hawk CA does not have a direct relationship with Alice; the Hawk CA probably does not even know that it is trusted by Alice. Alice will continue to trust certificates issued by the compromised CA until the news trickles down to her.

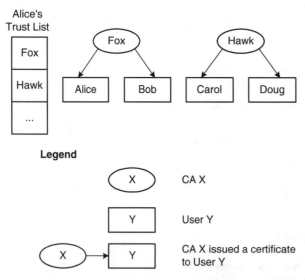

Figure 6.2 Supporting multiple CAs through a trust list.

Enterprise PKI Architectures

In this section, we present two enterprise PKI architectures. In these architectures, CAs establish trust relationships with other CAs from the same enterprise. The enterprise might be a company, a government agency, or a user community.

In the examples in this section, we assume that Alice, Bob, Carol, and Doug are all employed by a large company. Alice and Bob work in the Research and Development group, Carol is in the Legal group, and Doug is in Operations. The company is too large or complex to rely on a single CA; each of these groups will obtain its certificates from different CAs.

Hierarchical PKI

The traditional PKI architecture is the hierarchical PKI. In this architecture, multiple CAs provide PKI services, and the CAs are related through superior-subordinate relationships. In this architecture, all users trust the same central *root CA*. With the exception of the root CA, all the CAs have a single superior CA. CAs may have subordinate CAs or issue certificates to users. Each CA trust relationship is represented by a single certificate. The issuer is the superior CA; the subject is the subordinate.

To add a new CA to the PKI, one of the existing CAs issues a certificate to the new CA. Figure 6.3 shows a hierarchical PKI and three ways to add new CAs. The hierarchical PKI is shown as Figure 6.3 (a). In Figure 6.3 (b), the new CA was grafted directly under the root CA of the existing PKI; in Figure 6.3 (c), the new CA became a subordinate of CA2. Two hierarchical PKIs may be merged in the same fashion. In Figure 6.3 (d), an entire hierarchical PKI is added to the existing PKI under the root.

Certification paths are easy to develop in a hierarchy because every CA has a single superior CA. There is a simple, obvious, and deterministic path from a user's certificate back to the single trust point at the root. The certification paths are relatively short. The longest path is equal to the depth of the tree: a CA certificate for each subordinate CA, plus the user's certificate. Superior CAs may impose restrictions upon the subordinate's actions. These restrictions could be maintained through procedural mechanisms or imposed through the certificates themselves. In the latter case, the CA certificate will contain additional information to describe the restrictions. (The types of restrictions are discussed in detail in Chapter 7, "X.509 Certificates.")

In Figure 6.4, the R&D, Legal, and Ops CAs have joined a small hierarchical PKI. The root CA is the HQ CA. Alice sets her trust point to HQ, even though she obtained her certificate from the R&D CA. Alice can easily construct Carol's certification path. It contains two certificates, not just one. The certification path will be more difficult to analyze than a single certificate. The path contains more certificates, and the CA certificates contain additional information that must be processed.

Hierarchical PKIs handle the compromise of a single CA within the infrastructure easily, as long as it is not the root CA. If a CA is compromised, its superior CA simply revokes its certificate. Once the CA has been reestablished, it issues new certificates to all of its users. The superior issues a new certificate to the CA, containing the new public key, bringing it back into the hierarchy. During the interim, transactions between any

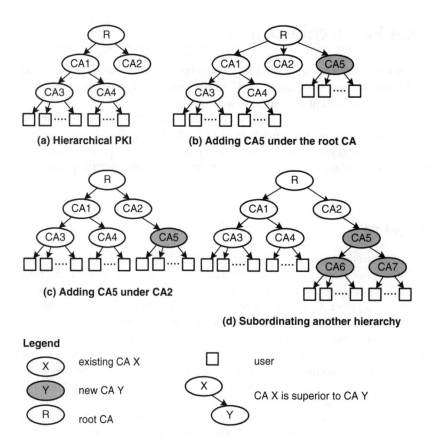

Figure 6.3   Expanding a hierarchical PKI.

two users outside the compromised part of the PKI can proceed. Of course, users in the compromised part of the hierarchy lose all services.

On the other hand, the compromise of the root CA has the same impact as in the single CA architecture. It is critical to inform all the users in the hierarchical PKI that the root CA has been compromised. Until the root CA is reestablished, issues new certificates to its subordinates, and distributes the new trust point information, users cannot use the PKI to establish secure communications. There is one advantage in comparison to the compromise of the single CA: The root CA will have to reissue a much smaller number of certificates. In addition, the root CA can operate offline, significantly reducing the likelihood of key compromise.

Mesh PKI

The mesh PKI architecture is the primary alternative to a hierarchy. This architecture is also referred to as the network PKI or a *web of trust*. In this architecture, multiple CAs provide PKI services, and the CAs are related through peer-to-peer relationships. Each user trusts a single CA; however, the trusted CA is not the same for all users.

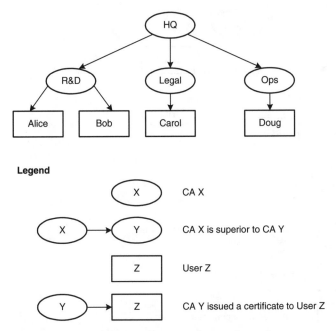

Figure 6.4 A hierarchical PKI for Alice and Carol.

In general, users will trust the CA that issued their certificate. CAs issue certificates to each other; a pair of certificates describes their bidirectional trust relationship.

A new CA can easily be added to a mesh PKI. The new CA exchanges certificates with at least one CA that is already a member of the mesh. However, path construction is particularly difficult in a mesh PKI. In a hierarchy, building a certification path from a user's certificate to a trust point is deterministic. In a mesh, this process is nondeterministic. Path discovery is more difficult since there are often multiple choices. Some of these choices lead to a valid path, but others result in useless dead-ends. Even worse, it is possible in a mesh PKI to construct an endless loop of certificates. The length of a path may be longer than in a typical hierarchical PKI. In the worst case, the path length can approach the number of CAs in the PKI.

Certificates issued in a mesh PKI are also more complex. Since the CAs have peer-to-peer relationships, they cannot impose conditions governing the types of certificates other CAs can issue. If a CA wishes to limit the trust, it must specify these limitations as certificate extensions in the certificates issued to all of its peers.

Mesh PKIs are very resilient since there are multiple trust points. Compromise of a single CA cannot bring down the entire PKI. CAs that issued certificates to the compromised CA simply revoke them, thereby removing the compromised CA from the PKI. Users associated with other CAs will still have a valid trust point, and can communicate securely with the remaining users in their PKI. In the best case, the PKI shrinks by a single CA and its associated user community. At worst, the PKI fragments into several smaller PKIs. Recovery from a compromise is simpler in a mesh CA than in a hierarchical PKI, primarily because it affects fewer users.

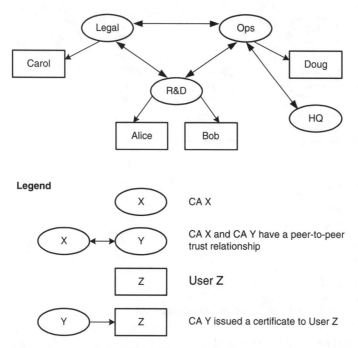

Figure 6.5   A mesh PKI for Alice and Carol.

In Figure 6.5, the CAs are incorporated into a mesh PKI. Alice and Bob trust the R&D CA. Carol trusts the Legal CA, and Doug trusts the Ops CA. It is more difficult for Alice to find and analyze a certification path for Carol than in a hierarchical PKI. The certification path may contain two or three certificates. It contains two if the path from the R&D CA directly to the Legal CA is used. However, it contains three certificates if the path through the Ops CA to the Legal CA is used. While attempting to find one of these valid paths, Alice may also follow other paths that result in dead-ends. For example, Alice might try a path that includes the HQ CA. The certificates will also be more complicated to process, since all limitations in trust relationships are expressed as additional information in the certificates.

Hybrid PKI Architectures

Thus far, we have described PKI architectures as competing solutions for an enterprise or user community. Of course, many applications will cross the boundaries between two communities or enterprises. PKIs must provide users with the tools they need to establish secure communications between users of different enterprise PKIs.

Pragmatically, the CA trust list, hierarchical PKI, and the mesh PKI architectures are often combined to create a hybrid PKI. Such hybrid PKIs allow organizations to apply the most appropriate architecture to different facets of an organization, and address the technical, political, and scaling issues that are encountered deploying PKIs.

In this section's examples, we assume that Alice and Bob are employed by Fox Consulting. Carol works for the R&D group in Hawk Data. Doug works in the Legal group at Dove, Incorporated. The three companies are working collaboratively. Each company operates its own PKI, each choosing a suitable architecture.

Consider the scenario shown in Figure 6.6. Alice and Bob received their certificates from the Fox Consulting CA. Carol received her certificate from the R&D group's CA in Hawk Data's hierarchical PKI. Doug obtained his certificate from the Legal group's CA in Dove, Incorporated's mesh PKI. Alice may use any of three hybrid PKI architectures to establish secure communications with Carol and Doug. The first architecture extends the trust list architecture to support certification paths of lengths greater than one. In the second architecture, CAs and enterprise PKIs establish peer-to-peer relationships to support secure communications between their users. The third architecture introduces the *Bridge CA* as a unifying component expressly designed to support the combination of PKIs.

Extended Trust List Architecture

The *extended trust list* architecture addresses the shortcomings of the simple trust list. A list of multiple trust points is maintained. Each trust point identifies a PKI that the user trusts, which may be a single CA, a hierarchy, or a mesh. Alice trusts certification paths that begin with any of the certificates in the trust list.

In this architecture, Alice adds one CA to her trust list for each trusted PKI. As shown in Figure 6.7, Alice must trust three CAs to communicate with Bob, Carol, and Doug. Alice trusts her own CA, the root of the Hawk Data hierarchy, and one CA in the Dove, Inc. mesh. Either peer-to-peer or hierarchical relationships may relate CAs within an enterprise PKI. Alice can easily add a new CA or entire enterprise PKI to her trust list. The complexity of the certificates depends upon the relationships incorporated in each enterprise PKI.

This architecture preserves the basic strength of the trust list. If Alice has a business need to trust users from a PKI that does not have a trust relationship with her own CA, the trust list provides a mechanism to quickly and easily satisfy this requirement. In addition, it adds the basic strength of the hierarchical and mesh PKIs. Alice can take

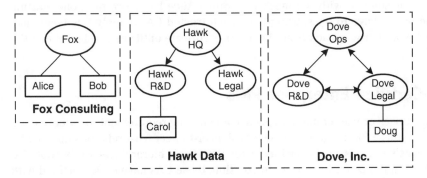

Figure 6.6 Three enterprise PKIs.

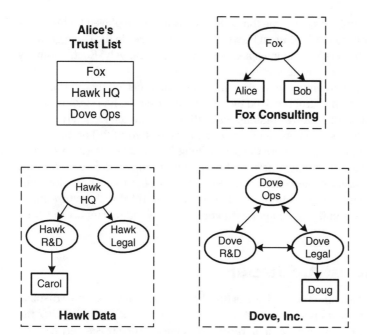

Figure 6.7   Supporting multiple PKIs through a trust list.

advantage of the trust relationships established by the CAs she trusts to establish security services with other communities of users. This should reduce the number of trust points that she must establish and keep updated.

The extended trust list architecture does not resolve the problems of trust list management and CA compromise. As with the trust list architecture, Alice may be motivated by expediency rather than security considerations when choosing her trust points. As the trust list grows, maintenance becomes increasingly difficult. As with the basic trust list, Alice may not receive timely notification of a CA compromise.

The extended trust list architecture also introduces new path construction problems. Since Alice cannot determine which of the trusted CAs could begin the certification path, path building is more complex. Alice cannot work forward, starting at the trusted CA, as she can with the mesh PKI. Since Alice has more than one starting point, she would have to try starting from each trusted CA to apply this technique. Alice must work her way back from the user's certificate until she reaches one of the trusted CAs.

Cross-Certified Enterprise PKIs

If two enterprises or user communities have an ongoing requirement for secure communications, these PKIs may wish to establish peer-to-peer trust relationships. In Figure 6.8, Alice's CA has cross-certified with the Hawk hierarchical PKI's root CA, and R&D CA in the Dove, Inc. mesh. In addition, these CAs have cross-certified with each other.

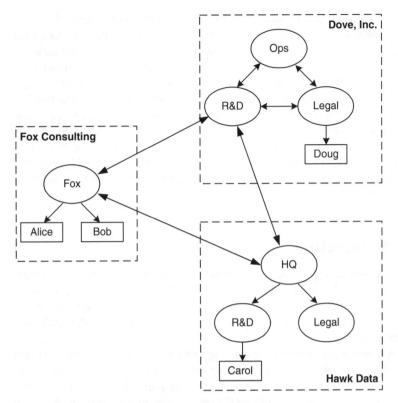

Figure 6.8 Three cross-certified enterprise PKIs.

Each user can maintain a single trust point. Alice, Bob, and Doug trust the CA that issued their certificates, and Carol trusts her root CA. While the cross-enterprise relationships are peer to peer, either peer-to-peer or hierarchical relationships relate CAs within the enterprise PKI.

Unlike the trust list, Alice cannot add a new PKI on her own. CA administrators must review the policies and practices of another CA before they cross-certify. On the other hand, the CA administrators are probably better qualified than Alice to determine if a CA or PKI is trustworthy. Once the CAs have cross-certified, Bob can also validate user certificates in the other PKI. Therefore, one administrator action enables secure communications for the whole user population. With the extended trust list architecture, both Bob and Alice need to update their own trust lists.

Certification paths in this environment may be quite complex. Since the resulting PKI includes both mesh and hierarchical sections, the path-building algorithms must combine both hierarchical and mesh certification path-building techniques to perform efficiently in this architecture. Certificates may be quite complex, and finding a valid path may be difficult. On the plus side, Alice is building paths from a single trust point.

Many of Alice's problems with CA compromise are resolved by this architecture. Alice is maintaining a single trust point, and she has a direct relationship with that CA. She can expect immediate notification if her own CA is compromised. Alice's CA has a direct relationship with the two cross-certified CAs. If either is compromised, Alice's CA will be notified and will revoke the appropriate certificate. In addition, if CAs within the other enterprise PKIs are compromised, they will be handled as discussed earlier.

This architecture is an appropriate solution when a small number of enterprise PKIs must establish trust relationships. In Figure 6.8, three peer-to-peer relationships and six CA certificates were required to establish these relationships. However, this number grows rapidly as the number of enterprise PKIs increases. Cross-certifying n enterprise PKIs requires $(n^2 - n)/2$ peer-to-peer relationships and $(n^2 - n)$ certificates. In Figure 6.9, there are eight enterprise PKIs. Cross-certifying each pair of PKIs requires 28 peer-to-peer relationships and 56 CA certificates. Since establishing these relationships requires a time-consuming review of policies and practices, this architecture rapidly becomes an intractable problem.

Bridge CA Architecture

The bridge CA architecture was designed to address the shortcomings of the extended trust list and cross-certified enterprise PKI architectures. The user cannot be expected to maintain current information on a large number of trust points. On the other hand, CA administrators need a mechanism to establish trust relationships with other PKIs in a more efficient fashion.

The bridge CA meets these requirements, acting as a sort of trust arbitrator. Unlike a mesh CA, the bridge CA does not issue certificates directly to users. Unlike a root CA in a hierarchy, the bridge CA is not intended for use as a trust point. All PKI users consider the bridge CA as an intermediary. The bridge CA establishes peer-to-peer relationships with different enterprise PKIs. These relationships can be combined to form a *bridge of trust* that connects the users from the different PKIs.

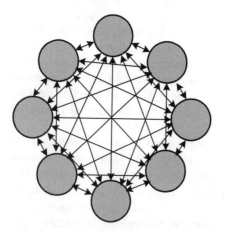

Figure 6.9   Eight cross-certified enterprise PKIs.

If the trust domain is implemented as a hierarchical PKI, the bridge CA will establish a relationship with the root CA. If the domain is implemented as a mesh PKI, the bridge CA will establish a relationship with only one of its CAs. In either case, the CA that enters into a trust relationship with the bridge CA is termed a *principal CA.*

In Figure 6.10, the bridge CA has established relationships with three enterprise PKIs. The first is Bob and Alice's CA, the second is Carol's hierarchical PKI, and the third is Doug's mesh PKI. None of the users trusts the bridge CA directly. Alice and Bob trust the CA that issued their certificates; they trust the bridge CA because the Fox CA issued a certificate to it. Carol's trust point is the root CA of her hierarchy; she trusts the bridge CA because the root CA issued a certificate to it. Doug trusts the CA in the mesh that issued his certificate; he trusts the bridge CA because there is a valid certification path from the CA that issued him a certificate to the bridge CA. Alice (or Bob) can use the bridge of trust that exists through the bridge CA to establish relationships with Carol and Doug.

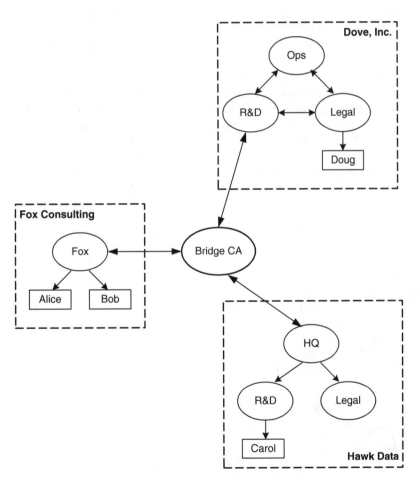

Figure 6.10   Connecting three enterprise PKIs with a bridge CA.

The trust relationships between the bridge CA and the principal CAs are all peer to peer. The trust relationships within the enterprise PKIs it connects are determined by their own architecture. Within the hierarchical PKI, trust relationships are superior-subordinate. Within the mesh PKI, the trust relationships are peer to peer.

It is easy to add new CAs, or entire enterprise PKIs, to a bridge-connected PKI. The change is transparent to the users, since no change in trust points is required. As the PKI grows, the number of trust relationships that must be established is far more manageable. In Figure 6.10, three trust relationships were established for three enterprise PKIs. This is the same as the cross-certified example shown in Figure 6.8. However, in Figure 6.11, a bridge CA is shown connecting eight enterprise PKIs. This required eight trust relationships, rather than the 28 required by the cross-certified example shown in Figure 6.9.

The bridge CA does not resolve the certification path construction or validation problems. Path construction is just as complex as in a mesh PKI, since some of the enterprise PKIs are themselves a mesh. Certificates issued to and by the bridge may be very complex to ensure that the trust relationship is accurately conveyed. This increases the complexity of the path validation software.

In a bridge CA architecture, the PKI can easily recover from compromise. If the principal CA from an enterprise PKI is compromised, the bridge CA revokes its certificate. This invalidates the trust relationship between that PKI and any of the other enterprise PKIs. The rest of the relationships are not affected. If the bridge CA itself is compromised, it notifies the principal CAs. Since none of the users has the bridge CA as a trust point, the principal CAs simply revoke the certificates they issued to the bridge CA. For completeness, the bridge CA can issue a CRL revoking the certificates it has issued as well. The result is a set of separate PKIs, so users from different PKIs will lose the ability to establish secure services. On the other hand, it is straightforward to reestablish the PKI after rebuilding the bridge CA.

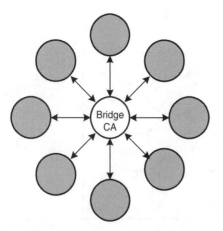

Figure 6.11   Connecting eight enterprise PKIs with a bridge CA.

Choosing the Best Architecture

What architecture should an organization choose? None of the architectures is perfect for all situations. Each PKI architecture has its own strengths and weaknesses. By understanding your organization and its requirements, you will be able to choose the architecture that best meets those needs.

A single CA is the sensible, straightforward solution for a small, homogeneous community. When the community can agree upon a single CA to issue all of their certificates, the problems associated with certification path development and validation disappear. Compromise of the CA is catastrophic, of course, and invalidates all of the certificates. As a result, the community loses all access to security services. On the other hand, such a close-knit community will be able to efficiently distribute the failure notice and rapidly rebuild the PKI.

A hierarchical PKI is the most elegant solution for an organization with a well-defined structure. The hierarchical PKI parallels the organization's structure, so authority is derived naturally. Certification path development and validation are straightforward. However, it can be very difficult to impose this structure on a collection of independently deployed CAs. If an organization intends to deploy a hierarchical PKI, it is best to deploy the root CA first. As subordinate CAs deploy, they can be incorporated into the hierarchy immediately, thereby avoiding thorny transition problems. Compromise of the root CA is a catastrophe; compromise of any other CA is straightforward to resolve. The root CA policies, practices, and physical protections should make compromise extremely unlikely.

A mesh PKI is a pragmatic, rather than elegant, solution for those organizations that do not have a well-defined structure. Developing a hierarchical PKI would be controversial, since the trust relationships are not widely agreed upon. The mesh PKI is more straightforward to deploy for these organizations, since the peer-to-peer relationships are not contentious. If CAs have been established beforehand by different parts of an organization, the mesh PKI will be the simplest to implement. If an organization needs a PKI that can survive CA compromise, the mesh PKI is best. Compromise of a single CA will be a catastrophe for its users, but transactions between other users of other CAs will be largely unaffected. The complexities of path development and path validation are the major weaknesses of the mesh PKI architecture.

When a cross-enterprise PKI is unavailable, trust lists are the work-around. Alice and Carol may want to protect their e-mail, but they cannot dictate what trust relationships are established between their organizations. Their respective PKIs may choose not to cross-certify. By maintaining trust lists of PKIs, Alice and Carol can still establish secure communication. In spite of their many limitations, trust lists are the solution that provides control to individual users. Because many organizations have not deployed PKIs yet, trust lists are the most widely used architecture.

Cross-certification of enterprise PKIs is a straightforward solution for small numbers of PKIs. This works when two organizations have well-established relationships. For example, two companies that have signed a contract for a long-term joint venture might cross-certify their PKIs. However, this solution is not acceptable when large numbers of parties need to work together, or where business relationships are dynamic.

Bridge CAs are an efficient solution for connecting a large number of enterprise PKIs. This model is ideally suited to today's dynamic business relationships. While each company has a limited set of business partners at any given moment, this set may be very fluid. Companies may rapidly establish and terminate these relationships. However, the companies within a particular industry are not so dynamic. The bridge CA establishes a single relationship for each enterprise PKI. As a side effect, relationships are established indirectly between every pair of enterprises that cross-certifies with the bridge CA. By establishing a bridge of trust between all PKIs, even if they have never worked together before, the bridge CA enables the dynamic business relationships required by today's economy.

X.509 Public Key Certificates

In Chapter 3, we listed nine properties that certificates would satisfy in an ideal world. The first of these properties was that a certificate "would be a purely digital object, so it can be distributed over the Internet and processed automatically." This was a bit of a simplification; to support automatic processing, certificates need to be digital objects and encoded in a standard format. A standard digital format for certificates allows Alice and Bob to process each other's certificates efficiently. The widely accepted standard format for public key certificates is the X.509 public key certificate.

The X.509 certificate format has evolved into a flexible and powerful mechanism. It may be used to convey a variety of information. Much of that information is optional, and the contents of mandatory fields may vary as well. It is important for PKI implementers to understand the choices they face, and the consequences of those choices. Unwise choices may hinder interoperability or prevent support for critical applications. The goal of this chapter is to educate readers so they can make informed decisions.

This chapter is organized into five major sections. First, we review the evolution of the X.509 standard. Understanding its history explains many implementation details. Second, basic building blocks that are reused repeatedly in the X.509 format are defined. The third section describes the mandatory certificate contents. The fourth section discusses the optional features. The final section provides baseline recommendations for the contents of various certificates.

Throughout this chapter, the ASN.1 structure definitions for the various data structures are included as a supplement to the text. These structure definitions describe the order and type of the various fields, and denote which fields are optional. Some brief notes on ASN.1 features used by X.509 are included in Appendix A, "ASN.1 Primer"; however, the reader does not need to be an ASN.1 expert to make informed choices! ASN.1 details are transparent to PKI users, and nearly transparent to PKI staff.

The ASN.1 details are a critical issue for PKI product developers of course. For the details of the X.509 ASN.1 format and encoding, see Peter Gutmann's *X.509 Style Guide* [GUTM00].

X.509 Certificate Evolution

The X.509 certificate is named after the document in which it was originally specified: CCITT Recommendation X.509 [X50988]. This document specifies the authentication framework for the X.500 Directory. X.509 was first published in 1988. The X.500 Directory requires strong authentication to ensure that only authorized users make modifications. In addition, when the Directory contains confidential information, authentication can be used to control Directory access.

Over time, the focus shifted from supporting the Directory to developing a general-purpose PKI. As a result, two upwardly compatible versions have been published since 1988 [X50997]. Version 2 certificates addressed a single issue: reuse of names. Version 3 of the X.509 certificate introduces certificate extensions. Extensions are used when the issuer wishes to include information not supported by the basic certificate fields. All modern PKI implementations generate and process X.509 version 3 (X.509 v3) certificates. The set of extensions used by implementations varies widely. A fourth edition of the X.509 standard was recently completed [X50900]. This edition does not modify the certificate format, but it does define several new extensions.

The Internet Engineering Task Force (IETF) profiled X.509 certificates for the Internet. The Internet Certificate and CRL Profile was published in March 1999 as RFC 2459 [HOUS99]. RFC 2459 identifies optional features of X.509 that are required for the Internet, and it discourages the use of other features. The IETF is currently updating RFC 2459.

We were heavily involved in the creation of RFC 2459, and we are also involved in the ongoing update. This text relies on the IETF specifications. Where the IETF Profile is more specific, the IETF requirements are described rather than the ISO specifications.

ASN.1 Building Blocks

This section describes five ASN.1 types that are used repeatedly in the X.509 certificate structure and the certificate extensions. Some of these building blocks were defined in other ISO or CCITT specifications; others were defined in X.509 itself.

Object Identifiers

Object identifiers (OIDs) are one of the basic ASN.1 data types. An OID is a sequence of integers that uniquely identifies an object or an *arc*. The IETF standard notation for OIDs [HOWE95] is the sequence of integers separated by periods (for example, 1.3.6

or 1.3.6.1). OIDs are allocated hierarchically. Each authority is responsible for assigning semantics to all subordinate OIDs. Authorities may also delegate subtrees, or arcs, to other authorities. In this way, each OID is guaranteed to be globally unique.

An alternative representation for OIDs is used in ASN.1 definitions. OIDs are assigned textual names, and are written as an ordered sequence of integers. For example, the U.S. Department of Defense arc can be written as:

```
dod ::= OBJECT IDENTIFIER { 1 3 6 }
```

An OID can also be specified using the name of an arc. For example:

```
internet ::= OBJECT IDENTIFIER { dod 1 }
```

When referring to standard OIDs in the text, we use the textual names. They are more descriptive. When a sequence of integers is needed, we use the dotted notation.

OIDs appear frequently in X.509 certificates. They are used to indicate cryptographic algorithms (for example, RSA or DSA), certificate policies, and extensions. Most of the necessary OIDs are already defined. However, almost every PKI deployment will require obtaining a few new OIDs. In particular, most PKIs will need at least one OID to encode the certificate policy. It is critical that OIDs are obtained from legitimate OID arc owners! Making up an OID will result in collisions, and the system that processes such a certificate will likely misinterpret it. Appendix B, "Object Identifiers," includes several legitimate sources for OIDs.

Algorithm Identifiers

The algorithm identifier is an ASN.1 structured type that conveys information about cryptographic algorithms and keys. The algorithm identifier is composed of an OID that identifies the algorithm and optional parameters.

The algorithm identifier ASN.1 syntax is:

```
AlgorithmIdentifier  ::=  SEQUENCE  {
    algorithm             OBJECT IDENTIFIER,
    parameters            ANY DEFINED BY algorithm OPTIONAL  }
```

Algorithm identifiers are used in two ways in X.509 certificates. First, algorithm identifiers indicate which digital signature algorithm was used to sign a certificate. For this use, algorithm parameters are not required. Second, algorithm identifiers indicate the algorithm associated with the subject public key. Some cryptographic algorithms, such as DSA and Diffie-Hellman, require parameters as well as a public key. The RSA algorithm does not require parameters. An RSA public key is identified by the OID 1.2.840.113549.1.1.1 along with a parameter value of NULL.

Directory String

The Directory String is an ASN.1 structured type used to represent textual information regardless of language or character set. The DirectoryString type is defined as a *choice* of five different ASN.1 base types: PrintableString, TeletexString, BMPString, UTF8String, and UniversalString. Different types support different languages, as shown in Table 7.1.

Table 7.1   Directory String Languages and Character Sets

STRING TYPE	SUPPORTED CHARACTER SETS AND LANGUAGES
PrintableString	This type supports most of the printable ASCII characters. Most notably, this type does not include the at sign character (@).
TeletexString	This type supports the T.61 character set. TeletexString is a superset of PrintableString and supports most northern European languages.
BMPString	BMP means basic multiplane, and it uses a 16-bit character encoding. BMPString supports a variety of languages.
UTF8String and UniversalString	UTF8String and UniversalString are semantically equivalent multibyte character encodings. Both of these string types support any language for which a digital encoding has been defined.

The ASN.1 syntax for DirectoryString is:

```
DirectoryString  ::=  CHOICE {
    teletexString        TeletexString (SIZE (1..MAX)),
    printableString      PrintableString (SIZE (1..MAX)),
    universalString      UniversalString (SIZE (1..MAX)),
    utf8String           UTF8String (SIZE (1.. MAX)),
    bmpString            BMPString (SIZE (1..MAX)) }
```

In theory, strings may be equivalent even if they are encoded using different string types. For example, the string "Bob Burton" may be encoded using any of the string types. To compare two such strings, one could translate both of them to UTF8, and then compare the translated strings. In practice, this is not done. Rather, strings are encoded in the most restrictive type that includes all the necessary characters, and strings encoded in different types are assumed different.

However, printable strings have specific processing rules. Printable strings are compared without regard to case after whitespace compression. When encoded as printable strings, the following text strings are considered equivalent: "Bob Burton", "BOB BURTON", and " Bob BuRtOn ".

Distinguished Names

The distinguished name (DN) is a structured type that supports a hierarchical naming system. The X.500 suite of standards was expected to result in a global Directory. This lofty goal required a name form that could be used to create globally unique names. Naming authorities manage their own name spaces, and only that authority assigns names in that space, ensuring collision-free names.

The ASN.1 syntax for distinguished names is surprisingly complicated. In fact, it is probably the most complicated ASN.1 in this book. It is included here for completeness:

```
Name   ::=  CHOICE  {
   RDNSequence  }

RDNSequence  ::=  SEQUENCE OF RelativeDistinguishedName

RelativeDistinguishedName  ::=  SET OF AttributeTypeAndValue

AttributeTypeAndValue  ::=  SEQUENCE  {
   type      AttributeType,
   value     AttributeValue  }

AttributeType  ::=  OBJECT IDENTIFIER

AttributeValue  ::=  ANY DEFINED BY AttributeType
```

DNs are an ordered list of naming attributes. Each attribute has a type and a value. The attribute type is encoded as an OID. In this book, DNs are written as "type 1=value 1; type 2=value 2; ... type n=value n", beginning at the root. There are two basic DN styles. The first style is constructed from X.500 naming attributes. The second style is based on the Internet Domain Name System (DNS). The most common X.500 naming attributes are country (written as c=), organization (o=), organizational unit (ou=), locality (l=), and common name (cn=). For example:

```
c=US; o=Fox Consulting; ou=R&D; cn=Alice Adams
c=US; o=Fox Consulting; l=Washington; cn=Bob Burton
c=UK; o=Hawk Data; ou=Legal; cn=Carol Cousins
```

The Internet community wants to use DNs that reflect their DNS names. The IETF-defined the domain component (dc=) naming attribute makes this possible. For example:

```
dc=com; dc=dove; dc=legal
dc=com; dc=dove; dc=legal; cn=Doug Dillon
```

A DN with zero naming attributes is called an *empty DN*.

General Names

The general name is a structured type that is used to encode any name form. The structure provides a choice of seven standard name forms, and it allows locally defined name forms.

The ASN.1 syntax for the general name is:

```
GeneralName  ::=  CHOICE  {
   otherName                 [0]   OtherName,
   rfc822Name                [1]   IA5String,
   dNSName                   [2]   IA5String,
   x400Address               [3]   ORAddress,
   directoryName             [4]   Name,
   ediPartyName              [5]   EDIPartyName,
   uniformResourceIdentifier [6]   IA5String,
```

```
        iPAddress                [7]  OCTET STRING,
        registeredID             [8]  OBJECT IDENTIFIER  }
OtherName  ::=  SEQUENCE  {
    type-id                  OBJECT IDENTIFIER,
    value              [0]  EXPLICIT ANY DEFINED BY type-id  }

EDIPartyName  ::=  SEQUENCE  {
    nameAssigner             [0]  DirectoryString OPTIONAL,
    partyName                [1]  DirectoryString  }
```

The seven standard name forms cover the most frequently employed name forms. Any other name form is handled by an OID to identify the name form followed by a name form-specific string. Other name is used for Kerberos principal names.

Time

Time is used to express date and time. It contains two alternative representations. UTC time contains a two-digit representation of the year, omitting the century digits. Generalized time contains a four-digit representation of the year. Very explicit rules determine which alternative is to be used to express any particular date and time value.

The ASN.1 syntax for Time is:

```
Time  ::=  CHOICE  {
    utcTime      UTCTime,        --   YYMMDDHHMMSSZ
    generalTime  GeneralizedTime --  YYYYMMDDHHMMSSZ
    }
```

UTC time must be used for dates between the year 1950 and the year 2049 (inclusive). X.509 certificates were not invented until the 1980s, so we are sure that no dates need to be represented within the certificate fields that are before 1950. The year field is interpreted as follows:

If YY is equal to or greater than 50, the year is 19YY.

If YY is less than 50, the year is 20YY.

Generalized time must be used for dates in the year 2050 or later.
Dates before the year 1950 cannot be expressed.
For UTC time and generalized time, The Internet Certificate and CRL profile [HOUS99] requires the values to be expressed in Greenwich Mean Time (Zulu) and include seconds. Seconds are explicitly stated, even if zero.

X.509 Certificates

X.509 Certificates (Figure 7.1) may be considered as three nested components. The first component is the *tamper-evident envelope*. The digital signature provides the tamper-evident wrapper. Inside the envelope, we find the *basic certificate content*. The basic

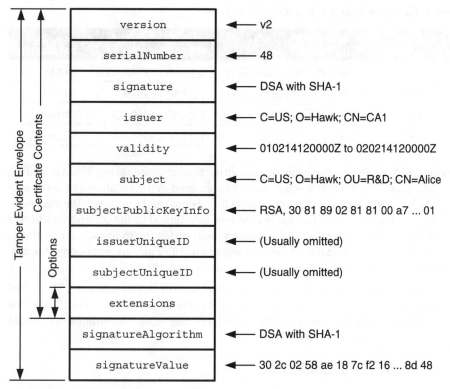

Figure 7.1 X.509 certificate structure.

certificate content includes the information that must be present in every certificate. The basic certificate content may include an optional *set of certificate extensions*. This component contains optional information. The vast majority of certificates generated today will include all three components. The following sections address each of the components in turn.

The Tamper-Evident Envelope

At the outermost level, certificates have just three fields: the to-be-signed certificate, the signature algorithm identifier, and the signature value. Consider the tamper-evident envelope as a transparent plastic envelope around the certificate content. The message is easily read, but it cannot be modified without tearing the envelope.

The certificate is defined by the following ASN.1 type definition:

```
Certificate  ::=  SEQUENCE  {
   tbsCertificate          TBSCertificate,
   signatureAlgorithm      AlgorithmIdentifier,
   signatureValue          BIT STRING  }
```

tbsCertificate. This field contains the signed certificate, and its structure is discussed in the next section.

Table 7.2 OIDs for Common Digital Signature Algorithms

PUBLIC KEY ALGORITHM	HASH FUNCTION	ALGORITHM IDENTIFIER	ALGORITHM OID	PARAMETERS
RSA	MD5	md5WithRSAEncryption	1.2.840.113549.1.1.4	NULL
RSA	SHA-1	sha1WithRSAEncryption	1.2.840.113549.1.1.5	NULL
DSA	SHA-1	id-dsa-with-sha1	1.2.840.10040.4.3	Absent
ECDSA	SHA-1	ecdsa-with-SHA1	1.2.840.10045.4.1	Absent

signatureAlgorithm. The signature algorithm field contains an algorithm identifier, and it identifies the digital signature algorithm used by the certificate issuer to sign the certificate. The optional parameters field is not used to validate the signature. This field is not inside the tamper-evident envelope, but the information in this field repeated is repeated in the signature field within the to-be-signed certificate, which is protected. Table 7.2 lists the object identifier and corresponding parameters field for the most common digital signature algorithms.

signatureValue. The signature value field contains the digital signature. The digital signature is computed using the ASN.1 DER encoded to-be-signed certificate. The resulting signature value is encoded as a bit string, using conventions defined for the specified signature algorithm.

Basic Certificate Content

The to-be-signed certificate is the real meat of the X.509 certificate; it contains all the basic certificate information. At a minimum, it contains six fields: the serial number, the certificate signature algorithm identifier, the certificate issuer name, the certificate validity period, the public key, and the subject name. The subject is the party that controls the corresponding private key. There are four optional fields: the version number, two unique identifiers, and the extensions. These optional fields appear only in version 2 and version 3 certificates.

The following ASN.1 syntax defines the basic certificate content. Following the definition, each of the fields in the structure is described.

```
TBSCertificate  ::=  SEQUENCE  {
    version             [0] EXPLICIT Version DEFAULT v1,
    serialNumber            CertificateSerialNumber,
    signature               AlgorithmIdentifier,
    issuer                  Name,
    validity                Validity,
    subject                 Name,
    subjectPublicKeyInfo    SubjectPublicKeyInfo,
    issuerUniqueID      [1] IMPLICIT UniqueIdentifier OPTIONAL,
                            -- If present, version shall be v2 or v3
    subjectUniqueID     [2] IMPLICIT UniqueIdentifier OPTIONAL,
                            -- If present, version shall be v2 or v3
    extensions          [3] EXPLICIT Extensions OPTIONAL  }
                            -- If present, version shall be v3
```

```
Version  ::=  INTEGER  {  v1(0), v2(1), v3(2)  }

CertificateSerialNumber  ::=  INTEGER

Validity  ::=  SEQUENCE  {
   notBefore        Time,
   notAfter         Time  }

UniqueIdentifier  ::=  BIT STRING

SubjectPublicKeyInfo  ::=  SEQUENCE  {
   algorithm           AlgorithmIdentifier,
   subjectPublicKey    BIT STRING  }

Extensions  ::=  SEQUENCE SIZE (1..MAX) OF Extension

Extension  ::=  SEQUENCE  {
   extnID      OBJECT IDENTIFIER,
   critical    BOOLEAN DEFAULT FALSE,
   extnValue   OCTET STRING  }
```

version. The optional version field describes the syntax of the certificate. When the version field is omitted, the certificate is encoded in the original, version 1, syntax. Version 1 certificates do not include the unique identifiers or extensions. When the certificate includes unique identifiers but not extensions, the version field indicates version 2. When the certificate includes extensions, as almost all modern certificates do, the version field indicates version 3.

serialNumber. The serial number is an integer assigned by the certificate issuer to each certificate. The serial number must be unique for each certificate generated by a particular issuer. The combination of the issuer name and serial number uniquely identifies any certificate.

signature. The signature field is an algorithm identifier. It is a copy of the signature algorithm contained in the signature algorithm field; however, the digital signature protects this value.

issuer. The issuer field contains the X.500 distinguished name of the certificate issuer. The Internet Certificate and CRL profile [HOUS99] requires the issuer field to contain a non-empty name. The distinguished name can include any attributes; however, for interoperability, issuer should be limited to the naming attributes described previously.

validity. The validity field has two components, indicating the dates on which the certificate becomes valid (notBefore) and the date on which the certificate expires (notAfter). The validity field represents dates in either UTCTime or Generalized-Time according to the rules provided earlier.

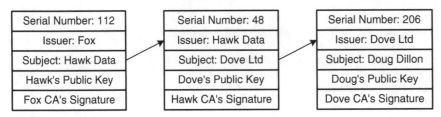

Figure 7.2 Chaining issuer and subject names.

subject. The subject field contains the distinguished name of the holder of the private key corresponding to the public key in this certificate. The subject may be a certification authority (CA) or an end entity. End entities can be human users, hardware devices, or anything else that might make use of the private key. The distinguished name can include any attributes; however, for interoperability, the subject name should be limited to the naming attributes described earlier. In the development of a certification path (discussed more fully in Chapter 10, "Building and Validating Certification Paths"), the subject names in CA certificates must match the issuer name in the certificate that follows. Figure 7.2 illustrates name chaining.

subjectPublicKeyInfo. The subject public key information field contains the subject's public key and algorithm identifier. Unlike the signature or signature algorithm fields, which also make use of algorithm identifiers, the parameters within this field convey important information about the public key. For example, the parameters field will contain the domain parameters (p, q, and g) associated with DSA or Diffie-Hellman public keys. Table 7.3 describes the contents for the most popular public key algorithms. DSA and ECDSA parameters are optional. If the parameters are omitted, then the subject and issuer have the same public key parameters. *Parameter inheritance* simply reduces the size of certificates by not repeating the same values over and over again.

The public key in this field, along with the optional algorithm parameters, is used to verify digital signatures or perform key management. If the certificate subject is a CA, then the public key is used to verify the digital signature on a certificate. The keys and

Table 7.3 OIDs and Parameters for Popular Public Key Algorithms

PUBLIC KEY ALGORITHM	ALGORITHM IDENTIFIER	ALGORITHM OID	PARAMETERS
RSA	rsaEncryption	1.2.840.113549.1.1.1	NULL
DSA	id-dsa	1.2.840.10040.4.1	Optional
Diffie-Hellman	dhPublicNumber	1.2.840.10046.2.1	Required
Elliptic Curve	id-ecPublicKey	1.2.840.10045.2.1	Optional
KEA	id-keyExchangeAlgorithm	2.16.840.1.101.2.1.1.22	Required

signatures within a certification path must chain in a manner similar to the names; that is, the public key in a CA certificate is used to verify the signature on the following certificate. Figure 7.3 builds on the Figure 7.2, adding public key and signature chaining.

issuerUniqueID and **subjectUniqueID**. These fields contain identifiers, and they only appear in version 2 or version 3 certificates. The subject and issuer unique identifiers are intended to handle the reuse of subject names or issuer names over time. However, this mechanism has proven to be an unsatisfactory solution. The Internet Certificate and CRL profile [HOUS99] recommends omission of these fields. Even so, implementations must parse these fields or reject certificates containing them.

extensions. This optional field only appears in version 3 certificates. If present, this field contains one or more certificate extensions. Each extension includes an extension identifier, a criticality flag, and an extension value. Common certificate extensions are described in the next section.

Certificate Extensions

Early PKI deployments clearly demonstrate that the basic certificate content described earlier is insufficient. Certificate users are unable to determine important information about the issuer, the subject, or the public key itself. The missing information can be divided into five groups. Each group is characterized by the questions that it answers.

Subject type. Is Bob a CA or an end entity?

Names and identity information. Are *alice@fox.com* and *c=US; o=Fox Consulting; cn=Alice Adams* the same person?

Key attributes. Can this public key be used for key transport? Can it also be used to verify a digital signature?

Policy information. Can I trust Alice's certificate? Is it appropriate for large value transactions?

Additional information. Where can I find certificates issued to the Fox Consulting CA? When can I obtain certificate revocation lists (CRLs) issued by the Fox Consulting CA?

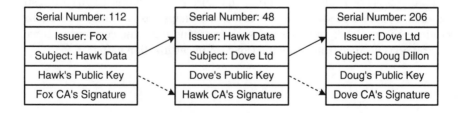

Legend
⟶ Names Match
----▶ Public Key Verifies Signature

Figure 7.3   Chaining public keys and signatures.

Certificate extensions allow the CA to include information not supported by the basic certificate content. Any organization may define a private extension to meet its particular business requirements. However, most requirements can be satisfied using standard extensions. Standard extensions are widely supported by commercial products. Standard extensions offer improved interoperability, and they are more cost effective than private extensions.

Extensions have three components: extension identifier, a criticality flag, and extension value. The extension identifier is an OID, and it indicates the format and semantics of the extension value. The criticality flag indicates the importance of the extension. When the criticality flag is set, the information is essential to certificate use. Therefore, if an unrecognized critical extension is encountered, the certificate must not be used. Alternatively, unrecognized non-critical extensions may be ignored.

ITU-T and IETF have defined several extensions for X.509 v3 certificates. They are specified in [X50997], [X50900], and [HOUS99]. This section identifies standard certificate extensions that will likely be used in the Internet PKI. These extensions have OIDs assigned by ITU-T in the certificate extension arc (id-ce), or by the IETF in the PKIX extension arc (id-pe).

```
id-ce  OBJECT IDENTIFIER  ::=  { joint-iso-ccitt(2) ds(5) 29 }
id-pe  OBJECT IDENTIFIER  ::=  { 1 3 6 1 5 5 7 1 }
```

Subject Type Extensions

The inability to determine whether a certificate belongs to a CA or an end entity makes certificate path construction more difficult. When Alice obtains certificates for both Bob and the Hawk Manufacturing CA, she cannot determine from the basic certificate content that Bob is not a CA. Therefore, she may try to use the certificate to construct a certification path. Eventually, she will discover that no certificates chain to Bob's distinguished name. The basic constraints extension resolves this issue.

Basic Constraints

Consider the mesh PKI illustrated in Figure 7.4. The basic constraints extension allows Fox to specify that Bob is an end entity, not a CA. It also allows Fox to specify that Hawk is a CA. This is not a complete solution. In Figure 7.4, Fox has issued a certificate to Hawk, and Hawk has issued a certificate to Dove. Perhaps Fox is willing to recognize user certificates from Hawk, but does not wish to extend the same courtesy to Dove. How can Fox prevent Alice from using the Dove CA in certification paths?

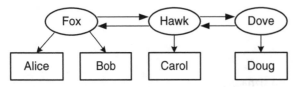

Figure 7.4   Simple mesh PKI.

To address this issue, the basic constraints extension also includes a path length constraint. This optional field contains an integer that indicates the maximum number of subsequent CA certificates in a certification path. If path length is specified as zero, Alice will only consider end entity certificates issued by Hawk. Thus, Alice considers any certification path that includes the CA certificate issued by Hawk to Dove invalid. Yet, Alice considers the end entity certificates issued by Hawk valid.

The basic constraints extension is identified by the id-ce-basicConstraints object identifier, and it has the following syntax:

```
id-ce-basicConstraints OBJECT IDENTIFIER ::=  { id-ce 19 }

BasicConstraints  ::=  SEQUENCE  {
   cA                      BOOLEAN DEFAULT FALSE,
   pathLenConstraint       INTEGER (0..MAX) OPTIONAL  }
```

The basic constraints extension may, at the option of the CA, be either critical or non-critical. However, the Internet Certificate and CRL Profile [HOUS99] suggests that this extension be marked critical in all CA certificates. Further, it recommends against the use of this extension in end entity certificates.

Name Extensions

In X.509 v1 certificates and X.509 v2 certificates, distinguished names were the only name form available. If a ubiquitous X.500 Directory had quickly emerged, this would be the only name form needed. Every system and user would have an entry in the X.500 Directory, and this name would be a unique identity. However, the global X.500 Directory did not emerge, and will probably not emerge as a unified system. Further, Internet expansion shows no signs of slowing, and X.500 Directory names are not the preferred name form on the Internet.

The alternative naming extensions, the subject alternative names and the issuer alternative names, allow additional names to be provided for the CA and the certificate subject. These alternative names can assume any form.

A second naming problem was encountered by early PKI deployments. When multiple CAs operated within a name space, they wanted to segment that name space, assigning a portion to each CA. Since the X.500 naming structure is hierarchical, this partitioning was simple and straightforward. For example, within the Hawk Data name space, one CA can serve the R&D group, and a second CA can serve the Manufacturing group. The first CA is assigned the name space C=US, o=Hawk Data; ou=Research. The second CA is assigned C=US, o=Hawk Data; ou=Manufacturing. Each CA can assign usernames by adding a common name without any fear of name collisions. However, it was not possible to enforce these name space assignments through the certificate contents.

The Privacy Enhanced Mail (PEM) PKI [KENT93] devised a *name subordination* rule that enforced these name constraints. It provided a very rigid name constraint, and privacy advocates were upset because anonymous and confidential electronic mail was very difficult under these rules.

The name constraints extension provides flexible controls. It can be used to implement PEM name subordination and other schemes as well.

Issuer Alternative Name

The issuer alternative name extension provides a list of general names. Generally, the names of CAs are not important to certificate users. The issuer information that is important to certificate users is addressed later in this chapter. However, this extension can advertise the electronic mail address of the CA.

The alternative issuer name extension is identified by the OID id-ce-issuerAltName, and it has the following syntax:

```
id-ce-issuerAltName OBJECT IDENTIFIER  ::=  { id-ce 18 }

IssuerAltName  ::=  GeneralNames

GeneralNames  ::=  SEQUENCE SIZE (1..MAX) OF GeneralName
```

This extension should never be critical.

Subject Alternative Name

The subject alternative name extension is extremely useful in end entity certificates. The electronic mail address and DNS name are commonly included in X.509 v3 certificates for human users. URLs and DNS names are commonly included in certificates for computers, especially servers. IP addresses and DNS names are commonly included in certificates for IPsec routers and servers.

Microsoft Windows 2000 uses the other name field to specify a Kerberos principal name for certificate subjects. The IETF Qualified Certificates specification [SANT00] uses the other name field to convey additional identification information. Qualified certificates are addressed further in Chapter 17, "Future Developments."

Generally, this extension is not included in certificates issued to CAs. When it is included, it can lead to surprising certification path rejections due to naming constraints. This is discussed in greater detail later in the chapter.

The subject alternative name extension is identified by the id-ce-subjectAltName object identifier, and it has the same syntax as the issuer alternative name extension:

```
id-ce-subjectAltName OBJECT IDENTIFIER  ::=  { id-ce 17 }

SubjectAltName  ::=  GeneralNames
```

This extension may be either critical or non-critical. If the subject field in the basic certificate content is a sequence of zero elements, it is said to be *empty*. When the subject name is empty, this extension must be included, and it must be marked critical. If the subject name is not empty, this extension should be marked non-critical.

Name Constraints

As noted earlier, X.509 v1 certificates and X.509 v2 certificates were expected to contain distinguished names assigned from the global X.500 Directory name space. At that time, most PKIs consisted of a single CA, and name collisions were not an issue. When, hierarchical PKIs emerged, the superior CAs assigned a portion of the name space to each subordinate CA, but these hierarchical PKIs could not enforce their name space limits without special processing rules. Name collisions issues multiplied when isolated CAs were cross-certified, forming mesh PKIs.

Consider again the PKI topology in Figure 7.4. Fox Consulting and Hawk Data may wish to trust each to manage its own name space, but they do not want the foreign CA to issue certificates for subjects in the local name space. That is, Fox Consulting trusts Hawk Data to issue certificates to Hawk employees. Yet, Fox Consulting wants to ensure that the Hawk Data CA cannot issue certificates to subjects claiming to be Fox Consulting employees. The name constraints extension offers a mechanism to implement these constraints.

The name constraints extension offers two constraint types: permitted subtrees and excluded subtrees. Permitted subtrees specify acceptable names, and excluded subtrees specify unacceptable names. Permitted subtrees could limit the Hawk Data to distinguished names that begin with C=US, o=Hawk Data, and electronic mail addresses that end with hawk.com. Excluded subtrees could prohibit Hawk Data's use of distinguished names that begin with C=US, o=Fox Consulting, and electronic mail addresses that end with fox.com. A name is acceptable only if it falls within one of the permitted subtrees and is not within any of the excluded subtrees.

Consider the following scenario: Hawk Data has two CAs that share the Hawk name space. The Hawk R&D CA issues a CA certificate to the Hawk Manufacturing CA. The Hawk Manufacturing CA issues certificates to employees in the legal group and the manufacturing group. How can the R&D CA protect its portion of the name space? The R&D CA has three ways in which it can use name constraints:

- Specify the entire Hawk Data name space in a permitted subtree, and specify the Hawk Data R&D name space in an excluded subtree. This is shown as Figure 7.5(a).

- Specify two permitted subtrees, one for the Hawk Data Manufacturing group and one for the Hawk Data Legal group. This is shown as Figure 7.5(b).

- Specify one excluded subtree for the Hawk Data R&D name space. This is shown as Figure 7.5(c).

Each of these strategies protects the Hawk Data R&D name space and recognizes certificates issued by the Hawk Data Manufacturing CA. However, each has somewhat different overall implications. Figure 7.5(c) is the weakest strategy. Recall from the discussion of the directory strings that few implementations compare names that employ different string types. Therefore, by encoding ou=R&D as a UTF8 string instead of a teletext string, the two strings will not be considered the same. By combining permitted and excluded subtrees, the same string types must be employed to pass the constraint.

The constraints shown in Figure 7.5(a) permit the Hawk Data Manufacturing CA to use names in any organization within Hawk Data except R&D. It could invent an Ops group, and these names would be acceptable. Sometimes this flexibility is desirable, and sometimes it is unacceptable. The constraints shown in Figure 7.5(b) limit the Hawk Data Manufacturing CA to use names within the Legal and Manufacturing groups.

The name constraints extension can specify constraints on any of the seven standard name forms, as well as locally defined names. When a name constraint is expressed for

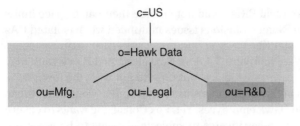

(a) one permitted subtree, one excluded subtree

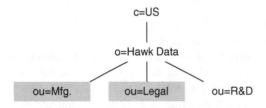

(b) two permitted subtrees

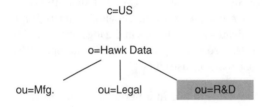

(c) one excluded subtree

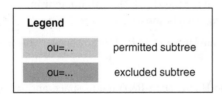

Figure 7.5 Name constraints alternatives.

distinguished names, it applies to both the subject name and the alternative subject names of the directory name form. Name constraints only appear in CA certificates. The Internet Certificate and CRL profile [HOUS99] defines the syntax and semantics for the specification of subtrees using electronic mail addresses, DNS names, IP addresses, and URIs.

Applying name constraints becomes very confusing when multiple name forms are present. If a certificate user can process more than one name form, then the name constraints must be satisfied for all of those name forms. If the only name in a certificate is a name form that has not been constrained, it is accepted. Since the Internet Certificate and CRL profile requires CA certificates to include a distinguished directory name in the subject field, this name constraint is always processed, and it is the best name form to constrain to control certification path construction.

The name constraints extension is identified by the id-ce-nameConstraints object identifier, and has the following syntax:

```
id-ce-nameConstraints OBJECT IDENTIFIER  ::=  { id-ce 30 }

NameConstraints  ::=  SEQUENCE {
   permittedSubtrees  [0]  GeneralSubtrees OPTIONAL,
   excludedSubtrees   [1]  GeneralSubtrees OPTIONAL  }

GeneralSubtrees  ::=  SEQUENCE SIZE (1..MAX) OF GeneralSubtree

GeneralSubtree  ::=  SEQUENCE  {
   base                 GeneralName,
   minimum        [0]  BaseDistance DEFAULT 0,
   maximum        [1]  BaseDistance OPTIONAL  }

BaseDistance  ::=  INTEGER (0..MAX)
```

This extension may, at the option of the CA, be either critical or non-critical.

Key Attributes

X.509 v1 certificates and X.509 v2 certificates specify the public key algorithm and parameters, but they do not offer any other key attributes. Most CAs and end entities have more than one public/private key pair, and they use different key pairs to implement different security services. To differentiate the public keys in different certificates, CAs employ four standard certificate extensions: key usage, extended key usage, authority key identifier, and the subject key identifier.

Key Usage

The key usage extension identifies the security services that a public key may be used to provide. This extension offers 9 security services, and the CA selects the appropriate combination. The 9 key usage choices are as follows:

keyCertSign. Key certificate sign indicates that the public key may be used to verify signatures on certificates.

cRLSign. CRL sign indicates that the public key may be used to verify signatures on CRLs (or other certificate status reporting mechanisms).

non-Repudiation. Non-repudiation indicates that the public key may be used to verify digital signatures intended to provide a non-repudiation security service. Non-repudiation protects against the signer falsely denying some action.

digitalSignature. Digital signature indicates that the public key may be used to verify signatures. This key usage is used whenever the security service is not covered by any of the three previous key usage values. For example, peer-entity authentication and data origin authentication employ this key usage value.

keyEncipherment. Key encipherment indicates that the public key may be used for key transport. This key usage value is used when an RSA key may be used for key management.

dataEncipherment. Data encipherment indicates that the public key may used to directly encrypt data, other than cryptographic keys.

keyAgreement. Key agreement indicates that the public key may be used for key agreement. This key usage value is used when a Diffie-Hellman key may be used for key management.

encipherOnly. Encipher only is used in conjunction with key agreement. This key usage value indicates that the symmetric key resulting from key agreement may only be used for encrypting data.

decipherOnly. Decipher only is used in conjunction with key agreement. This key usage value indicates that the symmetric key resulting from key agreement may only be used for decrypting data.

Any combination of these key usage values may be indicated; however, the meaning of some combinations is not well defined. The meaning of encipher only or decipher only is undefined in the absence of the key agreement. Setting both encipher only and decipher only is contradictory. Indicating the digital signature service for a Diffie-Hellman public key (or any other key management algorithm) is confusing at best.

The key usage extension is identified by the id-ce-keyUsage object identifier, and it has the following syntax:

```
id-ce-keyUsage OBJECT IDENTIFIER  ::=  { id-ce 15 }

KeyUsage  ::=  BIT STRING  {
    digitalSignature    (0),
    nonRepudiation      (1),
    keyEncipherment     (2),
    dataEncipherment    (3),
    keyAgreement        (4),
    keyCertSign         (5),
    cRLSign             (6),
    encipherOnly        (7),
    decipherOnly        (8)  }
```

This extension may, at the option of the CA, be either critical or non-critical. However, the Internet Certificate and CRL Profile [HOUS99] recommends that this extension always be critical.

Extended Key Usage

The extended key usage extension indicates specific applications for public keys. The extended key usage extension is composed of a sequence of OIDs, where each OID identifies a particular application context in which the public key may be used. For example, the id-kp-serverAuth OID (1.3.6.1.5.5.7.3.1) indicates that the public key may be used by a TLS Web server.

The extended key usage extension is identified by the id-ce-extKeyUsage object identifier, and has the following syntax:

```
id-ce-extKeyUsage OBJECT IDENTIFIER  ::=  { id-ce 37 }


ExtKeyUsageSyntax  ::=  SEQUENCE SIZE (1..MAX) OF KeyPurposeId


KeyPurposeId  ::=  OBJECT IDENTIFIER
```

This extension may, at the option of the certificate issuer, be either critical or noncritical.

Private Key Validity

The private key usage extension indicates the validity period of the private key associated with the public key contained in the certificate. For example, a private key may be useful for signing documents for six months. Yet, the signatures may need to be validated for two years. In this case, a two-year certificate validity period allows signature verification for the whole period, and a six-month period at the beginning of the two years in this extension indicates the signing lifetime of the private key. A timestamp to show when the signature was actually generated is necessary to enforce this constraint.

The private key usage period extension is identified by the id-ce-privateKeyUsagePeriod object identifier, and has the following syntax:

```
id-ce-privateKeyUsagePeriod OBJECT IDENTIFIER  ::=  { id-ce 16 }


PrivateKeyUsagePeriod  ::=  SEQUENCE  {
    notBefore          [0]  GeneralizedTime OPTIONAL,
    notAfter           [1]  GeneralizedTime OPTIONAL  }
```

Unlike many of the other certificate time values, UTC time is not permitted for private key validity. Generalized time is always used.

The Internet Certificate and CRL profile [HOUS99] recommends against inclusion of this extension, and it forbids marking this extension as critical. Since signature timestamps are not readily available, this extension has little utility.

Subject Key Identifier

The subject key identifier extension provides a means for identifying certificates containing a particular public key. The subject key identifier contains a string that names the key. If the subject has multiple certificates, especially if multiple CAs issue them, the subject key identifier provides a means to quickly identify the certificates containing the public key of interest.

The subject key identifier extension, when used in conjunction with the authority key identifier extension, enables efficient certificate path construction.

To avoid complicated identifier assignment mechanisms, yet provide a low probability of two keys with the same identifier, the key identifier is usually a one-way hash of the public key. The hash value may be truncated or folded to keep it short. The Internet Certificate and CRL Profile [HOUS99] offers two techniques for assigning key identifiers.

The subject key identifier extension is identified by the id-ce-issuerAltName object identifier, and it has the following syntax:

```
id-ce-subjectKeyIdentifier OBJECT IDENTIFIER  ::=  { id-ce 14 }

SubjectKeyIdentifier  ::=  KeyIdentifier

KeyIdentifier  ::=  OCTET STRING
```

This extension must always be non-critical.

Authority Key Identifier

The authority key identifier extension provides a means for identifying certificates signed by a particular CA private key. This extension aids certification path construction. If the CA has several certificate signing keys, this extension identifies the correct one to verify a particular certificate signature. Without such a pointer, each public key must be tried in succession until the signature verifies or until all possibilities are exhausted!

The authority key identifier points to a public key that can be used to verify the signature on this particular certificate. The authority key identifier may be the issuer name and serial number of a certificate or a string. If the authority key identifier extension contains an issuer name/serial number pair, then the identified certificate contains the public key. This form of chaining is illustrated in Figure 7.6(a). If the authority key identifier

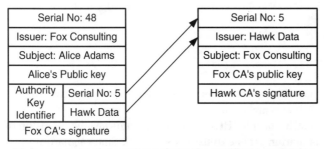

(a) **Issuer and serial number point to the certificate containing the public key needed to validate the certificate signature.**

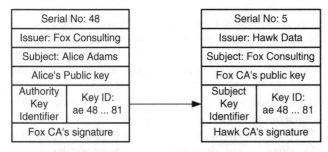

(b) **Authority key identifier in the subordinate certificate matches the subject key identifier in the parent certificate.**

Figure 7.6   Authority key identifiers aid certificate path construction.

extension contains a string, the CA certificates will contain the same string in the subject key identifier extension. This form of chaining is illustrated in Figure 7.6(b). Of course, both forms may be used at the same time.

The authority key identifier extension is identified by the id-ce-authorityKeyIdentifier object identifier, and has the following syntax:

```
id-ce-authorityKeyIdentifier OBJECT IDENTIFIER  ::=  { id-ce 35 }

AuthorityKeyIdentifier  ::=  SEQUENCE  {
   keyIdentifier                [0] KeyIdentifier OPTIONAL,
   authorityCertIssuer          [1] GeneralNames OPTIONAL,
   authorityCertSerialNumber    [2] CertificateSerialNumber OPTIONAL  }
```

This extension must always be non-critical.

Policy Information

In early PKI implementations, using X.509 v1 certificates and X.509 v2 certificates, each CA issued certificates under one and only one policy. The policy was implicit. Implicit policy information proved unacceptable. Organizations found that no one policy fit all needs. Further, it was, and still remains, inefficient to deploy a separate CA for every policy. It was difficult for certificate users to track which policy was used by each CA. Tracking issuer distinguished directory names to policies and policies to application requirements was too complicated; it was not implemented.

Two standard policy extensions fulfill these needs: the certificate policies extension and the policy mapping extension. The certificate policies extension indicates the policy or policies under which a certificate was issued. In a CA certificate, this indicates the policies under which the CA operates. In an end entity certificate, this indicates the policy (or policies) under which the certificate was issued. An object identifier, usually referred to as a *policy OID*, identifies the certificate policy. The policy mapping extension translates policy OIDs from one PKI to the equivalent policy OIDs in another PKI.

As with most flexible mechanisms, a means to impose limits is needed. How does a CA recognize another CA for some, but not all, of its policies? How does a CA declare that it is policy neutral? These questions, and others like them, lead to the policy constraints extension and the inhibit any-policy extension.

Certificate Policies

The certificate policies extension indicates the certificate policies under which the certificate was issued. The CA asserts that the procedures used to issue the certificate satisfy the listed policies. Certificate users must know which policy or policies are acceptable for their application. In end entity certificates, this extension describes the policies satisfied. In CA certificates, this extension defines the set of policies that can be included in subordinate certificates.

The certificate policies extension lists one or more policies, and each policy may include optional policy qualifiers. Policies are identified by an OID. The policy may indicate that the certificate is intended to be used with a particular application, such as electronic mail or contract signing. Alternatively, the policy may indicate the relative quality of a certificate, such as very good, good, or mediocre. Since the same certificate might be used for multiple applications, several policies might be identified in one certificate. Chapter 12, "Policies, Procedures, and PKI," addresses certificate policies in detail.

When a CA does not wish to limit the set of policies, it may include the special any-policy OID. The any-policy OID is useful when issuing certificates to a totally trusted CA. For example, two CAs within the same enterprise might accept any policy asserted by the other CA. In this case, any-policy OID accurately describes that relationship. The any-policy OID should never appear in end entity certificates.

The any-policy OID is defined as:

```
anyPolicy OBJECT IDENTIFIER  ::=  { 2 5 29 32 0 }
```

Each policy may optionally include a list of policy qualifiers. The qualifiers limit or modify the policy information. For example, the policy OID might indicate that a certificate can be used for secure electronic mail, and the qualifier might indicate that this certificate can only be used for internal mail. Like certificate policies themselves, certificate policy qualifiers are identified by an OID.

Policy qualifiers negatively impact interoperability. If the policy is not locally defined, then certificate users may not recognize a particular qualifier. Technologists, including the authors of this book, dislike this construct and strongly discourage its use. However, lawyers love qualifiers. Qualifiers offer a means to embed disclaimers, or pointers to disclaimers, in the certificate. Lawyers often use qualifiers as a means of providing notice.

As a compromise, the Internet Certificate and CRL Profile [HOUS99] specifies the syntax and OIDs for two policy qualifiers. One qualifier provides a pointer to the CA's *Certification Practices Statement* (CPS). The other qualifier provides text for a user notice. Implementers are expected to support these two qualifiers, so they may be used without unduly affecting interoperability.

The CPS pointer qualifier contains a pointer to the CA's CPS. The CPS is usually a 20- to 30-page document that describes the way the CA operates. Certificate users can read the CPS to determine whether a certificate is acceptable for their application. The CPS pointer is a URL to locate the document on the Internet. The CPS is described in detail in Chapter 12.

The user notice qualifier provides text to be displayed when the certificate is used. Application software is supposed to display the user notices from all certificates in a certification path. Duplicates may be reduced to a single entry. The user notice qualifier may include text (up to 200 characters), a pointer to the notice (a URL), or both. When the pointer is used, it names an organization and identifies a particular textual statement prepared by that organization. For example, it might identify the Fox Consulting organization and notice number 48. If the application locates the right statement, it should display it to the certificate user. If both explicit text and pointer qualifiers appear, the pointer has precedence. That is, the text from the pointer is displayed, but if it cannot be located, the explicit text is used.

If lawyers insist on the inclusion of a user notice, we recommend the explicit text. It is the least onerous to process, and it is more likely to actually be displayed.

Use of locally defined qualifiers is strongly discouraged. They greatly hamper interoperability.

The certificate policies extension is identified by the id-ce-certificatePolicies object identifier, and has the following syntax:

```
[id-ce-certificate Policies   OBJECT IDENTIFIER ::=  { id-ce 32 }
CertificatePolicies  ::=  SEQUENCE SIZE (1..MAX) OF PolicyInformation

PolicyInformation  ::=  SEQUENCE {
   policyIdentifier    CertPolicyId,
   policyQualifiers    SEQUENCE SIZE (1..MAX) OF
                             PolicyQualifierInfo OPTIONAL  }

CertPolicyId  ::=  OBJECT IDENTIFIER

PolicyQualifierInfo  ::=  SEQUENCE {
   policyQualifierId   PolicyQualifierId,
   qualifier           ANY DEFINED BY policyQualifierId  }

-- policyQualifierIds for Internet policy qualifiers

id-qt          OBJECT IDENTIFIER  ::=  { id-pkix 2 }
id-qt-cps      OBJECT IDENTIFIER  ::=  { id-qt 1 }
id-qt-unotice  OBJECT IDENTIFIER  ::=  { id-qt 2 }

PolicyQualifierId  ::=  OBJECT IDENTIFIER
                      ( id-qt-cps | id-qt-unotice )

Qualifier  ::=  CHOICE  {
   cPSuri             CPSuri,
   userNotice         UserNotice  }

CPSuri  ::=  IA5String

UserNotice  ::=  SEQUENCE {
   noticeRef          NoticeReference OPTIONAL,
   explicitText       DisplayText OPTIONAL  }

NoticeReference  ::=  SEQUENCE {
   organization       DisplayText,
   noticeNumbers      SEQUENCE OF INTEGER  }

DisplayText  ::=  CHOICE {
   visibleString      VisibleString (SIZE (1..200)),
   bmpString          BMPString (SIZE (1..200)),
   utf8String         UTF8String (SIZE (1..200))  }
```

This extension may, at the option of the CA, be either critical or non-critical.

Policy Mapping

The policy mapping extension is used in CA certificates to translate policy information between two policy domains. Generally, certificate users recognize only a handful of policy OIDs. Normally, these are the policy OIDs that appear in certificates issued by their own CA. When two CAs operate under different policies, their users will not be able to use the policy information. A policy mapping extension provides the translation needed to make the remote policy information useful. Policy mapping translates remote policy OIDs into local policy OIDs that the certificate user already knows.

The policy mapping extension contains a list of one or more OID pairs. Each pair includes an issuer domain policy OID and a subject domain policy OID. The extension indicates that the issuing CA considers its issuer domain policy equivalent to the subject domain policy used by the subject CA. By including this extension, the CA asserts: If the issuer domain policy is acceptable for your application, then the subject domain policy is also acceptable for your application.

Each issuer domain policy OID listed in the policy mapping extension should also be listed in a certificate policies extension in the same certificate. Further, the policy mapping extension may not be used to map the special any-policy OID.

Figure 7.7 demonstrates the utility of policy mapping. Alice trusts the Fox CA, and it issues certificates under the Fox Contracts and Fox Email policies. Carol obtains her certificate from the Hawk Data CA, which issues certificates under the Gold Hawk and Silver Hawk policies. Alice receives a signed contract from Carol, and needs to decide if the signature is acceptable. The Fox CA had determined that the Gold Hawk policy may be accepted in lieu of the Fox Contracts policy, and that both the Gold Hawk and Silver Hawk policies may be accepted in lieu of the Fox Email policy. By including the policy mapping extension in the certificate issued to the Hawk Data CA by the Fox CA, Alice can easily determine that the contract is acceptable if Carol's certificate was issued under the Gold Hawk policy.

The policy mapping extension does not translate certificate policy qualifiers. Whatever policy qualifiers were employed with the issuer domain policy must have the same meaning to the subject domain policy. This is further justification to avoid certificate policy qualifiers.

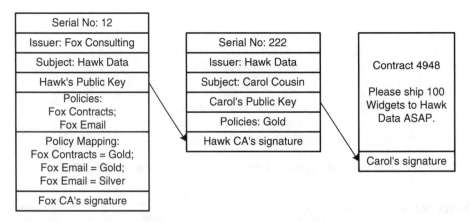

Figure 7.7   Policy mapping between Fox Consulting and Hawk Data.

The policy mapping extension is identified by the id-ce-policyMappings object identifier, and has the following syntax:

```
id-ce-policyMappings OBJECT IDENTIFIER  ::=  { id-ce 33 }

PolicyMappings  ::=  SEQUENCE SIZE (1..MAX) OF SEQUENCE  {
    issuerDomainPolicy       CertPolicyId,
    subjectDomainPolicy      CertPolicyId }
```

The syntax for CertPolicyId is defined earlier as part of the certificate policies extension. It is simply an OID.

This extension may, at the option of the CA, be either critical or non-critical. In general, this extension should be non-critical.

Policy Constraints

The policy constraints extension is used to impose limitations on valid certification paths. This extension can constrain path validation in two ways. First, it can be used to prohibit policy mapping. Second, it can require that each certificate in a path contain an acceptable policy OID. Either restriction can be imposed immediately, or the restriction can begin after the certification path reaches a specified length.

The policy constraints extension contains at least one of two optional fields: the inhibit policy mapping field and require explicit policy field. Both fields are defined as a skip certificate counter. The counter indicates the number of additional certificates that can appear in the certification path before the constraint takes effect. Usually, the counter is set to zero, causing the restriction to begin immediately.

When the inhibit policy mapping constraint is in effect, policy mapping extensions are ignored. The counter in the inhibit policy mapping field indicates the number of additional certificates that may appear in the certification path before policy mapping is no longer permitted. A counter value of one indicates that policy mapping may be processed in certificates issued by the subject of this certificate, but not in subsequent certificates.

When the require explicit policy constraint is in effect, all additional certificates in the path must include an acceptable policy identifier. The counter in the require explicit policy field indicates the number of additional certificates that can appear in the certification path before the constraint goes into effect. A counter value of three indicates that the constraint will go into effect after three subsequent certificates in the path.

The policy constraints extension is identified by the id-ce-policyConstraints object identifier, and has the following syntax:

```
id-ce-policyConstraints OBJECT IDENTIFIER  ::=  { id-ce 36 }

PolicyConstraints  ::=  SEQUENCE {
    requireExplicitPolicy    [0] SkipCerts OPTIONAL,
    inhibitPolicyMapping     [1] SkipCerts OPTIONAL  }

SkipCerts  ::=  INTEGER (0..MAX)
```

This extension may, at the option of the CA, be either critical or non-critical.

Inhibit Any-Policy

Like the policy constraints extension, the inhibit any-policy extension imposes additional limitations upon certification paths. This extension can only appear in certificates issued to CAs. The inhibit any-policy extension indicates that the special any-policy OID (2.5.29.32.0) is not considered a match for other certificate policies. A counter indicates the number of additional certificates that may appear in the certification path before any-policy is no longer permitted. A counter value of one indicates that any-policy may be processed in certificates issued by the subject of this certificate, but not in additional certificates in the path.

The inhibit any-policy extension is identified by the id-ce-inhibitAnyPolicy object identifier, and has the following syntax:

```
id-ce-inhibitAnyPolicy OBJECT IDENTIFIER  ::=  { id-ce 54 }

InhibitAnyPolicy  ::=  SkipCerts
```

The syntax for SkipCerts is defined earlier as part of the policy constraints extension. It is simply an integer.

This extension must be critical.

Additional Information

To validate a certificate, a certificate user must obtain the CA certificate to extract the public key to verify the certificate signature, and the certificate user must obtain the most recent CRL to determine if the certificate has been revoked. Early PKI developers assumed that an X.500 Directory would be available to disseminate certificates and CRLs. The issuer's distinguished names within the certificate provide the perfect search index for an X.500 Directory.

Of course, the ubiquitous X.500 Directory has not emerged. Instead, we find a large number of isolated or loosely connected repositories. Some are X.500 Directories serving a particular community, but most are LDAP directories. Most LDAP directories are stand-alone, and a few provide referrals to other LDAP directories. Other repositories are accessed using HTTP, FTP, finger, or electronic mail. To obtain certificates or CRLs, a certificate user needs the distinguished name, the address of the repository containing the information, and the access protocol. Each CA in a certification path may use a different repository.

From the certificate users' point of view, the X.500 Directory was an elegant solution. However, PKI deployment cannot wait for a global X.500 Directory to emerge. The benefits of PKI are too significant to be road-blocked by a single repository technology.

Several standard extensions provide certificate users with pointers to additional information, including issuer certificates, CRLs, delta CRLs, and online certificate status servers. Further, attributes associated with the certificate subject may be included directly in the certificate. The CRL distribution points extension, freshest CRL extension, authority information access extension, subject information access extension, and the subject directory attribute extension provide this additional information.

CRL Distribution Points

The CRL distribution points extension tells certificate users where and how to obtain CRLs needed to determine if the certificate is revoked. CRLs are discussed in detail in Chapter 8, "Certificate Revocation Lists."

The CRL distribution points extension contains one or more distribution points. Each distribution point describes one location for an appropriate CRL. A distribution point consists of three optional fields: the name of the distribution point, reasons flags, and the CRL issuer. While each component is optional, a distribution point must not consist solely of the reasons flags field. If the distribution point name is absent, the CRL issuer must be present, and it must include a distinguished directory name corresponding to an X.500 Directory or LDAP directory entry where the CRL is located. If the distribution point omits the CRL issuer, then the same CA that issued the certificate must issue the referenced CRL.

If the CRL distribution points extension contains a URI distribution point name, then the URI is a pointer to the current CRL for the associated reasons, and the CRL is issued by the associated CRL issuer. If the distribution point omits reasons, then the referenced CRL must include revocations for all reasons.

The CRL distribution points extension is identified by the id-ce-cRLDistribution-Points object identifier, and has the following syntax:

```
id-ce-cRLDistributionPoints OBJECT IDENTIFIER  ::=  { id-ce 31 }


cRLDistributionPoints  ::=  CRLDistPointsSyntax


CRLDistPointsSyntax  ::=  SEQUENCE SIZE (1..MAX) OF
                              DistributionPoint


DistributionPoint  ::=  SEQUENCE {
    distributionPoint      [0]  DistributionPointName OPTIONAL,
    reasons                [1]  ReasonFlags OPTIONAL,
    cRLIssuer              [2]  GeneralNames OPTIONAL  }


DistributionPointName  ::=  CHOICE {
    fullName               [0]  GeneralNames,
    nameRelativeToCRLIssuer [1]  RelativeDistinguishedName  }


ReasonFlags  ::=  BIT STRING {
    unused                 (0),
    keyCompromise          (1),
    cACompromise           (2),
    affiliationChanged     (3),
    superseded             (4),
    cessationOfOperation   (5),
    certificateHold        (6)  }
```

This extension may, at the option of the CA, be either critical or non-critical. However, the Internet Certificate and CRL profile [HOUS99] recommends that this extension be marked non-critical.

Freshest CRL

The freshest CRL extension could have been named the delta CRL distribution point extension. It identifies how delta CRL information is obtained. The same syntax is used for this extension and the CRL distribution points extension described in the previous section. The same conventions apply to both extensions.

As an alternative to including this extension in the certificate, it may be placed in a base CRL providing a pointer to the delta CRL that updates the base. We encourage the use of this extension in a CRL rather than a certificate simply to limit the size of the certificate.

The freshest CRL extension is identified by the id-ce-freshestCRL object identifier, and has the following syntax:

```
id-ce-freshestCRL OBJECT IDENTIFIER  ::=  { id-ce 46 }

FreshestCRL  ::=  CRLDistributionPoints
```

This extension must be non-critical. Implementations are not required to process delta CRLs.

Authority Information Access

The authority information access extension tells how to access CA information and services. This information and services may include CA policy data and online certificate status services. However, the location of CRLs is not specified in this extension; that information is provided by the CRL distribution points extension.

The authority information access extension contains a list of access descriptors. Each access descriptor describes the format and location of additional information provided by the CA. Two fields are used: the access method field and the access location field. The access method field contains an object identifier that specifies the type and format of the information. The access location field specifies the network location of the information. The retrieval mechanism may be implied by the access method or explicitly specified by the access location.

Two standard access descriptors have been defined. They are named by their access method OIDs: CA issuers (id-ad-caIssuers) and OCSP (id-ad-ocsp). Additional access descriptors may be defined in the future.

The CA issuers OID is used to name other CAs that have issued certificates to this CA. The list of CAs aids in certification path construction. When the CA issuers OID appears in the access method field, the access location field describes access protocol and location to obtain the list of CAs. The access location field contains a general name, as described much earlier in this chapter. If the uniform resource identifier (URI) field is populated, then a URL allowing the information to be fetched with HTTP, FTP, or LDAP is provided. If the directory name field is populated, then the Directory Access Protocol (DAP) can be used to fetch the information from an X.500 Directory. If the rfc822Name field is populated, then electronic mail is used to fetch the information. In practice, this extension is used to primarily with an LDAP directory.

The OCSP (Online Certificate Status Protocol) OID is used when the CA provides an OCSP responder to provide online certificate status information. OCSP may be used to determine whether a certificate is revoked. OCSP responders are discussed further in Chapter 17.

The authority information access extension is identified by the id-pe-authorityInfoAccess object identifier, and has the following syntax:

```
id-pe-authorityInfoAccess OBJECT IDENTIFIER  ::=  { id-pe 1 }

AuthorityInfoAccessSyntax  ::=  SEQUENCE SIZE (1..MAX) OF
                                   AccessDescription

AccessDescription  ::=  SEQUENCE  {
   accessMethod            OBJECT IDENTIFIER,
   accessLocation          GeneralName  }

id-ad OBJECT IDENTIFIER  ::=  { id-pkix 48 }

id-ad-ocsp OBJECT IDENTIFIER  ::=  { id-ad 1 }

id-ad-caIssuers OBJECT IDENTIFIER  ::=  { id-ad 2 }
```

This extension may be included in end entity or CA certificates, and it must be non-critical.

Subject Information Access

The subject information access extension is still under development by the IETF. It has the same syntax as the authority information access extension, except that it provides additional information about the subject instead of the CA.

So far, two standard access descriptors have been defined. They are named by their access method OIDs: timestamping (id-ad-timestamping) and CA repository (id-ad-ca Repository). Additional access descriptors are likely to be defined in the future.

The timestamping access descriptor is used when the certificate subject is a Time Stamp Authority (TSA). The access method tells how to contact the TSA to obtain a timestamp. Timestamps are discussed further in Chapter 17.

The CA repository access descriptor is used when the certificate subject is a CA. It tells where the CA publishes certificates and CRLs (if any). When the CA repository OID appears in the access method field, the access location field describes access protocol and location of the repository. The access location field contains a general name, as described much earlier in this chapter. If the uniform resource identifier (URI) field is populated, then a URL allowing the information to be fetched with HTTP, FTP, or LDAP is provided. If the directory name field is populated, then the Directory Access Protocol (DAP) can be used to fetch the information from an X.500 Directory. If the rfc822Name field is populated, then electronic mail is used to fetch the information. Other name forms are not defined in the context of the CA repository access descriptor.

The subject information access extension is identified by the id-pe-subjectInfoAccess object identifier, and has the following syntax:

```
id-pe-subjectInfoAccess OBJECT IDENTIFIER  ::=  { id-pe 11 }

SubjectInfoAccessSyntax  ::=  SEQUENCE SIZE (1..MAX) OF
                                   AccessDescription
```

```
AccessDescription   ::=   SEQUENCE  {
   accessMethod              OBJECT IDENTIFIER,
   accessLocation            GeneralName  }

id-ad OBJECT IDENTIFIER  ::=  { id-pkix 48 }

id-ad-timestamping OBJECT IDENTIFIER  ::=  { id-ad 3 }

id-ad-caRepository OBJECT IDENTIFIER  ::=  { id-ad 5 }
```

This extension must be non-critical.

Subject Directory Attributes

The subject directory attributes extension allows any attribute of the certificate subject to be included in the certificate. Any attribute that may be contained by an X.500 Directory or LDAP directory may be conveyed. The subject directory attributes extension contains a list of attributes; each attribute is identified by an OID and contains a value. The data type for each attribute value is determined by the OID.

Authorization information may be placed in this extension. The placement of authorization information in certificates is usually undesirable for two reasons. First, authorization information often does not have the same lifetime as the binding of the identity and the public key. When authorization information is placed in a certificate extension, the general result is the shortening of the certificate useful lifetime. Second, the CA is not usually authoritative for the authorization information. This results in additional steps for the CA to obtain authorization information from the authoritative source. Attribute certificates offer an alternative, and are discussed further in Chapter 17.

The subject directory attributes extension is identified by the id-ce-subjectDirectoryAttributes object identifier, and the syntax is defined as follows:

```
id-ce-subjectDirectoryAttributes OBJECT IDENTIFIER  ::=  { id-ce 9 }

SubjectDirectoryAttributes  ::=  SEQUENCE SIZE (1..MAX) OF Attribute
```

The syntax for Attribute is presented earlier in the distinguished name discussion. This extension must always be non-critical.

Generating and Using Certificates

In this section, we offer some guidance on certificate content. This guidance is intended to promote interoperability while providing sufficient information to support a variety of applications. We will cover three classes of certificates: user certificates, CA certificates, and self-issued certificates.

Unless explicitly noted, all certificates discussed in this section share the following properties regarding their certificate contents. The basic certificate contents are specified to maximize the probability that certificate users can process the certificate. To achieve this goal, the issuer must use commonly recognized algorithms and identify them with the standard OIDs. The CA must use naming attributes in the issuer name that all certificate users will recognize.

- The version number is three. X.509 v3 certificates are used.
- The serial number is a monotonically increasing integer value. This guarantees that the serial number is unique with respect to the issuing CA.
- The issuer name is populated with an X.500 distinguished name. The issuer name should be constructed using only the recommended distinguished name attributes identified in the directory name discussion earlier in the chapter. Wherever possible, use characters that can be represented with printable strings.
- The subject public key corresponds to a standard algorithm, and the algorithm is identified by one of the standard OIDs listed in Table 7.3.
- The signature field identifies a standard signature algorithm using one of the standard OIDs listed in Table 7.2.
- The unique identifier fields should not be present.

Some certificate extensions should appear in every certificate. These extensions help locate certificates and CRLs. All of these extensions are non-critical, so they should not reduce interoperability.

- Include an authority key identifier extension containing a key identifier. Inclusion of the issuer and serial number does not cause any harm, but it does increase the size of the certificate.
- Include a CRL distribution points extension that points to the locations where CRLs may be found.
- Include an authority information access extension specifying the repository in which the issuer's own CA certificates may be found.

End Entity Certificates

These certificates are issued to subjects that are not CAs. These certificates contain the public keys that will be used by a certificate user to verify a digital signature or perform key management. These certificates must contain sufficient information for the certificate user to determine whether the public key is appropriate for the intended application. The subject of an end entity certificate may be a human user or a system (such as a Web server or router). Our recommended certificate profile differs slightly in each case.

User Certificates

This user certificate profile includes naming information to support online applications, and naming information to support secure electronic mail. The recommended contents are as follows:

- The subject name is populated with a distinguished name. Either X.500 distinguished names or distinguished names comprised of domain components (a DNS-style name) is acceptable. The subject name should be constructed using only the recommended directory name attributes identified previously.
- The validity period should begin when the certificate is issued, and expire no more than three years later. Longer validity periods will lead to excessive CRL growth.

- Include the key usage extension as a critical extension. For signature public keys, both the digital signature and non-repudiation values should be asserted, and other key usage values should not be asserted. For Diffie-Hellman, Elliptic Curve Diffie-Hellman, or KEA public keys, only the key agreement value should be asserted. For RSA key transport keys, only the key encipherment value should be asserted.

- Include the certificate policies extension as a non-critical extension. The extension should specify a single policy, and that policy should not include any qualifiers. If qualifiers must be included to satisfy legal advisors, stick to the two discussed in this chapter.

- Include the subject alternative name extension as a non-critical extension. Include the user's electronic mail address (rfc822Name) to support S/MIME v3 applications.

Additional extensions may be included to meet local requirements, but these additional extensions should be non-critical.

System Certificates

This computer system certificate profile includes naming information to support online applications. The recommended contents are as follows:

- The subject name is populated with a distinguished name. Either X.500 distinguished names or distinguished names comprised of domain components (a DNS-style name) is acceptable. The subject name should be constructed using only the recommended directory name attributes identified previously.

- The validity period should begin when the certificate is issued, and expire no more than three years later. Longer validity periods will lead to excessive CRL growth.

- Include the key usage extension as a critical extension. For signature public keys, both the digital signature and non-repudiation values should be asserted, and other key usage values should not be asserted. For Diffie-Hellman, Elliptic Curve Diffie-Hellman, or KEA public keys, only the key agreement value should be asserted. For RSA key transport keys, only the key encipherment value should be asserted.

- Include the extended key usage extension as a non-critical extension if the system is a Web server supporting SSL or TLS, or the system is a router supporting IPsec. Assert the appropriate values for each protocol.

- Include the certificate policies extension as a non-critical extension. The extension should specify a single policy, and that policy should not include any qualifiers. If qualifiers must be included to satisfy legal advisors, stick to the two discussed in this chapter.

- Include the subject alternative name extension as a non-critical extension. Include the computer's DNS name (dNSname). If the system is a router supporting IPsec, the IP address may also be included (iPAddress).

Additional extensions may be included to meet local requirements, but these additional extensions should be non-critical.

CA Certificates

These certificates are issued to subjects that are CAs. These certificates will be part of certification paths. The public keys in these certificates will be used to verify the digital signatures on certificates and CRLs. These certificates must contain sufficient information for certificate users to construct certification paths and locate CRLs. The subject of a CA certificate may be another CA within the same enterprise PKI, a CA in a different enterprise PKI, or a bridge CA. Our recommended certificate profile differs slightly in each case.

CA Certificates within an Enterprise PKI

CA certificates within an enterprise PKI propagate simple trust relationships. Policy information is included in a non-critical extension to allow legacy implementations to accept the certificates without problems. Policy mapping is unnecessary, since the issuer and subject CAs are within the same enterprise. Since there are probably few limitations in the trust relationship, policy and name constraints are omitted.

- The subject name is populated with a distinguished name. Either X.500 distinguished names or distinguished names comprised of domain components (a DNS-style name) is acceptable. The subject name should be constructed using only the recommended directory name attributes identified previously. Further, any portion of the subject name that is the same as the issuer name should be encoded using the same string type.

- The validity period should begin when the certificate is issued, and after all certificates whose signatures can be verified by this key will expire. However, validity periods of more than five years are discouraged.

- The subject public key is associated with a signature algorithm. Diffie-Hellman, Elliptic Curve Diffie-Hellman, and KEA public keys should not be used. If an RSA key is used, it should not also be used for key transport. The algorithm identifier OID should be listed in Table 7.3.

- Include the basic constraints extensions as a critical extension. CA is TRUE. If the Enterprise PKI is a hierarchy, the path length value may be set.

- Include the key usage extension as a critical extension. The key certificate sign and CRL sign values are all asserted.

- Include the certificate policies extension as a non-critical extension. The extension should specify all of the policies that the subject CA may include in subordinate certificates. The policies specified should not include any qualifiers. If qualifiers must be included to satisfy legal advisors, stick to the two discussed in this chapter.

- Include the subject key identifier extension as a non-critical extension. The value of this extension should match the value of the key identifier in the authority key identifier extension of certificates issued by the subject CA.

- Include the subject information access extension as a non-critical extension, and specify the repository in which certificates issued by the subject can be found.

Additional extensions may be included to meet local requirements. These additional extensions should be non-critical.

CA Certificates between Enterprise PKIs

CA certificates that cross enterprise PKI boundaries describe more complex trust relationships. Policy information is included in a non-critical extension to allow legacy implementations to accept the certificates without problems. However, policy mapping information is required to translate policy information between the two enterprise PKIs. Name constraints are be used to protect name spaces.

- The subject name is populated with a distinguished name. Either X.500 distinguished names or distinguished names comprised of domain components (a DNS-style name) is acceptable. The subject name should be constructed using only the recommended directory name attributes identified previously. Further, any portion of the subject name that is the same as the issuer name should be encoded using the same string type.

- The validity period should begin when the certificate is issued, and after all certificates whose signatures can be verified by this key will expire. However, validity periods of more than five years are discouraged.

- The subject public key is associated with a signature algorithm. Diffie-Hellman, Elliptic Curve Diffie-Hellman, and KEA public keys should not be used. If an RSA key is used, it should not also be used for key transport. The algorithm identifier OID should be listed in Table 7.3.

- Include the basic constraints extensions as a critical extension. CA is TRUE. If the Enterprise PKI is a hierarchy, the path length value may be set.

- Include the key usage extension as a critical extension. The key certificate sign and CRL sign values are all asserted.

- Include the certificate policies extension as a non-critical extension. The extension should specify all of the policies that the subject CA may include in subordinate certificates. The policies specified should not have qualifiers. Since policy mapping will be used, policy qualifiers can be particularly disruptive. If policy qualifiers must be included to satisfy legal advisors, stick to the two discussed in this chapter.

- Include the policy mapping extension as a non-critical extension. The extension specifies the mapping between the issuer's policies and the subject's policies. Only specify mappings for issuer policies that appear in the certificate policies extension.

- Include the name constraints extension as a critical extension. Exclude subtrees for distinguished names associated with the local name space. This prevents the subject in the local enterprise PKI from accepting certificates in the remote enterprise PKI that include names from the local name space. Permit subtrees associated with the remote enterprise PKI.

- Include the subject key identifier extension as a non-critical extension. The value of this extension should match the value of the key identifier in the authority key identifier extension of certificates issued by the subject CA.

- Include the subject information access extension as a non-critical extension, and specify the repository in which certificates issued by the subject can be found.

Additional extensions may be included to meet local requirements. These additional extensions should be non-critical.

CA Certificates in a Bridge CA Environment

Where the subject is a bridge CA, the vast bulk of the requirements discussed earlier apply. However, in the bridge CA environment, the name spaces supported by the bridge CA are unpredictable. Therefore, the issuer should omit the permitted subtrees in the name constraints extension. The path length in the basic constraints extension should also be omitted since the length of certification paths cannot be predicted.

Self-Issued Certificates

Self-issued certificates are a special class of CA certificates. In this case, the issuer and the subject are the same. Self-issued certificates are used to establish trust points, distribute a new signing public key, and modify the set of certificate policies supported in a PKI.

Trust Point Establishment

A self-signed certificate is commonly used to distribute a public key and establish a trust point. Self-signed certificates are only certificates in the sense that they satisfy the X.509 format. They do not meet the general criteria for certificates presented in Chapter 3.

The signature on the self-signed certificate proves that the issuer has both the public and private keys. It does not prove anything else regarding the contents of the certificate. Self-signed certificates may only be trusted if the certificate user obtains them in a secure manner to ensure that they came from the correct authority, not a masquerade source.

Self-signed certificates can be X.509 v1. There is no need to include extensions. Trust point establishment is essentially an out-of-band activity. Generally, policy information is not included in self-signed certificates, especially at the root of a hierarchical PKI. Otherwise, a change in the set of policies would invalidate the trust point. Perhaps, in the future, self-signed certificates will use X.509 v3 certificates to establish policy-specific trust points. None of today's popular implementations could handle a policy-specific trust point.

Rollover Certificates

To introduce a new certificate or CRL signing key, a CA issues key rollover certificates. A CA issues a pair of key rollover certificates simultaneously. The first certificate contains the old public key, and it is signed with the new private key. The second certificate contains the new public key, and it is signed with the old private key. In this way, subscribers with certificates signed with the old private key, and subscribers with certificates signed with the new private key, can validate each other's certificates.

In both certificates, the issuer and subject names are identical. They are both CA certificates within the same enterprise PKI. Some differences from the normal CA certificate profile are discussed in the next two sections.

Old Signed With New

This rollover certificate allows the subscribers with certificates signed by the new private key to construct a valid certification path to the certificates previously signed with the old private key. The recommended certificate contents are as follows:

- The validity period begins when the certificate is issued, and ends after all certificates signed by the old private key expire.
- The subject public key is the old signature key.
- Include the basic constraints extensions as a critical extension. CA is TRUE, but the path length value is omitted.
- Include the authority key identifier extension as a non-critical extension. The information in the extension corresponds to the new public key.
- Include the subject key identifier extension as a non-critical extension. The value of this extension corresponds to the authority key identifier in certificates signed with the old private key.
- The signature value is generated using the new private key.

New Signed With Old

This rollover certificate allows the subscribers with certificates signed by the old private key to construct a valid certification path to the certificates signed with the new private key. The recommended contents are as follows:

- The validity period begins when the certificate is issued, and ends after all certificates signed by the old private key expire.
- The subject public key is the new signature key.
- Include the basic constraints extension as a critical extension. CA is TRUE, but the path length value is omitted.
- Include the authority key identifier extension as a non-critical extension. The information in the extension corresponds to the old public key.
- Include the subject key identifier extension as a non-critical extension. The value of this extension corresponds to the authority key identifier in certificates signed with the new private key.
- The signature value is generated using the old private key.

Policy Rollover Certificates

A CA issues policy rollover certificates to implement changes in the policy domain. Assume that a CA issues certificates under the red and white policies. Due to changes within an organization, new certificates will be issued under the gold, silver, and bronze policies. The CA wants to ensure that the existing subscribers can continue to operate during the transition. Even if the CA could instantly issue new certificates to all subscribers, every certificate user, including those outside the organization, would be forced to reconfigure their applications. A hard cut-over of this nature is an operational disaster. A soft cut-over is highly desirable.

Migration involves a pair of policy rollover certificates. The first certificate asserts the red and white policies, mapping them to gold, silver, and bronze policies. The second certificate asserts the gold, silver, and bronze policies, mapping them to the red and white policies.

Policy rollover often occurs in conjunction with key rollover. In such a case, the certificates use the profile from the previous sections with the modifications described in the next two sections.

Old Signed With New

This rollover certificate allows the subscribers with certificates issued under a new policy to construct a valid certification path to the certificates issued under the old policy. Since this is such a major transition, key rollover will likely be performed at the same time. The additional certificate profile recommendations are as follows:

- The certificate policies extension is included as a non-critical extension. The extension specifies all of the new policies that the CA will assert in certificates issued under the new private key. The policies specified do not have qualifiers.

- The policy mapping extension is included as a non-critical extension. The extension specifies the new policies as issuer domain policies, and it maps them to the old policies specified as subject domain policies.

New Signed With Old

This rollover certificate allows the subscribers with certificates issued under an old policy to construct a valid certification path to the certificates issued under the new policy. Since this is such a major transition, key rollover will likely be performed at the same time. The additional certificate profile recommendations are as follows:

- The certificate policies extension is included as a non-critical extension. The extension specifies all of the old policies that the CA asserted in certificates issued under the old private key. The policies specified do not have qualifiers.

- The policy mapping extension is included as a non-critical extension. The extension specifies the old policies as issuer domain policies, and it maps them to the new policies specified as subject domain policies.

CHAPTER 8

Certificate Revocation Lists

Recall the discussion of revoked credit cards in Chapter 3; we discussed the credit card hot list. When a certificate needs to be revoked, the certification authority (CA) puts the certificate serial number on a hot list, too. The hot list is called a *certificate revocation list* (CRL).

In Chapter 3, merchants checked the hot list for the credit card account number to determine whether the credit card was revoked. Similarly, certificate users check the CRL for the certificate serial number to determine whether the certificate is revoked. The CRL is signed by the CA to provide authentication and integrity of the CRL content.

CRLs may be used in a wide range of applications and environments. These environments encompass a very broad spectrum of operational requirements and assurance requirements. In this chapter, we discuss a common baseline that can be expected in every CRL, representations for frequently used attributes within the CRL, and provide guidance for effective and efficient CRL management.

Basic CRL Contents

Figure 8.1 illustrates the structure of the X.509 v2 CRL, and its syntax is listed next. The *tbs* prefix means *to be signed*. Therefore, the to-be-signed certificate list is the portion of the CRL that is ASN.1 DER encoded and digitally signed by the CRL issuer.

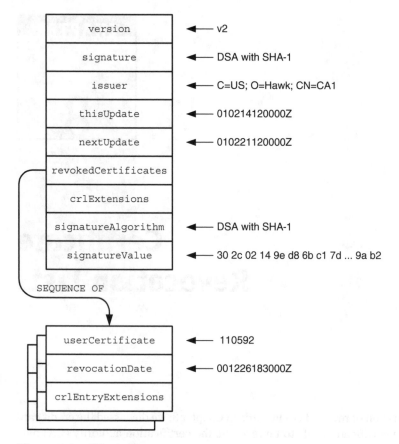

Figure 8.1   CRL structure.

```
CertificateList  ::=  SEQUENCE {
   tbsCertList               TBSCertList,
   signatureAlgorithm        AlgorithmIdentifier,
   signatureValue            BIT STRING  }

TBSCertList  ::=  SEQUENCE {
   version                   Version OPTIONAL,
                                 -- if present, version shall be v2
   signature                 AlgorithmIdentifier,
   issuer                    Name,
   thisUpdate                Time,
   nextUpdate                Time OPTIONAL,
   revokedCertificates       SEQUENCE OF SEQUENCE {
      userCertificate           CertificateSerialNumber,
      revocationDate            Time,
      crlEntryExtensions        Extensions OPTIONAL } OPTIONAL,
                                 -- if present, version shall be v2
   crlExtensions             [0]  EXPLICIT Extensions OPTIONAL }
                                 -- if present, version shall be v2
```

The top-level structure of the CRL parallels that described for certificates in the preceding chapter. The top-level structure of the CRL provides a tamper-evident envelope for the CRL content and is composed of three fields:

tbsCertList. The first field is the digitally signed CRL content. The fields within the to-be-signed certificate list are discussed in detail later in the chapter.

signatureAlgorithm. The signature algorithm field contains the algorithm identifier for the digital signature algorithm used by the CRL issuer to digitally sign the CRL. The algorithm identifier specifies the registered algorithm using an object identifier (OID). The optional parameters field is not used to validate the signature. The signature algorithm field must contain the same algorithm identifier as the signature field within the to-be-signed certificate list. As with the certificate structure discussed in the previous chapter, the digital signature covers one of these algorithm identifiers and not the other.

signatureValue. The signature value field contains a digital signature computed on the ASN.1 DER encoded to-be-signed certificate list. The signature value is ASN.1 encoded as a bit string.

Signed Certificate List

The to-be-signed certificate list contains the signature algorithm identifier, the CRL issuer, and the CRL issue date. It should always contain the date by which a new CRL will be issued, even though the syntax specifies the next update field as optional. Failure to include the next update field significantly complicates validation of a certificate. When there are no revoked certificates, the revoked certificates portion of the structure is absent. When one or more certificates are revoked, each entry on the revoked certificate list is defined by a structure containing the user certificate serial number, revocation date, and optional CRL entry extensions. The to-be-signed certificate list may also contain CRL extensions. CRL entry extensions provide information about a single revoked certificate, while CRL extensions provide information about the whole list.

version. The optional version field describes the syntax of the CRL. When extensions are used, which is usually the case, the field specifies version two (v2). CRL issuers may set the version field to v2 even if extensions are absent, so very few version one (v1) CRLs are actually in use today.

signature. The signature field contains the algorithm identifier for the digital signature algorithm used by the CRL issuer to sign the to-be-signed certificate list. This field must contain the same algorithm identifier as the signature algorithm field in the top-level structure of the CRL. The two algorithm identifiers are redundant; however, the digital signature covers one and not the other.

issuer. The issuer field contains the X.500 distinguished name of the CRL issuer. The Internet Certificate and CRL profile [HOUS99] requires the issuer field to contain a non-empty name. This is generally the identity of the CA; however, some CAs may choose to delegate some or all CRL functions to another authority by including a CRL Distribution Point extension in certificates. Such CRLs are called *Indirect CRLs* since the certificate issuer and the CRL issuer are different authorities.

Indirect CRLs are described in detail later in this chapter. Additional names, or aliases, for the CRL issuer may also appear in the issuer alternative name extension.

thisUpdate. The this-update field indicates the issue date of this CRL. There are two forms of date supported: UTC time and generalized time. CRL issuers must encode the this-update field as UTC time for dates through the year 2049, and CRL issuers must encode the this-update field as generalized time for dates in the year 2050 and beyond. This is the same rule as described in the previous chapter for the validity period in the certificate.

nextUpdate. The next-update field indicates the date by which the next CRL will be issued. The same two date forms are supported: UTC time and generalized time. The next CRL could be issued before the indicated date, but it must not be issued any later than the indicated date. As stated previously, CRL issuers ought to include this field, even though it is optional. CRL issuers should include a next-update time equal to or later than all previous CRLs issued for the same distribution point. If this simple rule is not followed, then clients trying to determine when to fetch an updated CRL from the repository may not check when an updated one is available.

revokedCertificates. The revoked certificates structure lists the revoked certificates. The revoked certificates structure is optional, but should only be absent when none of the unexpired certificates has been revoked. When there are no unexpired revoked certificates, the revoked certificates structure is absent; otherwise, the revoked certificates structure contains one entry for each revoked certificate. The structure contains the certificate serial numbers, time of revocation, and optional CRL entry extensions.

userCertificate. The user certificate field within the revoked certificate structure specifies the serial number of the revoked certificate. Certificates are uniquely identified by the combination of their certificate issuer name and their certificate serial number. Generally, the certificate issuer and the CRL issuer are the same authority, so the CRL structure is optimized for this case. That is, the issuer name is carried once in the issuer field, and it applies to the entire list of serial numbers. When the CRL issuer and the certificate issuer are different, the certificate issuer must be paired with each serial number. The certificate issuer CRL entry extension provides the certificate issuer name. This CRL entry extension, as well as the others, is described later in the chapter.

revocationDate. The revocation date field specifies the date on which the revocation occurred. The same two date forms are supported: UTC time and generalized time.

crlEntryExtensions. The CRL entry extensions field is used to provide additional information about single CRL entries. This field may only appear if the version is v2. The certificate issuer described previously is one example. This CRL entry extension and others are discussed later.

crlExtensions. The CRL extensions field is used to provide additional information about the whole CRL. Again, this field may only appear if the version is v2. CRL extensions are discussed in the next section.

CRL Extensions

ITU-T and ANSI X9 have defined several CRL extensions for X.509 v2 CRLs. They are specified in [X50997] and [X955]. Each extension in a CRL may be designated as critical or non-critical. A CRL validation fails if an unrecognized critical extension is encountered. However, unrecognized non-critical extensions may be ignored. The X.509 v2 CRL format allows communities to define private extensions to carry information unique to those communities. Communities are encouraged to define non-critical private extensions so that their CRLs can be readily validated by all implementations.

The following CRL extensions are the ones that should be properly handled by all implementations.

Authority Key Identifier

The authority key identifier extension provides a means of identifying the public key needed to validate the signature on the CRL. The identification can be based on either the key identifier (the subject key identifier extension from the CRL issuer's certificate) or on the issuer name and serial number (again, from the CRL issuer's certificate). This extension is especially useful where a CRL issuer has more than one signing key. In this case, the CRL issuer should have more than one certificate, one corresponding to each signing key.

CAs may choose to use different private keys for signing certificates and signing CRLs, and the corresponding public keys would each be certified. The subject name in those certificates would be the same. Therefore, the subject key identifier extension in these certificates is a good discriminator.

CRL issuers will regularly transition from one signing key to another. Usually, there will be an overlap in the validity period of the certificates associated with each of the signing keys. Therefore, during this overlap period, two certificates with the same subject name (and different public keys) will be valid. Again, the subject key identifier extension in these certificates is a way to quickly identify the proper certificate for a particular signature validation.

The authority key identifier extension is identified by the id-ce-authorityKey Identifier object identifier, and has the following syntax:

```
id-ce OBJECT IDENTIFIER  ::=  { joint-iso-ccitt(2) ds(5) 29 }

id-ce-authorityKeyIdentifier OBJECT IDENTIFIER ::=  { id-ce 35 }

AuthorityKeyIdentifier  ::=  SEQUENCE {
    keyIdentifier                [0] KeyIdentifier OPTIONAL,
    authorityCertIssuer          [1] GeneralNames OPTIONAL,
    authorityCertSerialNumber    [2] CertificateSerialNumber OPTIONAL  }

KeyIdentifier  ::=  OCTET STRING
```

The authority key identifier extension is always non-critical.

The Internet Certificate and CRL profile [HOUS99] requires CRL issuers to include this extension in CRLs to aid validators in locating the correct certificate. Further, the

Internet Certificate and CRL profile requires that the key identifier field be present, and it recommends that the key identifier be computed from the public key value. Two methods of computing the key identifier are suggested. The key identifier is mandated to enhance performance when the CRL issuer has multiple certificates.

The fields within the authority key identifier extension are used as follows:

keyIdentifier. This optional field contains the subject key identifier extension from the CRL issuer's certificate. We strongly encourage the inclusion of this optional field.

authorityCertIssuer. This optional field contains the issuer name or issuer alternative name of the CRL issuer's certificate. More than one name may be included. The Internet Certificate and CRL profile requires that CA certificates contain a non-empty issuer name, so if any name is present, this is the best name to use. If this field is present, the authority certificate serial number field must also be present.

authorityCertSerialNumber. This optional field contains the serial number of the CRL issuer's certificate. If this field is present, the authority certificate issuer field must also be present.

Issuer Alternative Name

The issuer alternative names extension allows additional name forms to be associated with the issuer of the CRL. Defined options include an RFC 822 name (an electronic mail address), a DNS name (an Internet host name), an IP address, and a URI (usually a WWW URL). Multiple instances of a name and multiple name forms may be included.

In the previous chapter, we discussed the inclusion of the issuer alternative name extension in certificates. The rules and recommendations made in the previous chapter apply to CRLs as well. The inclusion of these names is entirely optional.

The authority key identifier extension is identified by the id-ce-issuerAltName object identifier, and has the following syntax:

```
id-ce-issuerAltName OBJECT IDENTIFIER  ::=  { id-ce 18 }


IssuerAltName  ::=  GeneralNames
```

This extension may, at the option of the CRL issuer, be either critical or non-critical. However, since the Internet Certificate and CRL profile requires the CRL issuer field to be non-empty, we suggest that this extension always be non-critical.

CRL Number

The CRL number extension conveys a monotonically increasing sequence number for each CRL issued by a CRL issuer. This extension allows users to easily determine when a particular CRL supersedes another CRL from the same CRL issuer.

The Internet Certificate and CRL profile requires the inclusion of this extension in all CRLs.

The CRL number extension is identified by the id-ce-cRLNumber object identifier, and has the following syntax:

```
id-ce-cRLNumber OBJECT IDENTIFIER  ::=  { id-ce 20 }

cRLNumber  ::=  INTEGER (0..MAX)
```

The CRL number extension is always non-critical.

Delta CRL Indicator

The delta CRL indicator extension identifies a CRL as a delta CRL. A delta CRL contains updates to revocation information previously issued and distributed in a complete CRL. This earlier CRL is called the *base CRL*. In some environments, using delta CRLs can significantly reduce network load and processing time. A delta CRL will generally be smaller than the base CRL that it updates, so applications that obtain a delta CRL consume less network bandwidth than applications that obtain the corresponding complete CRL. Applications that store revocation information in a format other than the CRL structure can add new revocation information to such a local database without reprocessing the older information that is already in the database.

The delta CRL indicator extension contains a single value: the base CRL number. This value identifies the CRL number of the base CRL that was used as the foundation in the generation of this delta CRL. The referenced base CRL is a CRL that was explicitly issued as a CRL that is complete for a given scope. A scope might be a set of revocation reasons or a particular distribution point. The CRL containing the delta CRL indicator extension contains all updates to the certificate revocation status for that same scope. The combination of the delta CRL plus the CRL referenced in the base CRL number field is equivalent to a full CRL for the applicable scope at the time of publication of the delta CRL.

Since most certificate-using applications do not handle delta CRLs, we recommend that CRL issuers issue a complete CRL for the same scope whenever a delta CRL is issued. This practice provides the most recent revocation information available to all certificate users, those that handle delta CRLs and those that do not. The CRL number extension in both the delta CRL and the complete CRL must contain the same value. This is further indication that the delta CRL and the complete CRL convey the same revocation information.

When using delta CRLs, a certificate user can construct a CRL that is complete for the scope, at the current time, in either of the following ways:

- Retrieve the current delta CRL for that scope, and combine it with the previously issued base CRL that is complete for the same scope.

- Retrieve the current delta CRL for that scope, and combine it with a locally constructed CRL whose content is equivalent to the previously issued base CRL that is complete for the same scope.

In either case, the constructed CRL contains the same revocation information. To ensure that the constructed CRL is complete, the CRL number within the base CRL and the base CRL referenced in the delta CRL must be compared.

The delta CRL indicator extension is identified by the id-ce-deltaCRLIndicator object identifier, and has the following syntax:

```
id-ce-deltaCRLIndicator OBJECT IDENTIFIER  ::=  { id-ce 27 }

BaseCRLNumber  ::=  CRLNumber
```

The delta CRL indicator extension is always critical. Since the delta CRL does not contain a list of all of the unexpired revoked certificates, the criticality ensures that a certificate validation process does not accidentally use the incomplete list instead of a full list. The certificate validation process must recognize the extension or reject the delta CRL.

Issuing Distribution Point

The issuing distribution point extension identifies the CRL distribution point for a particular CRL, and it indicates whether the CRL covers revocation for end entity certificates only, CA certificates only, or a limited set of reason codes.

Each CRL distribution point does not have a different signing key; rather, one CRL issuer may support several CRL distribution points with a single signing key.

The reason codes associated with a CRL distribution point are specified in the only-some-reasons field. If only-some-reasons does not appear, the CRL distribution point contains revocations for all reason codes. CRL issuers may use CRL distribution points to partition the CRL based on compromise and routine revocation. In this case, the revocations with reason code key compromise (bit position one within reason flags) and CA compromise (bit position two) appear in one distribution point, and the revocations with other reason codes appear in a separate distribution point.

If the CRL is stored in the Directory, it is stored in the Directory entry corresponding to the CRL distribution point, which may be different from the Directory entry of the CA. The full-name alternative can be used to specify an arbitrary name in the Directory, or the name-relative-to-CRL-issuer alternative can be used to specify a name that is subordinate to the name in the issuer field.

When the full-name alternative contains a URI, the object is a pointer to the most current CRL. The URI schemes ftp, http, mailto, and ldap [BERN94, HOWE95] are defined for this purpose. The URI must include an absolute pathname to a host.

The issuing distribution point extension is identified by the id-ce-issuing DistributionPoint object identifier, and has the following syntax:

```
id-ce-issuingDistributionPoint OBJECT IDENTIFIER  ::=  { id-ce 28 }

issuingDistributionPoint  ::=  SEQUENCE  {
    distributionPoint      [0] DistributionPointName OPTIONAL,
    onlyContainsUserCerts  [1] BOOLEAN DEFAULT FALSE,
    onlyContainsCACerts    [2] BOOLEAN DEFAULT FALSE,
    onlySomeReasons        [3] ReasonFlags OPTIONAL,
    indirectCRL            [4] BOOLEAN DEFAULT FALSE  }
```

```
DistributionPointName   ::=  CHOICE  {
   fullName                [0] GeneralNames,
   nameRelativeToCRLIssuer [1] RelativeDistinguishedName  }

ReasonFlags  ::=  BIT STRING  {
   unused                  (0),
   keyCompromise           (1),
   cACompromise            (2),
   affiliationChanged      (3),
   superseded              (4),
   cessationOfOperation    (5),
   certificateHold         (6)  }
```

The issuing distribution point extension is always critical. Since the only-some-reasons field can be used to limit the scope of the unexpired revoked certificates listed, the criticality ensures that a certificate validation process does not accidentally use an incomplete list instead of a full list. The certificate validation process must recognize the extension or reject the CRL.

Freshest CRL

The freshest CRL extension identifies how to obtain delta CRL information for the base CRL that contains the extension. Given the base CRL, the delta CRL can be fetched and processed. This extension has exactly the same syntax as the CRL distribution point certificate extension and the freshest CRL certificate extension. All of the conventions discussed in the previous chapter apply.

The freshest CRL extension is identified by the id-ce-freshestCRL object identifier, and has the following syntax:

```
id-ce-freshestCRL OBJECT IDENTIFIER  ::=  { id-ce 46 }

FreshestCRL  ::=  CRLDistributionPoints
```

The freshest CRL extension is always non-critical. The certificate validation process is not required to support delta CRLs.

CRL Entry Extensions

ITU-T and ANSI X9 have defined several CRL entry extensions for X.509 v2 CRLs. They are specified in [X50997] and [X955], and they associate additional attributes with CRL entries. Each entry extension in a CRL entry may be designated as critical or non-critical. A CRL validation fails if an unrecognized critical entry extension is encountered. However, unrecognized non-critical entry extensions may be ignored. The X.509 v2 CRL format allows communities to define private extensions to carry information unique to those communities. Communities are encouraged to define non-critical private extensions so that their CRLs can be readily validated by all implementations.

The following CRL entry extensions are the ones that should be properly handled by all implementations.

Reason Code

The reason code entry extension identifies the reason for certificate revocation. We strongly encourage CRL issuers to include meaningful reason codes in CRL entries; however, the reason code entry extension should be absent instead of using unspecified (enumerated value of zero) as the reason code value.

The reason code entry extension is identified by the id-ce-cRLReason object identifier, and has the following syntax:

```
id-ce-cRLReason OBJECT IDENTIFIER ::= { id-ce 21 }

CRLReason  ::=  ENUMERATED  {
    unspecified            (0),
    keyCompromise          (1),
    cACompromise           (2),
    affiliationChanged     (3),
    superseded             (4),
    cessationOfOperation   (5),
    certificateHold        (6),
    removeFromCRL          (8)  }
```

The reason code entry extension is always non-critical.

Hold Instruction Code

The hold instruction code entry extension provides a registered instruction identifier that indicates the action to be taken after encountering a certificate that has been placed on hold.

The Internet Certificate and CRL profile [HOUS99] requires support for several instruction codes that have been defined by the financial industry. One can expect support for these instruction codes:

id-holdinstruction-callissuer. Applications that encounter this hold instruction must call the certificate issuer or reject the certificate. Most applications will not be in a position to make telephone calls, so the likely response is certificate rejection, which is the same response that would be made if this entry extension were absent. The intent is to allow some human discretion by the CA, but as a practical matter, most applications expect a "yes" or "no" from certificate path validation. This hold instruction suggests a third response: "please call the CA."

id-holdinstruction-reject. Applications that encounter this hold instruction must reject the certificate, which is the same response that would be made if this entry extension were absent.

id-holdinstruction-none. Applications that encounter this hold instruction must reject the certificate, which is the same response that would be made if this entry extension were absent. This hold instruction is semantically equivalent to the absence of a hold instruction code entry extension. For this reason, we strongly discourage its use. It is less confusing to omit the entry extension.

The hold instruction code entry extension is identified by the id-ce-hold InstructionCode object identifier, and has the following syntax:

```
id-ce-holdInstructionCode OBJECT IDENTIFIER  ::=  { id-ce 23 }


holdInstructionCode  ::=  OBJECT IDENTIFIER

— Hold instructions from ANSI X9.57
holdInstruction OBJECT IDENTIFIER  ::=
    { iso(1) member-body(2) us(840) x9-57(10040) 2 }
id-holdinstruction-none OBJECT IDENTIFIER  ::=
    { holdInstruction 1 }
id-holdinstruction-callissuer OBJECT IDENTIFIER  ::=
    { holdInstruction 2 }
id-holdinstruction-reject OBJECT IDENTIFIER  ::=
    { holdInstruction 3 }
```

The hold instruction code entry extension is always non-critical. The presence of a hold instruction is not likely to alter the behavior of the application. For this reason, it has very limited use. It may be of value when the human user presents a token, such as a smartcard, to another human, perhaps a cashier, as part of a transaction. In this case, the CA may use the call-issuer hold instruction to have the cashier call the CA, and the CA may direct the cashier to confiscate the token containing the private key that corresponds to the certificate.

Invalidity Date

The invalidity date entry extension provides the date on which it is known or suspected that the private key was compromised, or that the certificate otherwise became invalid. This date may be earlier than the revocation date in the CRL entry, which is the date on which the CRL issuer processed the revocation. When a revocation is first posted in a CRL, the invalidity date may precede the date of issue of earlier CRLs, but the revocation date should not precede the date of issue of earlier CRLs. Whenever this information is available, we strongly encourage CRL issuers to share it.

Unlike other dates represented in the CRL, the invalidity date is always expressed using the generalized time format. Values must be expressed in Greenwich Mean Time (Zulu).

The invalidity date entry extension is identified by the id-ce-invalidityDate object identifier, and has the following syntax:

```
id-ce-invalidityDate OBJECT IDENTIFIER  ::=  { id-ce 24 }

invalidityDate  ::=  GeneralizedTime
```

The invalidity date entry extension is always non-critical. The presence or absence of this entry extension does not impact the acceptance or rejection of a certificate; however, the invalidity date information may help resolve a dispute when the subject of a revoked certificate repudiates their participation in a transaction.

Certificate Issuer

The certificate issuer entry extension allows a CRL to include entries from more than one certificate issuer. As stated earlier, such CRLs are called indirect CRLs, and they have the indirect CRL flag set in the issuing distribution point extension. The certificate issuer entry extension identifies the certificate issuer associated with an entry in an indirect CRL. If this entry extension is not present in the first entry in an indirect CRL, the certificate issuer for that entry defaults to the CRL issuer. On subsequent CRL entries where the entry extension is not present, the certificate issuer for the entry is the same as that for the preceding entry.

The certificate issuer entry extension is identified by the id-ce-certificate Issuer object identifier, and has the following syntax:

```
id-ce-certificateIssuer OBJECT IDENTIFIER  ::=  { id-ce 29 }

certificateIssuer  ::=  GeneralNames
```

This certificate issuer entry extension is always critical. If a certificate validation process ignored this extension, it could not correctly attribute CRL entries to the correct certificates.

Generating and Using CRLs

In Chapter 5, "PKI Components and Users," we learned that the CA is responsible for maintaining the list of unexpired certificates that can no longer be trusted. The CRL is the usual means of letting certificate users know which certificates are no longer trustworthy. In the remainder of this chapter, we build on the details presented in the first part of this chapter, and we discuss the conventions for effective and efficient CRL management.

CRL Coverage

The CA issues a certificate after validating the information that it contains. If any of this information is incorrect or some event causes it to become invalid, the CA must revoke the certificate. Timely notification of the revocation is important so that certificate users do not rely on incorrect or invalid information.

The CA revokes a certificate by including the certificate serial number on the list of revoked certificates in the CRL.

The CRL syntax also permits the CA to suspend certificates. Suspension places a certificate on hold, and the CA may take the certificate off hold by removing the entry from a future CRL. The certificate-hold reason code indicates that the CA has suspended the certificate and might unsuspend it in the future.

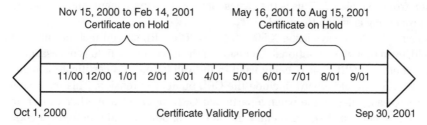

Figure 8.2 Timeline of certificate that is suspended twice.

Figure 8.2 shows the timeline of a certificate that is placed on hold twice before it expires. The swapping back and forth between valid and suspended causes severe difficulties with non-repudiation.

Let us consider a simple scenario. Alice uses her private key to sign a document. Many months later, the validity of Alice's digital signature is important to Bob. How can Bob determine if the signature was generated when Alice's certificate was valid or suspended? With extreme difficulty. First, Bob will need a method of determining the time that Alice signed the document. Without a trusted time source, this might be impossible. Second, Bob will need the CRLs issued just before and just after the document signing time to determine whether Alice's certificate was suspended at the time the signature was generated.

Certificate suspension should be avoided. When a CA suspends a certificate, the binding between the identity of the certificate subject and the public key is not placed on hold. Rather, some other attribute within the certificate is being suspended. Perhaps the confidence in the subject's ability to pay for electronic commerce purchases has become suspect. To avoid this situation, attributes that may lead to suspension should not be included in the certificate.

Such attributes can be included in attribute certificates, or they can be maintained in databases. Attribute certificates will be discussed in Chapter 17, "Future Developments." Databases can be indexed by the certificate subject or by the subject key identifier, and they can contain arbitrary information about the subject. For example, before accepting an electronic commerce transaction, the database can be queried to determine whether the subject is an acceptable business risk. Attribute certificates or databases offer an attractive alternative to the inclusion of attributes that may require suspension in a certificate.

In summary, avoid certificate suspension. The suspension of a certificate makes it quite difficult to retrospectively determine the validity of a signature. Move any attributes that might lead to certificate suspension to an attribute certificate or database so that there is never a need to suspend a certificate.

Full CRLs

Most CAs issue their own CRLs; that is, the CA is the certificate issuer and the CRL issuer. The CA will periodically issue a single CRL that covers its entire certificate population. Such CRLs are often called *full CRLs* because they contain all of the most recent information from a single CA. This is the easiest approach to implement, and the certificate user processing is straightforward.

CRL issuers should always issue X.509 v2 CRLs. The CRL should include the next update field, even though it is optional. Inclusion of the next update field is necessary to determine whether a CRL that is being used in the validation of a certificate is stale. Likewise, the CRL should always include the CRL number extension. This extension allows users to easily determine when a particular CRL supersedes another CRL from the same CRL issuer. Further, each entry in the CRL should include the reason code entry extension if the CRL issuer knows the reason.

Certificates should include the CRL distribution points extension to help certificate users locate the CRL.

Use of full CRLs does have some limitations.

- The Directory location of the full CRL is implied by the CA's distinguished name.

- The size of the CRL can get out of control. If a large number of certificates need to be revoked, the CRL can become quite large. Large CRLs require too much network bandwidth as many different certificate users individually retrieve them from the repository.

- The CRL may be issued and retrieved more frequently than necessary. If the certificate policy requires that key compromise revocation be distributed in one day, then a new full CRL must be issued each day. We assume that key compromise occurs less frequently than other reasons for revocation, but all of the reasons are represented in the full CRL, so the whole bundle must be issued daily. The next update field in the certificate will cause certificate users to fetch a new full CRL each day.

- A full CRL is needed from each CA. Each CA maintains its own certificate status information, and a full CRL is needed from each one. A certificate user may fetch many different CRLs to validate a single certificate path.

A combination of certificate extensions and CRL extensions can be used to overcome these limitations.

CRL Distribution Points

CRL distribution points have two primary purposes. They provide a flexible way of specifying the location where the most recent CRL may be obtained. They also provide a means of limiting the maximum size of the CRL. When a CRL includes an issuing distribution point extension, the certificate that is being validated must contain a CRL distribution point extension.

CRL Location

If a certificate does not include a CRL distribution point extension, then the CRL is assumed to be available in the Directory entry associated with the CA. That is, the certificate issuer distinguished name specifies the exact location in the Directory where the CRL can be found. Unfortunately, Directory deployment is not ubiquitous. Even when a Directory is available, access to it may not be permitted outside of the organization. Therefore, CRL distribution often cannot be accomplished with the Directory.

The many benefits provided by a public key infrastructure (PKI) should not be delayed waiting for a ubiquitous Directory. Rather, PKI should be deployed with alternate means of distributing certificates and CRLs. When (and if) a ubiquitous Directory does emerge, the certificates and CRL distribution can migrate to the Directory. Further, since many certificate validation implementations do not assume the presence of a Directory, the inclusion of a CRL distribution point that points to the appropriate Directory server and entry ensures that all implementations can locate the most recent CRL.

In the absence of a Directory, CRL distribution points are very important. They offer the alternative means of locating the CRL associated with a particular certificate. CRL distribution points are most often used with LDAP, HTTP, and anonymous FTP. In each case, the CRL distribution point included within the certificate contains the URL from which the CRL may be obtained.

CRL Size

If a certificate does not include a CRL distribution points extension, then the CRL located in the Directory is assumed to cover all of the unexpired certificates issued by the CA. If the CA issues a large number of certificates, then the number that are revoked may also be large. To keep the CRL from getting too large, the CA may divide the population among different CRLs. The CA may divide the population by subject type (for example, all CA certificates appear on one distribution point and end entities on another). Alternatively, the CA may use serial numbers or any other arbitrary means to determine which CRL will be used with a particular certificate. Since the CRL distribution points certificate extension includes an explicit pointer to the corresponding CRL location, there is no need for any party other than the CA to be aware of the CRL partitioning scheme employed.

Partitioning may also occur based on the reason for revocation. We hope that the number of revocations due to key compromise will always be significantly less than the number of revocations due to affiliation changes. The frequency with which the CRL associated with each of these reasons is issued need not be the same. Since the ramifications of key compromise are significantly more severe than the ramifications of a superseded certificate, the CRL that includes the key compromise reason code might be issued twice as often.

The two partitioning techniques may be used together. An example is shown in Figure 8.3. In this example, the urgent CRL distribution point handles the key compromise and CA compromise reason codes, and the forty-eighth routine distribution point handles the remaining reason codes. Because the Hawk subscribers want speedy notification when compromise occurs, the CRL stored in the urgent CRL distribution point is updated twice each day. Since compromise is an infrequent event, all of the certificates issued by the Hawk CA include the same distribution point for compromise notification, yet this CRL will remain small. On the other hand, the more frequent and less urgent revocation events could lead to a very large CRL. To avoid the CRL becoming too large, only 1000 certificates reference the same routine CRL distribution point. Consequently, even if all of the certificates needed to be revoked, the maximum size of one routine CRL will be 1000 entries. Each of the routine CRLs is updated weekly.

```
CRLDistributionPoints {
   DistributionPoint {
      distributionPoint = ldap://dir.hawk.com/CN=UrgentCRLDP,
                            O=Hawk,C=US$certificateRevocationList
      reasons           = keyCompromise, cACompromise
   }
   DistributionPoint {
      distributionPoint = ldap://dir.hawk.com/CN=RoutineCRLDP48,
                            O=Hawk,C=US$certificateRevocationList
      reasons           = unused, affiliationChanged, superseded,
                            cessationOfOperation, certificateHold
} }
```

Figure 8.3   CRL distribution points using reason code partitioning.

The CRL issuer must plan ahead to achieve CRL size reduction and speedy notification of important revocations. By creating a separate distribution point for each of the categories, the mechanism is simple and straightforward. However, after a certificate is issued, it is too late to take advantage of this mechanism. The CRL distribution points must be identified in the certificate.

Delta CRLs

Simulations of very large certificate-based systems show that a significant amount to bandwidth is spent retrieving revocation information. A delta CRL only contains changes from a specified base CRL. CRL issuers must ensure that the delta CRL accurately reflects all changes in the revocation information to the referenced base CRL. Delta CRLs reduce the size of the revocation information that is retrieved, thus reducing the bandwidth requirements.

Delta CRLs may be referenced by a certificate or by a base CRL. One (or both) must contain a freshest CRL extension. The delta CRL must contain a delta CRL indicator extension. In addition, the Internet Certificate and CRL profile [HOUS99] requires CRL issuers to issue base CRLs as well as delta CRLs. This approach ensures that a CRL is available for simple and straightforward CRL processing. Few certificate users are currently able to process delta CRLs.

The bandwidth reduction provided by delta CRLs comes at a cost: certificate validation complexity. This cost may be too high. Today, many applications do not perform revocation checking at all; they check only the certificate signature and the certificate validity period. With each release, these applications are getting more robust and complete. Revocation checking will significantly improve security of the applications. Simple and straightforward CRL checking is more likely to be added than complex, multitiered CRL checking.

Certificate suspension further complicates delta CRLs. If a CA supports the certificate-hold revocation reason code, the CRL issuer must follow these rules when generating delta CRLs:

1. If a certificate is listed as revoked with the certificate-hold reason code, on either a delta CRL or a base CRL, and the hold is subsequently released, then the certificate must be included in all subsequent delta CRLs. The certificate must be listed with the remove-from-CRL reason code unless the certificate is subsequently revoked again for one of the reasons included in the scope of the delta CRL, in which case the certificate must be listed with the reason code appropriate for the subsequent revocation.

2. If a certificate is listed as revoked with the certificate-hold reason code, on either a delta CRL or a base CRL, and the certificate is subsequently permanently revoked, then the certificate must be listed on all subsequent delta CRLs. The certificate should be listed with the reason code appropriate for the permanent revocation.

Delta CRLs provide very fresh information with low overhead. The CRL issuer workload increases to provide both base CRLs and delta CRLs. The CRL issuer must generate the same number of base CRLs, and must also generate the delta CRLs. Reduced network bandwidth results, but so does increased certificate validation complexity.

Indirect CRLs

CRL distribution points are used to implement indirect CRLs. Normally, the issuer of the certificate and the issuer of the CRL are the same authority. With indirect CRLs, each has a different issuer. Indirect CRLs are used when the certificate issuer delegates the CRL management to another authority, often called the *Indirect CRL Authority* (ICRLA).

If more than one CA delegates compromise revocations to an ICRLA, then only one authority needs to issue frequent CRLs. Thus, the CAs must have a secure mechanism for communicating compromise revocation information to the ICRLA. Each certificate must contain a CRL distribution point extension specifying the ICRLA and the indirect CRL location. Likewise, the CRLs issued by the ICRLA must include the issuing distribution point extension.

In a hierarchical PKI, indirect CRLs offer another potential benefit. Since the top levels of the hierarchy only issue certificates to other CAs, any revocation resulting from a compromise is a CA compromise. Therefore, if these CAs all delegate to the same ICRLA, then one CRL can cover several of the most often validated certificates. By consolidating these CRLs, which should almost always be empty anyway, the number of Directory or other repository interactions can be significantly reduced.

Figure 8.4 illustrates the indirect CRL. It contains an update to the CRL distribution points certificate extension in Figure 8.3. The urgent CRL distribution point is replaced with an indirect CRL.

CAs must trust the ICRLA; otherwise, delegation of the most time-critical revocations is misplaced. CAs must plan ahead and develop a secure communication capability with the ICRLA. Within a hierarchical PKI, the trust relationship is already in place, and secure communication is likely to be readily available. This is a modest cost that can result in significant network bandwidth reduction.

```
CRLDistributionPoints {
   DistributionPoint {
      distributionPoint = ldap://dir.hawk.com/CN=ICRLA,
                             O=Hawk,C=US$certificateRevocationList
      reasons           = keyCompromise, cACompromise
      cRLIssuer         = CN=ICRLA,O=Hawk,C=US
   }
   DistributionPoint {
      distributionPoint = ldap://dir.hawk.com/CN=CRLDP48,
                             O=Hawk,C=US$certificateRevocationList
      reasons           = unused, affiliationChanged, superseded,
                             cessationOfOperation, certificateHold
} }
```

Figure 8.4   CRL distribution points using an indirect CRL.

Repository Protocols

In Chapter 3, we discussed two analogies for digital certificates: the business card and the credit card. These are physical objects. The cards are held by their owners, and the owner usually presents it. A business card is usually personally presented by the person named on the card. A credit card may be physically presented to a merchant, or the credit card number and expiration date may be recited on the telephone or typed into a browser form.

As we will see in Chapter 13, "PKI-Enabled Applications," many security protocols include the transfer of certificates. However, this is where the analogy begins to break down. The relying party cannot depend upon the other party to supply all of the certificates and certificate revocation lists (CRLs) necessary for a particular transaction. When the private key is used to generate digital signatures, the signer can enclose his or her own certificate. However, he or she may not be able to include the appropriate CRL to support signature verification. The verification process might take place in the future, long after the current CRL has become stale.

Further, the relying party may need several certificates to construct a certification path. Since the relying parties may use a different trust point, the certificate owner cannot know which certificates will be needed. The relying party also needs CRLs to check the status of these certification authority (CA) certificates.

Certificate and CRL distribution can be provided because of another difference in our physical analogies. Credit card security depends upon the physical possession of that one card. The merchant possesses it briefly, if at all. This is not true of certificates and

CRLs. The relying party does not need to obtain the certificates or CRLs from the certificate owner, from the issuing CA, or any other specific party. The manner in which a certificate is obtained has no bearing on security.

In Chapter 5, "PKI Components and Users," we introduced the concept of a repository. A public key infrastructure (PKI) relies on a repository to store and distribute certificates and CRLs. We noted that a repository is a system, and it is known by its address and access protocol. One of the crucial decisions in any PKI deployment is the access protocol or protocols that will be used to access the repository. The access protocol will determine which responsibilities are assigned to the CA, relying party, and the repository.

In this chapter, we define a number of different attributes of repositories. We review the most common access protocols, identify the attributes that apply to them, and provide advice on choosing a repository.

Repository Attributes

Different repository access protocols have different attributes. We consider the following attributes:

Location transparency. With some repository protocols, a client goes to a single system for all information. If that server does not have the information, it goes to other servers to locate the information on behalf of the client. This complexity is hidden from the client. In other cases, the server simply provides a pointer that the client must follow to the correct repository server. Some protocols simply return an error if the information is not stored locally.

Performance and availability. Relying parties experience a delay when waiting for a repository to respond. To manage delays, a repository needs to scale as the number of subscribers grows and the frequency of information requests increases. If the repository does not respond, clients cannot obtain the needed security services. The repository should be designed to maximize availability, even when one or more components fail.

Anonymous versus authenticated access. In the most common model, a repository provides information without authenticating the client. In this case, the repository is a part of the infrastructure costs to an organization. This implies a business model in which the cost of the PKI is underwritten by an organization, or the costs are based on a fee for each certificate issued. As an alternative, an organization can charge a fee for repository access. This approach requires the repository to identify and authenticate each client. This model moves the cost from the certificate owner to relying parties.

Interoperability. Repositories interact with CAs, relying parties, and other repositories. CAs must post certificates and CRLs to the repository, and then relying parties fetch them. In distributed systems, repositories need to share information with each other. Interoperability affects product selection and ease of use.

Common Repository Protocols

There are several repository options to support a PKI. The traditional PKI choice is a Directory. There are several types of directory systems. However, there are other choices. Any protocol that can be used to distribute binary information can work. These protocols include FTP, HTTP, finger, electronic mail, and even the DNS system.

Directories

The traditional PKI repository is the Directory. A Directory is an online database of arbitrary information. Information about a particular person or object is called a Directory *entry*. Each entry is associated with an *object class*, which describes different *attributes* the entry is expected to contain. Object classes associated with people contain different attributes than object classes associated with computer equipment. To obtain information from a Directory, clients must know where to send the request, which entry they want, and which attributes from the entry they want. However, searches are supported if the exact entry name is not known.

Each entry is identified by a distinguished name. The distinguished name is used as the subject and issuer names in certificates. The client requests different attributes depending on the information (for example, certificate or CRL) that is required. Attributes are defined in several specifications, but the preferred source for PKI-related attributes is RFC 2587, the IETF PKIX LDAP v2 Schema [BOEY99]. RFC 2587 specifies the following attributes:

userCertificate. This attribute contains end entity certificates with a subject matching the entry distinguished name.

cACertificate. This attribute contains CA certificates with a subject matching the entry distinguished name.

certificateRevocationList. This attribute contains CRLs.

authorityRevocationList. This attribute contains CRLs that only cover certificates issued to other CAs.

deltaRevocationList. This attribute contains delta CRLs.

crossCertificatePair. This attribute contains a pair of CA certificates. The elements of this pair are referred to as *forward* and *reverse*. The forward and the reverse elements are present in a single attribute value. The subject of one certificate matches the entry distinguished name, and the issuer of the other certificate matches the entry distinguished name. The subject public key in one certificate verifies the digital signature on the other certificate, and vice versa. A cross certificate pair is shown in Figure 9.1.

RFC 2587 specifies three object classes: pkiUser, pkiCA, and cRLDistributionPoint. The contents of attributes for these object classes are as follows:

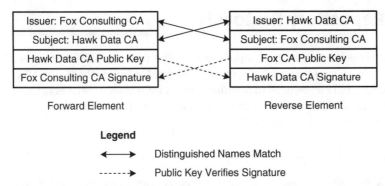

Forward Element   Reverse Element

Legend

⟷   Distinguished Names Match

------➤   Public Key Verifies Signature

Figure 9.1   Cross certificate pair.

pkiUser. This object class is used for certificate holder entries. PKI user entries must contain a user certificate attribute. All certificates whose subject name matches the name of the directory entry should be stored in this attribute.

pkiCA. This object class is used for CA entries. PKI CA entries may contain CA certificate, CRL, ARL, and cross certificate pair attributes. The CA certificate attribute contains CA certificates whose subject is the name associated with this entry. These certificates may be self-issued (for example, key rollover certificates) or issued by other CAs. The CRL attribute contains CRLs issued by the entry name. The ARL attribute contains CRLs that contain only CA certificates. The cross certificate pair attribute contains one or more CertificatePairs. The forward elements of the cross certificate pair attribute of a CA's directory entry store certificates issued to this CA by other CAs. The reverse elements of the cross certificate pair attribute may optionally contain a subset of certificates issued by this CA to other CAs.

cRLDistributionPoint. The cRLDistributionPoint object class may include CRL, ARL, and delta CRL attributes. The name of the directory entry will match the name in the CRL distribution points extension (see Chapter 7, "X.509 Public Key Certificates").

The X.500 Directory

In *Guidelines for Evaluation of X.500 Directory Products*, an X.500 Directory is described as "a distributed database, capable of storing information about people and objects in various nodes or servers distributed across a network" [TEBB95]. The various servers are called Directory Server Agents (DSAs), and clients are called Directory User Agents (DUAs). The DSA responds to DUA queries with the information or an error. Figure 9.2 depicts the conceptual view of an X.500 Directory.

The X.500 Directory uses two basic protocols: the Directory Access Protocol (DAP) and the Directory Service Protocol (DSP). DAP supports information requests from a DUA to a DSA. DSP supports information requests between DSAs. In general, DSAs are connected to support information sharing through *chaining*. DSAs may augment DSP with the Directory Information Shadowing Protocol (DISP). DISP may be used to replicate the contents (or a subset of the contents) of a DSA. This is generally referred to as *shadowing*.

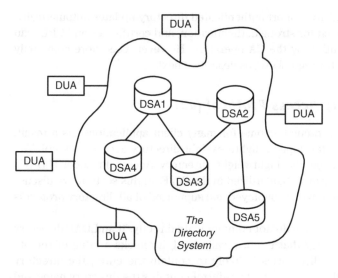

Figure 9.2   Conceptual view of an X.500 Directory.

From the DUA point of view, the entire database resides on a single system. That system is the DSA that handles its information requests. The number of DSAs and the manner in which they are connected is not visible to the DUA. Clearly, when chaining is used, the X.500 Directory provides transparency of location.

DSAs may also be connected indirectly through referrals. When DSAs are connected in this manner, the DSA does not attempt to satisfy queries for information in another DSA. Instead, the DSA returns the name of the DSA that contains the information to the requesting DUA. When referrals are used, the X.500 Directory does not provide transparency of location.

The distributed nature of the X.500 Directory provides for high availability. If one of the DSAs becomes unavailable, only the information that physically resides on that system becomes unavailable. (Of course, DUAs that request information from an out-of-service DSA must switch to another DSA or be denied access to the directory.) By shadowing information on more than one DSA, availability can be further enhanced.

Performance may vary based on the physical location of information and the manner in which the DSAs are connected. Reconsider Figure 9.2. If Alice directs her requests to DSA1 and Bob directs his requests to DSA5, they will experience very different performance when obtaining the same information. When the information is located on DSA1, Alice will get the information very quickly because it is local. Bob will have to wait while his request is forwarded to DSA2, then to DSA1, and the response works its way back. Average performance is optimized if the information they use frequently is on a nearby DSA.

DSAs may accept anonymous requests from DUAs, or they may authenticate requests with passwords or digital signatures. Authenticated requests support the cost recovery business model identified earlier. Authenticated requests are also important for controlling Directory updates.

CAs could include a DUA to support authenticated directory updates automatically. Digital signatures can be used for strong authentication, and certificates and CRLs can be posted without intervention by the CA operators. However, CAs more commonly support Directory updates through LDAP, as described next.

Lightweight Directory Access Protocol (v2)

The DAP protocol proved too cumbersome for many client applications. As a result, the University of Michigan developed a lighter-weight directory access protocol. The resulting protocol was named the Lightweight Directory Access Protocol (LDAP). LDAP was developed further and standardized in the IETF. In this section, we discuss LDAP version 2 (v2), the most widely deployed and supported of all directory protocols [YEON95].

In general, LDAP v2 directories do not communicate directly. If an LDAP directory receives a request for an entry that is not locally held, it checks a table of remote directories. If one of those directories is likely to contain the entry, the directory returns a referral to the other directory. The referral contains the directory name and the system that supports it. This simplifies directory implementation; there is no need for DSP.

However, this architecture does not provide transparency of location. A client must determine the physical location before it obtains any information. To make matters worse, few LDAP client implementations actually handle referrals. If certificates or CRLs are not available in the first LDAP directory checked, they will not be found. PKI repositories based on LDAP use a single repository or explicitly identify a particular repository through the CRL distribution points, authority information access, and subject information access certificate extensions.

This makes it difficult to scale the performance or availability of the system. Once their location is specified, the certificates and CRLs cannot be redistributed to balance the load. Scaling for LDAP directories is achieved with bigger, faster servers.

Some LDAP directory products use proprietary protocols to perform chaining and replication in an LDAP v2 environment. If an organization uses the same LDAP v2 product throughout its enterprise PKI, it may obtain the same benefits ascribed to X.500 Directories. However, the enterprise cannot count on other organizations using the identical products.

Most CA products include an LDAP client and can perform authenticated directory updates automatically. The authentication is based on a username and password. Certificates and CRLs can be posted without intervention by the CA operators.

X.500 Directory with LDAP

The glaring weakness of the X.500 Directory was the DAP protocol. The protocol worked, but was widely perceived as too cumbersome. As a result, client implementations generally support LDAP rather than DAP. Modern X.500 implementations replace or augment DAP with an LDAP front end. This solution has all the attributes of a powerful repository mechanism. As an X.500 Directory, it provides transparency of location, and may be scaled to meet organizational performance and availability requirements.

It supports both anonymous and authenticated access. It is interoperable with most CAs and PKI clients.

LDAP v3 with Extensions

The IETF has continued work on LDAP. LDAP v3 is the result, and a number of extensions are currently in development. When complete, these extensions will provide LDAP with protocols necessary to support chaining and replication. As stated earlier, this provides a powerful repository mechanism. When upgrading from an LDAP v2 repository to a more complete solution, LDAP v3 may require fewer adjustments.

FTP

The File Transfer Protocol (FTP) is defined in RFC 959 [POST85]. FTP servers have long been used to distribute information on the Internet. FTP servers may offer information anonymously, or they may require a username and password.

RFC 2585 defines data types and naming conventions for the transfer of certificates and CRLs using FTP [HOUS99c]. Files with a suffix of .cer contain exactly one certificate. Files with a suffix of .crl contain exactly one CRL. File names are specified as URIs within certificate extensions and CRL extensions. For example, ftp://ftp.fox .com/pki/id48.cer specifies a single certificate available for anonymous FTP from ftp .fox.com. RFC 2585 does not define data types that contain multiple values or a cross certificate pair.

FTP servers cannot provide transparency of location. They are simply not designed for implementation as a distributed system. This makes it difficult to respond to performance and availability issues. They can only be scaled with a bigger, faster FTP server.

FTP servers can track user activity by demanding a username and password for each user. In practice, this does not scale to large PKIs—there would be too many user accounts to administer. Anonymous FTP servers are better suited as a repository, but they are not well suited to support a cost-recovery model. They can log the IP addresses of the systems that request data, but it would be hard to generate a bill from system address alone.

Interoperability is also an issue. While FTP client code is widely available, it is not integrated into PKI clients for certificate and CRL retrieval. Few, if any, commercially available CAs can automatically populate the FTP server with certificates and CRLs. To populate the FTP repository requires a two-step process, as shown in Figure 9.3. The CA publishes the information into a directory, and then a utility program copies the certificates and CRLs from the directory to the file system of the FTP server.

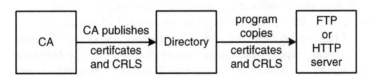

Figure 9.3 Two-step certificate publication.

HTTP

The Hypertext Transfer Protocol (HTTP) is defined in RFC 2068 [FIEL97]. RFC 2585 defines data types and naming conventions for the transfer of certificates and CRLs using HTTP [HOUS99c]. The naming conventions are the same as for FTP. File names are specified as URIs within certificate extensions and CRL extensions; for example, http://www.fox.com/pki/id48.cer.

HTTP can provide transparency of location. HTTP can be used to automatically redirect a request to a system on which the information currently resides.

This system is also scalable. It is common practice to build virtual Web servers that are actually composed of many different servers. While all clients use the same well-known URL (for example, http://www.cnn.com), different requests may be handled by different servers. This process is transparent to the client. This scheme permits the HTTP repository administrator to scale the system to meet current performance and availability requirements.

If the HTTP server implements SSL or TLS with client authentication, the server could identify and authenticate the origin of each request. This authentication permits the HTTP repository to support a pay-per-use model.

However, interoperability is an issue. Few, if any, commercially available CAs can automatically populate the HTTP server with certificates and CRLs. The approach shown in Figure 9.3 must be used to copy certificates and CRLs to a location where the HTTP server can use them. While HTTP client code is widely available, it is not integrated into many older PKI clients for certificate and CRL retrieval.

Electronic Mail

RFC 822 defines the format for another ubiquitous transfer protocol: electronic mail [CROC82]. Practically every client system supports electronic mail. Nearly every company has electronic mail servers. A client could request a certificate or CRL through the subject and body of an e-mail message. Certificates and CRLs can be returned as attachments in a reply using the MIME types specified in RFC 2585 [HOUS99c].

This seems to be a temptingly easy solution. However, the protocol does not have the attributes we seek in a repository protocol. Location is not really transparent (although mail forwarding can help). Once their location is specified in certificates, relying parties will always request information from the same mail servers. That does not bode well for availability or performance. Interoperability is a problem, as PKI clients do not integrate e-mail into the package as a supporting protocol. As shown in Figure 9.3, CAs can populate an e-mail repository using a two-step process.

It would be easy to authenticate the origin of each request, though. If signed e-mail (for example, S/MIME) is used for the requests, the repository can authenticate the requester as well [DUSS98a, RAMS99b]. This would permit support for a pay-per-use model.

There is no approved standard for electronic mail distribution of certificates and CRLs. In the absence of naming conventions and a well-established protocol, e-mail should not be used as a general-purpose mechanism for certificate and CRL distribution. However, e-mail offers significant advantages when employed to push freshly issued CRLs to selected users.

Domain Name System Support

One of the most successful distributed information retrieval systems is the Internet Domain Naming System (DNS). DNS is defined in RFCs 1034 and 1035 [MOCK87a, MOCK87b]. RFC 1035 states that "The goal of domain names is to provide a mechanism for naming resources in such a way that the names are usable in different hosts, networks, protocol families, internets, and administrative organizations." This system has achieved these goals, and researchers are constantly looking for new ways to leverage the success and capabilities of DNS.

There has been much discussion about using DNS to unify the many disjointed directories and specify the appropriate access protocols as an aid to clients. Rather than use DNS to transport certificates and CRLs, the concept requires new data types that identify a repository for some domain. When a client is processing e-mail from the fox.com domain, it would make a request to the DNS system. The response would identify the common PKI repository for Fox Consulting. This would simplify certificates, since these pointers could be omitted from the certificate. It would permit a PKI to change the repository access protocols it supports without reissuing certificates.

This idea has not yet been implemented, but the IETF has tentatively begun the process of standardizing this technique.

Border Repositories

Most repositories support other organizational information, not just certificates and CRLs. This is particularly true for directories. Often, these directories will contain a mix of public, proprietary, and confidential information. The certificates and CRLs are usually considered to be public information. They are intended for external distribution to support security services with external users. However, providing access to certificates and CRLs could place other proprietary and confidential information at risk.

The solution is to create two directories. One directory is internal, and it is protected from external access by network security controls. The second falls *outside the border*, and it is intended for external use. The external directory is called a *border directory*.

Figure 9.4 depicts a typical scenario. Fox Consulting has a firewall protecting its corporate network. Inside the firewall, there is an X.500 Directory containing private information, including employee telephone numbers, e-mail addresses, social security numbers, security clearances, and payment histories. Of course, it also contains certificates and the CRLs. Outside the firewall, there is a second X.500 Directory. This Directory shadows the certificate and CRL attributes from the internal directory. The Directory inside the Fox Consulting enclave pushes information to the border directory; the border directory does not modify the internal directory.

There are exceptions. Some organizations may consider certificates and CRLs confidential. This is often the case where information aggregation is considered a threat. For example, an intelligence agency would not want anyone to know how many analysts were assigned to each region. In this case, the repository may only expose the certificates associated with selected users in the border directory. Alternatively, the CA may issue two sets of certificates and publish the sanitized certificates in the border directory.

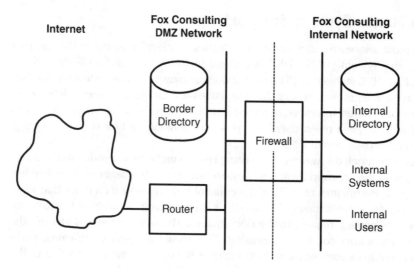

Figure 9.4   Border directory for Fox Consulting.

There is no reason why a border repository cannot be implemented with other protocols. However, the ability to chain a border repository to other organizations' directories is very attractive. The border repository is there to serve *external* users, who may have a hard time locating it. If the border directory is chained to their local directory, this problem is avoided.

Practical PKI Repositories

There is not a single correct PKI repository solution for every situation. There is no reason to pick a single protocol. Run as many protocols as needed to serve a wide diversity of clients and applications. Run the protocols simultaneously from the same system or from different ones. Operate multiple repositories to satisfy different communities.

The directory is still the pragmatic choice for PKI repositories. An X.500 Directory with an LDAP front end provides maximum scalability and interoperability. The transparency of location simplifies the client. As the PKI evolves and cross certifies with other PKIs that support X.500, the clients will instantly have access to all the required certificates. The X.500 Directory supports authenticated access, allowing a repository-based cost recovery model. On the other hand, authenticating access to publicly available data reduces system performance.

Small isolated PKIs can use an LDAP v2 directory. While this is not a long-term solution, a straightforward upgrade path exists. In the near future, LDAP v3 directories will offer replication and shadowing. LDAP v^3 clients will not have to reconfigure their repository address or access protocol.

If the organization is building a private PKI, an HTTP or FTP repository alone may be reasonable. Since most PKI components do not currently incorporate HTTP or FTP access, interoperability with external users will be limited. This problem may be overcome by operating a border directory as well. The best strategy is to implement a private directory as an initial step in a two-step publication process. The directory can also be used as a border directory, to achieve interoperability with external PKIs.

Border directories are a straightforward mechanism to share some of your information with the outside world while protecting your assets.

Here are two final thoughts, regardless of the protocol:

Don't implement a repository to support the PKI alone. Most organizations run information distribution systems for at least one of the repository protocols. If another part of your organization can support this function, let them. Once you implement the repository, other applications will find a use for it. The job will grow, distracting your attention from the operations of distinct PKI components.

Don't build a trusted repository if an untrusted repository meets your requirements. Running a trusted system is difficult. Remember, the data is tamper-evident. Use that to your advantage.

Building and Validating Certification Paths

The concept of the *certification path* was introduced in Chapter 3. Certification paths were revisited in Chapter 6 in relationship to PKI architectures. Certification paths are a fundamental public key infrastructure (PKI) construct, and this chapter examines them in more depth.

A certification path is a chain of certificates, where the issuer of the first certificate is a trust point, and the subject of the last certificate is the end entity. The last certificate in the chain, the end entity certificate, is the one being validated. This end entity certificate contains a public key that will be used to validate a signature or establish a symmetric key; it contains the identity and public key of interest. A PKI-enabled application must construct and validate a certification path before using a public key to verify a signature or establish a symmetric key.

Certification path construction and certification path validation are often performed as two independent steps. However, they can be combined into one more complicated process. In this chapter, we discuss certification path construction and then certification path validation. There are several certification path construction methods. We discuss the best methods for developing certification paths in each of the different PKI architectures presented in Chapter 6. Once a certification path is constructed, it is validated. Certification path validation is done the same way regardless of the PKI topology. We provide an overview of this algorithm.

Certification Path Construction

PKI-enabled applications must verify a certificate before using the public key inside the certificate for a cryptographic operation. The application cannot rely on the public key unless a valid certification path exists. The application is initialized to recognize paths that begin with one or more certification authorities (CAs). These CAs are known as *trust points*. The first step toward using the certificate is building a certification path between that certificate and one of the recognized trust points. The difficulty of this step reflects the complexity of the PKI architecture.

Simple PKI Architectures

In simple PKI architectures, certification paths consist of a single certificate. When there is a single CA, or all of the CAs are contained in the trust list, only one certificate is needed to connect a trust point to any valid subject. In this degenerate case, path construction is nonexistent. The single certificate is the entire path. This single certificate must still be validated, just like any other certification path.

Figure 10.1 shows certification paths for Alice and Bob in a simple PKI. As expected, each path is comprised of a single certificate. The notation [(Fox -> Alice)] indicates that the single certificate issued by the Fox CA to Alice comprises the whole path.

Hierarchical PKI Architectures

In hierarchies, certification paths originate at the root, and they terminate at the end entity. However, they are constructed in the opposite direction. Construction begins with the end entity certificate. This certificate has an issuer and an authority key identifier extension. Together, these values help locate the correct CA certificate. The issuer name is used to locate the CA certificates in the repository. The repository may contain several certificates that have been issued to the CA. The subject's authority key identifier in the end entity certificate matches the subject key identifier in exactly one certificate— the desired CA certificate. This simple process is repeated until a certificate issued by the root, the hierarchy trust point, is located.

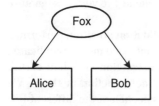

Certification Paths:
 Alice: [(Fox -> Alice)]
 Bob: [(Fox -> Bob)]

Figure 10.1   Certification paths in a simple PKI consist of a single certificate.

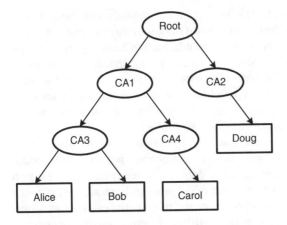

Certification Paths:
Alice: [(Root -> CA1); (CA1 -> CA3); (CA3 -> Alice)]
Bob: [(Root -> CA1); (CA1 -> CA3); (CA3 -> Bob)]
Carol: [(Root -> CA1); (CA1 -> CA4); (CA4 -> Carol)]
Doug: [(Root -> CA2); (CA2 -> Doug)]

Figure 10.2   Certification paths in a hierarchical PKI originate at the root.

Figure 10.2 shows certification paths for Alice, Bob, Carol, and Doug in a hierarchical PKI. Each end entity has one, and only one, certification path. Some certification paths are longer than others, but all of the paths start at the root. The notation `[(Root -> CA2); (CA2 -> Doug)]` indicates that two certificates comprise the path from the Root CA to Doug's certificate.

In hierarchies, the certification path that will be developed is completely predictable. In fact, the end entity could provide it as part of a security protocol so that it did not have to be reconstructed. In other PKI architectures, the trust point is not the same for each participant, so the certification path is not predictable.

Mesh PKI Architectures

In mesh architectures, different users will construct different certification paths. Recall that users generally consider the CA that issued their certificate to be the trust point. Therefore, when Alice constructs a certification path for Bob, it begins at the CA that issued her certificate, and ends with Bob's certificate. When Carol constructs a certification path for Bob, it begins at the CA that issued her certificate, and ends with Bob's certificate. These certification paths are different unless Alice and Carol obtained their certificates from the same CA.

In mesh architectures, end entity certificates are issued directly by their trust point. However, this CA may be different from the trust point for the entity constructing the path. Further, this CA will have many certificates; each issued by a different CA and each leading to a different portion of the mesh. For this reason, path construction begins at the trusted point and proceeds toward the issuer of the end entity certificate. The authority key identifier in a certificate will match the subject key identifier in a number of CA certificates, including the desired CA certificate. Since the authority key identifier extension is not a sufficient guide toward the goal, other attributes must be used as heuristics. Names provide the best guide, but information from any attribute can be used to help decide which of the possible certificates to try first. If that certificate does not lead to a complete certification path, then simply try the next one, and so on.

In some ways, developing a certification path in a mesh is like establishing an international telephone call or routing a packet through the Internet. Navigation may not be obvious, but there are algorithms available to solve the problem.

Since a mesh contains many bidirectional relationships between the CAs, there is usually more than one certification path between any end entity and a particular trust point. For this reason, certification path validation is often done at the same time as certification path construction, pruning invalid branches as part of the process. Even so, the existence of more than one valid certification path is common, and these paths can contain loops. A loop occurs when the same certificate is in the certification path more than once.

Caching certification path information can significantly enhance performance. Remembering that particular sequences of certificates provide a link between two portions of the mesh can avoid repeating significant trial-and-error path construction.

Figure 10.3 shows certification paths that Alice might construct for Bob, Carol, and Doug. More than one path is shown for Carol and Doug. Each path is valid, but some paths are longer than others. Finding the shortest possible path is not required, and finding it adds considerable complexity to the process. Generally, the first valid path located is used. For illustrative purposes, the third certification path listed for Doug contains a loop.

Extended Trust List Architectures

When extended trust lists are employed, implementations must be prepared to encounter hierarchical PKIs as well as mesh PKIs. One extended trust list entry could correspond to the root CA of a hierarchy, and another extended trust list entry could correspond to a CA within a mesh. The straightforward certification path construction approach can be used

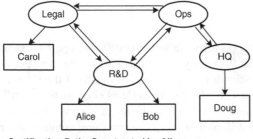

Certification Paths Constructed by Alice:
Bob: [(R&D -> Bob)]
Carol: [(R&D -> Ops); (Ops -> Legal); (Legal -> Carol)]
          [(R&D -> Legal); (Legal -> Carol)]
Doug: [(R&D -> Ops); (Ops -> HQ); (HQ -> Doug)]
          [(R&D -> Legal); (Legal -> Ops); (Ops -> HQ);
                   (HQ -> Doug)]
          [(R&D -> Ops); (Ops -> Legal); (Legal -> R&D);
                   (R&D -> Ops); (Ops -> HQ); (HQ -> Doug)]

Figure 10.3   Certification paths in a mesh PKI.

with a hierarchy, but the more complicated certification path construction approach must be used with a mesh. Unfortunately, given an end entity certificate, it is not readily apparent whether it belongs in a hierarchy or a mesh. Further, unless the certificate was issued directly by one of the trust points, it is not readily apparent from which trust point the certification path should begin.

One widely deployed implementation assumes that certificates belong to a hierarchy, employing the straightforward certification path development. If this path leads to one of the trusted points, then a valid path has been constructed. If not, then the implementation checks to see if the top of the partial certification path has been issued a certificate by any of the trust points. If so, then one certificate completes the path. If not, the implementation tries to build a path from each of the trust points to the top of the partial certification path.

For efficiency, this implementation builds a certificate cache. Within the cache, all possible certification paths are constructed and tagged with a quality value. Simple hierarchical paths are marked with a higher value than complex paths. Certification paths with the highest quality tags are selected. This approach leads to the selection of short certification paths at the expense of storage for the certificate cache and computation of all possible certification paths. Most importantly, it works in very complex topologies.

Implementations that support extended trust lists are flexible, and this flexibility allows them to work in just about any PKI environment. Implementations that are embedded in PKI-enabled applications should support extended trust lists to ensure that any certificate encountered can be used in certification path construction.

Cross-Certified PKI Architectures

PKI architectures that include cross-certificates have many similarities with mesh PKI architectures and extended trust list architectures. Again, different users construct different certification paths for the same end entity certificate. The path begins at the trust point associated with the native PKI. If Alice is part of a simple PKI or a mesh PKI, then the path will begin at the CA that issued her certificate. If Alice is part of a hierarchical PKI, then the path will begin at the root CA. One cross-certificate could connect to the root CA of a hierarchy, and another cross-certificate could connect to a CA within a mesh. As before, the straightforward certification path construction approach can be used within a hierarchy, but this breaks down once the foreign root is reached. At this point, the more complicated certification path construction approach associated with a mesh must be used to identify one or more cross-certificates to reach the trust point. Many implementations apply the straightforward certification path construction approach until multiple issuers are encountered, and then the more complicated certification path construction approach is applied beginning at the trust point. Since there is a single trust point, certification path construction is simpler than extended trust lists. This technique is most often used when the repository distinguishes between cross-certificates and other certificates. Directories provide this distinction.

Since a PKI may cross-certify with many different PKIs, and those PKIs may cross-certify among themselves, more than one certification path between for each end entity is likely. Further, these paths can contain loops.

Figure 10.4 shows certification paths that Alice might construct for Bob, Carol, and Doug. More than one path is shown for Carol and Doug. Each path is valid, but some

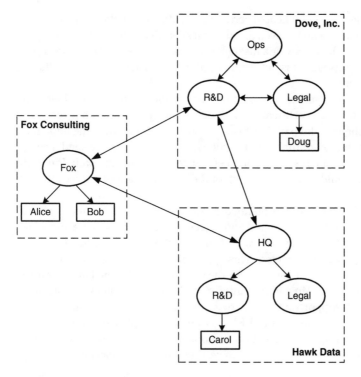

Certification Paths Constructed by Alice:
Bob: [(Fox -> Bob)]
Carol: [(Fox -> Hawk HQ); (Hawk HQ -> Hawk R&D); (Hawk R&D -> Carol)]
        [(Fox -> Dove R&D); (Dove R&D -> Hawk HQ);
                (Hawk HQ -> Hawk R&D); (Hawk R&D -> Carol)]
Doug: [(Fox -> Dove R&D); (Dove R&D -> Dove Legal);
                (Dove Legal-> Doug)]
        [(Fox -> Hawk HQ); (Hawk HQ -> Dove R&D);
                (Dove R&D -> Dove Legal); (Dove Legal -> Doug)]
        [(Fox -> Hawk HQ); (Hawk HQ -> Dove R&D);
                (Dove R&D -> Dove Ops); (Dove Ops -> Dove Legal);
                (Dove Legal -> Doug)]

Figure 10.4   Certification paths with cross certified PKIs.

paths are longer than others. As with mesh PKI architectures, finding the shortest path
adds considerable complexity to the process.

Bridge CA Architectures

Bridge CA architectures offer several improvements over the general cross-certified
PKI architecture. Different users still construct different certification paths for the same
end entity certificate, and the path still begins at the trust point associated with the
native PKI. However, there is only one cross-certificate linking the native PKI to all of
the foreign PKIs. This simplification aids certification path construction.

When simple PKIs and hierarchical PKIs are bridged, certification path construction
is only slightly more complex than a regular hierarchical PKI. As before, the straight-

forward certification path construction approach can be used within the hierarchy, but this time, when it breaks down, only one cross-certificate choice is available. This cross-certificate is issued by the bridge CA. One of the many certificates issued to the bridge CA will be issued by the single CA in a simple PKI or the hierarchy root CA. Locating the native trust point among the cross-certificates issued to the bridge CA is simple.

As with mesh architectures, caching certification path information can help. Remembering that particular sequences of certificates provide a link to a particular name space via the bridge CA can avoid repeating trial-and-error path construction.

When mesh PKIs are bridged, certification path construction within the mesh remains complex. However, since each of the foreign PKIs is likely to manage a separate name space, guesses about the most appropriate cross-certificate to use are usually correct. In addition, loops can only occur within the mesh itself. The bridge CA does not introduce the possibility of additional loops.

Figure 10.5 shows certification paths that Alice might construct for Bob, Carol, and Doug. More than one path is shown for Doug. There are multiple paths for Doug because he is a member of a mesh PKI.

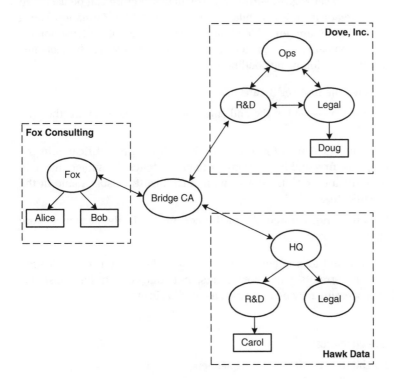

Certification Paths Constructed by Alice:
Bob: [(Fox -> Bob)]
Carol: [(Fox -> Bridge); (Bridge -> Hawk HQ); (Hawk HQ -> Hawk R&D);
           (Hawk R&D -> Carol)]
Doug: [(Fox -> Bridge); (Bridge -> Dove R&D); (Dove R&D -> Dove Legal);
           (Dove Legal-> Doug)]
      [(Fox -> Bridge); (Bridge -> Dove R&D); (Dove R&D -> Dove Ops);
           (Dove Ops -> Dove Legal); (Dove Legal-> Doug)]

Figure 10.5 Certification paths in enterprise PKIs with a bridge CA.

Certification Path Validation

Certification path validation verifies the binding between the subject identity, the subject public key, and any attributes of the subject that may be present in the certificate. Constraints contained within the certification path limit the possible identity values as well as the possible values for some attributes contained within the certificates.

This section provides an overview of certification path validation. Implementations employ many different algorithms to implement certification path validation. Some algorithms couple certification path construction and certification path validation, but most implement these as separate phases. In this section, we assume that the certification path construction is complete and that the resulting path needs to be validated.

The certification path must begin at a trust point. If this is not so, then certification path construction has failed. The trust point public key, the public key validity period, the trust point name, and any constraints imposed on certification paths associated with the trust point are inputs to certification path validation. In many implementations, this information is provided as a self-signed certificate. Any data structure can be used, but these implementations already include capabilities for extracting this information from a certificate, so these capabilities are reused to obtain information about the trust point.

Consider the certification path as a sequence of certificates. To be valid, the sequence of certificates must satisfy the following conditions:

- A trust point issued the first certificate.

- The last certificate was issued to the end entity of interest and contains the public key of interest.

- The issuer and subject names form a chain. For all of the certificates in the sequence except the first and last, the issuer name matches the subject name in the previous certificate and the subject name matches the issuer name in the subsequent certificate.

- The certificates have not expired. All of the certificates in the sequence were valid at the time of interest.

However, this set of conditions is necessary, but not sufficient, for a certification path to be valid. Basic constraints, name constraints, and policy constraints must also be considered. This processing may be described as four basic steps:

1. Initialization.

2. Basic certificate checking.

3. Preparation for the next certificate in the sequence.

4. Wrap-up.

Steps 1 and 4 are each performed once. Step 2 is performed for every certificate in the sequence, and step 3 is performed for all certificates in the path except the last one, the end entity certificate. Figure 10.6 provides a flowchart of these steps.

Certification path validation is most commonly performed to determine if a path is currently valid. This section describes processing when validating paths with respect to

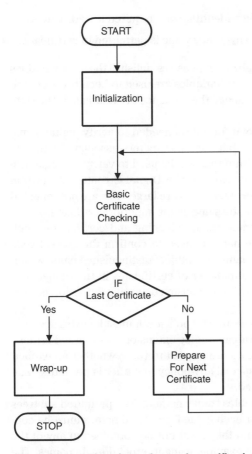

Figure 10.6 Flowchart of steps in certification path validation.

the current time. The algorithm can be adjusted to handle validation with respect to some earlier time.

Now, we describe each of the four processing steps in turn.

Initialization

Certification path validation requires several inputs. In some implementations, default values are provided from many of them. The default values are appropriate for specific applications. These values may not be appropriate for another application.

Inputs to certification path validation include:

- The prospective certification path.
- The set of acceptable certificate policy identifiers (often set to any-policy).
- The trust point information (often a self-signed certificate).
- An indicator of whether policy mapping is permitted in the certification path.

- An indicator of whether explicit policy identifiers are required in certificates.
- An indicator of whether the special any-policy value is permitted in certificates.

Based on the preceding inputs, the initialization phase establishes the state variables needed to validate the certification path. State variables are used to keep track of various constraints as the validation proceeds though the sequence of certificates. The state variables logically fall into four groups.

The first group of state variables tracks information needed to verify digital signatures. These state variables include the public key, parameters associated with the public key, and the digital signature algorithm that will be used to verify the signature on the next certificate in the sequence. Recall that the Digital Signature Algorithm (DSA) requires parameters, but since these parameters are large, they are not repeated in subordinate certificates if the values are the same as the superior certificate.

The second group of state variables tracks name chaining and certification path length. The expected issuer distinguished name is used to confirm the correct relationship between the issuer distinguished name and subject distinguished name within the sequence of certificates. The maximum number of certificates in the sequence is also tracked. The path length constraint within the basic constrains extension is used to adjust this state variable.

The third group of state variables tracks certificate policies. It must keep track of certificate policy identifiers, whether the certificate policy extension was marked critical, and the results of policy mapping. Indicators are needed to track whether an explicit policy identifier is required, whether the special any-policy identifier is permitted, and whether further policy mapping is permitted.

The fourth and final group of state variables tracks naming. The permitted subtrees and excluded subtrees must be tracked for each name form. Valid names must be contained in one of the permitted subtrees, and they must not be contained in any of the excluded name trees. Figure 10.7 shows an example using Internet domain names. The first invalid name shown is invalid because it is not within any of the permitted subtrees.

```
Permitted DNS Name Subtrees:    *.fox-consulting.com
                                *.hawk-data.com
                                *.dove-inc.com


Excluded DNS Name Subtrees:     *.legal.hawk-data.com
                                *.legal.dove-inc.com


Potential Subject DNS Names:    www.fox-consulting.com        [valid]
                                host.spyrus.com               [invalid]
                                post-office.hq.hawk-data.com  [valid]
                                mail.legal.hawk-data.com      [invalid]
                                legal-files.ops.dove-inc.com  [valid]
                                file-server.legal.dove-inc.com [invalid]
```

Figure 10.7   Sample name constraint validation using DNS names.

The second and third invalid names shown are invalid because they are within one of the excluded subtrees.

Once all of the state variables have been initialized, checking of the first certificate in the sequence is performed.

Basic Certificate Checking

Basic certificate checking is performed on all certificates in the sequence. Checks are made to determine whether the certificate is expired or revoked. Checks using each of the four groups of state variables are made to determine whether the certificate meets the constraints imposed by the inputs and the preceding certificates in the sequence. If any of these checks fail, then the certification path is invalid.

Check certificate validity. This check passes if the current date and time is between the not-before and the not-after dates specified in the certificate.

Check certificate revocation. This check passes if the issuer has not revoked the certificate. Certificate revocation lists (CRLs) provide the most common means of performing this check. Alternatively, some form of out-of-band certificate status check may be performed. CRLs are discussed further at the end of this chapter.

Check the certificate signature. Using the first group of state variables, confirm that the certificate signature can be validated with the issuer's public key using the correct parameters and digital signature algorithm.

Check name chaining. Using the second group of state variables, confirm that the certificate issuer's distinguished name matches the subject's distinguished name from the preceding certificate in the sequence.

Check certificate policies. The third group of state variables is used to make these checks. If the certificate policies extension is present, verify that the provided value is one of the expected values. If the certificate policies extension contains the special any-policy identifier, check the indicator to determine whether any-policy is permitted. If the certificate policies extension is absent, check the indicator to determine whether an explicit policy is required. Figure 10.8 illustrates certificate policy processing for several different certification paths. Alice constructed these certification paths from the topology shown in Figure 10.4. Path (a) is invalid because the first certificate in the sequence requires that subsequent certificates contain an explicit policy, but the second certificate does not include a certificate policy extension. Path (b) is invalid because the second certificate inhibits the use of any-policy, but the third certificate includes the any-policy identifier. Path (c) is valid. The first certificate requires explicit policy identifiers, and all of the certificates include them. The second certificate inhibits use of any policy, and subsequent certificates do not include the any-policy identifier.

Check name constraints. The fourth group of state variables is used to make these checks. Verify that the subject name is within one of the permitted subtrees for X.500 distinguished names, and verify that the subject name is not within any of

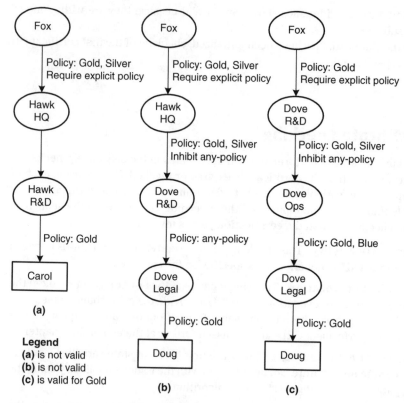

Figure 10.8 Certification path validation of policies.

the excluded subtrees for X.500 distinguished names. Also, verify that each of the subject alternative names is within one of the permitted subtrees for that name form, and verify that each of the subject alternative names is not within any of the excluded subtrees for that name form.

If any of the checks fail, then the certification path is invalid. If they all succeed, then the next step is determined by the placement of the certificate that just passed these checks within the sequence. If the certificate is the last one in the sequence, the wrap-up processing is the next step. If the certificate is not the last one, then preparation for the next certificate in the sequence is the next step.

Preparation for the Next Certificate

First, some straightforward CA certificate checking is performed. Then, state variables are updated to reflect the values in the certificate. There are several extensions that only appear in CA certificates; they are used to constrain subordinate certificates. Updating the state variables imposes the constraints on the subordinate certificates when subsequent basic certificate checking is performed.

Verify that the certificate is a CA certificate. Normally, the basic constraints extension contains this information; however, out-of-band means may also be employed. The certificate must contain a signature public key. Verify that it does, and that the key usage extension permits it to be used to sign certificates.

Check certification path length. Verify that the maximum certification path length has not been exceeded.

Update digital signature verification state variables. Set the public key, parameters associated with the public key, and the digital signature algorithm to the values contained in the certificate subject public key information field. If the subject public key information field does not include any public key parameters, and the previous certificate contained a public key associated with the same signature algorithm, then preserve the public key parameters used with the previous certificate. These parameters may have been inherited from a certificate earlier in the sequence.

Update name chaining and certification path length state variables. Set the expected issuer distinguished name to the certificate subject distinguished name. If the certificate issuer distinguished name and subject distinguished name are the same, then the certificate is *self-issued*. If the certificate is not self-issued, increment the certificate count state variable. Not counting self-issued certificates allows a CA to transition from an old signature key to a new signature key without invalidating any certificates as a result of an increased certification path length.

Perform policy mapping. The special any-policy identifier shall not be included in a policy mapping extension. If a CA tries to map from any-policy or to any-policy, the certification path is invalid. For other policy identifiers, update the certificate policies state variables, converting the specified issuer domain policy to the specified subject domain policy. Figure 10.9 shows several certification paths that include policy mapping. These certification paths were constructed from the topology shown in Figure 10.4. Alice constructed these paths, and Gold is the only certificate policy identifier that she considers acceptable. Path (a) is valid. Even though Carol's certificate was issued under the Cyan policy, the certification path provides a mapping from Gold to Cyan. Path (b) is not valid; no mapping is provided from Gold to Red. Path (c) is not valid. Doug's certificate is issued under the Gold policy, but Gold has been mapped to Silver. Had Doug's certificate been issued under the Silver policy, then Alice would consider it valid.

Update policy constraints. Based on the policy-related extensions, set the state variables to indicate whether subsequent certificates must contain explicit policy identifiers, may contain the any-policy identifier, or may contain policy mapping.

Update name constraints. If permitted subtrees are present in the certificate, set the state variables to the intersection of the previous permitted subtrees and the permitted subtrees indicated in the extension. If excluded subtrees are present in the certificate, set the state variables to the union of its previous excluded subtrees and the excluded subtrees indicated in the extension.

Process additional critical extensions. Recognize and process any additional critical extensions that are present in the certificate. If any critical extensions are unrecognized, then the certification path is invalid.

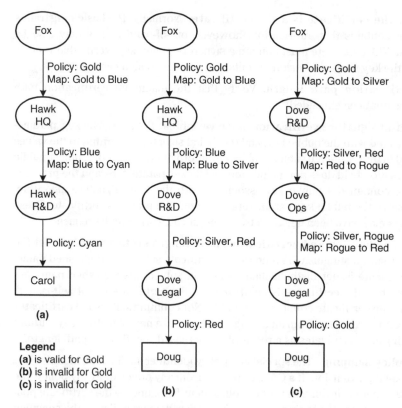

Figure 10.9   Certification paths that include policy mapping.

If any of the checks fail, then the certification path is invalid. If all of the checks succeed, advance to the next certificate in the sequence and perform the basic certificate checks.

Wrap-up

Complete processing of the end entity certificate. Then, set the output values based on the state variables.

Update digital signature verification state variables. Set the public key, parameters associated with the end entity public key, and the digital signature algorithm to the values contained in the certificate subject public key information field. If the end entity subject public key information field does not include any public key parameters, and the previous certificate contained a public key associated with the same signature algorithm, then preserve the public key parameters used with the previous certificate. These parameters may have been inherited from a certificate earlier in the sequence.

Determine satisfied certificate policies. Compute the intersection of the input set of acceptable certificate policy identifiers and the certificate policy state variables.

If the intersection is empty, then certificate path validation fails. If the intersection is not empty, set the state variables to the intersection.

Process additional critical extensions. Recognize and process any additional critical extensions that are present in the certificate. If any critical extensions are unrecognized, then the certification path is invalid.

Outputs from a successful certification path validation are derived from the state variables. The outputs include:

- The certificate policies, and any associated policy qualifiers, for the valid certification path.

- The end entity public key, parameters associated with the public key, and the public key algorithm.

CRL Validation

In the certification path validation processing described previously, it was necessary to determine whether each certificate in the sequence was revoked by its issuer. Often a CRL is checked to make this determination. In this section, we describe the processing necessary to determine whether a particular certificate is revoked using CRLs.

Revocation checking may be described as three sequential steps:

1. Initialization.
2. CRL checking.
3. Wrap-up.

Each step is performed once. Within step 2, several CRLs may be checked if necessary.

In some environments, it is not necessary to check all reason codes. For example, some environments are only concerned with CA compromise and key compromise of CA certificates. In this discussion, we check all reason codes. Also, the processing assumes that validation is with respect to the current time. The processing may be adjusted to check a subset of the reason codes or handle validation with respect to some earlier time.

Revocation processing requires two inputs:

- The certificate. The combination of certificate serial number and the issuer name are used to determine if the certificate is listed on a particular CRL. The basic constraints extension in the certificate is used to determine whether the certificate is associated with a CA or an end entity. The CRL distribution point and freshest CRL extensions in the certificate may specify the CRL to be used to determine revocation status.

- A delta-CRL indicator. This indicator determines whether delta CRLs should be considered.

Based on the inputs, the initialization phase establishes the needed state variables.

The reasons mask state variable contains the set of revocation reason codes supported by the CRLs and delta CRLs processed so far. The legal members of the set are the reason flags: unspecified, key compromise, CA compromise, affiliation changed, superseded, cessation of operation, and certificate hold. Initially, the reasons mask state variable is the empty set.

The certificate status state variable contains one of three alternative values. One value indicates that the certificate is revoked, as well as the reason for revocation. A second value indicates that the certificate is not revoked. The third possible value indicates that the certificate status could not be determined. Initially, the certificate status state variable is set to unrevoked. We assume that the certificate has not been revoked until we find evidence to the contrary.

Once initialization is complete, proceed to CRL checking.

CRL Processing

One or more CRL are checked. Checking proceeds until either the certificate status is determined to be revoked or sufficient CRLs have been checked to cover all reason codes.

Check each CRL pointed to by an entry in the CRL distribution points extension, while the reasons mask state variable does not indicate that all of the reasons have been checked and the certificate status indicates unrevoked. Process each CRL using the following six steps:

1. Fetch the CRL or locate it in the local CRL cache. The CRL may cover all of the reason codes or a subset of them. Confirm that processing the CRL will add members to the reasons mask state variable. If not, skip this CRL altogether. There are four cases to consider when determining which reason codes are covered by a particular CRL. Table 10.1 enumerates each case.

2. Verify the issuer of the CRL. If the certificate CRL distribution point extension entry includes a CRL issuer, then verify that the CRL issuer matches it. Otherwise, verify that the CRL issuer matches the certificate issuer. When Indirect CRLs are used, the certificate CRL distribution point extension entry includes a CRL issuer that is different from the certificate issuer.

Table 10.1 Determining Reason Code Coverage

CRL Reason Codes	Certificate CRL Distribution Points Extension Entry Reason Codes	Reason Codes Covered
Present	Present	Intersection of two reason code sets
Present	Omitted	CRL reason codes
Omitted	Present	Certificate CRL distribution point extension entry reason codes
Omitted	Omitted	All reason codes

3. Validate the CRL issuer signature. Obtain and validate the certification path for the CRL issuer, and use the CRL issuer's public key to validate the signature on the CRL. This might seem like a recursive nightmare. It could be, but generally, it is not. In most cases, the CRL issuer also issues one of the certificates in the path. If the same public key is used to sign both the CRL and the certificate, then the CRL issuer certification path is already constructed and validated. If the issuer used different keys, a single additional certificate may be required to build that path. When indirect CRLs are employed, a completely independent CRL issuer certification path may be needed.

4. Ensure the CRL is current. If the value of CRL next update field is before the current time, then either obtain an appropriate delta CRL to make the CRL current or discard the CRL. Also, if the delta CRL indicator input value is set and the freshest CRL extension is present, obtain the delta CRL corresponding to this base CRL. If a delta CRL was obtained for either of the previous reasons, then verify that the delta CRL addresses the same set of certificates and the same set of reason codes as the base CRL, verify that it was issued by the same authority as the base CRL, and verify that it was signed with the same public key as the base CRL. If all of these checks succeed, verify the signature on the delta CRL. If the signature is valid, combine the base CRL and delta CRL.

5. Update the reason mask state variable. Set the reasons mask state variable to the union of the current value and the reason code coverage for the CRL determined previously.

6. Search for the certificate serial number on the CRL. If the matching entry contains a certificate issuer CRL entry extension, the certificate issuer and the entry extension value must match. If the matching entry does not contain a certificate issuer CRL entry extension, the certificate issuer and the CRL issuer must match. If the certificate serial number and issuer names match, then the certificate is revoked. In this case, the certificate status state variable is set to reflect the reason for revocation.

If the reasons mask state variable does not indicate that all of the reasons have been checked and the certificate status state variable indicates unrevoked, then repeat the six steps with the next CRL from the CRL distribution points extension. If all of the entries in the CRL distribution points extension have been processed, and there are reason codes that remain unchecked, additional CRLs must be obtained. Usually, the certificate issuer's entry in the repository will contain CRLs. Repeat the six steps with any additional CRLs that are obtained. Finally, perform wrap-up processing.

Wrap-up

If all CRLs are exhausted and the reasons mask state variable does not indicate that all of the reasons have been checked, then set the certificate status state variable to undetermined. Most applications will treat this status the same as revoked, but others will prompt the user.

Processing is complete. Output the value of the certificate status state variable.

Merging Path Construction and Validation

At the beginning of this chapter, we mentioned that some implementations combine path construction and path validation into one operation. Why would an implementer choose to graft them together? Efficiency. First, path construction and path validation include some redundant operations, such as name chaining. These operations can be performed a single time in a combined operation. Second, by processing constraints during path construction, invalid paths can be rejected early, avoiding a significant number of useless fetches from the repository.

On the other hand, the combined operation is significantly more complex than path construction and path validation separately. This increased complexity often leads to implementation errors, and errors lead to maintenance issues. This increased complexity is unwarranted in a hierarchy since path construction is straightforward.

Summary

Certificate path construction and validation can be complicated, but it is vitally important. Applications should not use certificates, or the public keys contained in them, without first constructing and validating the certification path. Certification path construction can be difficult in some architectures, but it is not overwhelming. Routing an international telephone call is difficult for many of the same reasons. Such calls are handled routinely, and the vast bulk of the complexity is hidden from the caller. Certificate path validation is deterministic, so it is much easier. Simply use the algorithm and get the answer.

PKI Management Protocols

The certification authority (CA) is responsible for ensuring the correctness of certificates and CRLs that it generates. In Chapter 5, "PKI Components and Users," we discussed the consequences of this responsibility. The CA must verify certificate information before issuing the certificate, and the CA must maintain the list of certificates that are no longer valid. However, as we discussed in Chapter 5, the CA must also protect its private key from disclosure. That responsibility forces the CA to insulate itself from the other components of a public key infrastructure (PKI). So, how does the CA obtain certificate and revocation information? How can the CA be confident that the information is correct?

A CA needs to obtain the subscriber's public key, authenticate the subscriber's identity, verify that the subscriber possesses the corresponding private key, and verify any additional subscriber and key information before it signs a certificate. If the certificate contains incorrect information, a certificate user may establish security services with the wrong user, or employ the public key for an inappropriate application. A CA must also determine that the status of a certificate has changed before it adds the certificate to the CRL. If the CA adds a valid certificate to the CRL, subscribers are denied service. If the CA fails to add a certificate whose status has changed to the CRL, certificate users will accept the invalid certificate.

To meet these requirements, the CA must obtain trustworthy information from PKI participants. *PKI management protocols* are used by CAs to collect the information needed to issue certificates and CRLs. There are several different PKI management protocols. In this chapter, we begin by identifying the types of PKI transactions supported by PKI management protocols. Next, we identify the participants in these protocols. Then, we define a set of criteria for comparing management protocols. The criteria permit us to review and compare common management protocols. The chapter ends with some advice on selecting the best protocol or protocols for your PKI.

PKI Management Transactions

Management protocols support two basic types of transactions: *certificate requests* and *revocation requests*. The certificate request transactions may be subdivided into three classes of certificate requests:

- A *basic certificate request* from an end entity that is the subject of a currently valid signature certificate from the same CA.

- An *initial certificate request* from an end entity that is not the subject of a currently valid certificate from the CA.

- A *CA certificate request* from another CA. This transaction may be used to establish a subordinate CA in a hierarchy PKI, establish a peer CA in a mesh PKI, and perform one part of cross-certification.

Revocation requests may be subdivided based on the identity of the party requesting the revocation:

- The *basic revocation request* comes from the subject of the certificate to be revoked.

- An *external revocation request* comes from an entity other than the subject of the certificate to be revoked.

This chapter concentrates on these five transactions, which form the core of PKI management. Some PKI products support additional transactions. For example, some products allow a user to recover key management private keys in the event of loss or cryptographic module failure. Other transactions may be used to push data, such as a certificate or certificate revocation list (CRL), to other PKI components. A certificate might be pushed when the CA changes its private key. A CRL might be pushed when a cross-certified CA is compromised. Some business models require these additional transactions, but we will focus on the core transactions needed in every PKI.

Participants

As noted earlier, a CA needs to obtain trustworthy information before issuing or revoking a certificate. It may obtain this information from three PKI participants: a registration authority (RA), a current certificate holder, or the prospective certificate holder. The CA has a different relationship with each of these participants. These relationships shape the information flow.

A prospective certificate holder is essentially unknown to the CA, but has requested acceptance into the PKI. The potential subscriber would like the CA to issue a certificate containing a specific name (or names), public key, and policy attributes. The prospective certificate holder can provide this information in an initial certificate request, but the CA cannot ascertain from the data whether it should approve the request. The CA cannot determine from the data itself whether the name is appropriate. Without authenticating the subscriber's identity, the CA cannot verify the policy attributes. However, a CA can cryptographically verify that the requester has possession of the private key. For signature keys, the requester can simply digitally sign the request. For key management keys, a challenge-response mechanism may be required.

A certificate holder that possesses a currently valid certificate may request a new certificate. The requested certificate may have a different public key, include new names, or assert different policy information. The CA knows the subscriber's identity; otherwise, it would not have issued the current certificate. The current key pair may be used to authenticate the identity. As described previously, the CA can also cryptographically verify that the requester possesses the private key. However, the CA might not trust its subscribers to claim new names or policy attributes.

A certificate holder that possesses a currently valid certificate may also request revocation of one of his or her current certificates. As described previously, the CA knows the identity of the party that holds the private key, so it can readily authenticate the requester's identity. The CA should always revoke a certificate upon the request of the certificate holder, so the signed request contains all the information required by the CA. This does not necessarily mean that the CA trusts the subscriber for this information or that the subscriber is telling the truth. If the holder of a private key asserts that it is no longer valid, this request must be honored. If the signed request came from another source, then the private key has been compromised, and the certificate must be revoked any way.

The RA is empowered by the CA to collect information and verify its correctness. For certificate request operations, the RA may verify the prospective subscriber's identity, their e-mail address or other contact information, policy attributes (for example, small contract signature authority), or the type of cryptographic module that they possess (for example, hardware versus software). For revocation requests, the RA may identify the certificate subject and verify the reason for revocation. The RA is generally a certificate holder as well. RA digital signatures allow the CA to readily authenticate messages from the RA. An RA can review the documentation and determine whether a CA should honor a request.

Transaction Models

PKI management transactions must be designed so that the CA obtains reliable transaction information. For some transactions, the CA and the certificate holder can implement the transaction without assistance. These are *two-party transaction models*. In other cases, the transactions leverage an RA to fill in the gaps in the trust relationships between the CA and prospective subscriber. These are *three-party transaction models*. Different models will achieve different security objectives.

The simplest PKI transactions include two parties: the CA and the requester. Figure 11.1 depicts a generic two-party transaction model. To use this model, the requester must be the subject of a valid signature certificate, and the requester must know the CA's public key. Each message is digitally signed to authenticate the sender.

In this model, all information flows in the form of electronic messages. This type of transaction can be completed in a single round-trip or may include additional confirmation messages.

The simple two-party transaction model is widely used to implement both the basic certificate request and the revocation requests. The CA authenticates the requester identity based on the signed request. For revocation requests, the signature of the certificate holder or RA is all the confirmation that the CA needs to revoke the certificate. If the certificate holder is not requesting a change in his or her name or other security-relevant attributes, then the basic certificate request provides the CA with all of the information needed to issue the certificate.

However, the simple two-party model is insufficient for the initial certificate request. The CA requires further confirmation in order to trust the information received from the requester. This model is also insufficient when the certificate holder is requesting changes in particular attributes. For example, the user might be requesting a new name or might request a different certificate policy for the new certificate. To provide the CA with additional reliable information, we can either extend the two-party transaction model or turn to the three-party transaction model.

The extended two-party model is depicted as Figure 11.2. In this model, the requester generates a message, and then transmits it to the CA. The CA processes the message, and then generates a response. The CA generates a random encryption key, called the *authenticator*, and encrypts the response. The encrypted response is returned to the requester. The requester must obtain the authenticator to correctly process the message. The CA sends the authenticator to the requester through an out-of-band channel.

The out-of-band channel is designed to confirm the information provided by the requester. For example, the CA might confirm the electronic mail address of the requester by returning the authenticator in an e-mail message sent to that address. Similarly, the CA

Process:
1. Alice generates the signed request.
2. CA validates Alice's certification path and digital signature.
3. CA processes the request and generates a signed response.
4. Alice validates CA's certification path and digital signature, then processes the response.

Figure 11.1   Two-party transaction model.

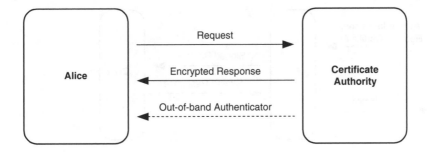

Process:
1. Alice generates the request.
2. CA verifies integrity, processes contents, and generates authenticator.
3. CA encrypts response using the authenticator and returns it.
4. Alice stores the encrypted response.
5. CA sends authenticator via out-of-band means.
6. Alice decrypts response.

Figure 11.2 Extending the two-party transaction model.

might confirm the postal address of the requester by returning the message by surface mail. The CA might confirm the requester's name by sending the authenticator via certified mail, where the recipient presents identification to the postal clerk to retrieve the message.

There is a variation to this model. Instead of encrypting the response, the CA stores the response in an online database and protects access to the data with a password. In this case, the password is the authenticator. As discussed earlier, the CA transmits the authenticator to the requester through an out-of-band channel. The selected out-of-band channel is designed to confirm the identity information in the request.

Extended two-party models are widely used because of their simplicity. However, they have several undesirable properties. The CA is generating a certificate without knowing whether the information it contains is valid. This action is in direct conflict with the CA's responsibilities (as described in Chapter 5). The CA cannot publish the certificate in a repository without confirmation that the subscriber was able to access the response. More satisfactory results can be achieved by delegating the burden for verifying subscriber information to an RA.

In this case, the CA, RA, and subscriber all participate in a three-party transaction model. The CA counts on the RA to verify the information it cannot accept directly from the subscriber. The CA uses the RA-validated information to issue and revoke certificates. There are many different transactions that employ the three-party model to issue certificates. Five examples are listed next. These examples are illustrative, not exhaustive.

- Alice generates a public/private key pair, and then Alice presents physical and electronic credentials to the RA. The RA reviews the credentials, and then the RA forwards the relevant information to the CA. The CA generates the certificate and returns it to the RA. This model is depicted in Figure 11.3.

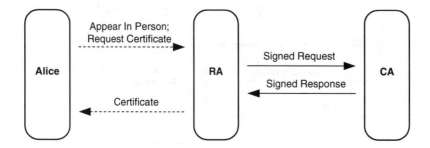

Process:
1. Alice generates public/private key pair, then appears in-person at the RA.
2. RA validates Alice's credentials, then generates signed request to CA.
3. CA validates RA's certification path and digital signature.
4. CA processes the request and generates a signed response.
5. RA validates CA's certification path and digital signature, then processes the response.
6. RA provides certificate to Alice.

Figure 11.3   RA performs in-person authentication.

- Alice presents physical credentials to the RA, which the RA reviews. The RA provides the client with a cryptographic module, such as a smartcard. Alice commands the cryptographic module to generate a public/private key pair. The cryptographic module retains control of the private key, and provides the public key to the RA for certification. On behalf of Alice, the RA requests a certificate from the CA. The CA generates the certificate, and returns it to the RA. The RA stores the certificate on the cryptographic module. This is very similar to Figure 11.3.

- Alice presents physical credentials to the RA and obtains an authenticator. Alice returns to her system and generates a public/private key pair. Alice requests a certificate from the CA, using the authenticator in the request. The CA generates the certificate, and the CA delivers the certificate directly to Alice. This model is depicted in Figure 11.4.

- Alice generates a public/private key pair and requests a certificate. The CA queues the certificate requests for RA review. The RA reviews the client information and approves or denies the request. If approved, the CA generates the certificate. This model is depicted in Figure 11.5.

- The RA obtains a cryptographic module, such as a smartcard, for Alice. The RA generates the public/private key pair on the cryptographic module, and then the RA requests a certificate from the CA. The CA generates the certificate for Alice and returns it to the RA. Alice comes to the RA and presents her credentials. The RA provides her with the cryptographic module. Finally, Alice changes the password to the cryptographic module so that no one else can access the private key stored in it. This is another variation on Figure 11.3.

As noted previously, there are numerous three-party transaction models. Selecting an appropriate model requires consideration of the type of information to be verified by the RA. This information is defined in the certification policy. This is discussed in Chapter 12, "Policies, Procedures, and PKI."

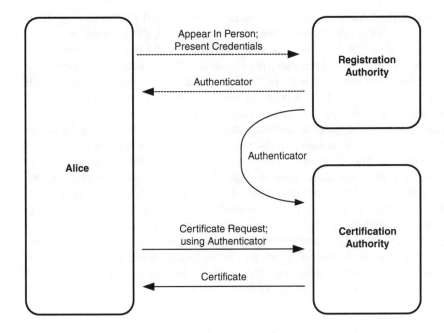

Process:
1. Alice appears in-person at the RA.
2. RA validates Alice's credentials, then generates authenticator.
3. RA provides authenticator to Alice and CA.
4. Alice generates public/private key pair, then sends public key and
   in a request to the CA using the authenticator.
5. CA validates authenticator, then processes the request.
6. CA provides certificate to Alice.

Figure 11.4   RA supplies an authenticator.

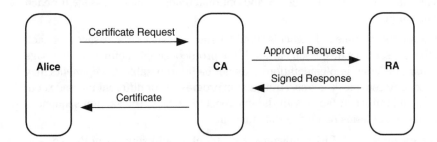

Process:
1. Alice generates public/private key pair, then sends certificate request to CA.
2. CA queues request for RA to validate Alice's credentials.
3. RA validates CA's certification path and digital signature.
4. RA processes the request and generates a signed approve/deny response.
5. CA validates RA's certification path and digital signature, then processes
   the response.
6. If RA approves, then CA generates certificate for Alice and sends it to her.

Figure 11.5   RA verifies the request after submission.

In Figure 11.3, the RA authenticates the request in person, so the RA can verify all the information in the certificate request. Once this is completed, the RA signs and transmits the request to the CA. The CA verifies the signature on the request, knows all the information is trustworthy, and generates the certificate. The CA may wish to verify that the requester has the private key or it may leave this validation to the RA. This model is an especially good choice if the CA requires the RA to verify that a prospective subscriber is using a particular type of hardware cryptographic module.

In Figure 11.4, an RA supplies an authenticator to the prospective certificate holder and the CA. The CA cannot be sure that the requester will put the appropriate information into the request. The RA must provide the validated name and policy attributes to the CA along with the authenticator for storage. The CA must verify the origin of the request and confirm that the certificate request matches the information provided by the RA. In this model, the RA does not get to confirm possession of the private key, so the CA must verify that the requester possesses the private key.

In Figure 11.5, the requester provides all information directly to the CA. The CA can directly verify that the requester possesses the private key. Additional information must be validated by the RA after submission. This model is especially useful when the CA must verify business information, such as a credit check.

Management Protocol Comparison Criteria

Management protocols can be compared in terms of the following criteria:

Completeness. The completeness of a protocol is a function of its message formats and transaction sequences.

Messages. Protocols should define the request, response, and error messages for each of the five transactions discussed in the previous section. Optionally, the protocol may define confirmation and other messages. Ideally, the protocol will clearly distinguish the mandatory and optional fields in each message for each transaction.

Transaction sequences. Protocols should define sequences of messages for each of the transactions discussed earlier. If the protocol simply defines the message formats, different implementations may not be interoperable. Components may expect different messages as a transaction progresses, or different message contents, and fail when faced with the unexpected. Ideally, transaction sequences are defined in terms of a finite state machine.

Transaction models. A PKI management protocol should support both two- and three-party transaction models. In particular, the utility of a three-party model where the requester appears at the RA in-person can be crucial in high-assurance PKI implementations. Flexibility to support a variety of three-party models is highly desirable.

Algorithm independence. The protocol should not be tied to any particular cryptographic algorithm. An organization may need to support different algorithms for different systems, and the algorithm suite will likely evolve over time. One of the most important aspects of algorithm independence is the ability of the CA to perform private key *proof-of-possession*. The CA needs to verify that the prospective subscriber has the private key that corresponds to the public key in the requested certificate. The prospective certificate holder cannot reveal the private key to the CA, so he or she must prove possession by performing cryptographic operations that require the private key. Ideally, the proof-of-possession operation should use the private key in its intended manner. That is, proof-of-possession for key transport private keys should involve decryption of a symmetric key, not generation of a digital signature.

Transaction complexity and efficiency. Simplicity and efficiency are desirable features in any protocol. Protocols should achieve their security objectives with the smallest possible number of messages. If a transaction requires more than one round-trip, then implementations need to maintain the state of all incomplete transactions. This increases implementation complexity.

Extensibility. PKI management protocols should be extensible to meet local requirements. No general protocol can be designed to meet every conceivable requirement. Different configurations, specific needs of hardware cryptographic modules, and other local requirements may require addition of nonstandard functionality. PKI management protocols should be designed to accommodate these local requirements.

Archival messages. PKI management protocols should permit CAs, RAs, and subscribers to archive proof that a particular transaction occurred. CAs may need to demonstrate at a future time that a certificate was issued based on verified information. Subscribers may need to prove that they requested revocation of their certificate. In some protocols, the messages transmitted permit the participants to prove they behaved properly. In others, the information is not available in a useful format.

Leverage existing code. This criteria addresses a pragmatic issue, rather than a security issue. Organizations have a limited number of software developers, and there is stiff competition for their time. A PKI management protocol that leverages existing code reduces development time and cost.

Common PKI Management Protocols

Five different protocols are commonly used to implement PKI management transactions. The first two protocols are based on the Public Key Cryptography Standard (PKCS) #10, Certification Request Syntax Standard [KALI98a]. PKCS #10 is the most common PKI management protocol, in combination with either the Secure Sockets Layer (SSL) [FREI96] or PKCS #7, the Cryptographic Message Syntax [KALI98b]. The third protocol is the Certificate Management Protocol (CMP) [ADAM99]. The fourth protocol is the Certificate Management Using CMS (CMC) [MYER00]. The final protocol is the Simple Certificate Enrollment Protocol (SCEP) [LIU00]. This section describes each of these protocols in turn, and identifies the strengths and weaknesses in terms of the criteria discussed previously.

PKCS #10

Public Key Cryptography Standard (PKCS) #10, Certification Request Syntax Standard, describes a message syntax for certification requests [KALI98a]. The certification request consists of a distinguished name (DN), the public key, an optional set of attributes, an algorithm identifier, and a digital signature. The optional attributes were designed to convey attributes for inclusion in the certificate (for example, an e-mail address), to provide the CA with additional information (for example, a postal address), and to establish a *challenge password* for use in a subsequent revocation request. The request is signed by the entity requesting certification using the corresponding private key. This signature is intended to achieve private key proof-of-possession. The PKCS #10 certification request format is depicted in Figure 11.6.

PKCS #10 is based, in part, on the certificate request message defined for the IETF Privacy-Enhanced Mail (PEM) standards [KALI93b]. When these specifications were developed, bandwidth was scarce, and many systems were not connected to the Internet. As with PEM, the authors of PKCS #10 expected many users to submit certificate requests on paper, faxing or mailing the request to the CA. This resulted in an implied requirement that a basic request fit on a single sheet of paper. To support such users, the number of mandatory fields was minimized.

When transmitted electronically, the signature on the PKCS #10 message is insufficient. This signature proves that the user generating the request has the corresponding private key. However, a CA that receives a PKCS #10 request requires additional information to authenticate the requester identity and verify that the request was received unaltered.

PKCS #10 defines the syntax of a single request message, not a full protocol. The contents or format of the response is outside the scope of PKCS #10, although a PKCS #7 [KALI98b] message is suggested as one possibility. Almost every PKCS #10 implementation employs PKCS #7 to return the certificate. The syntax and protocol used to request certificate revocation is also unspecified. PKCS #10 must be used with other message formats and protocols to provide functionality of a complete PKI management protocol.

PKCS #10 was not designed to be algorithm independent. The specification assumes the private key may be used to generate a digital signature, as is the case with the RSA

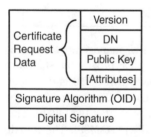

Legend:
[ ] Optional Field

Figure 11.6 PKCS #10 certificate request format.

algorithm. Proof-of-possession for key agreement algorithms, such as Diffie-Hellman, is outside the scope of the specification. However, proof-of-possession can be achieved with PKCS #10 using the optional attributes to convey additional information.[1]

In spite of these limitations, PKCS #10 remains the most widely used certificate request tool. The following sections describe two of the most common PKCS #10 usage scenarios. The first combines PKCS #10 with the Secure Sockets Layer (SSL) [FREI96]. The second combines PKCS #10 and PKCS #7.

PKCS #10 with SSL

The Web has become the standard interface for many Internet services, including PKI. Web pages can be used to guide the PKI user through the creation and submission of a PKCS #10 certificate request. However, the request cannot be submitted using the basic HTTP protocols. A CA that receives a PKCS #10 request over HTTP cannot authenticate the identity of the requester or be sure that the request was not altered by a man-in-the-middle. For this reason, this PKCS #10 request is submitted via an encrypted SSL connection.

The client and server establish a shared symmetric key. The details of symmetric key establishment are discussed further in Chapter 13, "PKI-Enabled Applications." The server provides a certificate as part of the SSL session establishment. This allows the client to authenticate the server, but the server cannot authenticate the client. In fact, since we are establishing the SSL session to transfer a PKCS #10 certificate request, the client may not have a certificate yet. The SSL connection provides confidentiality and integrity of the PKCS #10 request in transit to the CA. Only the server can decrypt it. The SSL connection also prevents a man-in-the-middle from altering the request.

SSL protection provides an incremental improvement, but it does not achieve all our goals. As described earlier, the CA cannot authenticate the identity of the requester. The CA can archive the request, but the CA cannot demonstrate that this request was received from a particular user. The SSL protocol protects the stream of data rather than distinct messages. As a result, the necessary information is not available to the CA.

The most common transaction model for PKCS #10 and SSL is the extended two-party model. The identity of the requester is verified by the delivery procedures after the certificate is issued. They are stored in a database or system, and may only be retrieved using a special authenticator. This authenticator is a one-time password that is shipped to the requester through an alternate channel, rather than as a Web page in the SSL session. The alternate channel is designed to confirm the identity information provided by the potential subscriber.

For example, the identity information may have included the potential subscriber's postal address. In this case, the authenticator is mailed to the potential subscriber at that address. If the potential subscriber does not receive the letter, then he or she cannot retrieve the certificate. More commonly, the identity information is an electronic mail address. The potential subscriber will receive the password in an e-mail message.

---

[1]Notably, Dave Solo submitted an Internet Draft to the PKIX Working Group that provides this capability with PKCS #10. The draft specification was not pursued since other management protocols under development provided the necessary proof-of-possession functionality.

If the potential subscriber does not have access to that e-mail address, then he or she will not be able to retrieve the certificate.

It is possible to construct a three-party transaction model using PKCS #10 and SSL. For example, a client could generate his or her own public/private key pair, create a PKCS #10 request, and hand carry it to an RA. The RA could verify the contents, establish an SSL session, and send the PKCS #10 request to the CA. The CA could issue the certificate, and then the CA could publish it or return it to the RA.

More commonly, a PKCS #10 and SSL implementation uses a three-party model in which the RA authenticates the request after it is submitted. Again, the client establishes an SSL session with the CA. The Web pages guide the client as it generates a key pair and creates a PKCS #10 request. The CA queues the certificate requests for RA review. The RA establishes an SSL session with the CA and logs in as the RA. The RA reviews the client information, compares it with out-of-band information, and approves or denies the request. If the RA approves the request, the CA generates the certificate. The certificate could be published in a directory or made available to the client using an authenticator as discussed previously.

Three-party models with different properties can also be achieved. These models use different message flows or augment PKCS #10 and SSL with additional mechanisms. For example, the SPYRUS WebReg product uses PKCS #10 between the subscriber and RA, and then the RA uses a signed certificate request format to request a certificate from the CA. This approach is described in further detail in Chapter 15.

PKCS#10 and SSL Summary

This protocol is the most widely used today, but it suffers from a number of weaknesses. Most importantly, PKCS #10 and SSL do not provide a syntax for revocation requests.

Completeness. PKCS #10 and SSL do not form a complete protocol. This protocol clearly defines the syntax for only one message—a certificate request. All other messages must be implemented in HTML or through Web forms. There are no well-defined messages for revocation (request or response), confirmation, or errors. Since there is only one well-defined message, there are no transaction sequences defined for this protocol.

RA participation models. PKCS #10 and SSL are generally used with two models. The first model is the extended two-party model in which identity information is authenticated by retrieving a certificate. Alternatively, the three-party model with postauthentication is also used. Other models can be supported by augmenting PKCS #10 and SSL with additional mechanisms.

Algorithm independence. The CA can verify that the end entity possesses the signature private key. The request format does not directly support proof-of-possession for key management private keys.

Transaction complexity and efficiency. The greatest strength of PKCS #10 is simplicity. As noted earlier, a PKCS#10 request is deliberately straightforward and simple. Systems may take advantage of the protection provided by SSL available in every Web browser. The protocol requires two round-trips.

Extensibility. Since this protocol leverages the capabilities of Web servers and browsers, it is relatively easy to extend the protocol to meet local requirements.

Forms can be designed to include any locally important information, and Web pages can be designed to support a variety of different configurations. For example, it is straightforward to support both Internet Explorer and Netscape Navigator client implementations.

Archival messages. This protocol does not provide appropriate information for archiving by the participants. The CAs can archive the digitally signed PKCS #10 request, but it does not include sufficient information. The RAs do not have any digitally signed information that they can use to demonstrate due diligence. The client obtains the certificate, but there is no other archival information. Users receive messages through the browser, so the user can print out the screen and file the paper.

Leverage existing code. Practically every client supports a Web browser. PKCS #10 is included in the most common cryptographic implementations (for example, Microsoft CryptoAPI and the Netscape cryptographic module). As a result, this protocol can be implemented with minimal development.

PKCS #7 and PKCS #10

PKCS #7 and #10 are independent specifications that may be used together to implement a protocol for issuing certificates. There is no standard specification describing this combination, but this section describes common practice.

PKCS #7 is the de facto standard specification for protecting messages with cryptography. PKCS #7 is the security foundation used by many protocols, including S/MIME v2 [DUSS98a, DUSS98b]. The basic PKCS #7 message format has only two fields: the content type and the content. PKCS #7 defines six content types: data, signedData, envelopedData, signedAndEnvelopedData, digestedData, and encryptedData. The content type is specified as an object identifier (OID), and defines the format of the content.

In general, PKI implementations rely on the signedData message format. The content includes six fields: the version, the algorithms used to generate the digital signatures, the content, certificates, CRLs, and signer information. The certificate and CRL fields are optional. The signedData message format is shown in Figure 11.7, where the content is a PKCS #10 request. Figure 11.7 shows a message that was signed three times; each represented by an independent signerInfo field.

The signerInfo consists of six fields: the version, the issuer and serial number of the certificate that contains the public key needed to verify the digital signature, authenticated attributes, the digital signature algorithm, the digital signature itself, and unauthenticated attributes. The authenticated attributes and unauthenticated attributes are both optional. The digital signature is generated using the signedData content and the signerInfo authenticated attributes, if any. In this fashion, all signatures include the signedData content. Each signer can supplement the content with different authenticated attributes. The signerInfo is depicted in Figure 11.8.

The PKCS #7 adds four important features to PKCS #10:

- By encapsulating PKCS #10 in PKCS #7, the message may be signed with a private key other than the one in the certification request. This permits the subscriber to sign the request with his or her current signature key or an RA to sign the request with its private key.

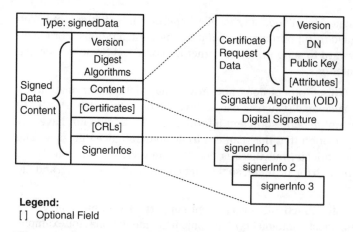

Legend:
[ ] Optional Field

Figure 11.7 PKCS #7 signedData encapsulating a PKCS #10 certificate request.

- In addition, the CA can use PKCS #7 to authenticate the certificate message returned to the subscriber. This provides the client or RA with archival proof that the certificate was issued.

- PKCS #7 can be used as a response message from the CA to the requester. If the certificate is issued, the CA can return the new subscriber certificate in a signed-Data message, as suggested in PKCS #10. Together, the two messages form a complete transaction sequence.

- The CA can retain the PKCS #7 signed message containing the PKCS #10 certificate request for archival purposes. The user can retain the signed PKCS #7 response message. Each participant has a signed message to archive as evidence.

PKCS #7 and #10 can, in combination, be used to support certificate issuance protocols that involve an RA directly or indirectly. For example, Alice can generate her own public/private key pair, create a PKCS #10 request, and hand carry the request to an RA. The RA verifies the contents by checking Alice's identification and the signature

Version
Issuer and Serial Number
Digest Algorithm
[Authenticated Attributes]
Encrypted Digest (Digital Signature)
[Unauthenticated Attributes]

Legend:
[ ] Optional Field

Figure 11.8 PKCS #7 signerInfo structure.

on the PKCS #10 request. The RA generates a signed PKCS #7 message for the CA. The CA authenticates the RA through the PKCS #7 signature, issues the certificate, and returns it in a PKCS #7 message to the RA (or Alice). The RA (or Alice) verifies the PKCS #7 signatures or the signature on the enclosed certificate to authenticate the identity of the CA.

PKCS #7 and #10 can also be used to support certificate issuance protocols when the user has a valid certificate. Again, Alice generates a new public/private key pair, and then creates a PKCS #10 request. This time, she generates a PKCS #7 message, signing it with her current signature key. The CA authenticates Alice through the PKCS #7 signature, issues the certificate containing the new public key, and returns it in a PKCS #7 message to Alice. Alice verifies the signature on the PKCS #7 message or certificate to authenticate the identity of the CA.

PKCS #7 and #10 Summary

The combination of PKCS #7 and #10 represents a significant improvement over PKCS #10 alone. We have a protocol that offers signed messages that may be archived. Proof-of-possession for signature keys in the PKCS #10 message can be preserved even if an RA signed the PKCS #7 message. We have a simple protocol, with a well-defined message flow for certificate issuance. The protocol is easy to implement, since most systems support the simple PKCS #7 and PKCS #10 formats.

Completeness. PKCS #7 and #10 describe both a request and response message for certificate request transactions. However, there are no messages defined for revocation requests. Confirmation and error messages are not defined. This protocol defines a single transaction sequence for certificate requests. This transaction requires one round-trip.

RA participation models. PKCS #7 and #10 can be used to implement a variety of transaction models. The first model is the extended two-party model in which identity information is authenticated by retrieving a certificate. Alternatively, the three-party model with post-authentication is also accommodated.

Algorithm independence. Proof-of-possession is supported for signature keys. Implementing proof-of-possession for key management keys cannot easily be achieved.

Transaction complexity and efficiency. This protocol's greatest strength is simplicity. As noted earlier, the PKCS #10 request is deliberately simple. Systems may take advantage of the PKCS #7 tools that are provided on typical clients and servers to implement this protocol. The basic protocols require one round-trip.

Extensibility. This protocol leverages the PKCS #7 message syntax. This syntax is inherently extensible. To add new information to any message, one simply adds an additional authenticated or unauthenticated attribute.

Archival messages. This protocol provides sufficient information for the CA to archive successful certificate request transactions. CAs can archive the PKCS #10 request encapsulated in a PKCS #7 signedData wrapper. For a basic certificate request, or an RA-authenticated initial request, this information justifies the CA action. However, the RA or client receives only the unsigned certificates-only message. The RA and client cannot demonstrate the origin of that message, although each certificate is easily traced to its issuer. The contents of the certificate and the CA's signature will be sufficient in most cases.

Leverage existing code   Since PKCS #7 is a basic building block for cryptographic applications, such as the S/MIME v2 electronic mail security protocol, it is implemented on many platforms. PKCS #10 is included in the most common cryptographic implementations. As a result, this protocol can be implemented without much code development.

Certificate Management Protocol (CMP)

When the IETF PKIX Working Group began development of a protocol for PKI management, they decided not to leverage PKCS #7 and #10. At the time, RSA Security held the copyright for the PKCS documents, so the IETF could not have change control.[2] In addition, the working group wanted to develop a comprehensive protocol to support a broad variety of models, including RA participation, and implement algorithm-independent proof-of-possession. At the time, it was unclear whether PKCS #7 and #10 were an appropriate starting point to meet these goals.

The PKIX working group developed a new protocol defined by the combination of RFCs 2510, the Certificate Management Protocol [ADAM99], and RFC 2511, the Certificate Request Management Framework [MYER99a]. RFC 2510 and RFC 2511 were approved in 1999. The resulting protocol is very comprehensive, can support practically any RA issuance model, and supports algorithm-independent proof-of-possession. The protocol also includes its own cryptographic message protection format, and it supports four different transport protocols.

The Certificate Management Protocol (CMP) message format is depicted in Figure 11.9. The message has four components: the *header*, the *body*, the *protection*, and the *extra certificates*. The protection and extra certificates components are optional. The protection component is used to protect the integrity of the header and body. It conveys a digital signature, message authentication code (MAC), or hashed message authentication code (HMAC). The protection field is only omitted if the header and body are integrity protected by some other means, such as PKCS #7 encapsulation. The extra certificate field can be used to deliver commonly needed certificates to the subscriber.

The header contains the name of the sender, the recipient, the message time, and indicates the cryptographic algorithm used to protect the message. The header may also contain optional nonces, key identifiers, a transaction identifier, a field for extra processing information, and a free text field for user information.

The body content is determined by the message type. CMP defines 24 message types, including:

Certificate request and response messages. CMP supports three pairs of certificate request and response messages. These messages may be used to request and deliver certificates to users. Different message types are used to indicate additional information about the type of certificate request. For example, the *initial request* and *initial response* messages are employed when a new user obtains his or her first certificate.

---

[2]Since that time, RSA Security has allowed the IETF to create derivative works based on many of the PKCS documents.

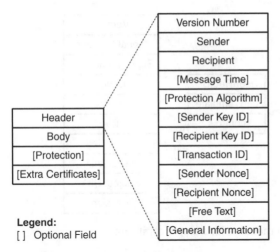

Figure 11.9   CMP message structure.

Cross-certification request and response messages. These messages may be used to request and deliver certificates to CAs.

Revocation request and response messages. These messages may be used to request revocation of certificates, and they confirm or deny the revocation request.

Key recovery request and response messages. These messages may be used to request and deliver private keys used for key management if they were backed up by the PKI.

Proof-of-possession challenge and response messages. These messages can be used to prove possession of private keys used for key agreement or key transport.

Certificate and CRL distribution messages. Four different messages may be used to announce issuance of a certificate or CRL.

Miscellaneous messages. These messages include a confirmation message, an error message, a general request message, and a nested message type to support multiple signers.

There are only 17 distinct ASN.1 types needed to encode the 24 message bodies. For instance, the body of the three certificate request messages and the cross-certification request are encoded using the same ASN.1 type. All certificate requests require the same types of information; the message type explicitly differentiates them.

Note that the message type was not indicated in the header. CMP indicates the body type through a trick of the ASN.1 syntax called *explicit tagging*. The outermost tag is replaced with a context-specific tag that defines the message body type. For instance, an initial certificate request is tagged with 0x80, while the basic certificate request is tagged with 0x82. While the messages use the same ASN.1 syntax, the CA can differentiate between the request types through this tag.

However, the ASN.1 types themselves are relatively complex. Figure 11.10 depicts the content of a certificate request for a single certificate using CRMF. The certificate request message consists of three major components: a CRMF, proof-of-possession, and

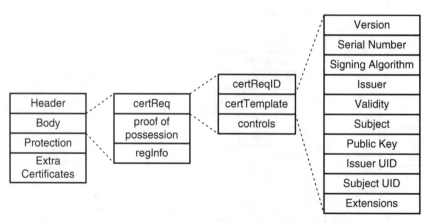

Figure 11.10   CMP certificate request message for a single certificate.

registration information. The CRMF contains a certificate request identifier, a certificate template, and controls. The certificate template includes all the certificate fields, including extensions. This approach permits the requester to specify the desired contents of any field in the certificate. This message format supports proof-of-possession for any key type. This approach is far more complex, and far more functional, than the PKCS #10 request format.

In addition, most CMP messages are designed to handle multiple requests in a single message. This feature permits a user with two key pairs (one for signature and another for key management) to submit a single request. This feature permits batch processing by RAs when large numbers of requests must be processed or when RAs operate primarily offline. There are many scenarios in which this is desirable. For example, a corporate spin-off may require mass revocation of users. Generation of thousands of separate requests would be inefficient. More commonly, a roving RA may visit several potential subscribers to accept certificate requests, queue them up, and submit them in mass at the end of the day.

CMP defines seven transaction sequences, employing both request and response messages. These message pairs support three types of certificate requests, a CA certificate request, revocation, and key recovery operations. A proof-of-possession challenge sequence is defined for use in conjunction with the certificate request messages. However, the complexity of the CMP messages means different implementations may not support the same combination of optional fields. As a result, interoperability cannot be guaranteed between conforming implementations.

However, the CMP specification also defines five specific transactions in detail. These transactions are mandatory for conforming implementations, and they are specified in sufficient detail to achieve interoperability. These transactions specify the message flow as well as the mandatory and optional fields for each of these messages for the following operations:

One-way cross-certification request/response. The cross-certification protocol is used when CAs wish to perform online cross-certification. This protocol may only be used if the CAs can authenticate the origin of the messages (possibly through out-of-band means). The transaction requires three messages: the requesting CA submits a *cross-certification request* message; the responding CA generates a *cross-certification response* message; and the requester submits a *confirmation* message. This transaction uses the basic two-party transaction model.

Initial registration and certification. The protocol implements a basic authenticated scheme. The initial registration request protocol is used when an end entity requests its initial certificate from a CA. In this protocol, the end entity requests certification of a locally generated public key (typically a signature key) using an *initialization request* message. The end entity must support proof-of-possession of the private key. The CA responds with an *initialization response* message containing a certificate, and the end entity replies with a *confirmation*. All messages are authenticated using a shared secret and a message authentication code (either a MAC or HMAC). This protocol uses a three-party transaction model, with the RA supplying an authenticator. This protocol follows the flow illustrated in Figure 11.5.

Certificate request. The certificate request protocol is used when an end entity that already holds a valid signature certificate requests a new certificate from its CA. This certificate may be a key management certificate or a new signature certificate. In this protocol, the end entity requests certification of a locally generated public key using a *certification request* message. The end entity must support proof-of-possession of the private key. The CA responds with a *certification response* message containing a certificate, and the end entity replies with a *confirmation*. These messages are authenticated using digital signatures. This protocol uses the basic two-party transaction model.

Key update request. The key update request protocol is used when an end entity that holds a valid certificate requests a new certificate for the same key pair from its CA. In this protocol, the end entity requests certification of the public key using a *key update request* message. The CA responds with a *key update response* message containing a certificate, and the end entity replies with a *confirmation*. In general, these messages are authenticated using digital signatures. This protocol uses the basic two-party transaction model.

PKI information request/response. In this protocol, an end entity sends a *general message* to the RA or CA requesting data needed for later PKI management operations. The RA/CA responds with *general response*. If an RA generates the response, then it will simply forward the equivalent message that it previously received from the CA, with the possible addition of extra certificates. These extra certificates do not invalidate the CA signature. The second message completes the protocol. That is, a *confirmation* message is not required. This protocol uses the basic two-party transaction model.

The syntax for the revocation protocol is not specified in detail, but the message flow is clear from the specification. The revocation protocol consists of two messages: a *revocation request* message to the CA followed by a *revocation response* message to the requester. The requester may be the certificate holder or an RA, depending upon local requirements.

Four of the six transactions require three messages. If the certification requests involve a challenge-response for proof-of-possession, those three requests demand five messages. However, the cross-certification protocol always involves a signature key, so challenge-response proof-of-possession is unnecessary. Only the *revocation request* and *information request* transactions can be completed in a single round-trip.

CMP Summary

CMP is a comprehensive protocol. It has all the desired security attributes, and CMP can support any conceivable PKI model for RA participation. These remarkable features increase complexity. By design, CMP did not leverage the established traditions, minimizing intellectual property concerns. This frustrates developers who must implement new software instead of reusing their existing code base. The stylistic differences between the PKCS-based protocols and CMP further magnify CMP implementation complexity.

Completeness. CMP is the most complete PKI management protocol to date. CMP describes both a request and response message for four classes of certificate request transactions, revocation request transactions, confirmation messages, and error messages. CMP also includes messages for additional functionality, such as challenge-response sequences, key recovery, central key generation, and general information requests. This protocol defines five transaction sequences in detail; unfortunately, additional transactions are more loosely defined.

Transaction models. This is an important strength of CMP. CMP can be used to implement any of the transaction models identified previously.

Proof-of-possession. CMP provides a thorough suite of proof-of-possession tools. Proof-of-possession may be implemented for digital signature keys or key management keys. Proof-of-possession may be established for key agreement private keys using challenge-response mechanisms. CAs can require that requesters prove possession of key transport or key agreement private keys by decrypting the new certificate and returning the hash in the confirmation message.

Transaction complexity and efficiency. CMP is a relatively complex protocol. It is not always clear which transaction or messages should be applied to a particular situation. Most transactions require more than one round-trip[3], and those involving a challenge-response may require three. A CA needs to maintain the state of every ongoing transaction and differentiate between the message flows. This adds complexity in the implementation. A complete CMP finite state machine would be a great help in resolving interoperability issues.

Extensibility. This protocol is extensible through the general information field. This field permits the inclusion of a type and value, so the data may be recognized by the other party in the transaction. Like an authenticated attribute in a PKCS #7 message, this information is protected by the digital signature on the message.

---

[3]Most certificate requests require a request message from the client (to the CA), a response message from the CA, and terminate with a confirmation message from the client. We call that one-and-a-half round-trips.

Archival messages. This is another strength of CMP. All the messages are cryptographically protected. In general, messages are digitally signed. In the case of initial certificate requests, a keyed hash is used to protect the message. In all the protocols, CAs generate signed responses that may be archived by the RA or client. RAs and clients generate confirmation messages in many transactions, permitting the CA to demonstrate acceptance.

Leverage existing code. This is the biggest issue with CMP. CMP is built upon an entirely new cryptographic message syntax. The message formats are relatively new. In general, implementing a PKI component based on CMP requires a fair amount of new code development.

Certificate Management using CMS (CMC)

Over time, the IETF PKIX Working Group grew and became more diverse. Not everyone was comfortable with the direction of the CMP protocol. A group emerged that felt that it was crucial to leverage the installed base of PKCS #7 and #10. To these vendors, CMP represented a radical departure from a working, deployed protocol. CMP defined too many messages, and the CMP transactions demanded too many round-trips. In their eyes, the comparative complexity of CMP overwhelmed the new functionality.

The PKIX Working Group fragmented into two camps. Those with a significant investment in CMP pointed out the weaknesses in PKCS #7 and #10, as well as the intellectual property issues. Those with a significant investment in PKCS #7 and #10 pointed out that a majority of PKIs used the RSA algorithm exclusively, and that most PKIs did not involve RAs in protocols directly. When RSA Security decided to relinquish change control for PKCS #7 and #10 to the IETF S/MIME Working Group, the major intellectual property issues were resolved.

Eventually, an uneasy truce was achieved. A second protocol would be permitted to enter the standards track. It was agreed, however, that the two protocols would share the same certificate request format. The second protocol would use the new CMS specification to provide cryptographic protection for messages. Further, the new protocol would also offer algorithm independence and include support for direct involvement of RAs.

The result was RFC 2797, Certificate Management Messages Over CMS (CMC) [MYER00a]. CMC references PKCS #10 for a basic certificate request format, and RFC 2511 for the more functional certificate request format used in CMP [MYER99a]. CMC relies on the Cryptographic Message Syntax, RFC 2630 [HOUS99a], for message encryption and signature. CMC also mandates support for RFC 2875, Diffie-Hellman Proof-of-Possession Algorithms [PRAF00].

As expected, CMC is reminiscent of PKCS #7 and #10. CMC permits the use of an unprotected PKCS #10 message for backward compatibility, and CMC permits a SignedData message with an empty content to convey certificates. This is often called a *certs-only* message. All other CMC messages are protected using CMS, and all of the CMC transactions can be completed in a single round-trip.

The CMC specification defines two new content types: PKI data and PKI response. The PKI data is essentially a request message, and the PKI response is the reply message from the CA. The CMC specification employs the CMS signed data and enveloped data content types to provide protection. Most CMC messages do not require confidentiality. Messages are constructed by encapsulating the PKI data or PKI response message in a CMS signed data content. This is depicted in Figure 11.11 (a).

There are occasions in which a PKI request or response message must be encrypted. The encryption prevents any information about the enrollment from being accessible to unauthorized entities. Confidentiality is provided by encapsulating the signed PKI message in a CMS enveloped data content type. This is shown in Figure 11.11 (b). CMC recommends that a second signed data encapsulation be used outside of the enveloped data layer. This is shown in Figure 11.11 (c). Figure 11.11 shows the encapsulation of PKI data, but all of the same options may be used for PKI response.

Control attributes are carried as part of both PKI requests and responses. Each control attribute is identified by a unique object identifier (OID). The encoding of the control attribute data depends on the OID. Processing systems first detect the OID, and then process the corresponding control attribute value prior to processing the message body.

In CMC, control attributes determine the overall control flow. If a PKI data message includes an unrecognized control attribute, the message must be rejected.

CMC defines 24 control attributes. These control attributes provide many of the features found in the CMP header, such as nonces and transaction identifiers. They are also used to implement proof-of-possession, pass arbitrary data, and indicate which extensions should appear in a certificate.

CMC specifies only two complete transactions: the simple enrollment protocol and the full enrollment protocol. These transactions each require two messages. It is incumbent upon the CA to determine which type of certificate request has been received based on the content of the message. Beyond that, transmission of PKI data messages is expected to result in the reception of a PKI response message. Even if systems implement all 24 control attributes, they may not use them in the same manner.

CMC Summary

CMC is far more complex than PKCS #7 and #10, but CMC is still less complicated than CMP. CMC supports the basic management protocol with or without RA participation. Reusing the CMS message protection provides an elegant model for applying cryptographic protection. CMS can be used to perform proof-of-possession for key management private keys. CMS signed and unsigned attributes provide an easy method to

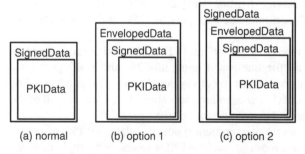

Figure 11.11   Protecting CMC PKI data with CMS content types.

extend CMC. Reusing the CMS message protection and the PKCS #10 request format provides opportunities to reuse existing code.

Completeness. CMC defines request and response messages for two classes of certificate request transactions and one class of revocation request transactions. CMC specifies only two real transactions: the simple enrollment protocol and the full enrollment protocol. CMC does not fully specify a revocation transaction, and support for this transaction is not mandatory.

Transaction models. CMC can be used to implement any of the transaction models identified earlier.

Proof-of-possession. CMC supports proof-of-possession for all types of private keys. However, CMC provides fewer mechanisms to choose from than CMP.

Transaction complexity and efficiency. CMC finds a middle ground in complexity. CMC is between CMP and PKCS #7 and #10. There are a small number of messages, but a substantial number of control attributes. It is not always clear which control attributes should be employed. Explicitly defined transactions, including a finite state machine, would greatly assist implementers. Most transactions can be implemented in exactly one round-trip, which simplifies implementations by eliminating the need for state at the CA.

Extensibility. This protocol is extensible through the CMS signed and unsigned attributes. These attributes permit the inclusion of a type and value, so the protocol control information may be recognized by the other party in the transaction. Extending the protocol requires only the selection or definition of attributes to convey the appropriate information.

Archival messages. This is another strength of CMC. Most of the messages are cryptographically protected by digital signatures. In general, messages are digitally signed, although initial certificate requests using the PKCS #10 format may be unprotected. The CA generates signed responses that may be archived by the RA or client.

Leverage existing code. This is another strength of CMC. CMC is built upon CMS, and PKCS #10 is one option for the body of certificate request messages. CMS and PKCS #10 are widely available. However, the full certificate request message syntax and revocation messages are not based on existing code. Unlike PKCS #7 and #10, CMC cannot be implemented without significant code development.

Simple Certificate Enrollment Protocol (SCEP)

The Simple Certificate Enrollment Protocol (SCEP) was developed by Cisco Systems "to support the secure issuance of certificates to network devices in a scalable manner, using existing technology whenever possible" [LIU00]. The existing technology includes the RSA algorithm, the DES algorithm, PKCS #7 and #10 message formats, HTTP, and LDAP. The protocol supports four different transactions: distribution of CA and RA public keys, certificate requests, certificate queries, and CRL queries. The latter two transactions are actually repository functions, but they are included in the SCEP specification. The protocol also supports out-of-band revocation requests by establishing a revocation challenge password during the certificate request.

SCEP requires that end systems obtain three pieces of information as an initial condition: the CA IP address or domain name, the CA HTTP script path, and the URL for CRL queries if CRLs will be obtained from a directory. The end system uses an unprotected HTTP Get operation to obtain CA and RA certificates. At this point, the end system must contact the CA operator through out-of-band means and verify the hash of the certificate to ensure the integrity of this operation.

End entities begin the certificate generation process by generating their own public/private key pair. At this point, they issue themselves a self-signed certificate. This certificate will be used for both authentication and key management, so it is limited to algorithms that can perform both functions (for example, RSA). This provides each entity with a temporary, but syntactically acceptable, X.509 certificate. This step is required, since all messages in the certificate request protocol are protected by a digital signature, or signed and encrypted using PKCS #7. PKCS #7 assumes that a public key certificate is available; PKCS #7 requires an issuer name and serial number to identify the certificate.

The protocol implements two models for enrollment: manual authentication and authentication based on a preshared secret. For manual authentication, the certificate request is submitted to the CA. The CA does not respond until the CA operator verifies the requester's identity information through an out-of-band procedure. This is basically the three-party transaction model with RA authentication after the request, as in Figure 11.5. For preshared secret authentication, the requester supplies the password to authenticate the request. This is the three-party transaction model with RA provided authenticator, as in Figure 11.4. In both cases, the certificate request is a PKCS #7 signed and enveloped data message with a PKCS #10 certification request as the content. The request must be encrypted, since the request includes a challenge password to support a future revocation request.

Note that the security of these authentication alternatives is independent of the temporary certificate. For the manual case, the authentication is based on the out-of-band procedures. For the preshared secret case, the security is based on the procedures used to distribute the shared secret.

SCEP requires support for revocation, but this operation is implemented manually. To revoke a certificate, the network device administrator calls the CA operator on the telephone. The CA operator will ask for the revocation challenge password established during certificate issuance. If the correct password is supplied, the CA will revoke the certificate.

Certificate and CRL access can be achieved by using the LDAP protocol or by using the query messages defined in SCEP. The current SCEP specification states that the use of HTTP for certificate and CRL access, and support for CRL distribution points, will be specified in a future version.

SCEP Summary

SCEP is an application-specific PKI management protocol. The scope of SCEP is limited to issuing certificates to network devices, and retrieving certificates and CRLs from a repository. It meets these requirements, and no more.

Message formats. SCEP defines request and response messages for certificate requests. SCEP does not define messages to support revocation requests. SCEP does define two messages for certificate retrieval and one for CRL retrieval. SCEP uses the response message from the certificate request as the response for the certificate and CRL retrieval messages.

Transactions and transaction models. SCEP specifies two certificate request transactions, each of which corresponds to the initial certificate request transaction. The transactions implement different three-party transaction models. SCEP was not designed to implement any generic transaction model.

Algorithm independence. SCEP is defined for only the RSA asymmetric algorithm. It makes no attempt to address proof-of-possession for key agreement private keys. SCEP assumes a single public/private key pair for both signature and key management.

Transaction complexity and efficiency. SCEP is a very simple protocol.

Extensibility. SCEP is extensible through the PKCS #7 authenticated attributes. Attributes permit the inclusion of a type and value, so the data may be recognized by the other party in the transaction. Extending the protocol requires only the selection or definition of attributes to convey the appropriate information.

Archival messages. SCEP is not particularly strong in this area. Certificate request transactions are cryptographically protected by digital signatures. However, other messages are not well defined, so they cannot be archived.

Leverage existing code. This is another strength of SCEP. SCEP leverages PKCS #7, PKCS #10, HTTP, and LDAP to construct a PKI management protocol. These are common building blocks. A system that includes these components would require relatively little new code development.

Selecting PKI Management Protocols

Selecting a PKI management protocol is one of the most perplexing aspects of PKI deployment. There are two protocols that can meet core requirements: CMP and CMC. However, the three PKCS #10-based protocols (PKCS #10 with SSL, PKCS #7 and #10, and SCEP) have the greatest installed base. CMP is not compatible with this installed base. CMC has some interoperability with this base, but there are very few products currently available. SCEP provides the least functionality of the newer protocols, but the support for routers provides significant momentum.

PKCS #10 with SSL and PKCS #7 and #10 are the PKI legacy systems. They have very limited functionality and lack many of the desired attributes. There are many examples of PKIs that have worked around these limitations. It seems shortsighted to build new PKIs on this foundation, even in the face of many stronger choices.

SCEP has a very focused and limited scope. It meets its stated goals, but no more. SCEP is sufficient for its constituency: enabling firewalls, routers, and virtual private networks (VPNs). SCEP falls far short for a PKI serving a more diverse community. However, SCEP has made inroads with its core constituency. SCEP should not be considered a legacy protocol; we will be seeing SCEP in use for years.

CMP is clearly the industrial-strength solution. It specifies more messages and transactions than the rest of the protocols combined. CMP includes all five core transactions, and adds additional features, including key management private key recovery. However, the complexity of CMP has slowed its acceptance in the marketplace.

CMC is not quite as comprehensive as CMP, but it specifies sufficient messages and transactions to meet our core requirements. CMC has a better opportunity to leverage the installed base of PKI clients, especially Netscape Communicator and Microsoft Internet Explorer. However, there are few full implementations of CMC currently available.

There are a number of pragmatic considerations that should be factored into the selection of a PKI management protocol. These factors include the security objectives for the PKI, the types of platforms used by subscribers and relying parties, and the availability of PKI-enabled applications.

Chapter 12 discusses certificate policies in detail. Development of a certificate policy will define the security objectives for a PKI, and determine which transaction models apply. Protocols with limited functionality may not effectively implement certain policies. It may be appropriate to defer selecting a PKI product until the security policy objectives and transaction models have been established.

Not all protocols are supported on all platforms. Availability of client software that will interoperate with this CA and the supported transaction models are irrelevant. The availability of client software should be factored into the selection of a management protocol as well. Of course, the end goal for PKI is to support application security services. The availability of PKI-enabled applications that use the client software should be factored into the selection of a management protocol as well.

The best solution is a CA that supports multiple protocols. This is not unreasonable; some PKI product vendors already support CMP and PKCS #7 and #10, for example. At a minimum, a CA should support PKCS #7 and #10, SCEP, and either CMP or CMC. Client systems could support any one (or two) of these protocols to be compatible with any CA product. This compatibility permits selection of the best-of-breed client software.

CHAPTER

12

Policies, Procedures, and PKI

The bulk of this book focuses on the technical mechanisms of a public key infrastructure (PKI). In computer security, however, technical mechanisms are insufficient on their own. These mechanisms are used in combination with a set of *procedures* to implement a particular *security policy*. This chapter is about developing sound policies and procedures for PKI implementations.

Specifically, this chapter is about two types of documents that describe the policies and procedures associated with a PKI. The first document is known as a *Certificate Policy* (CP), and the second is called a *Certification Practices Statement* (CPS). These documents share a common format, but have different audiences and different goals. In this chapter, we describe the format and explain the differences in content between these documents.

Of course, most users will not refer to the certificate policy or certification practice statement directly. They obtain the policy information they need indirectly, by processing the three policy extensions (certificate policies, policy mapping, and policy constraints, as described in Chapter 7, "X.509 Public Key Certificates") in the certificates. A direct relationship exists between the contents of these extensions and the documents described in this chapter.

We begin the chapter by introducing the concepts of security policy and procedures. Next, we describe the difference between a CP and a CPS, and their relationship to the certificate policy extensions. We describe the contents of a CP and a CPS, identifying the most important features. We introduce the concept of compliance audit is introduced, where the operations of the PKI are audited to ensure that the CP and CPS are being followed. We close the chapter with our recommendations for developing a CP and CPS.

Introduction to Policy and Procedures

A policy is a set of rules established to govern a certain aspect of organizational behavior. Policies describe *what* must be done to satisfy the business objectives, legal requirements, or corporate culture of an organization. In this chapter, we are concerned with security policies. A security policy describes the goals, responsibilities, and overall requirements for the protection of specific resources (for example, important computer systems or proprietary data).

Policy alone is insufficient to meet the organization's requirements. Security policies must be implemented through a combination of security mechanisms and procedures. An organization utilizes security mechanisms, such as locks on doors or network firewalls, as *tools* to implement a policy. However, security mechanisms will only produce the desired results if they are configured and maintained properly. Procedures are the steps that the system administrators and users follow when establishing and maintaining security mechanisms and when using the system. Procedures are *how* we achieve the security requirements described in our policy, and are directly linked with the mechanisms we use.

To illustrate the differences, let's consider the following scenario: An automotive manufacturer wants to protect new car designs from its competitors. The company decides that only the R&D group should have access to the building in which new car designs are developed.

The company has decided on a magnetic stripe card reader to restrict access to the building. The door will unlock automatically when a member of the R&D group swipes his or her identification card through the reader. When the door closes, it will lock automatically. The door will remain locked if the user presents an identification card for another group or company.

The company hires a contractor to install the new card reader during the one-week company-wide Christmas holiday. The contractor is provided with a recent R&D group organizational chart. The contractor encodes data onto the magnetic stripe cards and mails them to the homes of the R&D group members with instructions. The instructions describe how to use the card reader to open the door. On the second day of January, the card reader is in operation and the new car designs are safe. Right?

In this example, the automotive manufacturer has a reasonable security policy: Only members of the R&D group are permitted to enter the building in which new car designs are developed. The mechanism they selected to enforce this policy was a magnetic stripe card reader. The procedures were to have a contractor encode the cards and mail them to each person on the R&D group organizational chart.

So, how safe is that new car design? Not very. The company has a simple and reasonable policy. However, this combination of mechanisms and procedures is a rather poor implementation of this policy.

The mechanism does not prevent multiple people from entering the door at once. If an industrial spy times his or her arrival well, the spy can follow a member of the R&D

group through the door. The mechanism identifies R&D personnel solely through the possession of the card. If the spy obtains the identification card for any R&D person, he or she can gain access to the building.

The procedures compound these problems. The contractor could have forged additional identification cards and given them to the spy. That organizational chart might be out of date, so cards might have been mailed to the home of a deceased or recently fired employee. The spy could go through the mail of an R&D employee who is out of town and steal the identification card.

The company could improve the implementation of its policy by strengthening its mechanism, its procedures, or both. By adding a turnstile, the company could ensure that only one party enters the building for each card presented. By adding a keypad to the card reader, the company can require members to enter a PIN to go with the card. Now the spy must obtain a card and learn the user's PIN to gain entry. Further improvement is possible by adding a biometric device to the card reader. Now the spy needs the user's fingerprint or retina scan to gain entry.

Even if the company cannot install turnstiles or upgrade the card reader, it can improve through better procedures. First, users could be educated on the need to shut the door behind them. Without this education, it seems rude to force the next person to use his or her own card to open the door. Second, card delivery procedures can be created to reduce the risk of cards falling into the wrong hands. In-person pickup or registered mail with delivery confirmation can be used to verify identity before cards are delivered. Third, the company could use its own security staff to issue the magnetic cards. It could restrict the cards to personnel on a list provided by management or the corporate personnel database. The company could issue the cards to those personnel in person after verifying their identity.

To ensure that a security system provides adequate protection, the combination of policies, procedures, and mechanisms must be examined. Adequate protection will be different for different applications. The late-model parts department, which maintains an inventory of replacement parts for recent model years, would certainly require less protection than new model development, for example. Consequently, a particular security mechanism or system might be appropriate for one application and not for another. An assessment of threats and risks, placed in the context of the organizational culture, helps to define the most appropriate and most cost-effective security solutions.

In this book, the security system is a PKI. The technical mechanism is sound, but differences in policy and procedure will affect which certificates are acceptable for a particular application. The policies and procedures apply to the operations of the CAs, the RAs, the repository, and the subscribers themselves. Relying parties decide whether the certificate may be used for their application based in part on the policies and procedures used by the certificate issuer.

Policy and PKI

PKI policies and procedures information is conveyed through three basic tools: the certificate policy (CP), the certification practices statement (CPS), and the certificate policies extensions (as described in Chapter 7). Each of these tools fulfills the needs of different audiences. In this section, we clarify the differences between these tools. First, we describe a CP and a CPS. Then, we relate them to the policy information in the certificate extensions.

As noted earlier, CPs must address the components of a PKI *in total*. In the following section, we discuss CPs, CPSes, and their relationship to the operation of certification authorities (CAs) and their supporting components. Rather than introduce a new term, or continually state "CAs and their supporting components," we refer to the CA alone. The operations of associated registration authorities (RAs), repositories, and other supporting components are also included in the policy.

Certificate Policies and Certification Practice Statements

The CP is a high-level document that describes a security policy for issuing certificates and maintaining certificate status information. This security policy describes the operation of the CA, as well as the users' responsibilities for the requesting, using, and handling of certificates and keys. The CP asserts that this security policy shall be implemented from certificate generation until its expiration or revocation. It does not specify how the policy shall be implemented. For example, a CP might state: "All subscribers shall be authenticated in person by an RA before a certificate is issued." The CP excludes all operational details, since they may evolve over time. For example, the CP would not identify the physical location of the CA or the products used in the CA. By excluding these details, the CP becomes a very stable and high-level document. It is reasonable to assume that a CP could be used for 10 years or more.

The scope of a CP may be the operations of a single CA and its supporting components. This is generally the case when a single CA serves an enterprise or a CA participates in a mesh PKI. Since the CA issues the subscriber certificates, and serves as the trust point, a CP covering the operations of the CA is meaningful. Multiple CAs may operate under a single CP. This will often be the case when multiple CAs are maintained by a single enterprise (for example, company or government agency) and jointly support a single community of users through a mesh PKI.

Alternatively, the scope of a CP may be the operations of a hierarchical PKI for this policy. Since the CA that issues the subscriber certificates is different from the trust point, describing the policy of a single CA is insufficient to determine the level of security provided. In this case, the CP must address the operations of the root CA and all the CAs that issue certificates under this policy. Different hierarchical PKIs could share a single CP as well. For example, different health care organizations could implement hierarchical PKIs that implemented the same industry-standard policy. This is not a common occurrence today, but could be in the future. For the sake of clarity, the figures and discussion in the remainder of this chapter assume that a CP covers the operations of a single CA.

Different people will use the CP for different reasons. For example, the CP will be used to guide the development of the CPS for each CA that operates under its provisions. CAs from other enterprise PKIs will review the CP before cross-certification. Auditors and accreditors will use the CP as the basis for their review of CA operations.

Application owners will review a CP to determine whether these certificates are appropriate for their application.

The CPS is a highly detailed document that describes how a CA implements a specific CP. The CPS identifies the CP and specifies the mechanisms and procedures that are used to achieve the security policy. The CPS asserts that the specified products will be used in combination with the specified procedures. The CPS might state: "Users will receive their certificates and smartcards from the RA after presenting the following credentials in person: (1) current driver's license, (2) work identification card, (3) blood sample, and (4) hair sample." A CPS includes sufficient operational details to demonstrate that the CP can be satisfied by this combination of mechanisms and procedures.

Each CPS applies to a single CA.[1] The CPS may be considered the overall operations manual for the CA. Specific portions of the CPS may be extracted to form the CA Operator's Guide, RA Manual, PKI Users Guide, or other role-specific documentation. Auditors and accreditors will use the CPS to supplement the CP during their review of CA operations. This may occur periodically as a matter of policy or could be performed whenever cross-certification occurs. Note that a CPS does not need to be published. The combination of a CP and the results of an accreditation process should be sufficient for external parties.

The CP, CPS, and Policy Extensions

As described in Chapter 7, certificate users obtain policy information in the form of object identifiers (OIDs). Each policy OID in a certificate maps to a single CP. When a CP is developed, a unique policy OID is assigned as described in Appendix B, "Object Identifiers." Only slight modifications can be made to a CP without assigning a new OID. The procedure for changing the CP, and how to obtain the most current information, is contained within the CP itself. A very large number of policies could, and probably will, be defined over time. CPSes are related to policy OIDs through the CP they implement. Each CP may be implemented by many different CPSes, and one CPS could meet the requirements of more than one CP.

Figure 12.1 illustrates these relationships for three different CAs issuing certificates under a single policy. Each CA issues its certificates under the Fox Certificate Policy #1, or Fox CP-1. All of these certificates will carry the same policy OID in the certificate policies extension. Each CA has its own unique CPS reflecting different combinations of mechanisms and procedures appropriate to each CA.

Mechanisms may differ based on the clientele they support or the available facilities. For example, assume the Legal group uses Apple Macintoshes, the Operations group uses Wintel systems, and the R&D group relies on UNIX workstations. These differences could influence the selection of PKI products. Alternatively, the Operations group may operate secure computing facilities that can house a CA, while the R&D group does not. To meet the requirements in the CP, the R&D group may need more robust security mechanisms or procedures.

---

[1]A large PKI may have several CAs that are practically clones. In this case, it may be more efficient to develop a single CPS that applies to all the clone CAs. However, this specification must include separate information (for example, location or contact information) for each CA within the PKI.

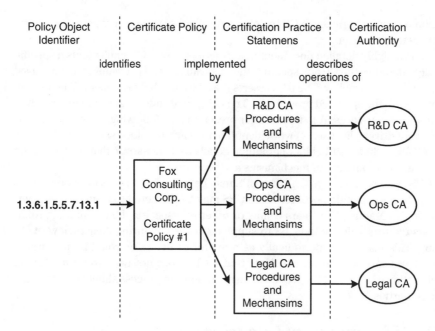

Figure 12.1 Three CAs implement a single policy.

In this scenario, all of the CAs are part of the same enterprise PKI. They share a single policy, but the procedures and mechanisms used by each CA may be very different. Each CA may use a different product, be protected by different physical controls, and rely on different identification procedures. However, the same security goals are achieved in each case. Users throughout the Fox Consulting Corporation will recognize the Policy OID and know whether the certificate is acceptable for its application. For example, Fox CP-1 may be appropriate for e-mail.

Of course, Fox Consulting may need to support a wide variety of applications. Fox CP-1 may not be acceptable for signing contracts. Consequently, an enterprise PKI may issue certificates under more than one policy. In Figure 12.2, Fox Consulting uses two policies. The R&D CA issues under Fox CP-1, and the Legal CA issues under Fox CP-2. The Ops CA issues under both policies. Note that the Ops CA maintains a single CPS that satisfies both CP-1 and CP-2. Recall that the CPS acts as an operations manual. If there is more than one CPS, it will be more difficult for the CA staff to perform its functions correctly.

The Ops CA may issue certificates to users with the policy OID for Fox CP-1, Fox CP-2, or both. Where policies are application specific, it may be reasonable to issue certificates with both policies. That is, if Fox CP-1 is the e-mail policy and Fox CP-2 is the contract signing policy, Alice's certificate may need to specify both policies. On the other hand, policies may be oriented toward the level of assurance; that is, Fox CP-1 may be "low assurance" and Fox CP-2 may be "high assurance." Low-risk applications, such as e-mail, could accept certificates asserting CP-1 *or* CP-2. High-risk applications,

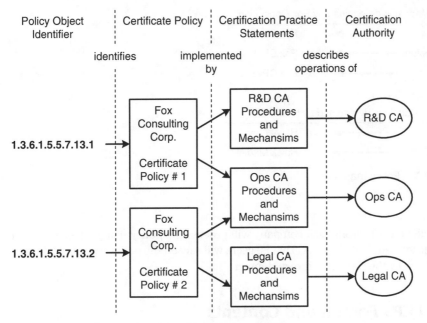

Figure 12.2   Three Fox CAs issue under two policies.

such as contract signing, might require CP-2. In this case, Alice's certificate would assert either CP-1 or CP-2, but not both.

No user will recognize all the policy OIDs that exist. A user is probably familiar with a more limited set of policies that are in use in his or her local CA or enterprise PKI. We will call this set of policies the *user's policy domain*. For Alice and Bob, Fox CP-1 and Fox CP-2 form their policy domain.

There may be CPs used in other enterprise PKIs that are consistent with the policies in Alice's and Bob's policy domain, but Alice and Bob cannot make this determination. Assume that Hawk, Ltd. has a single CA that issues certificate under three policies: Hawk High, Hawk Medium, and Hawk Low. If Bob and Alice encounter Hawk certificates, they will not recognize the respective policy OIDs. They cannot tell which of the policies (if any) would be acceptable for their application.

A Fox CA can translate policy information from other domains into policy information that Fox users can recognize through the policy mapping extension. Fox Consulting may determine that Hawk High may be accepted as Fox CP-2 and Hawk Medium and Low may both be accepted as Fox CP-1. On the other hand, Hawk, Ltd. may determine that Fox CP-1 may be accepted as Hawk Low, Fox CP-2 may be accepted as Hawk Medium, and none of the Fox corporate policies meets the requirements of Hawk High. As a result, applications that require the Hawk High policy will not be able to accept any Fox certificates.

Figure 12.3 demonstrates one of the key features of policy mapping. Policy mapping need not be symmetric! Fox Consulting and Hawk, Ltd. need not agree on which policies

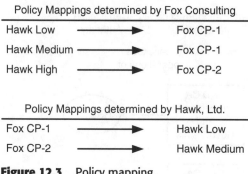

Policy Mappings determined by Fox Consulting

Hawk Low   ⟶   Fox CP-1

Hawk Medium ⟶ Fox CP-1

Hawk High   ⟶   Fox CP-2

Policy Mappings determined by Hawk, Ltd.

Fox CP-1   ⟶   Hawk Low

Fox CP-2   ⟶   Hawk Medium

Figure 12.3   Policy mapping.

are equivalent. Users from each company will process the policy mapping extension in the certificate issued by their CA. That is, users will rely on the policy mapping information provided by the CAs in their own domain.

CP and CPS Format and Contents

A CP and a CPS are commonly written in a single standard format. RFC 2527, the *Certificate Policy and Certification Practices Framework*, established the recognized format for both a CP and a CPS. RFC 2527 may be obtained from ftp://ftp.ietf.org/rfc/rfc2527.txt. RFC 2527 proposes an outline with eight major sections and 185 second- and third-level topics. Most CPs and CPSes are written to this outline, since the standard format has a number of distinct advantages.

By adhering to a well-defined format, the CP writer is less likely to forget something important. It would be easy to overlook a few of the 185 topic areas identified in RFC 2527 without the outline. Of course, the author may determine that some topics do not apply to his or her situation. The CP author should explicitly indicate this by adhering to the outline and stating "No Stipulation" where appropriate. If a topic is simply omitted, it will be unclear to the reader whether the topic was out of scope or overlooked. Similarly, a CP author may decide that additional topics need to be added to the framework defined in RFC 2527 to meet the requirements of his or her organization.

We have stated many times that CAs should not establish trust relationships without understanding each other's policies. Adhering to the standard CP format will simplify cross-certification with CAs that implement other policies. CAs that intend to cross-certify can compare their CPs and quickly evaluate the differences. This information can be used to determine policy mappings, which can be represented in a policy mapping extension. By inserting these mappings, a CA's subscribers can interpret policies in other CA's certificates according to its local policies. This process will be performed each time a CA cross-certifies with a CA using new policies.

Using the same format for the CP and CPS also makes it easy to review them side by side. Comparison of a CP and CPS is necessary to ensure that the procedures and mechanisms specified in the CPS faithfully implement the policy.

Highlights of the RFC 2527 Format

RFC 2527 established an outline with the following major sections:

- Introduction
- General Provisions
- Identification and Authentication
- Operational Requirements
- Physical, Procedural, and Personnel Security Controls
- Technical Security Controls
- Certificate and CRL Profiles
- Specification Administration

Next, we summarize the contents of each section, highlighting crucial issues that should be addressed in every CP and CPS. For complete details, the reader should refer to RFC 2527.

Introduction

The "Introduction" provides an overview of the use of the certificates issued under this policy. This section will not tell the reader if certificates are appropriate for a particular application, but you may be able to eliminate them from consideration.

This section explains how to identify certificates issued under this policy. Most commonly, this is achieved through an OID in the certificate policies extension as described in Chapter 7. The policy might also apply to a CA, or a subtree of a hierarchical PKI, that issues certificates under a single policy. In this case, the policy can be identified by the issuer name. For example, the policy could state: "This policy applies to all certificates issued by the Fox Consulting Operations CA and its subordinates."

This section also identifies the user community and the applications that the policy is intended to support. A CA may issue certificates to members of the Red-Headed League, employees of Fox Consulting, or members of the NATO forces. The CA may issue the certificates to protect everyday e-mail, financial transactions, or military secrets.

This section describes the types of entities involved in the operation of the CA and the roles they perform. These components include CAs, RAs, subscribers, and relying parties. They may also include entities that oversee operations of a component, maintain the CP, or other administrative functions.

This section ends with contact information for the people who administer the CA, maintain the policy, and approve the corresponding CPSes. In a CP, this contact information should identify the telephone numbers or mail addresses associated with the organizations that perform these functions. More specific information could result in frequent revisions. In a CPS, the actual personnel might be named.

General Provisions

The "General Provisions" section captures legal and general practices information. This section describes the obligations imposed by this policy on the CA, its RAs, subscribers, relying parties, and repositories. For computer scientists and engineers, this section may seem dry and boring. However, the information that it contains is absolutely critical to cross-certification, risk or loss management, and liability.

One of the most important topics addressed in this section is the compliance audit. A policy is only a paper document. The information is only useful if it accurately describes the protections in place when the certificates were issued. This section describes the frequency of compliance audits, who performs the audit, the auditor's qualifications, the auditor's relationship to the CA, topics covered by the audit, actions taken as a result of any deficiencies in the audit, and how to communicate the results of the audit. Regular compliance audits by a knowledgeable third party are your best guarantee that a certificate policy is properly implemented and enforced.

Other important topics in this section include the obligations, liabilities, and financial responsibility of the various PKI components (including the subscriber and the relying party). For example, the policy might state that a relying party must check the status of a certificate on the latest CRL before each use. A relying party that fails to meet its obligations may have little recourse if the transaction turns out to be fraudulent. This section also specifies any limitations in the liability accepted by a CA or RA, and who bears the financial responsibility if use of these certificates results in a loss. If a user is relying on these certificates for financial transactions, this section determines whether the PKI accepts some of the liability or the relying party bears all liability itself. This section also specifies the legal jurisdiction and dispute resolution procedures in case issues arise. For example, the policy may specify: "the laws of the state of Massachusetts shall apply." Alternatively, the policy might require that disputes must be submitted for binding arbitration.

This section describes how information is disseminated. A CA's obligations (if any) to publish its CP, CPS[2], certificates, and the current status of those certificates are defined here. For example, this section might state "The CA shall publish the list of revoked unexpired certificates in *The New York Times* once a month." The availability and timeliness of this information impact the scope of applications that can be supported.

A CA may also receive requests for other types of information. Law enforcement may wish to establish the identity of a certificate holder if a certificate was used in the commission of a crime. Also, a court may issue a subpoena for similar information. For example, signed e-mail could be introduced as evidence of adultery in a divorce case. The circumstances under which a CA will release such information are described in this section.

This section also covers fees for services, the refund policy, and the warranty. Depending upon the business model, there may be a cost associated with obtaining a new certificate, retrieving a certificate from a repository, checking its status, or obtaining policy information. If there is a cost, there should also be a refund policy. CAs that charge for services generally offer warranties as well. Warranties usually set a limit on liability. The liability limitations come in many flavors: two examples are aggregated and per case. With aggregation, claims are fulfilled until a ceiling value is reached. After that, no further claims are fulfilled. With per case, a ceiling value is imposed on each claim, but each case is independent.

---

[2] It is unclear if a CPS should ever be published in full, since it may provide an attacker with useful information. For example, the CPS would identify the information retained in audit trails. Publication of a sanitized CPS extract seems a reasonable compromise.

Identification and Authentication

The "Identification and Authentication" section handles one of the most important aspects of PKI policy: the procedures that are used to identify users before issuing or revoking a certificate. The strength of these procedures determines the degree to which a relying party can depend upon the identification information in the certificate.

The initial registration procedures, which are used to establish the identity of a user obtaining his or her first certificate, are of particular importance. The primary role of a certificate, after all, is binding the subject and his or her public key. These procedures vary widely and differ in the strength of that binding and the type of identity they establish.

A user may be identified based on an e-mail address, by presenting identification to collect certified mail, or by presenting identification during a face-to-face appearance at an RA (or a CA). Since it is easier to gain access to another user's e-mail than to forge government-issued identification cards, the first procedure creates a relatively weak binding. The identities that are authenticated differ as well. The first procedure authenticates the subject as "the user that can read mail delivered to alice.adams@fox.com." The second and third procedures authenticate the subject as "the person whose photograph is on the driver's license issued to Alice Adams." Depending upon the application, different types of identity information may be more important.

After initial registration, different procedures may be employed. A CA can authenticate a user through use of a digital signature key, for example. An entirely different set of procedures may be employed for revocation. For example, a CA might honor a revocation request if it was made by telephone from an internal line or if it appears on company letterhead with a handwritten signature.

A second critical issue appears in this section, although it is not reflected in the section's title. This feature is the semantics, if any, of names. Names in certificates must be unique to the user (or system) that holds the private key, but there are no requirements regarding the semantics. That is, two certificates issued by the same CA to "Santa Claus" must correspond to the same person, but that person's legal name may not be Santa Claus. As long as the Fox Consulting CA issues certificates to just one user with the name "Santa Claus," it is immaterial whether that user is actually Alice Adams or Bob Burton. Names could also be arbitrarily assigned numbers.

In reality, most certificates are issued with meaningful names. This section specifies the semantics of names, if any, that appear in these certificates. If Bob Burton applies for a certificate, the CA is unlikely to approve "Santa Claus" as the subject name. The rules specified in this section will determine whether the certificate uses the name Bob Burton or Robert Burton. The rules also specify the rules for name assignment when the preferred name is already in use. In large organizations, there may be a number of people named Bob Burton. The CA can differentiate through middle initials, middle names, or DN qualifiers.

Operational Requirements

The "Operational Requirements" section focuses on the procedures performed to ensure that the CA issues and revokes certificates only when appropriate. The previous section was devoted to the verification of identity for issuing and revoking certificates. The CA may know the requester's identity, but could still refuse the request. Often, additional procedures must be performed before a CA performs these actions.

For example, a particular policy may only apply to contract managers and accountants. The CA may not issue this certificate to a user based on identity alone. The CA also needs to verify that the user is a contract manager or a company accountant. The policy specifies how the CA verifies that the user is entitled to such a certificate. This requirement may be achieved as part of the RA function or performed independently to achieve separation of duties, as described in the following section.

Certificate revocation is likely to have operational requirements as well. A CA may revoke the user's certificate upon request by other parties. For example, a user's manager may be authorized to request revocation. The procedure followed by a CA to determine whether the requester is the user's manager is an operational requirement specified in this section.

Physical, Procedural, and Personnel Security Controls

The security of a PKI also reflects where the equipment is installed, the procedures followed by the people who operate the equipment, and the way those people are selected. A fire (or firebomb) could destroy the CA and the backup tapes. Poorly trained CA operators may not generate backup tapes at all. Untrustworthy RAs might accept a bribe to falsely authenticate a user's identity. The *non-technical security controls* that protect a PKI from these threats are the focus of this section.

Physical controls protect the PKI components from unauthorized access and environmental threats. This section should, at a minimum, address the following topics:

- Physical access controls to restrict the entry and exit of personnel (for example, from the room housing the CA).

- Environmental controls such as uninterruptible power supplies, fire extinguishers, and drainage systems, to protect against utility failures, fires, and plumbing leaks.

- Offsite backup to ensure that backups are available to reconstruct the CA if other physical controls have failed.

- Site location and construction techniques to guard against structural collapse from storms or bombs.

- Waste disposal to prevent dumpster diving.

Procedural controls implement a series of checks and balances that ensure the CA staff does its job, and only its job. The actions of individual staff members, both intentional and unintentional, can adversely impact the security achieved in the PKI. Procedural controls should be designed to enforce the concepts of *least privilege* and *separation of duties*. Least privilege restricts staff member access privileges (for example, the programs they can execute or files they can modify) to the minimum necessary to perform the job. Separation of duties divides critical functions among different staff members, ensuring that no one individual has enough information or access to perform a fraudulent activity. Some important examples are listed next.

- No single staff member should be able to generate a new CA key pair. This can be implemented procedurally. For example, different staff members could be required to open the door, sign on to the CA, and sign on to the cryptographic module. This can also be achieved using a cryptographic module that supports n of m control. For example, the module might require that three of the five security officers be present and authorize generation of a new key pair.

- Regular audit trail review deters intentional malicious actions or fraudulent activities by staff members by increasing the probability of detection. The staff member who reviews the audit trail should not have any other operational PKI duties. This prevents the auditor from personally committing fraud and then approving the audit trail.

- Staff members who authorize issuing certificates to a subject should not be permitted to verify the subject's identity. This prevents staff members from issuing a certificate with an inappropriate identity.

Another important aspect of procedural controls is training. Are CA and RA staff well trained in the use of the PKI components? Are they aware of the procedures they are supposed to follow? Does the company provide up-to-date documentation? Staff members may be dedicated and motivated, but they will make mistakes if they are not equipped with the right information.

Procedural controls are designed to prevent a single staff member from adversely impacting the security of the PKI. Staff members could work together, though, to circumvent the procedural controls. For example, staff members could conspire to issue fraudulent certificates, which are used to authorize million-dollar contracts with mythical corporations. Even if this is detected during audit trail review, it may be too late to prevent the damage. The best protection from this threat is an honest and responsible staff.

Personnel controls are designed to ensure that staff members are trustworthy. A very effective tool for personnel control is background screening. This type of screening helps to expose potential problem employees. For example, people who are in financial trouble may be more easily motivated to violate procedures. Disgruntled employees may want to get even with the company. Background checks and credit checks may help to ensure that the PKI is staffed with trustworthy people who do not have a significant motivation to defraud the company.

Technical Security Controls

Technical security controls are security controls designed into the computer systems. Technical controls can be used to enforce operational and procedural controls, as well as provide automated protection against computer hackers, viruses, and Trojan Horse programs. The technical, operational, and procedural controls must be consistent to ensure that the PKI's security goals are met.

Perhaps the most important technical controls are those used to protect the CA's private keys. A CA's cryptographic module should be independently validated as secure and correct. FIPS 140-1 Level 2 or Level 3 hardware cryptographic modules [FIPS140] are appropriate for most CA implementations. Hardware cryptographic modules do not rely on the operating system for protection, and the private key is never in host memory.

Of course, other PKI components must protect their private keys as well. Software cryptographic modules and FIPS 140-1 Level 1 or Level 2 hardware are appropriate in most RAs. Secure key management is critical to ensure that all private keys and activation data are protected and used only by authorized personnel. The type and level of cryptographic module appropriate for a user depends upon his or her applications. However, all cryptographic modules should be validated at the FIPS 140-1 Level 1 or higher.

The CA must rely on the operating system and application software for some security. CA databases are maintained in files and processed in the host memory. These databases may identify the set of recognized RAs, contain the certificate and CRL profile, or the list of unexpired but revoked certificates. If an attacker can modify this information, he or she may be able to achieve his or her goals without access to the private key.

At a minimum, the CA operating system should incorporate all current security patches and be securely configured. Operating system vendors are the primary source for security patches and configuration information. Computer Security Incident Response teams, such as the Computer Emergency Response Team (CERT) or Federal Computer Incident Response Capability (FedCIRC), are another source for this information. FedCIRC maintains a list of current patches at http://www.fedcirc.gov.

Third-party validation of operating systems and application software can provide additional assurance. The primary vehicle for this validation is now a Common Criteria Protection Profile. Several protection profiles have been developed to address the security of PKI Components. Both SPYRUS and the National Institute of Standards and Technology (NIST) have published Protection Profiles for CAs and RAs. ANSI X9 is drawing from this previous work to create a Protection Profile for PKI components used in the banking industry. You can find additional information about the Common Criteria at http://csrc.nist.gov. Information about the SPYRUS Protection Profile is available at http://www.spyrus.com/documents/cims, and information about the NIST Protection Profile is available at http://csrc.nist.gov/pki.

Another crucial aspect of the technical security controls is network security. It is not prudent to install a CA in a concrete bunker but connect it to the Internet without additional protection. In general, a CA should be isolated from non-PKI equipment by a firewall. Systems that are separated from the CA by a firewall are limited to typical PKI transactions in any attack on the CA. Systems that share an unprotected network with the CA may use the types of unsafe protocols prevented by a firewall to launch an attack.

Certificate and CRL Profiles

The "Certificate and CRL Profiles" section describes the contents of certificates and CRLs issued under this policy. One important aspect is the set of algorithm identifiers that will be used to identify public keys and signatures. The set of X.509 certificate extensions that will (or may) be included in the certificates and CRLs is listed. This section also states whether the CA issues delta CRLs, CRLs at multiple distribution points, or relies on another CA to issue indirect CRLs.

This section must be reviewed before interoperation to ensure that certificates and CRLs contain sufficient information for local users. Local users may not be prepared to process certificates and CRLs conforming to this profile. Encoding of names, policy information, and CRL types, in particular, may prevent interoperability.

Specification Administration

If you are reading a CP or CPS, you would like to be sure that you have the current copy and that the CPS in use accurately implements the corresponding CP. The "Specification Administration" section describes who has change control for the document, publication and notification procedures for new versions, and the CPS approval procedures.

Compliance Audits and Accreditation

Compliance audits for CAs have traditionally been performed as SAS 70 audits. SAS No. 70, *Reports on the Processing of Transactions by Service Organizations*, provides guidance to an auditor when a user organization uses a service provider to process transactions that will "be reflected in the user organization's financial statements" [AICPA00]. This has not been totally satisfactory when applied to CAs. For example, the SAS 70 audit does not address the mechanisms that protect the CA's private key. There are several projects under way to develop PKI-specific third-party accreditation techniques to replace the SAS 70 audit.

The CA Trust project is the most ambitious North American project for third-party accreditation. This project combined the efforts of the American Institute of Certified Public Accountants (AICPA) and Canadian Institute of Chartered Accountants (CICA). The AICPA and CICA are developing a series of accreditation processes for electronic commerce sites called WebTrust. The *WebTrust for CAs* process focuses on the control objectives identified in ANSI X9.79 PKI Practices and Policy Framework. Several CAs have now been accredited against version 1.0 of the WebTrust Program for Certification Authorities. More information is available at http://www.aicpa.org.

In the European Union, recent regulations require that member states develop systems for supervision of CAs. Some systems will require government supervision; others may be voluntary or co-regulatory schemes. The *tScheme project* in the United Kingdom is developing a co-regulatory scheme. A non-for-profit company, tScheme Ltd., has been established and will perform the CA approval processes against criteria established by the Alliance for Electronic Business (AEB). Other mechanisms are under development in other countries.

The Information Security Committee of the American Bar Association (ABA) is currently developing the PKI Assessment Guidelines (PAG) [ABA-1]. The PAG addresses both technical and business requirements in a legal framework. This document builds upon RFC 2527 and the ABA's Digital Signature Guidelines to support parties that need to assess the trustworthiness of a PKI [ABA-2]. The PAG contains detailed requirements and practices provisions in the format of RFC 2527. These provisions will be very helpful to CP and CPS authors as well. The PAG defines two types of PKI assessments: the first type is performed before the CA begins to issue certificates; the second is performed on a regular basis to demonstrate sustained compliance to a CP or other applicable documents. This document is still incomplete, and is not yet publicly available. Upon completion, the PAG should prove to be an important addition to our tools for PKI assessment.

In summary, accreditation and compliance auditing are crucial to establishing consumer confidence. They also ease the process of cross-certification, providing assurance that a CA implements its stated certificate policies.

Advice for Policy Authors

Development of a certificate policy for an enterprise requires the integration of technical, legal, and business considerations into a single document. Successfully integrating these disparate viewpoints is an inherently political exercise. Acceptance of a CP will require significant buy-in from key players in the organization: the organizational security officer, the legal department, the owners of the most significant applications, and systems support. Not all of these groups will choose to be directly involved, but it is best to invite participation from each.

The first step in developing a CP is to understand the business objectives and requirements that created the need for a PKI. It is also important to review the concept of operations for the business and the proposed system architecture. All of these together will define the scope and other significant parameters for the PKI. The organizational Security Policy should be a significant source of information in this step.

Then, analyze the data and applications that your organization needs to protect, and assess the threats and risks to that data. Consider the impact of security compromise. Laws require some organizations to protect privacy data about their customers. In this case, a security breach might result in fines or civil judgements. In other cases, disclosure may give a competitor an advantage. For example, the competitor may change its own product development schedule to ensure that its new product is first to market. An intelligence operative's life might depend on the secrecy. Disclosure of financial transaction data may have other consequences. Are these one-hundred-dollar or one-million-dollar consequences? Developing a CP without asking these questions is a recipe for disaster.

The CP *must* be appropriate for the data and applications it is intended to support. If the CP is not appropriate, the PKI will be too expensive, or will leave critical data and applications at risk. There is a cost associated with implementing a PKI, and there is a correlation between the level of security and the cost. A higher assurance CP will require more personnel and specify more complex procedures. If an organization is protecting low-risk applications, a lower assurance CP may provide acceptable levels of security at lower cost. On the other hand, a low assurance PKI cannot adequately protect higher risk data and applications.

If the range of sensitivity is too great, it may be appropriate to specify more than one CP. For example, a company may wish to support financial payments of up to a million dollars and also maintain a virtual private network (VPN) for sales employees who telecommute. Successfully masquerading as a company accountant with financial responsibility would clearly be lucrative. The CP that covers those certificates should be stringent. Competitors would like to obtain the company's complete sales data, but the utility of information transmitted by a single salesperson is relatively low. The CP that covers the sales VPN certificates could be much more relaxed.

This company may not be well served by a single CP. If the CP is appropriate for the sales staff, the financial transactions will be placed at risk. If the CP is appropriate for the accountants, it may be too complex or expensive to issue certificates to the sales staff. The company has two choices: implement two distinct policies to meet the requirements of each community or support both at the *higher* security level. The company should analyze the costs and benefits of each strategy, and decide up front if two different CPs are required.

This information can also be used to analyze the costs and benefits of liability insurance. The CA operator may obtain an insurance policy to cover liability claims that are a result of errors and omissions by the CA staff. If the value of the data is particularly high, or the applications cross organizational boundaries, liability insurance may be appropriate.

The second step in developing a CP is to obtain a copy of RFC 2527 and several sample policies that share your objectives. RFC 2527 is the framework for your CP, but not every feature in the outline will apply to your organization. Reading through sample policies will help you assemble a policy that makes sense for your organization. It will also demonstrate due diligence.

RFC 2527 can be obtained from ftp://ftp.ietf.org/rfc/rfc2527.txt. There are numerous sites for publicly available policies. Government agencies can look to NIST Computer Security Objects Registry at http://csrc.nist.gov/csor. One section of the registry is devoted to registration of PKI certificate policies. Most public CAs, such as VeriSign or Digital Signature Trust, publish their policies as well.

If the PKI expects to cross-certify with other existing PKIs, research the certificate and CRL profiles that those PKIs employ. Making your certificate profile consistent with theirs will reduce interoperability problems later. Key aspects are algorithms, critical extensions, and the means of locating revocation data.

The third step is to draft a CP (or CPs) that makes sense for your organization. In the example presented earlier, it makes sense for the company accountants to use strong hardware cryptographic modules validated against FIPS 140-1 Level 2 or higher. On the other hand, the sales staff might be well served by software cryptographic modules validated as meeting FIPS 140-1 Level 1. The CP for accountants should require in-person identity proofing by the company security office. That might not work for the sales staff, though. If members of the sales staff are distributed across the country, they can be authenticated by the Post Office using certified mail.

The fourth step is to decide whether to operate the CA or procure CA services. To operate a CA, the organization may need a physically secure site for its operations and a remote site to store backups. Does your organization have a site with suitable physical controls in place or an installation that could easily be modified to satisfy those requirements? If not, building a new facility is obviously an expensive undertaking. It may be cost-effective to outsource operations of certain PKI components while performing others locally. For example, RA or repository operations may be implemented locally, while the CA operations are outsourced.

If you decide to operate the CA, now is the time to select products that can be used to implement your policy. PKI products are developed with certain policy goals in mind. For example, some products are developed with in-person proofing in mind. Others assume a remote proofing model. Without a CP in hand, it can be difficult to ensure that the selected products are appropriate for the high-level policy.

The PKI products should be able to support all objectives specified in the Identification and Authentication, Operational Requirements, and Technical Security Controls sections of the CP. If the product does not support these objectives, the CA staff will have to implement complex procedures to overcome the product's shortcomings. Additional complexity in the CPS will translate into higher operating costs.

The final documentation step is developing a CPS. If you are going to operate the CA, the CPS identifies the physical sites that will be used. It maps the roles in the CP to the roles and procedures supported by the PKI products and physical controls. The CPS specifies how the controls provided by the PKI products will be used to meet the objectives described in the CP's Authentication, Operational Requirements, and Technical Security Controls sections. If you are procuring services, the service provider has probably written the CPS already. The service provider must demonstrate that its controls and procedures meet your CP.

Now, you are ready to begin fielding your PKI. Begin by training your staff and fielding the PKI for a limited set of users. This includes extracting pertinent portions of the CP and CPS, and ensuring that the appropriate users have the documentation and understand their use. For example, the human resources department must implement the screening procedures. A security awareness plan should also be developed to make sure that operations stay consistent over time. This is particularly important for those in trusted roles, such as the CA operators, RA operators, and system administrators.

Often, initial experiences will result in revisions to the CPS. By limiting the initial set of users, the majority of users can benefit from the experiences of your pioneers. Once the CPS has been finalized, it is time for third-party accreditation. As noted previously, this accreditation is crucial to establishing confidence with users and other CAs.

CHAPTER

13

PKI-Enabled Applications

In this chapter, we explore PKI-enabled applications. Whole books are dedicated to each of these applications, so the coverage here is admittedly superficial. We focus on the role that PKI plays in each application. PKI is central to the handling of digital signatures and symmetric key management.

We explore:

S/MIMEv3. S/MIME version 3 provides security for Internet electronic mail. It can be used to digitally sign and encrypt mail messages. Protection is provided from the message originator to one or more message recipients.

TLS. Transport Layer Security provides authentication and encryption for a communications stream. The communications stream from the client to the server and the communications stream from the server to the client are both protected. TLS is most often used to protect Web content, but it can be used with any stream-oriented application protocol.

IPsec. Internet Protocol Security provides authentication and encryption for individual datagrams. Placement at the network layer (Layer 3) allows IPsec to protect communication from client to server or from one border of an organizational enclave to another.

S/MIMEv3

S/MIME provides security for electronic mail. Electronic mail, or e-mail, is arguably the most widely used Internet service, and it is used in a variety of ways. Since this is such an important networking service, there have been many attempts to standardize secure e-mail solutions: PEM [LINN93, KENT93, BALE93, KALI93b], MOSS [GALV95, CROC95], PGP [ATKI96, ELKI96], OpenPGP [CALL98], and S/MIME. All of them work, and all of them leverage a PKI in one form or another. For a variety of reasons, S/MIME seems to be the solution that is being widely implemented and deployed.

RSA Data Security originally published the S/MIME version 2 (S/MIMEv2) specifications [DUSS98a, DUSS98b], but to achieve broader acceptance, they released the specifications to the IETF. The IETF is not a rubber stamp for specifications developed in other forums. The IETF made several improvements, and created S/MIMEv3 [RAMS99a, RAMS99b, HOFF99].

```
Content-Type: application/pkcs7-mime;
        smime-type=signed-data; name=smime.p7m
Content-Transfer-Encoding: base64
Content-Disposition: attachment; filename=smime.p7m

Certificates and CRLs
One or more digital signatures
Authenticated attributes for each signature, like
        ML Expansion History, Content Description, etc

    Content-Type: application/pkcs7-mime;
            smime-type=enveloped-data; name=smime.p7m
    Content-Transfer-Encoding: binary
    Content-Disposition: attachment; filename=smime.p7m

    Certificates and CRLs
    Recipient and mail list tokens

        Content-Type: application/pkcs7-mime;
                smime-type=signed-data; name=smime.p7m
        Content-Transfer-Encoding: binary
        Content-Disposition: attachment; filename=smime.p7m

        Certificates and CRLs
        One or more digital signatures
        Authenticated attributes for each signature, like
                Receipt Request, Security Label, Signing Time, etc

            Content-Type: text/plain

            Hello, world.
```

Figure 13.1   S/MIMEv3 triple-wrapped message.

Message Signature and Encryption

Both S/MIMEv2 and S/MIMEv3 define two MIME wrappers: one for digital signatures and one for encryption. Both wrappers build on the cryptographic message syntax defined in PKCS#7 [KALI98, HOUS99a]. Digital signatures use the signed-data structure. In addition to signing the content, this structure binds attributes to the content. Encryption uses the enveloped-data structure.

Figure 13.1 illustrates the use of three MIME wrappers. The outermost MIME wrapper and the innermost MIME wrapper provide digital signatures, and the middle MIME wrapper provides encryption. All three MIME wrappers are rarely present. Triple wrapping is used when a message must be digitally signed, then encrypted, and then have attributes bound to the ciphertext. Outer attributes may be provided by the message originator or intermediate mail list agents (MLAs).

There are two ways to MIME encode a signed-data wrapper: `multipart/signed` and `application/pkcs7-mime`. Figure 13.2 shows a signed message using the `multipart/signed` MIME type, and Figure 13.3 shows a signed message using the `application/pkcs7-mime` MIME type. The originator should select the appropriate MIME type based on the capabilities of the intended recipients. If some of the recipients are not S/MIME-enabled, then the `multipart/signed` MIME type should be used since it carries the signed content in one part and the signed-data structure in another part. Recipients without S/MIME capabilities will be able to view the signed content, even if the MIME processing is handled by a remote translating gateway.

```
Content-Type: multipart/signed;
   protocol="application/pkcs7-signature";
   micalg=sha1; boundary=boundary48


--boundary48
Content-Type: text/plain

This format is preferred. Recipients that cannot verify
signatures or decode CMS ASN.1 objects can still read the
message content.

--boundary48
Content-Type: application/pkcs7-signature; name=smime.p7s
Content-Transfer-Encoding: base64
Content-Disposition: attachment; filename=smime.p7s

ghyHhHUujhJhjH77n8HHGTrfvbnj756tbB9HG4VQpfyF467GhIGfHfYT6
4VQpfyF467GhIGfHfYT6jH77n8HHGghyHhHUujhJh756tbB9HGTrfvbnj
n8HHGTrfvhJhjH776tbB9HG4VQbnj7567GhIGfHfYT6ghyHhHUujpfyF4
7GhIGfHfYT64VQbnj756
--boundary48?
```

Figure 13.2 Sample signed message using the `multipart/signed` type.

```
Content-Type: application/pkcs7-mime; smime-type=signed-data;
   name=smime.p7m
Content-Transfer-Encoding: base64
Content-Disposition: attachment; filename=smime.p7m

567GhIGfHfYT6ghyHhHUujpfyF4f8HHGTrfvhJhjH776tbB9HG4VQbnj7
77n8HHGT9HG4VQpfyF467GhIGfHfYT6rfvbnj756tbBghyHhHUujhJhjH
HUujhJh4VQpfyF467GhIGfHfYGTrfvbnjT6jH7756tbB9H7n8HHGghyHh
6YT64V0GhIGfHfQbnj75
```

Figure 13.3   Sample signed message using the `application/pkcs7-mime` type.

Unfortunately, some message transfer systems alter messages that they process, and such manipulation will invalidate the digital signature that S/MIME-enabled recipients will try to validate. The `application/pkcs7-mime` MIME wrapper avoids these manipulations by encapsulating the message content. Unfortunately, only S/MIME-enabled recipients will be able to extract the content.

Only one MIME type is defined for encryption: `application/pkcs7-mime`. Figure 13.4 shows an encrypted message using the `application/pkcs7-mime` MIME type. An S/MIME-enabled recipient is needed to decrypt the content, so there is no need for more than one encryption MIME type.

Enhanced Security Services

S/MIMEv3 supports four important features that were not available in S/MIMEv2:

- Digitally signed receipts
- Security labels
- Mail lists
- Flexible key management

```
Content-Type: application/pkcs7-mime; smime-type=enveloped-data;
   name=smime.p7m
Content-Transfer-Encoding: base64
Content-Disposition: attachment; filename=smime.p7m

rfvbnj756tbBghyHhHUujhJhjH77n8HHGT9HG4VQpfyF467GhIGfHfYT6
7n8HHGghyHhHUujhJh4VQpfyF467GhIGfHfYGTrfvbnjT6jH7756tbB9H
f8HHGTrfvhJhjH776tbB9HG4VQbnj7567GhIGfHfYT6ghyHhHUujpfyF4
0GhIGfHfQbnj756YT64V
```

Figure 13.4   Sample encrypted message.

Digitally signed receipts allow an originator to request a receipt from one or more recipients. When the recipient returns a valid receipt, the originator has proof that the original message was received without modification. The recipient cannot generate a valid receipt unless the originator signed the original message and the recipient was able to validate that signature. Receipts are important in electronic commerce. When Alice sends a purchase order to Bob by e-mail, the receipt returned by Bob gives Alice proof that her purchase order was received without error. Alice specifies that she wants to receive a digitally signed receipt by including a receipt request signed attribute in her message. Bob uses a special signed content to return the receipt. The *signed-receipt* content always uses the `application/pkcs7-mime` MIME type, since the receipt recipient must be S/MIME-enabled.

Security labels allow an originator to specify handling requirements for the message content. Most often, the security label indicates that the message content contains proprietary information or government classified information. Different security labels may appear in the inner signature and the outer signature. A security label in the inner signature specifies the handling requirements for the message plaintext. A security label in the outer signature specifies the handling requirements for the ciphertext. One could imagine one handling requirement for ciphertext when a weak encryption algorithm is used, and a second, less constraining, handling requirement when a strong encryption algorithm is used.

The originator processing to send an encrypted message to a large distribution can be quite time consuming. The originator encrypts the message once under a symmetric key. Then, the originator must encrypt the symmetric key separately, using public key cryptography, for each intended recipient. When the number of recipients is large, it may be desirable to delegate the processing to a trusted server. Such a server is called a *Mail List Agent* (MLA). The originator sends the encrypted message to a single recipient, the MLA, and then the MLA performs the lengthy processing to send the encrypted message to the whole distribution. The MLA need not decrypt the message content to perform its processing, but the MLA does have access to the key that was used to perform the encryption. The originator must select a MLA that is *trusted* to distribute the message only to the intended recipients. Figure 13.5 illustrates the difference in message processing when the originator performs all of the processing and when a MLA is involved. Delegation is not likely for only three recipients, but we did not want to clutter the figure with hundreds of recipients.

MLAs can also be used to conserve bandwidth on expensive network links. Suppose that some of the recipients are in North America, some are in Australia, and the rest are in Europe. An MLA can be set up in each of these regions, subordinate to a master MLA. Alice sends an encrypted message to the master MLA, the master MLA sends the encrypted message to each of the regional MLAs, and finally, each regional MLA sends the encrypted message to the local recipients. In this way, the message only traverses each intercontinental link once. The use of nested MLAs can lead to administrator errors. For example, if the Australian MLA recipient list includes the European MLA, and the European MLA recipient list includes the Australian MLA, the same message could loop forever. To detect and break such loops, MLAs always include an outer signature that includes the *mail list expansion history* signed attribute. When an MLA receives a message, it checks the expansion history to determine if it has already processed this

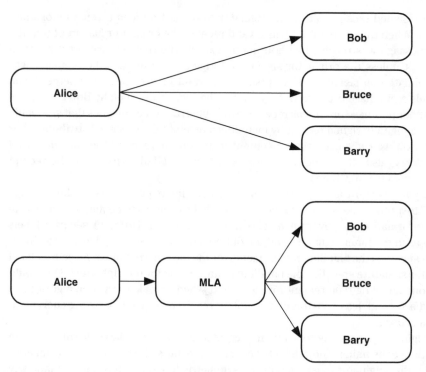

Figure 13.5 The originator delegates time-consuming processing of an encrypted message with a large number of recipients to a Mail List Agent.

particular message. If the MLA has already processed this particular message, it is simply discarded, and the loop is broken. The outer signature provides integrity for the mail list expansion history.

S/MIMEv2 supports only RSA key transport for the secure transfer of the *content-encryption key* from the originator to the recipient. S/MIMEv3 also supports RSA key transport, but it also supports key agreement mechanisms and out-of-band distribution of symmetric *key-encryption keys*. Key agreement mechanisms include the Diffie-Hellman algorithm discussed in Chapter 2, "Cryptography Primer." Out-of-band distribution of key-encryption keys is especially desirable when used in conjunction with MLAs. An MLA can periodically distribute a key-encryption key to its recipients. Then, the MLA can use that symmetric key to efficiently distribute messages to the recipients. Expensive public key operations are only performed to distribute the symmetric key-encryption key. Inexpensive symmetric key operations are used to process user messages.

PKI Support

Certificates are central to all of the services offered by S/MIME (both versions 2 and 3). Encryption, signature, and receipt processing all rely on the binding of an e-mail address to the public key. The e-mail address (also called the RFC 822 address) should be present in the subject alternative name extension (using the rfc822Name name form). Unfortunately, S/MIMEv2 was designed before certificates included extensions, so a less desirable alternative must also be supported. When the subject alternative name extension does not include an e-mail address (rfc822Name), the subject distinguished name can include the e-mail address attribute (emailAddress). Figure 13.6 contains a flow chart used by many S/MIME implementations to determine if the identity contained in a certificate matches a particular e-mail address.

For encryption, the originator must be sure that the key management public key used to distribute the content-encryption key belongs to the intended recipient. If the incorrect public key is used, then an unintended party will have the ability to decrypt the message content. Similarly, the MLA relies on the proper binding of the recipient identity and the key management public key to distribute symmetric key-encryption keys only to the mail list members. The originator and MLA compare the identity in the certificate with the e-mail address of the intended recipient.

For signatures, the recipient must be sure that the signature public key used to verify the message signature belongs to the originator. The recipient must compare the e-mail

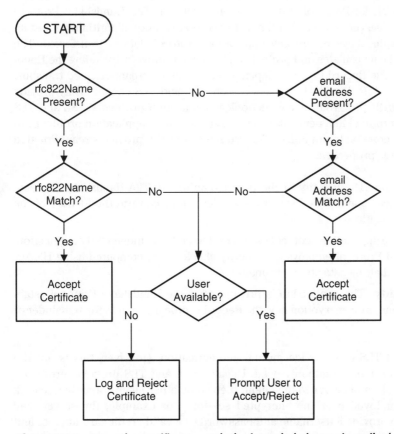

Figure 13.6   Does the certificate match the intended electronic mail address?

address from the SENDER or the FROM header fields in the received message with the e-mail address in the certificate.

For receipts, the receipt validator must be sure that the signature public key used to verify the receipt signature belongs to the receipt signer. The receipt validator must compare the e-mail address from the receipt request to the e-mail address in the certificate.

Transport Layer Security (TLS)

TLS provides security for stream-oriented application-to-application communications; most commonly communication between a Web browser and a Web server. After e-mail, the Web is the most widely used Internet service.

Netscape originally published the Secure Sockets Layer (SSL) [FREI96] specification. Attempting to gain broader acceptance, Netscape released the specifications to the IETF. The IETF process does not simply publish specifications developed elsewhere, so the IETF made several improvements. The result is the TLS [DIER99] specification.

The goal of both SSL and TLS is to provide authentication, integrity, and confidentiality between two communicating applications. The protocols are composed of two layers: the Handshake Protocol and the Record Protocol. The Handshake Protocol authenticates the server and the client, negotiates an encryption algorithm, and establishes cryptographic keys before any application protocol data is transferred. The Record Protocol encapsulates and protects higher-level protocols, including the Handshake Protocol. The Record Protocol depends on a reliable, stream-oriented transport protocol such as TCP [POST81]. For this reason, SSL and TLS cannot easily provide protection for UDP [POST80] or connectionless application protocols. SSL and TLS are application-protocol independent, so any stream-oriented application protocol can transparently operate on top of SSL or TLS. Both SSL and TLS provide stream-oriented security with three properties:

Authentication. The identity of the peer is confirmed. The Handshake Protocol uses certificates and digital signature verification to confirm the identity of the remote application.

Integrity. The application protocol data is protected from undetected modification. The Record Protocol employs an integrity check value, computed using HMAC, to confirm that the data stream is unaltered.

Confidentiality. The connection is private. After the Handshake Protocol establishes a symmetric encryption key, the Record Protocol encrypts the remainder of the session.

Both SSL and TLS can provide mutual authentication. However, this is not the way that they are most commonly used. Usually, SSL and TLS provide certificate-based authentication of server to the client; then some other means of authenticating the client is employed over the encrypted session. For example, the server may ask the client to provide a username and password or a valid credit card number and expiration date.

Handshake Protocol

The Handshake Protocol is comprised of three subprotocols that allow peers to agree upon security parameters for the Record Protocol, authenticate themselves, instantiate negotiated security parameters, and report error conditions to each other.

The Handshake Protocol is responsible for negotiating a session for the Record Protocol, which consists of the following items:

Session identifier. An arbitrary byte sequence chosen by the server to identify a session.

Peer certificate. X.509 certificate of the peer. This element may be absent if authentication is not performed.

Compression method. The algorithm used to compress data prior to encryption.

Cipher spec. Specifies the bulk data encryption algorithm (such as Triple-DES) and the HMAC one-way hash algorithm (such as SHA-1). It also defines cryptographic attributes (such as hash size).

Master secret. A large secret value shared between the client and server.

Is resumable. A flag indicating whether the session can be used to initiate new connections.

These items are then used to set Record Protocol security parameters. The resumption feature allows many protected connections to be established from the single handshake. This feature is used to reduce the overhead, and is especially important when a client and server have several short connections.

The cryptographic parameters are produced by the Handshake Protocol. When a client and server first start communicating, they agree on a protocol version, select cryptographic algorithms, optionally authenticate each other, and use public key cryptography to establish shared secret values. The Handshake Protocol involves the following six steps. Figure 13.7 illustrates the protocol messages that implement these six steps.

1. Exchange *hello messages* to negotiate algorithms and exchange random values.

2. Exchange cryptographic parameters to agree on the *premaster secret*.

3. Optionally exchange certificates and cryptographic information to authenticate the client and server to each other.

4. Generate a *master secret* from the premaster secret and exchanged random values.

5. Provide security parameters to the Record Protocol layer.

6. Confirm that the peer has calculated the same security parameters and that the handshake occurred without tampering.

To improve performance by avoiding pipeline stalls, the change cipher spec message is an independent TLS Protocol content type, and it is not actually a TLS Handshake Protocol message. Figure 13.7 includes the change cipher spec message to show the logical flow.

When the client wants to resume a previous session or duplicate an existing session, the client sends a client hello message that includes the Session ID of the session to be

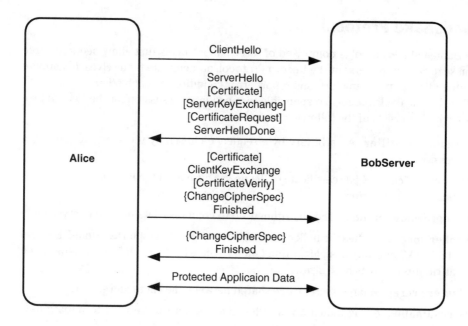

Legend:
[ ]   Optional Handshake Protocol message
{ }   Not really part of the Handshake Protocol

Figure 13.7   TLS Handshake Protocol.

resumed. If the server still has the session parameters in its cache and the server is willing to reestablish the connection, the server sends a server hello message with the same Session ID value. At this point, both the client and server send change cipher spec messages and finished messages.

One should not rely on the Handshake Protocol to always negotiate the strongest possible protection for a connection between two peers. Charlie, employing a man-in-the-middle attack, may be able to convince two peers to select an insecure set of parameters. For example, Charlie might cause the peers to negotiate an unauthenticated connection. To avoid man-in-the-middle attacks, the application protocol must be cognizant of its security requirements and not transmit on the protected stream unless those requirements are met. Of course, this is in conflict with transparently layering applications on SSL and TLS. To preserve transparency, all of the options offered in the negotiation should meet the application protocol security requirements. The SSL and TLS protocols are secure to the level of the cipher suite that is selected. If a Triple-DES symmetric key is transferred using a 1024-bit RSA key from a validated certificate, then one can expect very reasonable cryptographic security.

The certificate and key exchange messages convey the data necessary to establish the premaster secret. When RSA is employed, the client generates the random premaster secret value and encrypts it in the server's RSA public key. When Diffie-Hellman is employed, the client and server exchange public keys; then the result of the classic Diffie-Hellman key agreement computation is used as the premaster secret.

A *pseudorandom function* (PRF) built from SHA-1 [FIPS180] and MD5 [RIVE92] is used to generate the master secret and symmetric keying material. Two different one-way hash functions are used to ensure security even if one of the algorithms is found to have a flaw. The first use of the PRF generates the master secret from the premaster secret and the random values from the client hello message and the server hello message. The second use of the PRF generates two symmetric keys, two IVs, and two MAC secret values from the master secret and the random values from the client hello message and the server hello message. In a resumed session, the master secret from the parent session is used, but new random values are used, resulting in different keying material.

The Record Protocol uses one symmetric key, one IV, and one MAC secret value to protect the traffic from client to server. The Record Protocol uses the other symmetric key, the other IV, and the other MAC secret value to protect the traffic from server to client. Obviously, both client and server need all six secret values for correct operation of the Record Protocol.

Record Protocol

The Record Protocol is composed of several sublayers. It processes application protocol data by fragmenting the data into manageable blocks, optionally compressing the data, computing the integrity check value, encrypting the output from the previous sublayer, and finally transmitting the result. Received data is processed in the opposite order. It is decrypted, integrity checked, optionally decompressed, reassembled, and then delivered to the application.

The Fragmentation sublayer breaks information into records. A record is 16,384 bytes or less. Application protocol message boundaries may not be preserved. Multiple application protocol messages of the same content type may be aggregated into a single record; also, a single application protocol message may be fragmented into several records.

The Compression sublayer performs compression and decompression on all fragments. Initially, the compression method is *null*, but a real compression algorithm can be negotiated. Compression must not lose data.

The Payload Protection sublayer computes an integrity check value on the compressed record, and then encrypts the compressed record and the integrity check value. The integrity check value is referred to as a Message Authentication Code (MAC), even though a keyed hash (HMAC) is used. On reception, decryption recovers the plaintext, and the MAC is recomputed to verify the integrity of the plaintext. The MAC computation also includes an implicit sequence number to detect missing, extra, or repeated compressed records.

When encryption employs a block cipher with a mode that requires an initialization vector (IV), such as Cipher Block Chaining (CBC) mode, the IV for the first record is generated when the security parameters are set by the Handshake Protocol. The IV for subsequent records is the last ciphertext block from the previous record. This technique avoids the transmission of explicit IVs.

Figure 13.8 shows a TLS Record Protocol data unit with all of the sublayer protocol control information. The Payload Protection sublayer includes a header and a trailer;

Protection Head: ContentType ProtocolVersion Length	Compression: ContentType ProtocolVersion Length	Fragmentation: ContentType ProtocolVersion Length	Application Protocol Data	Protection Tail: MAC Pad (Optional) Pad Length (Optional)

Figure 13.8   TLS Record Protocol.

the pad and pad length fields are only present when a block cipher is used for encryption. There is no need for padding when a stream cipher, such as RC4, is used.

PKI Support

Certificates are central to all of the authentication and key management services offered by both TLS and SSL. These services rely on the binding of an identity to the public key. The Domain Name Service (DNS) name (such as, www.spyrus.com or csrc.ncsl.nist.gov) is the preferred name form, and it should be present in the subject alternative name extension (using the dNSName name form). The DNS name is especially well suited for identification of Web servers, but is far from ideal for the identification of a human user at the keyboard of a Web browser. The common name within the subject distinguished name is used for identification when the DNS name is not present. Figure 13.9 contains a flow chart used by many TLS implementations to determine if the identity contained in a certificate matches a particular DNS name.

Recall that the Handshake Protocol certificate and key exchange messages convey the data necessary to establish the premaster secret. Authentication is one result of this exchange. Usually, the server provides a certificate and the client does not, resulting in the authentication of the server to the client, but the client remains anonymous. The server can insist on client authentication by sending the Handshake Protocol certificate request message. In this situation, the client must also have a certificate and present it to the server. Usually, the client presents a signature certificate and a digitally signed Handshake Protocol certificate verify message to demonstrate that the client can generate signatures using the private key that corresponds to the public key contained in the signature certificate.

Certificates should also include the key usage extension. This extension indicates the appropriate uses for the public key contained in the certificate. TLS includes several key usage extension rules:

- The digital signature key usage must be set to allow signature verification.

- The key encipherment key usage must be set to allow RSA encryption.

- The key agreement key usage must be set to allow Diffie-Hellman operations.

The client must be sure that the public key belongs to the server. If the incorrect public key is used, then an unintended party can obtain the premaster secret and have the ability to compute the master secret and all of the symmetric secret values derived from it. The certificate provides the needed binding of the public key to the server's identity.

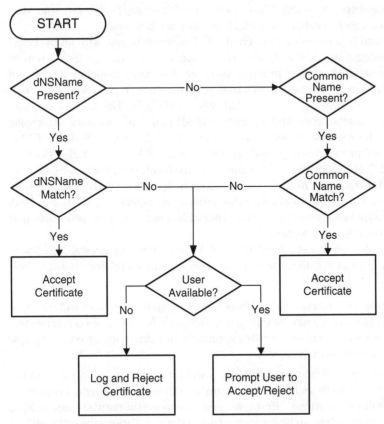

Figure 13.9   Does the certificate match the intended identity?

When client authentication is desired, the server must be sure that the public key belongs to the client. Usually, client authentication is performed to confirm the identity of the client so that the server can make an access control decision. If the incorrect public key is used, then access may be granted to an inappropriate party, or an appropriate party will be denied access. The certificate provides the needed binding of the public key to the client's identity.

IPsec

IPsec provides security for individual IP (Layer 3) datagrams. All Internet traffic is carried by IP datagrams. IPsec protects communication from one machine to another, or it protects communications from one border of an organizational enclave to another. IPsec is the security protocol used to implement *virtual private networks* (VPNs). There were many proprietary solutions developed before the IETF began development of the IPsec specification. Many of these proprietary solutions were studied in the development of

IPsec, but none was selected. Rather, IPsec is a hybrid of the many proprietary solutions. The result is a comprehensive, but complex, IP security architecture.

IPsec is described in a series of 10 documents. The series begins with an overview of the IPsec architecture [KENT98a]. *Security associations* form the foundation of the cryptographic security services provided by IPsec. A security association is shared symmetric keying material and attributes that govern its use. Next, the *Authentication Header* (AH) is specified [KENT98b, MADS98a, MADS98b]. The AH protocol provides IP datagram authentication and integrity, and AH optionally provides anti-replay protection. Next, the *Encapsulating Security Payload* (ESP) is specified [KENT98c, MADS98c]. The ESP protocol may provide IP datagram confidentiality, authentication, and integrity, and ESP optionally provides limited address hiding and/or anti-replay protection. Finally, the *Internet Key Exchange* (IKE) is specified [HARK98, MAUG98, PIPE98, ORMA98]. The IKE protocol provides security associations for AH and ESP. Basically, IKE establishes symmetric keying material and negotiates the attributes that will govern the use of that keying material.

There are several ways to implement IPsec in a host, router, or firewall. An IPsec-enabled router or firewall is called a *security gateway*. Common implementation alternatives include:

Integration into the native stack. Many operating system vendors will integrate IPsec capabilities directly into their IP stack. Access to the IP source code is needed, so third-party vendors cannot use this approach. In many popular operating systems, this code resides in the kernel.

Replacement stack. A third-party vendor may write a complete replacement for the original stack that includes IPsec capabilities in addition to the original communication capabilities. Significant effort is needed to recreate the native IP capabilities, and the operating system architecture may make the installation quite difficult.

Bump-in-the-stack implementations. A third-party vendor may insert an IPsec implementation into the native IP stack. IPsec is inserted between the native IP and the local network drivers. Source code access for the IP stack is not required, making this implementation approach especially appropriate for legacy systems. APIs can make this approach much more straightforward, and avoids the tedious task of reverse engineering module interfaces.

Bump-in-the-wire implementations. Outboard cryptographic processors are commonly used in military and financial industry network security systems. Bump-in-the-wire implementations are usually dual-port devices with high-quality IPsec capabilities and minimal communications capabilities. The bump-in-the-wire device usually has an IP address of its own. When providing security services for a single host, the bump-in-the-wire device may be quite analogous to a bump-in-the-stack implementation. However, when providing security services for a router or firewall, the bump-in-the-wire device must operate as a security gateway.

Security Associations

Security associations are simplex—they apply to communication in a single direction. Two security associations are needed to secure normal bidirectional communications, one for incoming datagrams and one for outgoing datagrams. The security association attributes vary for each protected connection. The security association can name the security protocol (AH or ESP), specify symmetric algorithms and their mode of operation, include authentication keys and encryption keys, define key validity periods, and identify peer IP addresses. These security association attributes direct the processing of incoming security protocol packets, and they direct the security protocol processing for outgoing packets.

A security association is uniquely identified by three items: a *security parameter index* (SPI), a destination IP address, and a security protocol identifier (identifying either AH or ESP). The SPI is an identifier that is carried in AH and ESP to identify the security association. The destination IP address identifies the IPsec peer. In principle, the destination IP address may be a unicast address, a broadcast address, or a multicast group address. However, IKE is currently defined only for unicast addresses. Support for broadcast addresses and multicast group addresses presently requires manual key distribution to all destinations.

Two types of security associations are defined for both AH and ESP: *transport mode* and *tunnel mode*. Figure 13.10 shows when each type of security association must be employed. Figure 13.11 shows two protocol stacks, one employing transport mode and the other employing tunnel mode.

A transport mode security association provides protection between two hosts. In transport mode, the AH or ESP security protocol header appears between the IP header and the higher-layer protocol such as TCP or UDP. Transport mode ESP protects only the higher-layer protocol; it does not protect any part of the IP header. Transport mode AH protects the higher-layer protocol and also protects selected portions of the IP header.

A tunnel mode security association provides protection to an IP tunnel. If either end of a security association is a router or firewall, a tunnel mode security association must be employed. Tunnel mode security associations avoid potential problems with fragmentation and reassembly of AH and ESP packets and problems when multiple paths exist to the same destination behind the IPsec-aware router or firewall. In tunnel mode, the AH or ESP security protocol header appears between two IP headers. The outer IP header specifies the IPsec processing destination, and the inner IP header specifies the ultimate destination for the unprotected datagram. Tunnel mode ESP protects the inner IP header and higher-layer protocol; it does not protect any part of the outer IP header. Tunnel mode AH protects the inner IP header, the higher-layer protocol, and selected portions of the outer IP header.

	Host	Router or firewall
Host	Transport mode or tunnel mode	Tunnel mode
Router or firewall	Tunnel mode	Tunnel mode

Figure 13.10   Security association type used for different communicating peers.

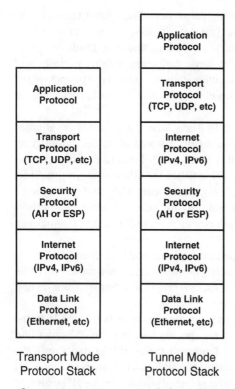

Transport Mode
Protocol Stack

Tunnel Mode
Protocol Stack

Figure 13.11 Transport mode and tunnel mode protocol stacks.

Authentication Header (AH)

The AH security protocol provides integrity for an individual IP datagram, and it authenticates the datagram source, either by source IP address or by end-user name. AH provides integrity for selected portions of the IP header in addition to the higher-layer protocol. AH also offers anti-replay service (really a partial sequence integrity service) to the receiver. This service helps counter denial-of-service attacks. AH does not provide confidentiality.

Either the MD5 or the SHA-1 one-way hash function is combined with a symmetric shared secret to compute an integrity check value.

Figure 13.12 illustrates a typical AH protocol data unit. AH contains five fields:

Next Header. The next header field tells which higher-layer protocol is encapsulated by AH. In tunnel mode, the next header field will always indicate IP (either IPv4 or IPv6). In transport mode, the next header field will usually indicate TCP, UDP, or ICMP.

Length. The length field tells the size of the AH protocol header. The size depends on the one-way hash function employed since the integrity check value is contained in the only variable length field.

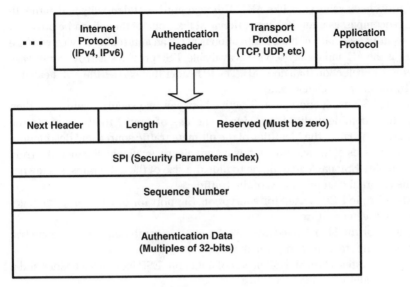

Figure 13.12 AH protocol header.

SPI. The SPI (security parameter index) field contains a 32-bit arbitrary value that identifies the security association. The SPI and the destination IP address uniquely identify the AH security association for this datagram.

Sequence Number. The sequence number field contains the anti-replay sequence number. It contains an unsigned 32-bit monotonically increasing counter value. The sender must include this value; the receiver may either process it or ignore it.

Authentication Data. The authentication data field contains the integrity check value for this datagram. The field is variable length, but it must be a multiple of 32 bits in length.

On transmission, the sequence number is incremented, and then portions of the IP header and the higher-layer protocol are hashed along with the symmetric shared secret to create the integrity check value. On reception, the same calculation is performed. If the calculated integrity check value does not match the one received in the AH protocol, the datagram is discarded. Also, if the security association indicates that the anti-replay facility is in use, then the sequence number must fall within the expected range and it must not duplicate any prior value. If either check fails, the datagram is discarded.

Encapsulating Security Payload

The Encapsulating Security Payload (ESP) protocol can provide confidentiality, authentication, and integrity. ESP provides confidentiality by encrypting the payload (and part of the ESP Header and ESP Trailer). The strength of the confidentiality service depends primarily on the encryption algorithm employed. ESP provides authentication and integrity using an integrity check value (just like AH). Although both confidentiality and authentication (which encompasses integrity) are optional, at least one of them must be provided in each ESP security association. If authentication is used, an anti-replay service with the same features as the AH anti-replay service is available. ESP provides narrower authentication and integrity protection than does AH. The IP header that carries the ESP header is not covered by the integrity check value.

If tunnel mode ESP using encryption is active between two security gateways, then partial traffic flow confidentiality is provided. The use of tunnel mode encrypts the inner IP headers, concealing the identities of the ultimate traffic source and destination. However, the addresses of the security gateways are clearly available. Further, the truly paranoid can employ ESP payload padding to hide the size of the datagrams, somewhat concealing the external characteristics of the traffic.

Either DES or Triple-DES is used for encryption. Support for other encryption algorithms is likely in the near future.

Either the MD5 or the SHA-1 one-way hash function is combined with a symmetric shared secret to compute an integrity check value.

Figure 13.13 illustrates a typical ESP protocol data unit. ESP includes a header and a trailer. The ESP Header contains two fields:

SPI. The SPI (security parameter index) field contains a 32-bit arbitrary value that identifies the security association. The SPI and the destination IP address uniquely identify the ESP security association for this datagram.

Sequence Number. The sequence number field contains the anti-replay sequence number. It contains an unsigned 32-bit monotonically increasing counter value. The sender must include this value; the receiver may either process it or ignore it.

The ESP Trailer contains four fields:

Padding. The padding field ensures that the size of the data to be encrypted is a multiple of the cryptographic block size and that the next header field ends on a 32-bit boundary.

Pad Length. The length field tells the size of the padding. The size depends on the encryption algorithm employed and the extent of traffic flow confidentiality that is desired.

Next Header. The next header field tells which higher-layer protocol is encapsulated by ESP. In tunnel mode, the next header field will always indicate IP (either IPv4 or IPv6). In transport mode, the next header field will usually indicate TCP, UDP, or ICMP.

Authentication Data. The authentication data field contains the integrity check value for this datagram. The field is a variable length, but it must be a multiple of 32 bits in length. If authentication and integrity are not desired, then the authentication data field is absent (or zero bits long).

On transmission, the sequence number is incremented, and then the ESP Header, the higher-layer protocol, and the ESP Trailer, except the authentication data, are hashed along with the symmetric shared secret to create the integrity check value. Next, the higher-layer protocol and ESP Trailer, except the authentication data, are encrypted.

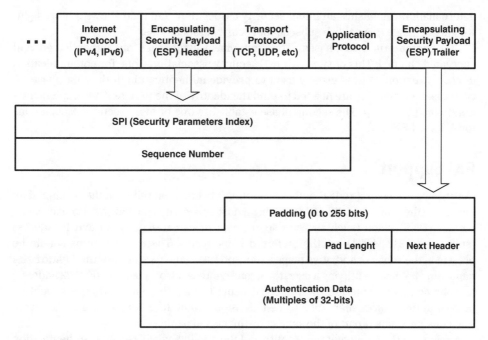

Figure 13.13   ESP protocol header and trailer.

If an initialization vector (IV) is needed, it is carried as a prefix to the ciphertext. On reception, decryption is performed, and then the same integrity check value calculation is performed. If the calculated integrity check value does not match the one received in the ESP Trailer, then the datagram is discarded. Also, if the security association indicates that the anti-replay facility is in use, then the sequence number must fall within the expected range and it must not duplicate any prior value. If either check fails, then the datagram is discarded.

Internet Key Exchange (IKE)

Widespread use of IPsec requires scalable, automated security association management. The on-demand creation of security associations and the anti-replay features of AH and ESP require an automated solution. The Internet Key Exchange (IKE) protocol is the automated solution. IKE is a subset of ISAKMP [MAUG98] and OAKLEY [ORMA98].

The Internet Security Association and Key Management Protocol (ISAKMP) is a complex and comprehensive key management protocol. ISAKMP provide a cryptographic mechanism independent authentication and key exchange framework. IKE selects a core set of features from ISAKMP and selects OAKLEY as the means for symmetric key establishment.

IKE uses OAKLEY to establish a shared symmetric key between two IPsec implementations. OAKLEY includes a variant of Diffie-Hellman key agreement. OAKLEY key determination establishes an initial security association, and then allows a more light-weight exchange to establish subsequent security associations.

IKE operates in two phases. The first phase establishes an authenticated and encrypted channel. This creates two IKE security associations, one for communication in each direction. DSA is usually used to provide authentication in the first phase. In both cases, certificates are needed to bind the identity of the remote IPsec implementation to the public key. The second phase establishes one or more security associations for AH and ESP.

PKI Support

Certificates are central to IKE authentication. Authentication relies on the binding of an identity to the public key. When identifying a host or security gateway, the Domain Name Service (DNS) name (such as www.spyrus.com or csrc.ncsl.nist.gov) and IP address (such as 207.212.34.221) are the preferred name forms. These name forms should be present in the subject alternative name extension (using the dNSName or the iPAddress name form). When identifying a user, the e-mail address (also called the RFC 822 address) and the common name are the preferred name forms. The e-mail address should be present in the subject alternative name extension (using the rfc822Name name form). The common name is part of the subject distinguished name.

A failure in the binding of the identity and the public key will result in authentication failures. An IKE authentication failure could result in key establishment with the wrong IPsec implementation. As a result, an unauthorized individual (or whole subnet of computers) could be admitted access to a VPN.

Certificates should also include the key usage extension. This extension indicates the appropriate uses for the public key contained in the certificate. When DSA is employed, the digital signature key usage must be set to allow signature verification.

Certificates should also include the extended key usage extension. This extension indicates the appropriate applications that the public key was intended to support. IPsec is one of the applications that can be explicitly listed.

Summary

Certificates are central to the security services provided by S/MIME, TLS, and IPsec.

S/MIME identifies users with certificates. Authentication, integrity, non-repudiation, and confidentiality services depend on certificates. Certificates support message encryption, message signature, and receipt signature.

TLS identifies users and servers with certificates. Authentication, integrity, and confidentiality services depend on certificates. Certificates support stream encryption, stream authentication, and stream integrity.

IPsec identifies users, hosts, and security gateways with certificates. Authentication services depend on certificates. Certificates authenticate the exchange of ephemeral Diffie-Hellman public keys, which are used to establish share symmetric keys. These keys are used to provide authentication, integrity, and confidentiality services for individual datagrams.

Defense Message System 1.0

You know the pioneers from all of the arrows in their backs. Public key infrastructure (PKI) is no exception.

The U.S. Military was one of the first organizations to implement and deploy PKI. As we have mentioned several times before, no one implements PKI for its own sake. For the U.S. Military, PKI was needed to support secure (digitally signed and encrypted) electronic messaging. Don Heckman created the Defense Message System (DMS) PKI architecture in February 1994. Don built on some of the efforts that came before, most notably the Internet Privacy-Enhanced Mail (PEM) [LINN89a, KENT89, LINN89b] and Secure Data Network System (SDNS) [SDN701a, SDN702, SDN703] certificate-based key management architectures, and he created a concept that would be used for decades.

As with any long project, DMS has changed the names of many different system components over the years. In this chapter, we use the most current terminology. We hope that this will avoid confusion associated with several different names for the same thing.

First, we describe the DMS 1.0 PKI architecture. Then, building on this background, we discuss the successes and shortcomings of this PKI deployment.

DMS 1.0 Architecture

We provide an overview of the DMS 1.0 PKI architecture. The discussion includes the cryptographic environment, PKI architecture, certificate and CRL profiles, repositories, certificate management, management protocols, failure recovery, and applications.

Cryptographic Environment

DMS uses algorithms approved by the National Security Agency (NSA) to provide confidentiality, integrity, authentication, and non-repudiation (of origin as well as receipt). DMS uses:

- The Digital Signature Algorithm (DSA) for digital signatures
- The Secure Hash Algorithm (SHA-1) as a one-way hash function
- The Key Exchange Algorithm (KEA) for key agreement
- The SKIPJACK algorithm for symmetric encryption

In 1994, SKIPJACK and KEA were classified algorithms. On June 23, 1998, the Department of Defense announced the declassification of SKIPJACK and KEA. The algorithm specifications are available on the Web [NIST98].

All four algorithms are implemented in the FORTEZZA Crypto Card. DMS uses this personal, portable cryptographic token, built primarily by SPYRUS, to securely store keying material and certificates for each DMS user. The FORTEZZA Crypto Card is a PCMCIA card; it is roughly the size of four credit cards stacked on top of each other. The FORTEZZA Crypto Card also includes a trust list with a single certificate, referred to as *slot zero*. Only the certification authority (CA) knows the *System Security Officer Personal Identification Number* (SSO PIN) necessary to update slot zero. DMS uses a hierarchical PKI, and the public key for the single trusted root CA is stored in slot zero.

FORTEZZA Crypto Card initialization and management is performed at the *Certification Authority Workstation* (CAW). The DMS PKI architecture supports worldwide deployment, not just within the Military, but also within other parts of the Government. The PKI can support millions of users. Although the PKI was designed to support the DMS electronic mail environment, it can be used to support a variety of applications.

PKI Architecture

The DMS 1.0 PKI uses a hierarchical structure with several levels of certificate issuers. It supports many user communities, each needing to communicate with each other. Due to their policies, some communities are relatively autonomous, but still need to communicate with users outside their community. To accommodate communication between the communities, a single policy agnostic root CA is shared by all of the communities. This root CA is called the *Policy Approval Authority* (PAA). The *Policy Creation Authority* (PCA) is subordinate to the PAA. The PCA sets the certification policy or policies for a community. Each PCA establishes CAs. The PCA establishes any number of CAs, depending on the quantity and geographic dispersion of the user community. Deployment of CAs is also contingent on the user community policies. For example, a PCA supporting three policies could enable one CA for each policy. Since X.509 v1 certificates cannot include a certification policy extension, the enforcement of this separation is completely procedural. Figure 14.1 depicts the hierarchy.

The PAA generates its own key pairs, and it signs a certificate for itself. This self-signed certificate contains the PAA X.500 Distinguished Name and the PAA public key. This self-signed certificate is placed in slot zero of each FORTEZZA Crypto Card, establishing the single trust point for the collection of communities. Since users do not know the SSO PIN

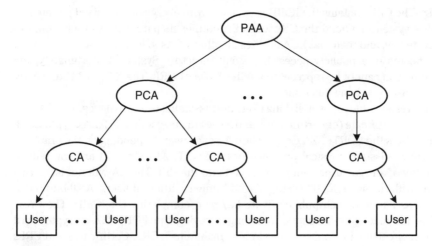

Figure 14.1 DMS 1.0 hierarchical PKI.

for their FORTEZZA Crypto Card, users cannot accidentally or maliciously change the trust point.

The FORTEZZA Crypto Card carries the entire certification path of the user. The PAA, PCA, CA, and user certificates are stored on the FORTEZZA Crypto Card. The certificates are also posted in a publicly accessible X.500 Directory System.

The PAA is a simple and straightforward program. It does not include network protocols. The source code is small enough to be reviewed and understood by one skilled programmer. The simplicity provides confidence that the program is robust and does not perform unexpected functions.

The PAA provides the means for communication among communities, yet each PCA retains control of its community. The PAA is responsible for authenticating PCAs, and then issuing certificates to them. The PCA generates its own key pairs, and then the public key is written to a floppy and carried to the PAA. The PAA reads the PCA public key from the floppy. The PAA ensures that each PCA has a unique X.500 Distinguished Name, and the PAA assigns a 20-bit unique identifier to each PCA. The 20-bit unique identifier is a portion of the unique *Key Material Identifier* (KMID) assigned to each public/private key pair. The PAA generates a certificate for the PCA and writes it to a floppy, which is then carried to the PCA. PAA certificate signing procedures ensure that a rogue PCA cannot be introduced into the PKI. The PAA does not issue CRLs; therefore, it remains offline most of the time. Being offline protects the PAA and the root key stored on its FORTEZZA Crypto Card from many potential attacks.

The PCA is responsible for establishing and enforcing policies within its community. As stated earlier, the X.509 v1 certificate does not have the means to convey policy. Therefore, this policy enforcement is purely procedural. The PCA is also responsible for establishing subordinate CAs, then issuing a FORTEZZA Crypto Card and certificate to each one. The PCA initializes the FORTEZZA Crypto Card for each CA. Again, physical presence of the FORTEZZA Crypto Card reduces the possibility of a rogue CA being introduced into the PKI. The PCA assigns a 20-bit unique identifier to each CA. The 20-bit unique identifier is another portion of the unique KMID assigned by the CA to each public/private key pair. The PCA is responsible for issuing a CRL as well as a *Compromised Key*

List (CKL). The CKL contains the KMID associated with every compromised private key in the entire system. To build the CKL, each CA notifies its parent PCA of any compromised private key, and then that PCA notifies all other PCAs. Like certificates and CRLs, CKLs are posted in a publicly accessible X.500 Directory System. Unfortunately, the revocation reason cannot be represented in the X.509 v1 CRL. The X.509 v2 CRL clearly represents reasons, solving this issue.

The CA is responsible for establishing users and assigning user privileges. The CA generates the user certificate (or certificates), and issues the user a FORTEZZA Crypto Card. The CA initializes the FORTEZZA Crypto Card for each user. Depending on the practices of the certificate issuer, physical presence of the FORTEZZA Crypto Card can reduce the possibility of a rogue user being introduced into the PKI. The CA will not issue two certificates with the same X.500 Distinguished Name to different users. A 20-bit unique identifier is assigned to each public/private key pair, completing the KMID. The CA is responsible for managing its users, including rekeying the FORTEZZA Crypto Card before the user certificate expires. The CA also maintains a CRL. Certificates and CRLs are posted in a publicly accessible X.500 Directory System. The CA must notify the PCA of any compromised user private keys for inclusion on the CKL.

There are two types of DMS users: *individual* and *organizational.* Organizational users represent an organization, and they can commit organizational resources. DMS signed messages sent by an organizational user are easily differentiated from ones sent by an individual user, since a privilege is associated with the DSA public key.

The DMS 1.0 PKI architecture also includes an optional *Local Registration Authority* (LRA), although it is purely a procedural mechanism to streamline CAW processing. A user might enroll with an LRA; then the LRA sends the certificate application to the CAW for processing. The certificate issuer will process the certificate application at the CAW and generate a FORTEZZA Crypto Card and *User Personal Identification Number* (User PIN). The certificate issuer will send the FORTEZZA Crypto Card to the LRA, who will physically deliver it to the user. The certificate issuer will send the User PIN directly to the user.

Certificate and CRL Profiles

DMS 1.0 employs X.509 v1 certificates. X.509 v1 certificates do not readily support all of the DMS 1.0 requirements, so some unique features were shoehorned into the certificates. These unique certificates are often called *MISSI v1 certificates.* The system was designed before X.509 v3 certificates were invented. In fact, many of the lessons learned in DMS 1.0 guided the design of X.509 v3 certificates.

A DMS 1.0 X.509 v1 certificate contains the user's X.500 Distinguished Name, a KMID, the user's security clearance, two public keys, and privileges associated with each of the public keys. The X.500 Distinguished Name is carried in the subject field, and the rest of the data is carried in the subject public key information field. Figure 14.2 illustrates the method used to pack all of this data into the subject public key information field. Since the subject public key field is defined as a bit string, the packing of additional data into the fields is straightforward. The first portion of the structure is associated with the KEA public key, and the second portion of the structure is associated with the DSA public key.

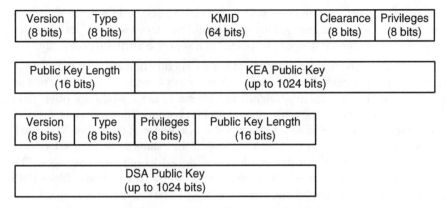

Figure 14.2   Subject public key field in DMS 1.0 certificates.

KEA Version. The first version field specifies the format of the data contained in the KEA portion of the structure. This allows for future modifications to the structure, if required. The value is zero.

KEA Type. The first type field specifies the following public key is used with KEA. The value is one.

KMID. The KMID field contains a systemwide unique value. The KMID is composed of four components: a 4-bit reserved value, set to zero; a 20-bit PCA value; a 20-bit CA value; and a 20-bit user value. This structure ensures that a universally unique KMID is assigned to each KEA key. The KMID is placed on the CKL if either the KEA or DSA private key is compromised.

KEA Clearance. The Clearance field has a structure that allows it to be a multiple of eight bits in length, but in practice, it is always exactly eight bits long. The last octet of the field has its most significant bit set to zero, while the other octets of the field contain a one in the most significant bit position. The remaining 7 bits of each octet are interpreted as a bit-mapped set of authorizations. The clearance bit mask is defined in Figure 14.3. The values in the bit mask map to the hierarchical classification levels assigned to information according to the harm that

Clearance Values	Bit Position
Extension Flag (set to zero)	7 [MSB]
Unclassified	6
Unclassified but Sensitive	5
Confidential	4
Secret	3
Top Secret	2
[Reserved]	1
[Reserved]	0 [LSB]

Figure 14.3   Security clearance bit mask.

unauthorized disclosure would cause to the United States. In a X.509 v3 certificate environment, clearance information would be placed in a subject directory attributes extension, or it would be placed in a separate attribute certificate.

KEA Privileges. The first privileges field has a structure that allows it to be a multiple of 8 bits in length, but in practice, it is always exactly 8 bits long. The last octet of the field has its most significant bit set to zero, while the other field octets contain a one in the most significant bit position. The remaining 7 bits of each octet are interpreted as a bit-mapped set of authorizations. The KEA privilege bit mask is defined in Figure 14.4. Three of the values in the bit mask map to the hierarchical message priorities levels assigned to military messages. The third position in the bit mask value identifies a special server that bridges DMS to the legacy military messaging communications system, called AUTODIN.

KEA Public Key Length. The KEA public key length field contains the length (in octets) of the following KEA public key field. In practice, it is always set to 128.

KEA Public Key. The KEA public key field contains the KEA public key.

DSA Version. The second version field specifies the format of the data contained in the DSA portion of the structure. This allows for future modifications to the structure, if required. The value is zero.

DSAType. The second type field specifies the following public key is used with DSA. The value is two.

DSAPrivileges. The second privileges field has a structure that allows it to be a multiple of 8 bits in length, but in practice, it is always exactly 8 bits long. The last octet of the field has its most significant bit set to zero, while the other octets of the field contain a one in the most significant bit position. The remaining 7 bits of each octet are interpreted as a bit-mapped set of authorizations. The DSA privilege bit mask is defined in Figure 14.5. Five of the values in the bit mask map to roles in the system. The first position in the bit mask value regulates signing. This capability allows an administrative assistant to decrypt and read messages for his or her boss, but the administrative assistant cannot generate a signed message claiming to come from his or her boss. In a X.509 v3 certificate environment, the Certification Authority flag would be placed in a basic constrains extension, and the read-only flag would be handled by a key usage extension.

Privilege Values	Bit Position
Extension Flag (set to zero)	7 [MSB]
Critic/Flash (Urgent)	6
Immediate/Priority (Normal)	5
Routine/Deferred (Non-Urgent)	4
Multi-Function Interpreter	3
[Reserved]	2
[Reserved]	1
[Reserved]	0 [LSB]

Figure 14-4 KEA privilege bit mask.

```
Privilege Values                              Bit Position
Extension Flag (set to zero)                  7 [MSB]
Organizational Releaser                       6
Policy Creation Authority                     5
Certification Authority                       4
Local Management Authority                    3
Configuration Vector Authority                2
No Signature Capability/Read Only             1
[Reserved]                                    0 [LSB]
```

Figure 14.5   DSA privilege bit mask.

DSA Public Key Length. The second public key length field contains the length (in octets) of the following DSA public key field. In practice, it is always set to 128.

DSA Public Key. The DSA public key field contains the DSA public key.

Repositories

As stated previously, DMS stores certificates and CRLs in an X.500 Directory.

Separate roles create the Directory entry and issue the certificate. Separating these functions makes it much more difficult for a rogue CA to issue certificates to unauthorized users. Thus, only the Directory administrator can create an entry in the Directory, and the user entry must be created before the CAW generates a certificate. Coordination between the certificate issuer and the Directory administrator is necessary to avoid errors when the CAW tries to post the user certificate. The certificate issuer and the Directory administrator must use exactly the same spelling for all portions of the subject distinguished name. Typographical errors lead to certificates that cannot be posted and must be revoked.

Certificate Management

The CAW was developed by BBN under contract to NSA. The CAW is used to implement the PAA, PCAs, and CAs. The CAW runs on the SCO\Secureware trusted UNIX operating system on an Intel-based hardware platform. The CAW has a network connection, enabling X.500 directory access. The CAW functionality includes generation and distribution of certificates, CRLs, and CKLs; programming FORTEZZA Crypto Cards; and audit.

A trusted operating system is needed to implement strong role segregation. The CAW has three roles: certificate issuer (or *CAW Operator*), *CAW Administrator*, and *CAW Site Security Officer*. Each of these three roles has separate duties, making it extremely difficult for a single person with physical access to attack the CAW. Security testing demonstrated that the CAW is extremely difficult to successfully penetrate. A successful CAW penetration is considered the issuance of a bogus certificate or CRL.

The certificate issuer, CAW Administrator, and CAW Site Security Officer are trusted roles. One person may not have more than two of these roles. Each person receives training in the proper operation of the CAW.

Certificate issuers register users. User registration policy and procedures are different in each organization. User registration builds on the procedures that organizations already employ to identify employees and their roles, responsibilities, and privileges. As part of registration, the human user must offer proof of his or her identity, such as a picture identification card. The certificate issuer must document the information provided at user registration, including the source of clearance and privilege information. Many hours were spent designing the forms to reduce the likelihood of mistakes.

DMS imposes a restriction on X.500 Distinguished Names that an issuer can assign to a subject: the subject distinguished name must be subordinate to the issuer distinguished name. *Subordinate* means that the subject distinguished name contains every component except the last component of the issuer distinguished name. Certificate users must confirm this subordinate relationship as part of certificate validation. Validation fails if this relationship is not present. This rule prevents one issuer from registering users who appear to be part of another community. Figure 14.6 illustrates name subordination. The valid subject distinguished name contains the same initial five components as the issuer distinguished name; however, the fifth component of the invalid subject distinguished name does not match the fifth component as the issuer distinguished name. In an X.509 v3 certificate environment, name subordination would be enforced with a name constraints extension.

For each certificate, the CA must:

1. Assign a unique subject distinguished name that is subordinate to the issuer distinguished name.

2. Assign a locally unique 20-bit value that is combined with the 20-bit value from the PAA and the 20-bit value from the PCA to form a KMID that is unique within the entire system.

3. Generate the user's KEA and DSA key pairs on the FORTEZZA Crypto Card.

4. Determine the user's clearance and privilege bit mask values.

5. Build and sign the certificate.

```
Issuer Distinguished Name
C=US;O=U.S. Government;OU=DoD;OU=Air Force;OU=7CG;CN=CA Number 48


Valid Subject Distinguished Name
C=US;O=U.S. Government;OU=DoD;OU=Air Force;OU=7CG;OU=CMM;CN=Howard Berg


Invalid Subject Distinguished Name
C=US;O=U.S. Government;OU=DoD;OU=Air Force;OU=1ISG;OU=CMM;CN=Howard Berg
```

Figure 14.6   Valid and invalid subordinate distinguished names.

Once the user certificate is signed, the CA stores it in a local database, posts it to the X.500 Directory, and programs it on the user's FORTEZZA Crypto Card. Part of programming the FORTEZZA Crypto Card includes the storage of the PAA self-signed certificate in slot zero. The rest of the user's certification path is also stored on the FORTEZZA Crypto Card.

As part of programming the FORTEZZA Crypto Card, a User PIN is assigned. The user needs the User PIN to unlock the FORTEZZA Crypto Card and access the cryptographic functions that it implements. The CA delivers the FORTEZZA Crypto Card and the User PIN to the user, using separate paths.

In DMS, the user public/private key pairs are updated every five years. The CA will not issue a certificate with a validity period longer than five years to ensure that the keys are not used too long. Usually, the certificate lifetime is three years, which corresponds to the duration of the normal military assignment. To accomplish key update, the user returns his or her FORTEZZA Crypto Card to the CA that issued the original certificate. The CA then generates a new key pair, signs the new user certificate, and returns the FORTEZZA Crypto Card containing the new certificate back to the user. The CA also posts the new certificate into the X.500 Directory.

When keys and certificates are updated, the FORTEZZA Crypto Card maintains the new and the previous public/private key pairs, as well as their corresponding certificates. Retaining the old generation of keys and certificates ensures that users will be able to decrypt messages that were sent to them using the older keys.

Management Protocols

DMS 1.0 did not include any management protocols. All transactions were performed out-of-band. This was quickly recognized as a shortcoming. At this point in time, there were no standard certificate management protocols, so Dave Solo invented one for DMS 2.0: the *MISSI Management Protocol* (MMP) [SDN908]. Enabling communications between superior and subordinate CAs was the major requirement.

MMP has many of the same properties as CMC [MYER00], discussed in Chapter 11, "PKI Management Protocols." MMP defines a message content for communications between components of the PKI. The MMP content is encapsulated in the Message Security Protocol [SDN701a, SDN701b, SDN701c], which provides integrity, authentication, and confidentiality.

The use of secure electronic mail for PKI management traffic is especially well suited for DMS. The messaging infrastructure is ubiquitous. Further, firewalls are in place to allow messages to safely flow in and out of protected enclaves. This allows the CAW serving the users within the enclave to be housed within the enclave itself.

One feature that is unique to MMP, and unavailable in CMC, is the reporting of key compromise for inclusion in the CKL. CMC presumes the use of X.509 v2 CRLs that include revocation reason codes, making CKLs unnecessary.

Failure Recovery

Should a FORTEZZA Crypto Card fail, the private keys that are stored inside are lost. The loss of PAA, PCA, or CA keying material would have major ramifications to all DMS users. For example, the loss of a CA's FORTEZZA Crypto Card would require all of that CA's users to obtain new certificates. Even though the loss of the CA signing key does not invalidate the already issued certificates, it does prevent the CA from issuing any more CRLs. Without current CRLs, the existing certificates cannot be considered valid. To prevent such a loss, the FORTEZZA Crypto Card is duplicated and securely retained. Duplication is achieved by special commands that encrypt the private keying material stored on one FORTEZZA Crypto Card for decryption and storage inside another FORTEZZA Crypto Card, and it requires the involvement of two people. This technique ensures that the backup is done correctly, even if one of the people is malicious.

User FORTEZZA Crypto Card information may be securely retained at the discretion of the CA. In practice, KEA private keys are retained to facilitate data recovery, but DSA keys are not retained. Therefore, when a user FORTEZZA Crypto Card does fail, the user is given a new FORTEZZA Crypto Card, the KEA public/private keys are restored, new DSA public/private keys are generated, and new certificates are created. This allows the user to decrypt any previously encrypted traffic. Signatures generated by the user can still be validated with the old certificate, but new signatures must be validated with the new certificate.

Applications

DMS 1.0 has one primary application: X.400 messaging. The *Message Security Protocol* (MSP) [HOUS95, SDN701] is used to protect the message content. MSP provides the same security services as S/MIME v3 [RAMS99a, RAMS99b, HOFF99], discussed in Chapter 13, "PKI-Enabled Applications." However, MSP and S/MIME v3 bundle the security services differently. When a user sends a message, the user may elect to sign it, encrypt it, or sign and encrypt it. When the message is encrypted, MSP provides confidentiality, integrity, authentication, and label-based access control. Inclusion of a security label in an encrypted message is required. When the message is signed, MSP provides the major components of non-repudiation with proof of origin. The originator of a signed message may request a signed receipt from one or more recipients. When the recipient returns a signed receipt, MSP provides the major components of non-repudiation with proof of delivery.

Once the PKI was deployed to support secure messaging, additional uses were found, including Web security. Secure messaging remains the primary use. The algorithms implemented by the FORTEZZA Crypto Card are not widely supported in commercial products, and the placement of two public keys in the certificate subject public key information field is not widely supported either. Despite these issues, both Netscape and Microsoft choose to support the FORTEZZA Crypto Card in their Web security products.

Successes and Shortcomings

Despite the fact that the DMS 1.0 was one of the first PKI deployments, the developers did many things right. These things should be emulated. However, some choices had unpleasant ramifications, and these should be avoided.

The hierarchical PKI with a single, offline, policy agnostic root CA is scalable, and it readily supports multiple certification policies. As we will see, this topology has been used in other successful PKI deployments. It offers a robust foundation.

Unfortunately, the DMS CP cannot be represented in the X.509 v1 certificate. The only way for a certificate validator to determine the policy is to follow the certification path to the PCA, and then use the PCA distinguished name to infer the policy. No DMS software uses this error-prone technique. The X.509 v3 certificate policy extension solves this issue by conveying certificate policy identifiers. The lack of this information has forced the entire DMS community to implement roughly the same policy, even though the PKI topology readily supports multiple policies. The inability to include policy identifiers in certificates has prevented some user communities with distinct policy requirements from using DMS 1.0 (and DMS 2.0). Support for X.509 v3 certificates is part of DMS 3.0, so these user communities will be included in the future.

The use of hardware to protect the PAA, PCA, and CA private keys is prudent. Hardware provides significant protection against disclosure of the private key. Further, the FORTEZZA Crypto Card ensures that an authorized certificate issuer (that is, a human who knows the PIN) is operating the CAW. The hardware cannot ensure that only valid certificates are signed. However, the CAW architecture, building on the trusted operating system, provides many assurances in this area.

Similarly, the use of hardware to protect user private keys is prudent. The FORTEZZA Crypto Card offered four benefits beyond private key protection. First, it provides two-factor user authentication. The user must possess the FORTEZZA Crypto Card, and the user must know the PIN. Second, it provides a high-integrity means to distribute the trust point (the PAA public key) to all of the users. Third, it provides a personal and portable key container. The user can easily transfer the personal private keys to any workstation. Fourth, the user's certificate path was part of the mobile container. While this information does not need protection, carrying this information reduces the number of X.500 Directory queries, and it enables the simple and straightforward inclusion of these certificates in signed and encrypted messages. Inclusion of the user certificate path in messages simplifies recipient validation and further reduces the number of X.500 Directory queries.

The involvement of two people in a private key duplication along with other safeguards provide technical controls that limit the damage that a hostile CAW operator can cause.

Unfortunately, the FORTEZZA Crypto Card also has some deployment headaches. Many computers do not have PCMCIA adapters, so they must be purchased and added. The PCMCIA adapter can cost several times more than the FORTEZZA Crypto Card itself. In addition, device drivers are needed for every operating system variety. Installing the PCMCIA adapters and configuring the appropriate device drivers requires a skilled technician. These trained technicians are in short supply.

The CAW was developed before the DMS Certification Policy (CP) was written. Fortunately, the designers anticipated many of the policy elements and included significant flexibility. As a result, the DMS CP is fully implemented by the combination of the trained certificate issuer and the CAW hardware and software. The DMS CP requires the certificate issuer to validate the identity of the user. No computer program can perform this function. The realization that the human user is an important part of policy implementation cannot be overlooked. This is true in this PKI and every other PKI that requires face-to-face enrollment.

Unfortunately, with flexibility comes complexity. The CAW Graphical User Interface (GUI) is very complex. The GUI complexity leads to additional certificate issuer training requirements. Despite the additional training, the GUI complexity results in a significant number of human data entry errors. When these errors result in the issuance of an incorrect certificate, it must be revoked, and the user FORTEZZA Crypto Card must be reprogrammed. These errors affect the entire user community by making the CRL larger. Simplification of the CAW GUI could reduce training costs and reduce CRL size.

The use of an LRA could also reduce the GUI-related errors. By providing an LRA with a registration tool, the LRA performs the data entry on behalf of the CA. Then, the LRA electronically sends the data to the certificate issuer for automated processing at the CAW, minimizing the chance of data entry errors. Further, profiles and templates were added in later CAW versions to reduce data entry errors.

The Military deployed about 400 CAWs. In general, two certificate issuers are trained for each CAW. In large organizations, these can be full-time positions, but they are usually part-time duties. The personnel and training costs for the 800 certificate issuers were not anticipated by the original DMS plan. A way to reduce these costs must be found.

The DMS certificate includes authorization information. The certificate issuer is not usually in a role to know the authorizations of every user in the community that he or she supports. Additional processes and procedures are used to obtain this information to include it in the certificate. Obtaining authorization information further complicates the training requirements for certificate issuers. An architecture that allowed the certificate issuer to create an identity certificate (binding the user identity to a public key) and authorization issuers to create attribute certificates (binding the user identity to a set of authorizations) would significantly reduce these costs. Attribute certificates are discussed further in Chapter 17, "Future Developments."

The CKL is unique to the DMS 1.0 (and DMS 2.0) PKI. The means of bundling subject public keys and authorization information is also unique to the DMS PKI. It is included in DMS 1.0 and DMS 2.0, and it will remain part of DMS 3.0. The use of unique structures ensures that the DMS user community could not employ a commercial-off-the-shelf product. Other nonsecurity DMS unique features also have this impact. The use of nonstandard structures increases the client software costs.

The CKL also requires communications between infrastructure components that might not otherwise be needed. However, the CKL capability can be achieved with a combination of X.509 v3 certificate extensions and X.509 v2 CRL extensions. The use of CRL distribution points and indirect CRL capabilities offers a standard-based alternative. DMS 3.0 will adopt this standards-based approach.

The bundling of key management and digital signature keys into one certificate has both benefits and complications. The benefits include:

- A single certificate with two public keys is smaller than two certificates.

- In environments without Directory support, the sending of a signed message permits the recipient to reply with an encrypted message. This simple and straightforward bootstrap technique has allowed the DMS 1.0 PKI to support Directory-impaired application environments.

- Some PKI-enabled applications, such as SSL, use a single key pair for both signature and key management. It is relatively easy to modify such applications to support a single certificate containing two public keys. Yet, the major disadvantages associated with the use of a single key pair are avoided.

The complications include:

- Compromise of one of the private keys requires revocation of the certificate containing both public keys, preventing use of the uncompromised key until a new certificate is issued. Since both of the private keys are stored on the same FORTEZZA Crypto Card, the assumption that both are compromised if one of them is compromised is probably valid. This assumption will not be true in other environments.

- The ramifications associated with loss or disclosure of a signature key are different from loss or disclosure of a key management key. Using separate key pairs in separate certificates permits a balanced and flexible response. Further, key recovery for key management private keys without providing key recovery for signature keys is more complicated when the two keys are tightly linked. Key recovery is more straightforward with two separate certificates.

- Different validity periods for each key pair may be appropriate in some application environments. This cannot be accomplished if the two public keys are in one certificate.

- The message originator never needs the signature public key of the message recipient. Further, by including the signature certificate in the signed message, the recipient never needs to search for the originator signature certificate. For these reasons, one might choose to omit user signature certificates from the repository. Bundling the two keys into one certificate removes this alternative.

The name subordination technique was copied from PEM [KENT89]. Unfortunately, these checks are not routinely part of X.509 v1 certificate validation. Further, cross-certification with non-DMS communities cannot be done safely without a robust means of limiting the name space of a particular CA. The X.509 v3 name constraints extension will solve this issue. Again, support for X.509 v3 certificates is part of DMS 3.0.

Lessons Learned

The DMS 1.0 PKI has many lessons. They include:

Use X.509 v3 certificates. DMS 1.0 did not have X.509 v3 certificates, and specialized software was needed to implement certification policies and name constraints. Unique mechanisms can be expensive.

Use X.509 v2 CRLs. DMS 1.0 did not have X.509 v2 CRLs, and specialized software was needed to implement rapid notification of key compromise. Unique mechanisms, like CKLs, can be expensive, and they can impose complex administrative requirements on certificates.

Avoid special certificate validation rules. The certificate validation should be based on the certificate content, not special validation rules. Name subordination should be enforced using the name constraints extension. Implementation of special rules requires specialized software. If complex user software setup is needed, expect user problems and greater technical support costs.

Use two certificates. There are advantages to bundling two public keys into a single certificate; however, there are more advantages to two single-key certificates, one containing a signature key and the other containing a key management key.

Use hardware to protect important keys. Use hardware to protect all PKI component keys. The incremental cost is not significant. Depending on the value of information and the consequences from disclosure, the use of hardware may be warranted to protect user keys. In DMS 1.0, hardware protects both PKI infrastructure keys and user keys.

Create secure backup copies of CA signing keys. Loss or failure of a hardware cryptographic module that contains the CA signing key creates major operational problems. In the worst case, all certificates issued by a particular CA must be reissued. These problems can be avoided by duplicating the CA signing key in a spare hardware cryptographic module. This backup module must be protected with strong physical security and robust procedures. If an attacker were to obtain the backup module and the authentication data necessary to make use of the signing key stored within it, certificates and CRLs that are indistinguishable from the genuine article could be generated.

Consider manpower. The people needed to operate and maintain the PKI components represent a real cost. The costs associated with these people must be factored into any deployment plan. The training of these people must also be considered.

Separate RA and CA functions. User registration must be as easy as possible for the user and for the certificate issuer.

Limit identity certificate information. User attributes should be managed separately. Inclusion of too many user attributes will reduce the useful lifetime of the certificate and increase the likelihood of revocation. User attributes can be placed in attribute certificates, directories, or databases.

Consider certificate life cycle. DMS 1.0 required each user to bring his or her FORTEZZA Crypto Card to the CAW for every update. This solution does not scale, and it frustrates the users. Enabling electronic interactions with the PKI after enrollment is desirable.

CHAPTER 15

California Independent Service Operator

The California Independent Service Operator (CAISO) used a very methodical approach to select its technology providers. CAISO wanted the best-of-breed products for its entire system. It did not want the best collection of suppliers that a particular system integrator could meld into a team. CAISO established a contract with each of the chosen technology providers; then it established a contract with a system integrator to construct a system from the best-of-breed products.

CAISO conducted an extensive review of all available products. Three CAISO employees ranked each product based on present capabilities, current development activities, and planned features. Each product was rated against the CAISO requirements. Ten points were given for inclusion of mandatory features, seven points for inclusion of desirable features, and so on. In the end, all three graders had the same ordering of the products. Of course, the exact values were different. The products with the highest grades were selected.

CAISO operates the electric power grid for most of California. The first phase of the CAISO project is a closed PKI supporting energy trading, auctions, and generation. Since the concept of digital signatures and certificate policy was (and still is) very new to the energy industry, Steve Dougherty, CAISO Director of Information Security Services, wanted to gain experience with PKI technology without waiting for acceptance of digital signature law. Since over 50 different companies and a few regulatory agencies participate in the overall system, Steve did not want to delay the system deployment while attorneys from each participant reviewed the CP and CPS. Consensus within such a large and diverse group in a relatively new technology area would not be easy to reach. To avoid many issues, non-repudiation is not part of the service offered by the PKI. CAISO relies on existing tariffs for the legal and liabilities foundation. CAISO simply requires compliance with the CP and CPS as a condition of participation in the energy system.

Later phases of the CAISO project, once the digital signature legal infrastructure matures, will embrace non-repudiation. In the future, applications will sign schedules and bids, bringing non-repudiation into the system. All of the applications will be modified to digitally sign their transactions. Archiving each digitally signed transaction will also be part of this upgrade.

The PKI supports every aspect of CAISO's mission. It was designed to support all phases of the CAISO project. While the certificate policy does not presently support non-repudiation, the PKI design will readily accommodate non-repudiation once the applications begin digitally signing transactions and the legal infrastructure is available. Today, the PKI supports:

- Command and control of the power grid
- Brokerage of electric power
- Administrative communications

Three different certification policies are used, one for each aspect of the mission. All three policies are part of a single hierarchical PKI.

KPMG supported CAISO throughout the effort. Brad Fisher, a partner at KPMG, assembled the skilled PKI development team. Jon Graff designed the PKI architecture. Rena Mears and Michael Fagen helped with the PKI development and drafted the CP and CPS. Peter Walker managed the RFI, RFC, RFP, and RFQ process, leading to the selection of SPYRUS as the PKI technology provider, SPYRUS as the cryptographic hardware provider, and SAIC as the system integrator.

The SAIC system integration team helped CAISO with every aspect of the system deployment. Mike Walker, the SAIC Project Manager, and Terri Bush were instrumental in the PKI deployment. With the help of Jim Reynante, Mike and Teri also provided assistance to application vendors with the PKI integration. Jim also set up the PKI system hardware, ensuring a secure configuration. Maria Eleana Garcia set up the PKI software, instantiating the CAISO PKI system.

In this chapter, we describe the CAISO PKI architecture. Then, building on this background, we discuss the successes and shortcomings of this PKI deployment.

CAISO Architecture

We provide an overview of the CAISO PKI architecture. The discussion includes the cryptographic environment, PKI architecture, certificate and CRL profiles, certificate management, certification policies, management protocols, failure recovery, and applications.

Cryptographic Environment

CAISO uses commercial algorithms to provide authentication, integrity, and confidentiality services for mission-critical applications. CAISO uses:

- RSA for digital signatures and key management
- MD5 and SHA-1 for one-way hash functions
- RC2 and RC4 for symmetric encryption

The CAISO PKI uses the FORTEZZA algorithm suite to provide authentication, integrity, and confidentiality for communications between PKI components. The CAISO PKI uses:

- DSA for digital signatures
- SHA-1 as a one-way hash function
- Key Exchange Algorithm (KEA) for key management
- SKIPJACK for symmetric encryption

The user algorithms are implemented in both hardware and software. Some components in the CAISO system require hardware protection of the keying material, but software protection is sufficient for other system components. For control of the power grid, the SPYRUS LYNKS Privacy Card (a PCMCIA card) is used to protect the keys and execute the algorithms. For brokerage of electricity, the SPYRUS Rosetta smartcard is used to protect the RSA keys and execute the RSA algorithm; the other algorithms are executed in software. For administrative communications and one-time Internet auctions, Netscape browser software is used to protect the keys and execute the algorithms.

The Internet auction application was custom developed by Trading Dynamics for CAISO. When the project started, Trading Dynamics knew very little about public key cryptography or PKI. With Jahan Moreh from Michigan Group as a tutor, Trading Dynamics developed a solid application, and the first successful auction for futures trading of congestion for paths along the power grid ran in 1999. This success led to the purchase of Trading Dynamics by Ariba, and this application is the auction solution offered by Ariba.

Private keys for PKI components should be protected at least as well as any of the subscriber keys. To this end, the CAISO CAs and RAs use the LYNKS Privacy Card to protect keys and execute the algorithms.

LYNKS Privacy Card and Rosetta smartcard initialization and management is performed at the SPYRUS PKI *Registration Authority* (RA). User LYNKS Privacy Cards generate their own RSA public/private keys. User Rosetta smartcards do not generate their own RSA public/private keys. While these smartcards are capable of generating RSA public/private keys, they take several minutes to do so. For this reason, the RA LYNKS Privacy Card generates a RSA public/private key pair, which is then securely transferred into the Rosetta smartcard. Special commands in the LYNKS Privacy Card and in the Rosetta smartcard allow this secure operation. The Netscape browser generates its own keying material; then a Web interface, called *WebReg*, is used to certify the pubic key.

PKI Architecture

The CAISO PKI uses a hierarchical structure. The structure is very similar to the one employed by DMS 1.0. It supports four policies, one for each aspect of their mission plus an additional policy exclusively for testing. The root CA is called the *Policy Approval Authority* (PAA). One *Policy Creation Authority* (PCA) is subordinate to the PAA. The PCA defines all four CAISO policies, called *Test, Basic, Medium,* and *High.* Unlike the DMS 1.0 PCA, the CAISO PCA supports multiple policies simultaneously. The certificate policies extension determines the applicable policy rather than PKI topology. One Certification Authority (CA) is subordinate to the PCA for each policy. One or more RAs support each CA. A Web server application, called WebReg, provides communications support to the RA serving Basic CA.

Figure 15.1 depicts the hierarchy of CAISO operational policy CAs; the Test CA is omitted for clarity. Aldo Nevarez, CAISO Senior Information Security Manager, is responsible for the development, implementation, and operation of the components shown. In addition to the PKI, Aldo is also responsible for the overall security architecture, security policies, and standards. Tom Litney and Jim Burden, Security Engineers at CAISO, were responsible for developing and implementing the network security architecture, including the PKI. They were instrumental in selecting SPYRUS as the PKI supplier and SAIC as the system integrator. Leslie DeAnda managed the team resources and then became lead CA and RA administrator.

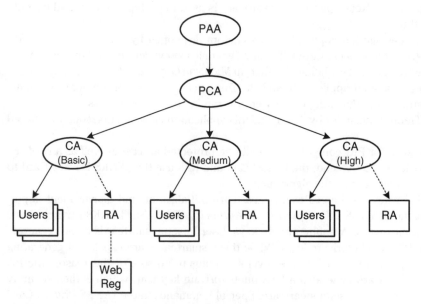

Figure 15.1 User view of the CAISO hierarchical PKI.

The CAISO hierarchy is realized through two sets of certificates. CAISO applications use RSA public keys contained in certificates that are signed with the RSA signature algorithm. The RSA hierarchy is referred to as the *user domain*. Internal PKI communications use DSA and KEA public keys contained in certificates that are signed with the DSA signature algorithm. The DSA hierarchy is referred to as the *infrastructure domain*.

Figure 15.2 depicts these domains. RAs are not included in the user domain, and users are not included in the infrastructure domain. RAs do not participate in CAISO applications. Users do not participate in CAISO internal PKI communications. The infrastructure domain and user domain are linked by the PAA.

Separation of the infrastructure domain from the user domain provides continuity of operations for the PKI. In the telephone system, there is an analogous separation between user calls and system commands. This separation ensures that telephone users cannot accidentally or maliciously harm the telephone systems. In the PKI, the infrastructure domain provides similar assurances. That is, the PKI continues to operate, even if there is catastrophic user key compromise. Enrollment and revocation require an operational infrastructure certificate path, and the use of a separate certificate path to protect PKI component communications guarantees that users cannot accidentally or maliciously jeopardize these protected communications.

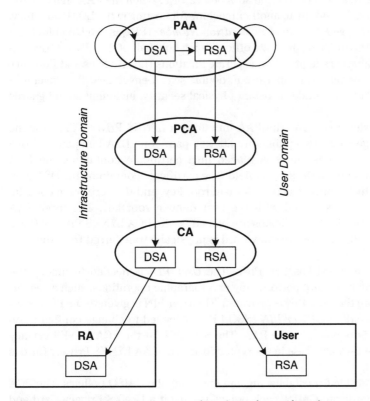

Figure 15.2   CAISO infrastructure domain and user domain.

The PAA provides a highly secure root. The PAA generates two public/private key pairs. The first is called the *infrastructure domain root key*; the second is called the *user domain root key*. The CAISO system uses a DSA key pair for the infrastructure domain root key, and it uses an RSA key pair for the user domain root key. The PAA places each of the public keys in a certificate and signs it with the corresponding private key, creating two self-signed certificates. The user domain root key is placed in a third certificate that is signed by the infrastructure domain root key. The third certificate links the infrastructure and user domains. All three certificates contain the PAA X.500 Distinguished Name for both the subject and issuer names. All three certificates are placed on the PAA LYNKS Privacy Card.

The self-signed certificate containing the user domain root key serves as the single trust point for user certificate path validation. The self-signed certificate containing the infrastructure domain root key serves as the single trust point for PKI component certificate path validation. PKI components can construct valid certificate paths in the user domain by following the PAA linking certificate.

Users never see certificates within the infrastructure domain; they are not posted to the LDAP directory. Only certificates in the user domain are posted in the LDAP directory.

The PAA is primarily offline and powered-down; it is not connected to the network. Being offline protects the PAA and the root keys from many potential attacks. The PAA is brought up to create a PCA or to issue an X.509 v2 CRL. When the PAA signs a CRL, the CRL is transferred on a floppy to another machine for posting in the LDAP directory. Further, a split-knowledge *Personal Identification Number* (PIN) is used to unlock the PAA LYNKS Privacy Card. Two corporate officers each hold half of the PIN, and backup copies of the PIN values are kept in two separate locations (Los Angeles and Folsom). The backup copies are kept in tamper-proof, double-sealed envelopes. The envelopes are stored in fireproof safes under constant physical security, including armed guards and video cameras.

The PAA establishes the PCA. The PAA initializes a LYNKS Privacy Card for the PCA, causing it to generate two public/private key pairs, one DSA key pair and one RSA key pair. Each of these keys is placed in a certificate containing the PCA X.500 Distinguished Name in the subject field. The certificate containing the DSA public key is signed with the infrastructure domain root key, and the certificate containing the RSA public key is signed with the user domain root key. The three PAA certificates and the two PCA certificates are placed on the PCA LYNKS Privacy Card. Then, the initialized PCA LYNKS Privacy Card is physically transferred from the PAA to the PCA.

The LYNKS Privacy Card has two PINs. The *User PIN* is needed to unlock the LYNKS Privacy Card; it will not perform any cryptographic operations, such as generate signatures, before the User PIN is provided. The User PIN is given to the PCA operator. The *System Security Officer PIN* (SSO PIN) is needed to change configuration information, and it is retained by the PAA. The SSO PIN for the PCA LYNKS Privacy Card is stored in the PAA database in encrypted form. The PAA LYNKS Privacy Card is needed to decrypt it.

The PCA is responsible for establishing and enforcing the CAISO policies. The PCA establishes one subordinate CA for each policy, issuing it a LYNKS Privacy Card and several X.509 v3 certificates. The PCA is primarily offline, since it does not issue any end-user certificates. The PCA issues an X.509 v2 CRL, and posts it in the LDAP directory. As with the PAA, a split-knowledge PIN is used to unlock the PCA LYNKS Privacy Card. A corporate director and a corporate attorney each hold half of the PIN. Again, backup copies of the PIN values are kept in two separate locations; sealed in tamper-proof, double-sealed envelopes; and stored in fireproof safes under constant physical security.

The PAA LYNKS Privacy Card, which contains both the infrastructure domain root private key and the user domain root key and the PCA LYNKS Privacy Card, are stored in separate dual-custody safes. The disk drives for the PAA and PCA computers are also stored in the dual-custody safes to completely ensure the integrity of the databases. This storage technique prevents any *one* person from restarting either the PAA or PCA. The PAA safe and the PCA safe are under the custody of separate people. This separation prevents the PAA operators from performing PCA tasks and vice versa.

The PCA establishes four CAs, one for each of the CAISO policies (Test, Basic, Medium, and High). The PCA initializes a LYNKS Privacy Card for each CA, causing it to generate two public/private key pairs, one DSA/KEA key pair and one RSA key pair. Since the DSA signature algorithm and the KEA key agreement algorithm are based on the same mathematics, one key pair can be used with both algorithms. Each of these keys is placed in a certificate containing the CA X.500 Distinguished Name. The certificate containing the DSA/KEA public key belongs to the infrastructure domain certification path, and the certificate containing the RSA public key belongs to the user domain certification path. The three PAA certificates, the two PCA certificates, and the two CA certificates are placed on the CA LYNKS Privacy Card. Then, the initialized CA LYNKS Privacy Card is physically transferred from the PCA to the CA. The User PIN for the CA LYNKS Privacy Card is provided to the CA operator; however, the SSO PIN for the CA LYNKS Privacy Card is stored, in encrypted form, in the PCA database.

The CA is responsible for issuing end-user X.509 v3 certificates under a single policy. The CA is constantly online; it automatically responds to certificate requests from the RA. Digitally signed and encrypted electronic mail is used for communications between the CA and the RA. The CA is a lights-out server. Once it is up and running, little human interaction is needed to keep it operational. If it shuts down for any reason, such as power failure, a human is needed to restart it. The human must provide the User PIN for the LYNKS Privacy Card. The CA also maintains an X.509 v2 CRL. Certificates and CRLs are posted in the LDAP directory.

The CA establishes at least one RA; more RAs may be established if the workload warrants. The CA initializes a LYNKS Privacy Card for each RA, causing it to generate one DSA/KEA key pair. The public key is placed in a certificate containing the RA X.500 Distinguished Name. The certificate belongs to the infrastructure domain certification path. The PAA DSA certificate containing the infrastructure domain root key, the PCA DSA certificate, the CA DSA/KEA certificate, and the RA DSA/KEA certificate are placed on the RA LYNKS Privacy Card. No user domain certificates are needed on the RA LYNKS Privacy Card. Then, the initialized RA LYNKS Privacy Card is physically transferred from the CA to the RA. The User PIN for the RA LYNKS Privacy Card is provided to the RA operator; however, the SSO PIN for the RA LYNKS Privacy Card is stored, in encrypted form, in the CA database.

The RA is responsible for enrolling end users according to the CAISO policy associated with its superior CA. The RA has a policy-specific module, called the *programmable policy module* (PPM), that implements much of the policy. The PPM alters the RA GUI to ensure that required information is provided. Further, the PPM provides environment-specific information without RA operator interaction. The PPM simplifies the RA operator's task, reducing errors. The RA generates certificate requests, and sends them to the CA using encrypted and signed e-mail. Once the CA has decrypted and validated the certificate request, it generates the signed certificate and returns it to the RA using encrypted and signed e-mail. The CA also posts the certificate to the LDAP directory. Then, the RA delivers the certificate to the end user. If the RA is initializing a hardware token for the user, then the RA loads the certificate onto the hardware token. If the user is employing software cryptography, the RA simply notifies the user, and the user fetches the certificate directly from the LDAP directory where the CA posted it.

WebReg provides an easy way for users who are using software cryptography to enroll. The user connects to the CAISO Registration Web page and provides all of the information that the RA needs to generate a certificate request, including the user's e-mail address and the user's public key, which is extracted directly from the browser by a script. The script generates a PKCS #10 certificate request. The RA periodically checks the Web server for new enrollment requests, validates them, and generates a certificate request for the CA. Once the CA returns the certificate, the RA sends it to the user by e-mail. In the near future, the LDAP Directory entries will be replicated in a separate server outside the firewall. This will allow users to easily download their own certificate, certificates of other users, and CRLs.

CAISO users operate the California power grid, sell power on behalf of power generators, buy power on behalf of utility companies, and administratively operate CAISO. These map directly to the High, Medium, and Basic certification policies. Like any other system, the CAISO system is constantly being upgraded, and to support testing of upgrades, CAISO also has a Test certification policy.

High. CAISO protects power grid command and control communications. The Generator Communications Project (GCP) CA provides certificates to protect direct communications and control for generation dispatch control. The power grid control operates on the private Energy Communication Network (ECN). Certificates are used to establish SSL sessions, mutually authenticating communicating parties and providing confidentiality and integrity for exchanged data and generation dispatch control. Certificate identity information provides the basis for access control decisions. PKI components and subscribers' cryptographic modules must be rated at FIPS 140-1 level 2 or higher.

Medium. CAISO protects power brokerage transactions. The Medium Assurance CA provides certificates to external entities that have business dealing with CAISO to enable electronic business transactions. The transaction may take place on a private network or the public Internet. External entities connect with a CAISO server and enter permitted transactions. Additionally, CAISO employees and contractors connect with the servers to observe and participate in the transactions. The CAISO brokerage processes about $50 billion in transactions annually. PKI component cryptographic modules must be rated at FIPS 140-1 level 2 or higher, and subscriber cryptographic modules must be rated at FIPS 140-1 level 1 or higher.

Basic. CAISO protects administrative communications, futures trading auctions, load shedding, and *reliability must run* (RMR) generation settlements. The Basic Assurance CA provides certificates to external entities that have business dealings with CAISO, CAISO employees, CAISO contractors, CAISO systems, and CAISO applications for identity authentication and for secure session establishment. PKI component cryptographic modules must be rated at FIPS 140-1 level 2 or higher, but there is no stipulation regarding subscriber cryptographic modules.

Test. Testing can be accomplished without generating certificates that might accidentally be accepted by other parts of the CAISO system.

Certificate and CRL Profiles

The CAISO PKI employs X.509 v3 certificates and X.509 v2 CRLs.

CAISO user certificates contain an X.500 Distinguished Name and a public key. The X.500 Distinguished Name is carried in the subject field, and one component of the X.500 Distinguished Name contains the electronic mail address. Figure 15.3 includes a sample CAISO X.500 Distinguished Name; the same subject name is used in the sample certificate shown in Figure 15.4. It is preferable to carry the electronic mail address in the subject alternative name extension; however, this older technique is used to support applications that do support the subject alternative name extension. The Netscape S/MIME v2 implementation is the primary concern. When CAISO is able to upgrade to S/MIME v3, support for this older technique will no longer be needed.

CAISO user certificates include several extensions. CAISO user certificates include a certificate policies extension that is used to determine which CAISO applications may accept this certificate. They include a key usage extension that identifies the security services that may be implemented using the public key. They include a non-critical Netscape Certificate Type private extension that helps the Netscape browser handle the certificates more smoothly.

Figure 15.4 shows a user certificate issued by the CAISO Basic CA. The DumpASN1 tool written by Peter Gutmann was used to create the figure. Each line in the figure represents an ASN.1 certificate field. The left margin contains three numbers. The first number is the byte offset into the certificate. The second number is two hexadecimal digits containing the ASN.1 tag byte. The third number is the field length. The whole certificate is 938 bytes.

```
 E = rhousley@caiso.com
CN = DEMO_CAISO_Russ Housley
SN = 000
OU = Basic
 O = CAISO
 C = US
```

Figure 15.3 Sample CAISO user X.500 Distinguished Name.

```
  0 30  938: SEQUENCE {
  4 30  658:   SEQUENCE {
  8 A0    3:     [0] {
 10 02    1:       INTEGER 2
    :             }
 13 02    2:     INTEGER 584
 17 30   13:     SEQUENCE {
 19 06    9:       OBJECT IDENTIFIER
    :               md5withRSAEncryption (1 2 840 113549 1 1 4)
 30 05    0:       NULL
    :             }
 32 30   65:     SEQUENCE {
 34 31   11:       SET {
 36 30    9:         SEQUENCE {
 38 06    3:           OBJECT IDENTIFIER countryName (2 5 4 6)
 43 13    2:           PrintableString 'US'
    :                 } }
 47 31   14:       SET {
 49 30   12:         SEQUENCE {
 51 06    3:           OBJECT IDENTIFIER organizationName (2 5 4 10)
 56 13    5:           PrintableString 'CAISO'
    :                 } }
 63 31   14:       SET {
 65 30   12:         SEQUENCE {
 67 06    3:           OBJECT IDENTIFIER organizationalUnitName (2 5 4 11)
 72 13    5:           PrintableString 'Basic'
    :                 } }
 79 31   18:       SET {
 81 30   16:         SEQUENCE {
 83 06    3:           OBJECT IDENTIFIER commonName (2 5 4 3)
 88 14    9:           TeletexString 'Basic_CA1'
    :                 } } }
 99 30   30:     SEQUENCE {
101 17   13:       UTCTime '001001230000Z'
116 17   13:       UTCTime '011001230000Z'
    :             }
131 30  128:     SEQUENCE {
134 31   11:       SET {
136 30    9:         SEQUENCE {
138 06    3:           OBJECT IDENTIFIER countryName (2 5 4 6)
143 13    2:           PrintableString 'US'
    :                 } }
147 31   14:       SET {
149 30   12:         SEQUENCE {
151 06    3:           OBJECT IDENTIFIER organizationName (2 5 4 10)
156 13    5:           PrintableString 'CAISO'
    :                 } }
```

Figure 15.4   Sample CAISO user certificate.

```
163 31   14:        SET {
165 30   12:          SEQUENCE {
167 06    3:            OBJECT IDENTIFIER organizationalUnitName (2 5 4 11)
172 13    5:            PrintableString 'Basic'
         :            } }
179 31   12:        SET {
181 30   10:          SEQUENCE {
183 06    3:            OBJECT IDENTIFIER serialNumber (2 5 4 5)
188 13    3:            PrintableString '000'
         :            } }
193 31   32:        SET {
195 30   30:          SEQUENCE {
197 06    3:            OBJECT IDENTIFIER commonName (2 5 4 3)
202 14   23:            TeletexString 'DEMO_CAISO_Russ Housley'
         :            } }
227 31   33:        SET {
229 30   31:          SEQUENCE {
231 06    9:            OBJECT IDENTIFIER
         :              emailAddress (1 2 840 113549 1 9 1)
242 16   18:            IA5String 'rhousley@caiso.com'
         :            } } }
262 30  159:      SEQUENCE {
265 30   13:        SEQUENCE {
267 06    9:          OBJECT IDENTIFIER rsaEncryption (1 2 840 113549 1 1 1)
278 05    0:          NULL
         :          }
280 03  141:        BIT STRING no unused bits, encapsulates {
284 30  137:            SEQUENCE {
287 02  129:              INTEGER
         :                  00 A7 C4 11 C4 E2 DE 6D 30 F1 90 17 E1 99 E2 76
         :                  FF B2 AC 5A C0 F7 83 DD 96 E1 C4 4B D7 CC D9 08
         :                  1D C0 7A 4D BE 46 8C F1 89 B1 63 97 D7 BB 3B 3C
         :                  B4 26 DB F1 0D ED E4 8F FC E7 00 8A 11 C4 56 89
         :                  B1 69 A1 86 06 2E 24 E1 2B ED 63 2C EF A4 52 E1
         :                  8A B6 07 07 B2 3E F6 C6 FA 7D 93 FD A7 DC A7 B0
         :                  9E C9 0A BB 20 7C CC FF A2 E2 AB C8 73 A9 D3 42
         :                  B5 1A BA 82 C0 0E BC 95 51 53 62 12 DB 6B 55 F1
         :                  89
419 02    3:              INTEGER
         :                  01 00 01
         :            }   } }
424 A3  239:      [3] {
427 30  236:        SEQUENCE {
430 30   17:          SEQUENCE {
432 06    3:            OBJECT IDENTIFIER subjectKeyIdentifier (2 5 29 14)
437 04   10:            OCTET STRING
         :                04 08 0B 4E 7B CC 7F CA 34 A7
         :            }
```

Figure 15.4   Continued

(continues)

```
449 30   91:        SEQUENCE {
451 06    3:          OBJECT IDENTIFIER authorityKeyIdentifier (2 5 29 35)
456 04   84:          OCTET STRING, encapsulates {
458 30   82:            SEQUENCE {
460 80    8:              [0]
          :                08 A3 B5 E8 89 73 D8 16
470 A1   67:              [1] {
472 A4   65:                [4] {
474 30   63:                  SEQUENCE {
476 31   11:                    SET {
478 30    9:                      SEQUENCE {
480 06    3:                        OBJECT IDENTIFIER
          :                          countryName (2 5 4 6)
485 13    2:                        PrintableString 'US'
          :                        } }
489 31   14:                    SET {
491 30   12:                      SEQUENCE {
493 06    3:                        OBJECT IDENTIFIER
          :                          organizationName (2 5 4 10)
498 13    5:                        PrintableString 'CAISO'
          :                        } }
505 31   11:                    SET {
507 30    9:                      SEQUENCE {
509 06    3:                        OBJECT IDENTIFIER
          :                          organizationalUnitName (2 5 4 11)
514 13    2:                        PrintableString 'IT'
          :                        } }
518 31   19:                    SET {
520 30   17:                      SEQUENCE {
522 06    3:                        OBJECT IDENTIFIER
          :                          commonName (2 5 4 3)
527 14   10:                        TeletexString 'CAISO_PCA1'
          :                        } } } } }
539 82    1:                [2]
          :                  12
          :              }   } }
542 30   86:        SEQUENCE {
544 06    3:          OBJECT IDENTIFIER certificatePolicies (2 5 29 32)
549 04   79:          OCTET STRING, encapsulates {
551 30   77:            SEQUENCE {
553 30   75:              SEQUENCE {
555 06   11:                OBJECT IDENTIFIER '1 3 6 1 4 1 3907 1 1 1 4'
568 30   60:                SEQUENCE {
570 30   58:                  SEQUENCE {
572 06    8:                    OBJECT IDENTIFIER
          :                      cps (1 3 6 1 5 5 7 2 1)
```

Figure 15.4 Continued

```
582 16   46:                          IA5String
         :                              'http://www.caiso.com/pubinfo/info-
         :                                security/cps'
         :                      }  } } } } }
630 30   17:              SEQUENCE {
632 06    9:                OBJECT IDENTIFIER
         :                    netscape-cert-type (2 16 840 1 113730 1 1)
643 04    4:                OCTET STRING, encapsulates {
645 03    2:                  BIT STRING no unused bits
         :                      '00000101'B
         :                  }  }
649 30   15:              SEQUENCE {
651 06    3:                OBJECT IDENTIFIER keyUsage (2 5 29 15)
656 01    1:                BOOLEAN TRUE (critical extension)
659 04    5:                OCTET STRING, encapsulates {
661 03    3:                  BIT STRING 7 unused bits
         :                      '000000101'B
         :              } } } }    }
666 30   13:      SEQUENCE {
668 06    9:        OBJECT IDENTIFIER
         :            md5withRSAEncryption (1 2 840 113549 1 1 4)
679 05    0:        NULL
         :          }
681 03  257:      BIT STRING no unused bits
         :          73 F3 24 5A B5 B5 D2 FB 2E 52 A5 F6 1B 40 FE 11
         :          EC DC EA 52 3F 51 1C 58 AF A7 FA 43 E3 0A 1E 38
         :          5A 86 42 4E 92 04 13 F3 C9 CE 1B 5D EE 9C DB 65
         :          0F D6 A0 20 23 D9 AD 1C D7 F9 FD 82 A5 BC 3D 13
         :          9B DA 43 26 80 7B A6 49 2E 89 15 B6 E3 01 1E 86
         :          CB D2 9D F6 31 36 B2 01 AA 0E EC 11 B4 1F 89 40
         :          3D 30 7B 61 C8 2E FB B0 BD AF 64 E2 76 98 F4 E2
         :          B9 8D CF 88 19 0E 8E 3B 82 0F 94 5D C4 37 D5 27
         :          7F A2 7E 8B 15 23 3B FA 3F 97 30 5F 9A DE 2F 2D
         :          01 E4 08 82 70 B1 F3 55 2B FE 10 BE 13 0C F7 27
         :          BC 7D AD 0C 07 17 55 F5 A6 D6 FA 8E DB 13 A1 0B
         :          8B 1C 38 47 61 C4 48 7C D2 DA 28 B3 B2 1B 34 AB
         :          EE BD 3A 6A 60 F5 DC 1B A9 69 B3 6A BA C8 2D D7
         :          1F D1 67 49 A6 95 7D 27 CC 1D 8E B0 AA 4A DA BC
         :          EE FD 31 55 E6 4A D1 F0 9D 86 C4 D4 B8 DC BB 82
         :          34 16 49 97 70 D0 B8 F9 83 0A FA 78 2C 35 C5 DA
         :      }
```

Figure 15.4 Continued

Repositories

As we have already said, CAISO stores certificates and CRLs in an LDAP directory. However, a firewall separates the network of the CA systems and LDAP Directory from other internal and external networks. Since the firewall blocks LDAP connections, the LDAP Directory is not publicly available.

Since the LDAP directory is not accessible by external entities, a server inside the CA system enclave *pushes* the most recent CRL to all CAISO application servers. CAISO recognizes that this approach does not scale as the number of application servers and other certificate users increases. Therefore, CAISO plans to replicate the certificates and CRLs in a publicly available LDAP directory outside the enclave. The approach that CAISO plans to use is similar to the Border Directory concept discussed in Chapter 9, "Repository Protocols."

Certificate Management

CAISO does not support certificate suspension.

CAISO uses the SPYRUS PKI. The PAA, PCA, and CAs each run on separate Windows NT 4.0 systems. Each CA has a Microsoft SQL Server database. The PCA and CA systems are connected to the private network, enabling electronic mail and LDAP directory access. E-mail is permitted to flow between the CA systems and external networks; this communication is needed for the CA and RA to communicate. The firewall permits communications only between specific IP addresses on specific sockets, enabling the CA and RA to communicate, but disabling all other communications.

The PAA LYNKS Privacy Card and the PCA LYNKS Privacy Card are stored in separate dual-custody safes. The PAA safe and the PCA safe are under the custody of separate people. Therefore, two people must cooperate to issue the PAA CRL or to create a new PCA. Two different people must cooperate to issue the PCA CRL or to create a new CA. These procedural measures help ensure the integrity of the hierarchical PKI. The CAISO CP specifies the background and training requirements for each of these people.

The CAISO CP [CAISO99a] and CPS [CAISO99b, CAISO99c, CAISO99d] documents are available to everyone on the Web at http://www.caiso.com/pubinfo/info-secutity/cps.

This Web page also contains a simple one-page document [CAISO99e] that highlights user security responsibilities. This document is a good idea. The CPS is not written for the average system user, and it mostly describes the responsibilities of the CA. Distilling the user responsibilities into a single page, written in simple language, makes this information accessible.

Companion Web pages offer other important information:

- The PAA, PCA, Medium Assurance CA, and Basic Assurance CA certificates are available for download. A document providing step-by-step instructions for installing the certificates in the Netscape browser is with them. These instructions add the PAA certificate to the trust list.

- Instructions for installation of the SPYRUS Personal Access Reader (a smartcard reader) on the user's workstation are available.

- Instructions for obtaining a certificate with the Netscape browser are available.

All CAISO issued certificates include subject X.500 Distinguished Names and begin with `c=US` and `o=CAISO`. CAISO imposes no further restrictions on subject X.500 Distinguished Names. Of course, appropriate proof of identity must be provided, and CAISO reserves the right to add numbers to the end of a common name to avoid duplication with a previously registered name.

The High Assurance CA provides devices and applications with LYNKS Privacy Cards to protect their private keys and perform cryptographic operations. As part of programming a LYNKS Privacy Card, a PIN is assigned. The user needs the PIN to unlock the LYNKS Privacy Card and access the keys and cryptographic functions. The High Assurance CA delivers the LYNKS Privacy Card and the PIN to the user, using separate paths.

Similarly, the Medium Assurance CA provides users with Rosetta smartcards to protect their private keys and perform RSA operations. As part of programming a smartcard, a PIN is assigned. The user needs the PIN to unlock the smartcard and access the keys and cryptographic functions. The Medium Assurance CA delivers the smartcard and the PIN to the user, using separate paths.

User public and private keys have a maximum life of one year. Therefore, expiration of a certificate is an expected event. Requests for a new certificate must be communicated to the CA in the same manner as a request for a completely new certificate. No automatic renewal processes are employed.

Table 15.1 summarizes the lifetime and key size for the public and private keys in the CAISO system.

The CAISO CAs are audited frequently to ensure compliance with the CP and CPS. Audit will be conducted, as a minimum, every two years. One of every three inspections is conducted by an agency external to CAISO. These audits provide confidence that the overall system is being operated correctly.

PriceWaterHouse Coopers conduct external agency audits for CAISO. In December 1999, during an EDP Audit, 160 findings were documented, 62 of which were PKI related. The PKI-related findings were primarily related to procedure and process documentation. A few had to do with awareness and user education. By September 2000, CAISO addressed all 62 PKI-related findings. Not only did CAISO do a tremendous job on the architecture design and product selection, they also did an excellent job documenting every aspect of the PKI process. This detailed documentation augments the CAISO CPSes.

Table 15.1 CAISO Key Sizes and Lifetimes

PKI ENTITY	KEY SIZE	KEY LIFETIME
PAA	2048 bits	20 years
PCA	2048 bits	10 years
CA	2048 bits	5 years
RA	1024 bits	1 year
User	1024 bits	1 year

The preliminary work for a Level 2 SAS70 audit was done in September 2000. The initial observations did not include any PKI- or security-related issues. The full-fledged SAS70 audit was completed in December 2000, and the results will be presented to the CAISO Board in January 2001 (after the manuscript for this book is complete).

Management Protocols

Communications between the CA and RA do not use a standard protocol. An enhanced and extended form of the *MISSI Management Protocol* (MMP) [SDN908] is used. MMP defines a message content for communications between components of the PKI. The enhancements permit the RA to obtain information for the CA database that is needed for administration of the LYNKS Privacy Card and the Rosetta smartcard. All MMP messages are carried as the protected content in signed and encrypted electronic mail messages.

The use of secure e-mail for PKI management traffic is especially well suited for the CAISO environment. The firewall allows e-mail to flow in and out of the protected enclave. This allows the RA to be outside the protected enclave, and near the users that it is serving.

Infrastructure domain keys are used to protect the MMP messages. The infrastructure domain certificates have a unique certificate policy identifier and a unique subject public key algorithm identifier. For this reason, neither the CA nor the RA can mistake a user domain certificate for an infrastructure domain certificate. The effect is a closed community for the management of the PKI.

Since the RA and CA comprise a closed system, the use of a nonstandard protocol does not adversely impact interoperability or scalability. Even so, SPYRUS plans to replace MMP with CMC [MYER00] in a future release. Since MMP and CMC have many of the same properties, CMC should be a straightforward substitution. CMC is discussed in Chapter 11, "PKI Management Protocols."

PKCS #10, also discussed in Chapter 11, is used for user enrollment when the user does not have a hardware token (either a LYNKS Privacy Card or a Rosetta smartcard). PKCS #10 is the most widely supported certificate enrollment protocol, and is built into the Netscape browser. The browser using WebReg generates the PKCS #10 request, then the RA validates the request and translates it into an MMP certificate request for the CA.

After the CA issues the certificate, it is returned to the RA and posted in the LDAP directory. The CA or RA ensures that the new subscriber has received its certificate in one of the following ways:

Electronic mail. The certificate can be sent directly to the user by e-mail. This approach is only employed if the e-mail system supports notification to the sender when a particular message is read. In this case, the notification constitutes user acceptance of the certificate.

Web download. The new subscriber can download the certificate from a Web server. The Web page provides the new subscriber with an opportunity to accept or reject the certificate. In this case, clicking the Accept button constitutes user acceptance of the certificate.

Physical delivery. The certificate can be physically delivered on a LYNKS Privacy Card, Rosetta smartcard, or floppy disk. In this case, the new subscriber must sign a letter acknowledging the receipt of the certificate.

Failure Recovery

CAISO does not use a key recovery or key escrow service.

CAISO performs a CA database backup daily. The backup tapes are stored in a safe and bonded storage facility. If a disaster occurs at the Folsom facility, making the CAs, RAs, WebReg, and the LDAP Directory unavailable, CAISO will follow a documented procedure to bring the PKI back up in Alhambra. Standby hardware is already installed in a secure facility in Alhambra. CAISO will retrieve the CA backup LYNKS Privacy Cards and the most current backup tapes to operate the PKI from the Alhambra facility until operations can be restored in Folsom. CAISO has successfully tested the setup in Alhambra.

Applications

CAISO applications provide command and control of the power grid, electric power brokerage, and administrative communications. Peer-to-peer communications are protected with SSL, and electronic mail communications are protected with S/MIME. We will explore the Generator Communications Project (GCP), which provides command and control of the power grid.

CAISO initiated the GCP to establish a direct communications and control system for generation dispatch control. CAISO selected the Remote Intelligent Gateway (RIG) system for direct communications and control. The RIG provides data collection and data transmission between generator sites as well as other monitoring and supervisory control sites. Data transmission occurs over the Energy Communication Network (ECN). Communicating parties include the *Master RIG*, the *Field RIG*, and an operator workstation known as the *Man-Machine Interface* (MMI). Each party requires a digital certificate issued by the GCP CA to interact with each other. Figure 15.5 shows the RIG system components.

The RIG security subsystem satisfies the CAISO security requirements by performing the functions listed next. Note that the security functions apply only when the RIG uses the ECN to communicate with another party. Other communication interfaces, such as serial lines, are not protected. Interestingly, unprotected Voice over IP (VOIP) is also enabled.

- Using SSL, the RIG provides confidentiality and integrity of all data originating or terminating at a RIG network interface.

- Using SSL and X.509 v3 certificates, the RIG mutually authenticates communicating parties.

- The RIG provides control access to all data based on the authenticated identity of the requester.

- The RIG keeps an audit record of security-related events.

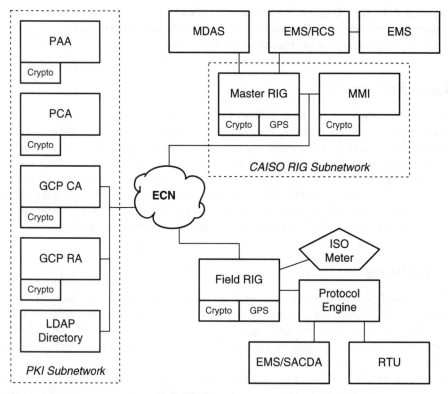

Figure 15.5   Components of the CAISO RIG system.

Successes and Shortcomings

The methodical approach employed by CAISO led to a very successful PKI deployment. Much of the CAISO documentation is publicly available, so it is pretty easy to follow in their footsteps.

The hierarchical PKI is scalable, and it readily supports multiple certification policies. If the CAISO PKI needs to support an additional project, several alternatives are available. If the new project fits within one of the currently deployed certification policies, then additional RAs can be added to support the enrollment of the new users. If the new project requires a new policy, a new CA or a new PCA and CA could be added.

The CAISO certification policies are easily represented in the X.509 v3 certificate with the certificate policies extension. Setting the certificate policies extension as critical ensures that it is not ignored.

Since all CAISO certificates have a common prefix, there is no need for name constraints. CAISO is the naming authority for all of the names contained in certificates that they issue.

The use of hardware to protect the PAA, PCA, and CA private keys is prudent. The use of 2048-bit RSA keys for these relatively long-lived certificates is also prudent.

Hardware provides significant protection against disclosure of the private key, and the long key length makes disclosure through cryptographic analysis of the public key extremely unlikely. Further, the LYNKS Privacy Card ensures that an authorized CA operator is starting the CA. The hardware cannot ensure that only valid certificates are signed. However, the CA architecture and the RA PPM provide assurances in this area.

Similarly, the use of hardware to protect high-value user private keys is prudent. The LYNKS Privacy Card and the Rosetta smartcard offer four benefits beyond private key protection. First, they provide two-factor user authentication. The user must possess a card, and the user must know the PIN. Second, they provide a high-integrity means to distribute the trust point (the PAA public key). Third, they provide a personal and portable key container. The user can easily transfer the personal private keys to any workstation. Fourth, the user's certificate path is part of the mobile container. While this information does not need protection, carrying this information reduces the setup necessary at each workstation.

Unfortunately, the LYNKS Privacy Card also has some deployment headaches. Many computers do not have PCMCIA adapters, so they must be purchased and added. Also, the interface library and drivers are not available on every operating system and hardware platform. The interface library for the LYNKS Privacy Card was ported to the RIG real-time operating system (VxWorks) for this project. A PCMCIA adapter can cost several times more than the LYNKS Privacy Card itself. Further, installing the PCMCIA adapters and configuring the appropriate device driver and interface library requires a skilled technician. These trained technicians are in short supply.

The involvement of two people in the operation of the PAA and the PCA greatly reduces the likelihood that inappropriate PCA or CA certificates will be issued.

Many RAs can support a single CA. In this way, the number of CAs is kept small, yet the number of people facilitating enrollment is scaled to match the size of the user population. Keeping the number of CAs small reduces the number of LDAP Directory interactions, and reduces the size of certificate caches.

The CAISO CP requires the RA operator to validate the identity of the user. No computer program can perform this function. The human user is an important part of CP implementation where face-to-face enrollment is required. The RA PPM provides an enrollment GUI that is simple and straightforward. This GUI reduces the likelihood of human enrollment errors.

CAISO certificates do not include authorization information. The RA operator does not usually know the authorizations of every user. The authenticated identity within the certificate is used to make identity-based access control decisions. Application owners maintain the user authorizations for their own applications. This separation of authentication and access control ensures that privilege changes do not lead to certificate revocation.

Many SSL and S/MIME implementations use a single RSA key pair for both key management and digital signature. Since the CAISO PKI does not support non-repudiation or key recovery, many of the concerns associated with the use of a single key pair for both functions are alleviated. In our view, the use of two separate keys is still preferable, since it would allow additional uses of the PKI without reviewing these potential concerns.

Separation of the infrastructure domain from the user domain ensures that the PKI can operate in the face of catastrophic user key compromise. Enrollment and revocation requires an operational certificate chain. The use of separate certificate chains to protect these communications guarantees that users cannot accidentally or maliciously jeopardize these protected communications.

CAISO uses RSA 2048-bit signing keys for the PAA, PCA, and CA. These offer very strong signatures. Unfortunately, they are used with a one-way hash function that is considerably weaker. This is not surprising since stronger one-way hash functions were not available when the system was deployed. As soon as all of the CAISO subscriber applications can be upgraded to support one of the newer, stronger one-way hash functions, the PAA, PCA, and CA certificates should be reissued to provide balanced security. The new one-way hash functions are discussed further in Chapter 17.

Lessons Learned

The CAISO PKI has many lessons. They include:

Use X.509 v3 certificates. Support for multiple CAISO certification policies is readily supported by the X.509 v3 certificate syntax. Also, the key usage extension clearly indicates that non-repudiation is not provided.

Use X.509 v2 CRLs. The use of X.509 v2 CRLs allows the CA to state the reason for revocation.

Use two certificates. One certificate containing a signature key and another certificate containing a key management key is the preferred approach. A single certificate containing one key that is used for signature and key management is acceptable when neither non-repudiation nor key recovery is provided by the PKI.

Use hardware to protect important keys. Use hardware to protect all PKI component keys, including RA keys. The incremental cost is not significant. Also, use hardware to protect valuable user keys. Consider the consequences of disclosure to determine if hardware protection is warranted to protect user keys.

Support standard enrollment protocols. Standard enrollment protocols make the PKI available to the widest possible client base. When a hardware token is provided to the subscriber, the certificate can be loaded onto the token before it is delivered. In this case, standard enrollment protocols can still be important for certificate renewal.

Consider user certificate acceptance. By having the subscriber review the content of the certificate at the time it is issued, errors may be detected before the certificate is used. Further, by incorporating such a review into the enrollment process, subsequent disputes regarding the content of the certificate can be avoided.

Consider manpower. The people needed to operate and maintain the PKI components represent a real cost, especially in areas when dual custody is required. The costs associated with these people must be considered. Also, select easily customized human interfaces to minimize the training expenses.

Conduct audits. Audits, especially audits conducted by an outside agent, will increase confidence that the PKI is being operated in accordance with the CP and the CPS. Both subscribers and management will benefit from the assurance that the PKI is being operated correctly.

Test backup procedures. Try recovery procedures. Make sure that they are sufficient to restore normal operations after a hardware failure or natural disaster.

CHAPTER

16

The Federal Bridge CA Project

The prospect of a unified—or at least interoperable—federal public key infrastructure (PKI) has tantalized U.S. government agencies for nearly a decade. With the security services provided by such a PKI, federal agencies could implement a wide variety of internal and cross-agency applications. As the agencies' business partners become members of PKIs, government services can be offered electronically and more efficiently. The business partners range from private industry and the citizenry to state, local, and foreign governments. In 1991, six U.S. agencies jointly funded a PKI study by the Mitre Corporation. Since that time, the project has faced a wide range of both technical and political challenges. It is finally positioned for success.

When the project commenced, the X.509 v2 certificate was the state of the art. PKI architectures were either a single certification authority (CA) or a strict hierarchy. A hierarchical PKI seemed an obvious choice for the implementation of a federal PKI. A steering group composed of federal agency representatives was formed in 1993. A technical working group was formed the following year to resolve technical issues. Numerous agencies joined the effort, and a federal PKI seemed near.

Unfortunately, political and technical problems associated with hierarchies proved insurmountable. Several agencies wanted to operate the root, and selecting one agency became a contentious political issue. Federal agencies have considerable autonomy in their information technology programs, and they were not ready to surrender that autonomy to the agency operating the federal root CA. In addition, PKIs at that time were all homogeneous systems. That is, all the CAs and registration authorities (RAs) in a PKI came from a single vendor. The agencies were unable or unwilling to make the necessary decisions to implement a hierarchical federal PKI.

A number of agencies grew impatient and forged off on their own. First, they implemented pilots. Soon, they began to field operational PKIs to secure their internal applications. PKIs were deployed (or planned) by different agencies using a single CA, a mesh, or a hierarchical PKI architecture. Different agencies chose different cryptographic algorithm suites to suit their local requirements. Any federal PKI would have to leverage these existing PKIs to succeed, which ruled out a government-wide hierarchy.

The only alternative appeared to be a broadly cross-certified PKI, but this approach presented operational problems. The federal government has 14 cabinet-level agencies, and numerous smaller agencies.[1] If only the cabinet-level agencies fielded a PKI and the principal CAs were to cross-certify, each agency would have to cross-certify with 13 other agency PKIs. These CAs would also need to cross-certify with business partners (which may include state and local governments as well as private companies). This places an enormous burden on the staff of the principal CAs.

The bridge CA concept was conceived to overcome these types of hurdles. As you may recall from Chapter 6, "PKI Architectures," the bridge CA does not operate as a root CA. Politically, the selection of a bridge CA is less emotionally charged. The bridge CA reduces the operational workload at the agency principal CA, requiring a single cross-certification to establish trust paths throughout the PKI. Later in this chapter, we describe how the bridge CA can also reduce the problems created by heterogeneous products and multiple cryptographic algorithm suites.

In this chapter, we present the architecture for the federal PKI and discuss the successes and shortcomings of this architecture. We also present the lessons to be learned from the Federal Bridge CA (FBCA) project.

Federal PKI Architecture

This section provides an overview of the federal PKI architecture. The discussion covers the cryptographic environment, FBCA architecture, the certificate and CRL profiles, repositories, certificate management, and recovery from CA compromise.

Cryptographic Environment

The Department of Commerce issues Federal Information Processing Standards (FIPS). FIPS publications include cryptographic standards for the processing of sensitive but unclassified information. FIPS 186, the Digital Signature Standard (DSS), specifies the suite of approved digital signature algorithms [FIPS186]. The current version of DSS, FIPS 186-2, permits use of four different signature algorithms: the Digital Signature Algorithm (DSA), Rivest-Shamir-Adelman (RSA), the Reversible Digital Signature Algorithm (rDSA), and the Elliptic Curve Digital Signature Algorithm (ECDSA).[2]

---

[1] www.whitehouse.gov has links to 136 different agency and commission Web sites.

[2] The RSA and rDSA signature algorithms are closely related. The recognized specification for the RSA signature algorithm is the Public Key Crypto Standard #1 (PKCS #1). The rDSA algorithm is specified by American National Standards Institute (ANSI) X9.31. The two algorithms pad the hash value differently before encrypting it with the signer's private key.

The National Institute of Standards and Technology (NIST) is currently developing a FIPS for key management using public key cryptography. As with FIPS 186-2, this standard is expected to approve a suite of public key algorithms. The suite of algorithms is expected to support both key agreement and key transport. Key agreement algorithms are likely to include Diffie-Hellman and Elliptic Curve Diffie-Hellman. RSA is likely to be approved for key transport.[3]

Federal agencies may use software or hardware cryptographic modules, as they deem appropriate. Whether hardware or software, federal agencies are required by FIPS 140-1, *Security Requirements for Cryptographic Modules* [FIPS140], to use validated cryptographic modules. An accredited laboratory tests the cryptographic module, and then the test reports are reviewed and approved by NIST and the Canadian government's Communications Security Establishment (CSE).

The federal PKI must be able to accommodate this mix of cryptographic algorithms and support this broad range of cryptographic modules. This presents a number of technical challenges. Users who support the same algorithm should be able to communicate securely even if they do not support all of the algorithms used in the federal PKI. William Burr proposed a set of rules for multiple algorithm support in the federal PKI in [Burr98][4]:

1. All user signature certificates must be consistent, meaning that the signature algorithm and algorithm of the public key are the same. For example, an RSA-signed certificate containing an RSA key is consistent. An RSA-signed certificate containing a DSA key is not consistent.

2. Two users who share a signature algorithm should not have to process inconsistent certificates to validate a path. That is, two users who agree upon a signature algorithm (for example, both sign with DSA) should not be required to process other algorithms to validate certification paths.

3. When two users sign with different algorithms (for example, DSA and RSA), the certification path should include exactly one inconsistent certificate. The inconsistent certificate is used to switch algorithms. Figure 16.1 illustrates a certification path that satisfies this requirement, but the path shown in Figure 16.2 does not. Figure 16.1 shows a path that begins with DSA, certifies an RSA key, and switches algorithms in the second CA certificate. If Alice supports both DSA and RSA, she can validate this path. Figure 16.2 illustrates a path that begins with DSA, switches to ECDSA, and ends with RSA. This path has two certificates that are not consistent. Alice must support three signature algorithms to validate the path. If Alice does not support ECDSA, she cannot validate the path, even if she supports both DSA and RSA.

---

[3] As with signatures, several related versions of RSA can be used to implement a key transport algorithm. The most widely recognized specification for the RSA encryption algorithm is the Public Key Crypto Standard #1 (PKCS #1). The American National Standards Institute has specified an alternative version as American National Standards Institute (ANSI) X9.44. The two algorithms pad the symmetric key differently before encrypting it with the recipient's public key.

[4] These three rules are an adaptation of the requirements and processing rules described in [Burr98], and reflect their application to the bridge CA architecture.

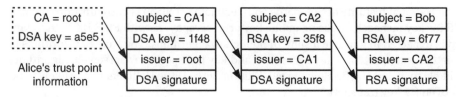

Figure 16.1   A certificate path with one inconsistent certificate.

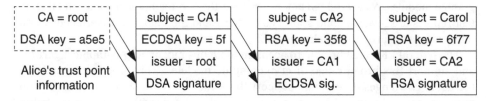

Figure 16.2   A certificate path with two inconsistent certificates.

The bridge CA concept can be extended to meet these requirements. In Figure 16.3, a bridge is composed of three separate CAs, or *nodes*, each supporting a particular signature algorithm. Each node is cross-certified with every other node in a mesh arrangement. Enterprise PKIs are cross-certified with the bridge CA node that signs with the same algorithm. As a result, Alice and Bob can construct and validate certification paths to each other's certificate using only DSA. To construct and validate a path to Doug's certificate, Alice must verify both RSA and DSA signatures. The only inconsistent certificate in the path is the certificate issued by BCA-1 to BCA-2. As long as all certificates from an enterprise PKI are signed with the same algorithm, this architecture will satisfy the three requirements described previously.

PKI Architecture

The Federal Bridge CA (FBCA) has been operating in a test and demonstration environment since early 2000. This section discusses the FBCA architecture as realized in the Electronic Messaging Association (EMA) Challenge 2000. The EMA Challenge was a large-scale demonstration of PKI interoperability at the EMA conference in April 2000. Based on the success of this testing, development of the production FBCA is underway, and it should be operational early in 2001.

At the EMA Challenge, the FBCA was composed of two CAs inside the *bridge CA membrane* and an X.500 directory system with an LDAP front end. The CAs were commercial products from Entrust Technologies and GTE CyberTrust. The two CAs within the bridge were cross-certified.

Six principal CAs were cross-certified with the prototype FBCA. Five principal CAs cross-certified with the Entrust CA, and one cross-certified with the CyberTrust CA. One of the principal CAs was itself a bridge CA that cross-certified with three additional enterprise PKIs. The completed PKI had a total of 18 CAs, representing six enterprise

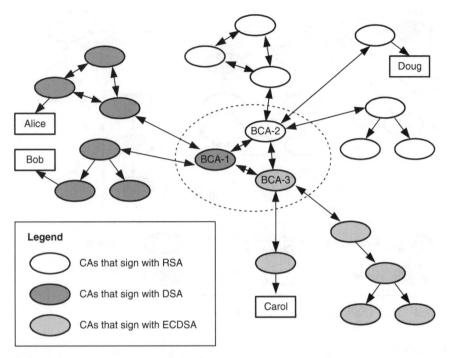

Figure 16.3   Extending the bridge CA to support multiple algorithms.

PKIs. The CAs included product offerings from SPYRUS and Entrust. The DoD PKI also included the DMS 2.0 CAW developed by Motorola and a special-purpose bridge CA developed by Cygnacom Solutions. The PKIs represented users from NIST, the Department of Defense, NASA, the Government of Canada (GoC), and the State of Georgia. The completed architecture is shown in Figure 16.4.

The PeerLogic i500 directory product provided the repository of the FBCA. The bridge directory serves two functions. The bridge directory is configured for anonymous access, and contains the directory entries for the bridge CAs. These entries include attributes for CA certificates, cross-certificate pairs, and CRLs.

The bridge directory serves as the central point in the federal PKI directory system. Each enterprise PKI has its own X.500 directory, which is chained to the bridge directory. Any user queries that cannot be satisfied by a local directory are chained to the bridge directory. The bridge directory satisfies the request if the user is looking for attributes associated with a bridge CA. Otherwise, the request is further chained to the directory associated with the appropriate enterprise PKI.

Agencies are not restricted to this repository architecture. The advantage of this architecture is the minimal number of directory chaining relationships. Agencies are free to establish direct chaining relationships for performance and to guard against denial-of-service attacks.

At the EMA Challenge 2000, the directory system consisted of six X.500 directories. Four of the directories corresponded to a single enterprise PKI. One directory supported two enterprise PKIs for NIST. The final directory was the FBCA directory. Products from

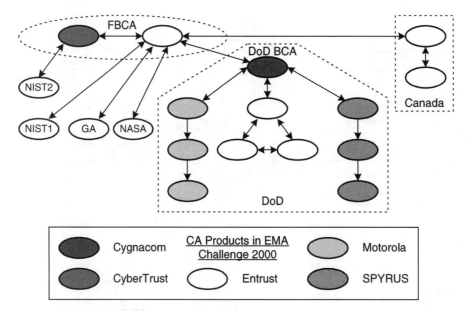

Figure 16.4 EMA Challenge bridge CA architecture.

Chromatix, Control Data Systems, Nexor, and PeerLogic were employed. The completed directory architecture is shown in Figure 16.5.

Certificate Policies

Government agency PKIs will support a broad range of applications. Some agencies will be using PKI-enabled security services to protect financial applications. Other agencies are using PKI to implement virtual private networks (VPNs) for telecommuters. Still others are targeting security for internal electronic mail and internal workflow processes. As a result, government agencies are implementing a wide variety of certificate policies.

As noted in Chapter 12, "Policies, Procedures, and PKI," certificate policies may be oriented toward a general level of assurance or indicate appropriate applications. The FBCA determined that the level of assurance approach was most appropriate for the federal government. Application-oriented policy information is most relevant in a local context. The idea that a certificate is strong or weak has utility in a global context. However, a single level of assurance is clearly insufficient.

The GoC established a four-level assurance certificate policy in 1997. The FBCA reviewed this set of well-defined certificate policies, and determined that this model fit the needs of federal agencies as well. In addition, the GoC PKI is likely to be one of the first foreign government PKIs to cross-certify with the FBCA. The U.S. Government chose to establish a four-level policy for the FBCA that is consistent with the four levels of assurance defined by the GoC [FBCA00a]. Four distinct object identifiers (OIDs)

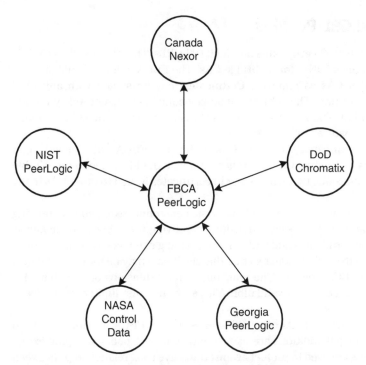

Figure 16.5   The EMA Challenge directory architecture.

were obtained from NIST's Computer Security Objects Registry (CSOR). They are listed in Table 16.1 in decreasing levels of assurance.

When the FBCA cross-certifies with an agency principal CA, it will use the policy mapping extension to indicate which subject domain policies may be accepted as the FBCA policies. Principal CAs are expected to use the policy mapping extension to indicate which FBCA policies may be accepted by its users as equivalent to the local policy. Alternatively, agencies that have not already deployed a PKI can use the FBCA policies in their own PKI.

Table 16.1   FBCA Certificate Policy OIDs

LEVEL OF ASSURANCE	OID NAME	OID
High	fbca-high	2.16.840.1.101.3.2.1.3.4
Medium	fbca-medium	2.16.840.1.101.3.2.1.3.3
Basic	fbca-basic	2.16.840.1.101.3.2.1.3.2
Rudimentary	fbca-rudimentary	2.16.840.1.101.3.2.1.3.1

Certificate and CRL Profiles

The FBCA will issue X.509 v3 certificates and X.509 v2 CRLs. The FBCA will use X.500-style Distinguished Names (DNs) for all bridge CAs. The FBCA will use X.500 or DNS-style DNs for principal CAs as required. Certificates may be signed with any FIPS approved signature algorithm. The subject public key contains a signature key for any FIPS approved algorithm. The FBCA only issues CA certificates so the subject public key will always be a signature key.

The contents of certificates issued by CAs within the FBCA will depend upon whether the subject is a principal CA or another CA inside the FBCA membrane. Table 16.2 lists certificate extensions that will appear in certificates issued to other CAs in the FBCA membrane.

Only two critical extensions are required: the basic constraints extension, identifying the subject as a CA; and the key usage extension, identifying the subject public key as appropriate for signing certificates and CRLs. The remaining extensions are non-critical. The certificate policies extension indicates that this certificate may be used to validate a path under any of the FBCA policies. The remaining three extensions provide hints for certification path construction and validation. There are no trust limitations between CAs within the FBCA membrane.

Table 16.3 describes the contents of certificates issued by FBCA membrane CAs to principal CAs. The principal additions are name constraints and policy mapping extensions. Name constraints are used to protect against transitive trust relationships between an agency PKI and an external CA by restricting names to the agency name space. Certificate policies and policy mapping are used to translate locally relevant policy information into FBCA policies. The path length may be included if the enterprise PKIs uses a hierarchical architecture.

Principal CAs may include any information they deem important in certificates they issue to the FBCA. Table 16.4 contains the suggested contents for certificates issued

Table 16.2 Extensions in FBCA Internal Certificates

EXTENSION	CRITICALITY	CONTENTS
Basic constraints	Critical	CA=true; path length is omitted
Key usage	Critical	The keyCertSign, cRLSign, digitalSignature, and nonRedpudiation bits are asserted.
Certificate policies	Non-critical	fbca-high, fbca-medium, fbca-basic, and fbca-rudimentary included.
CRL distribution points	Non-critical	Identifies the X.500 directory entry containing the CRL.
Authority key identifier	Non-critical	Bit string identifying the key used to sign the certificate.
Subject key identifier	Non-critical	Bit string identifying the public key in the certificate.

Table 16.3 Extensions in Certificates Issued to Principal CAs

EXTENSION	CRITICALITY	CONTENTS
Basic constraints	Critical	CA=true; if the principal CA is the root of a hierarchy, path length=maximum number of CAs in a path.
Key usage	Critical	The keyCertSign, cRLSign, digitalSignature, and nonRedpudiation bits are asserted.
Name constraints	Critical	Permitted subtrees for X.500 distinguished names is set to the agency's name space (for example, c=US; o=U.S. Government; ou=Commerce).
Policy mapping	Noncritical	Any or all of {fbca-high, fbca-medium, fbca-basic, and fbca-rudimentary} may appear as issuer domain policies mapping to agency policies.
Certificate policies	Non-critical	All FBCA policies asserted in policy mapping must be asserted in this extension.
CRL distribution points	Non-critical	Identifies the X.500 directory entry containing the CRL.
Authority key identifier	Non-critical	Bit string identifying the key used to sign the certificate.
Subject key identifier	Non-critical	Bit string identifying the public key in the certificate.

Table 16.4 Suggested Contents of Certificates Issued by Principal CAs to the FBCA

EXTENSION	CRITICALITY	CONTENTS
Basic constraints	Critical	CA=true; pathlength is omitted.
Key usage	Critical	The keyCertSign, cRLSign, digitalSignature, and nonRedpudiation bits are asserted.
Name constraints	Critical	Excluded subtrees for X.500 distinguished names is set to the agency's name space (for example, c=US; o=U.S. Government; ou=Commerce).
Policy mapping	Non-critical	Any or all of {fbca-high, fbca-medium, fbca-basic, and fbca-rudimentary} may appear as subject domain policies mapping to agency policies.
Certificate policies	Non-critical	All FBCA policies asserted in policy mapping must be asserted in this extension.
CRL distribution points	Non-critical	Identifies the X.500 directory entry containing the CRL.
Authority key identifier	Non-critical	Bit string identifying the key used to sign the certificate.
Subject key identifier	Non-critical	Bit string identifying the public key in the certificate.

by principal CAs to the FBCA. The path length is generally omitted since some enterprise PKIs use mesh architectures. Alternatively, a relatively large number (greater than 5) could be stated to cap the certification path construction delay experienced when no path can be found. Name constraints are used to protect against other CAs using the agency's name space. Certificate policies and policy mapping are used to translate FBCA policies into locally relevant policy information.

Repositories

Federal agencies have put a great deal of effort into a government-wide X.500 Directory. This is reflected in the strategy for repositories within the federal PKI: a fully chained hub-and-spoke X.500 Directory system. The bridge CA runs an X.500 Directory, and each agency PKI maintains an X.500 Directory. Agency directories need not be chained directly; each can chain to the bridge directory, as in Figure 16.6. Each agency directory considers the FBCA directory authoritative for the entire U.S. Government name space. The FBCA directory considers each agency directory authoritative for its own name space.

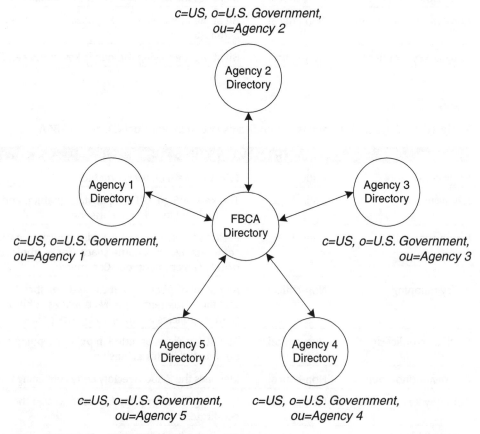

Figure 16.6 The FBCA X.500 Directory system.

This solution will work for internal connections. However, the FBCA will eventually facilitate security services with all government business partners. The government cannot insist that every company or state implement an X.500 Directory or use names in a consistent directory information tree. The federal PKI is planning to support disjoint repository systems in the future. The authority information access, subject information access, and CRL distribution points extensions can be used to achieve this goal.

Certificate Management

The CAs inside the FBCA membrane are generally offline. They are only turned on for four operations: to cross-certify with a new CA inside the FBCA membrane, to cross-certify with a new agency principal CA, to generate a new CRL, and to perform system backup. The CAs are not connected to a network or to any other machines.

The isolation of these CAs provides protection against many types of attacks, but it creates logistical problems. Every operation, except backup, requires updates to the bridge directory system. Practically every CA can perform this function automatically, but in the FBCA this must be performed via floppy disk. Every cross-certification requires out-of-band information exchange. Some CAs, most notably Entrust, are designed to automate the cross-certification process. The FBCA staff cannot take advantage of these features in an offline environment. This is not expected to present a serious problem since the number of certificates issued will be very small.

The CAs within the FBCA membrane are required to use FIPS 140-1 Level 3 or 4 hardware cryptographic modules [FIPS140], but may sign with any FIPS-approved algorithm.

Management Protocols

Unlike the DMS or CAISO PKIs, the federal PKI is an extremely heterogeneous environment. Agencies will continue to procure and deploy the PKI products that best meet their local requirements. As noted in Chapter 11, "PKI Management Protocols," management protocols are one of the most immature aspects of PKI technology. Interoperability between CA products is extremely limited unless both CAs were implemented with the same version of the same product. Establishing the necessary CA certificates between two dissimilar CAs is time consuming and frustrating.

The FBCA architecture reduces this to a manageable problem. They must cross-certify with one external CA, one of the CAs in the FBCA membrane. They do not need to cross-certify with any additional agencies. However, this places a substantial burden on the FBCA staff, as they are required to perform this process with each participating agency. Unfortunately, there is no single CA product that could be employed by the FBCA that could easily achieve cross-certification with all products.

The chairman of the Federal PKI Steering Committee, Rich Guida, recognized the need for a management protocol analog to the multiple cryptographic algorithm solution. In Figure 16.7, a bridge CA is composed of three separate CAs, each supporting a particular certificate management protocol. Enterprise PKIs cross-certify with the bridge CA that supports the same cross-certification management protocol. This greatly simplifies the technical procedures that must be followed when an agency PKI cross-certifies with the bridge CA. The collection of CAs that compose the bridge CA are cross-certified

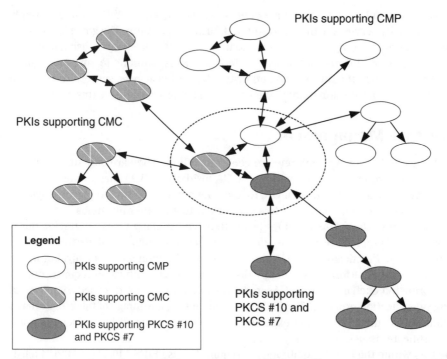

PKIs supporting CMP

PKIs supporting CMC

Legend

PKIs supporting CMP

PKIs supporting CMC

PKIs supporting PKCS #10 and PKCS #7

PKIs supporting PKCS #10 and PKCS #7

Figure 16.7 Extending the FBCA to support multiple certificate management protocols.

among themselves. Cross-certification of CAs within the bridge membrane is likely to be difficult to accomplish. Fortunately, there are very few of them, and they will not need to be repeated for many years.

Supporting both multiple algorithms and multiple management protocols could require a larger, and possibly cumbersome, number of CAs within the FBCA membrane. In the worst case, a separate CA for each combination of signature algorithm and enrollment protocol will be required. For example, to support the RSA and DSA algorithms as well as the CMP and CMC management protocols, four CAs within the bridge membrane could be required. Adding support for the ECDSA algorithm and support for the PKCS #7 and #10 enrollment protocol would require nine CAs within the bridge membrane. If a single CA product supports multiple protocols (for example, both SCEP and CMC), then the number of nodes required diminishes.

One of the greatest advantages of the bridge CA architecture is straightforward failure recovery. If an agency PKI is compromised, the FBCA simply revokes one certificate, the CA certificate issued to the agency principal CA. This effectively removes all certificates issued by that agency from the federal PKI. Yet, subscribers associated with other agencies are unaffected. Any two users certified by other agency PKIs can still enjoy security services. Only users associated with the offending agency PKI are inconvenienced. This scenario is illustrated in Figure 16.8. Carol's enterprise PKI has been compromised, and its certificate revoked by bridge CA 3 (BCA3). Alice can construct and validate a certification path for Bob, but not for Carol.

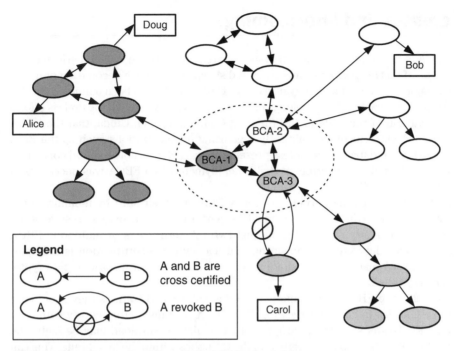

Figure 16.8 Revocation of a principal CA by the bridge.

If a CA within the bridge is compromised, all CA certificates issued to the compromised CA must be revoked. This will require $m + n - 1$ revocations, where m is the number of agency PKIs cross-certified with that particular CA and n is the number of CAs in the bridge membrane. Subscribers of those m agency PKIs will still be able to enjoy security services within their own PKIs. Subscribers associated with other agency PKIs (those that have cross-certified with the remaining CAs in the bridge membrane) can enjoy security services with each other. Consider the topology in Figure 16.8. If BCA-1 has been revoked, Alice and Doug can enjoy security services since they are in the same agency PKI. Carol and Bob can enjoy security services since their agencies cross-certified with bridge CAs that were not revoked. However, Alice cannot enjoy security services with Carol or Doug since her agency has revoked its certificate to the bridge CA.

Applications

The major interagency applications will be secure electronic mail (S/MIME), virtual private networks, and secure Web pages. Within agencies, PKIs are being used to implement digital signatures for workflow processes and perform public key-based user authentication. The federal PKI is also expected to secure services between the federal government and allied national governments (for example, Canada), state governments, local governments, and contractors.

Successes and Shortcomings

The FBCA is fielding the production system. Extensive testing has been performed. In the course of this testing, some successes and shortcomings have become apparent.

The major impediment to deploying a bridge CA-based PKI has been political. A bridge CA serves many masters, but it belongs to no one. It was only through the tireless efforts of the chairman of the Federal PKI Steering Committee, Rich Guida, that the FBCA has moved from concept to reality. By organizing demonstrations such as the EMA Challenge 2000 and making countless presentations, Rich was able to build consensus throughout the federal government that a deployment of an FBCA was necessary to support a federal PKI.

The FBCA reduces the burden on agency PKIs and their staff by minimizing the number of cross-certifications that must be performed. An agency's trust relationship can be efficiently managed using just two CA certificates. A multinode FBCA further reduces the burden by ensuring that agency cross-certification is only performed between machines that share a common management protocol and cryptographic algorithms.

CAs within the FBCA membrane will need a well-trained staff, as they shoulder a significant burden in cross-certification. The FBCA staff must cross-certify with each agency PKI. This is straightforward, but the cumulative workload may be high. The bridge CA staff must also cross-certify all the CA nodes within the membrane. This can be a significant problem, since the CAs will implement different cryptographic algorithms or management protocols.

The burden in constructing and validating paths falls squarely on the client systems. Clients may need to implement multiple signature algorithms to validate all possible paths. Clients need complex certification path construction software to build paths. The average desktop computer has sufficient power to construct and validate a seven-certificate path in a few seconds.[5] However, not all PKI products include this functionality.

A fully chained X.500 Directory system reduces the complexity of certification path building for client systems. In this architecture, each client directs all queries to the local X.500 Directory. Queries that cannot be satisfied locally are handled through chaining, which is transparent to the client. The availability and performance of this directory system will be critical to the performance of PKI-enabled secure applications.

A fully chained X.500 Directory system requires prior agreement on the structure of names and allocation of name spaces. If two PKIs have established overlapping name spaces, they cannot chain their directories. X.500 Directory systems are also more complex to administer than other types of repositories. In the future, the federal PKI may wish to cross-certify with external organizations or federal agencies that have implemented LDAP or other isolated repositories. Either way, the federal PKI will eventually have to face disjoint repositories.

---

[5] These statistics reflect the worst case, where none of the required certificates is in the system cache. If the certificates are already on the local system, path validation time is negligible.

The FBCA is a resilient architecture. Failure or compromise of any particular CA can be handled smoothly. Failure always inconveniences the smallest possible number of subscribers.

FBCAs can themselves be cross-certified. The EMA Challenge 2000 PKI included prototypes of both the FBCA and the DoD bridge CA. This added complexity did not impact application performance.

Administration and oversight of the FBCA is performed by consensus. Selection of a particular agency to oversee FBCA operations would be nearly as political as selecting an agency to operate a root CA. The U.S. Government has created several committees to advise and oversee operations of the FBCA. Agencies that cross-certify with the FBCA become members of a Federal PKI Policy Authority. This authority reviews and votes on subsequent applications for cross-certification. A steering committee and three additional working groups have been formed to address technical, legal, and business issues. See http://gits-sec.treas.gov or http://cioc-pki.treas.gov for additional information.

Lessons Learned

The FBCA has many lessons. They include:

Bridge CAs can unite PKIs with different architectures. The FBCA has connected single CAs, hierarchical PKIs, mesh PKIs, and even bridged PKI architectures into a seamless PKI.

Client software is critical. With a few exceptions, commercial products are not quite ready for a PKI as complex as the federal PKI. To completely realize the promise of the FBCA, client software must support multiple cryptographic algorithms, construct certification paths in a complex architecture, and include robust support for the policy mapping and name constraints. Due to the high visibility of the FBCA project, most PKI vendors are adding the necessary features to meet this goal.

Funding is difficult for bridge CAs. Bridge CAs do not belong to any particular enterprise, so they are difficult to fund. Political and promotional activities, such as the EMA Challenge, are necessary to gain sufficient visibility and support. Leadership and vision of the people in charge can make or break a bridge CA project.

Heterogeneous commercial products can implement a bridged PKI. While cross-certification can be painful and frustrating, the FBCA has demonstrated that a truly heterogeneous PKI can be integrated into one seamless heterogeneous system. CAs from nearly any vendor can be accommodated.

X.500 can simplify certificate retrieval. Fully chained X.500 systems remove the mystery from certificate retrieval. Clients simply query the local directory, and the remaining operations are transparent. Commercial X.500 Directory systems can be used to create heterogeneous directory systems.

A single cross-certification standard is needed. If a standard cross-certification mechanism was implemented by all vendors, the number of CAs within the bridge membrane could be reduced.

Bridge CAs could be operated more efficiently if network connectivity was permitted. Judicious use of firewalls and border directories might permit the FBCA to operate a LAN for the bridge CA nodes and an internal directory. This architecture could simplify operations without introducing unacceptable risk.

Administration and oversight of bridge CAs requires consensus. Rather than select a single entity to oversee the bridge, operations are monitored by the constituents.

Policy review is crucial. Policy review must be performed prior to issuing certificates so that policy mapping can be determined. It may not be possible to map between application-oriented policies and assurance-oriented policies.

Coordinate policy development. Review potential business partner CPs while you are developing your own CP. Comparison of independently developed CPs is always time consuming.

CHAPTER

17

Future Developments

This book has focused on features that are widely available in today's public key infrastructure (PKI) products. However, PKI is still a young field. As it matures, new features and concepts are continuously incorporated into products. Without a crystal ball, we cannot predict which features will prove important. However, in this chapter we make some educated guesses.

This chapter examines features that may become important or common in PKIs over the next few years. The chapter is organized to mirror the presentation of material in this book, rather than relative order of importance.

Cryptography

PKI and PKI-enabled applications rely on cryptography. As that field develops, PKI must change to stay current with the popular algorithms. There are many developments in every area of cryptography.

Table 17.1 lists the cryptographic algorithms in wide use today.

Applications and protocols that employ cryptography typically strive for uniform security from all classes of algorithms. The security of the system is equivalent to the strength of the weakest algorithm.

The most widely publicized development in the area of cryptography was the selection of the Rjindael algorithm by the National Institute of Standards and Technology

Table 17.1 Widely Deployed Cryptographic Algorithms

Hash algorithms	MD5 (128 bits)
	SHA-1 (160 bits)
Signature algorithms	RSA (1024 bits; occasionally 2048 bits)
	DSA (1024 bits)
Key management algorithms	RSA (1024 bits; occasionally 2048 bits)
	Diffie-Hellman (1024 bits; occasionally 2048 bits)
Encryption algorithms	DES (56 bits)
	Triple-DES (112 and 168 bits)
	RC2 and RC4 (40 and 128 bits)

(NIST) as the new Advanced Encryption Standard (AES). AES is expected to replace DES and Triple-DES as the internationally recognized standard for symmetric encryption. AES provides for symmetric encryption using 128-bit, 192-bit, and 256-bit keys. AES raises the bar for all other cryptographic techniques. AES will likely be published as a FIPS Publication in 2001.

Political changes are also making strong cryptography more freely available. The realization that electronic commerce cannot become ubiquitous without strong cryptography has lead to sweeping changes in the import and export controls on cryptography. As a result, quality implementations of strong algorithms are becoming available to almost everyone.

While AES is a symmetric algorithm, its development is having a substantial impact on PKI products. PKI components use symmetric cryptography in management operations; specifically, PKI management operations to recover encryption keys or obtain centrally generated keys. More importantly, PKI-enabled applications will be making use of AES in their applications. Therefore, the strength of the public/private keys needs to be increased to match the strength of AES.

Certificates and certificate revocation lists (CRLs) are digitally signed. Most PKI management messages are signed as well. The strength of a digital signature depends on two algorithms: the one-way hash function and the digital signature algorithm. As a rule of thumb for one-way hash functions, the hash value should be twice the size of the symmetric key offering the strength needed. For example, SHA-1 [FIPS180], with its 160-bit hash value, offers the same strength as an 80-bit symmetric key. MD5 [RIVE92], with its 128-bit hash value, offers the same strength as a 64-bit symmetric key. Both of these functions fall short of the security we need to complement AES.

NIST published three new hash functions, one to complement each of the three AES key sizes: SHA-256, SHA-394, and SHA-512 [SHA-256]. These algorithms are currently undergoing public review, but they appear to be both secure and efficient. Like AES, these new one-way hash functions will likely become a FIPS Publication in 2001. We expect to see the first implementations in products about the time this book is published.

Establishing rough equivalence for public key algorithms is considerably more complex. There is no rule of thumb that is widely accepted. Some researchers base *work factor* estimates on the number of computer operations needed to determine the private

Table 17.2 Comparative Algorithm Strength

SYMMETRIC KEY LENGTH	SYMMETRIC ALGORITHM	ONE-WAY HASH FUNCTION	RSA/DSA/ DIFFIE-HELLMAN KEY LENGTH	PRIME FIELD ELLIPTIC CURVE KEY LENGTH	BINARY FIELD ELLIPTIC CURVE KEY LENGTH
56	DES	MD5	768	–	–
80	SKIPJACK	SHA-1	1,024	$\|p\| = 192$	$m = 163$
112	Triple-DES	None	2,048	$\|p\| = 224$	$m = 233$
128	AES-128	SHA-256	3,200	$\|p\| = 256$	$m = 283$
192	AES-192	SHA-384	7,500	$\|p\| = 384$	$m = 409$
256	AES-256	SHA-512	15,000	$\|p\| = 521$	$m = 571$

key from the public key. Other researchers base work factor estimates on the amount of memory necessary to determine the private key from the public key.

Implementers must determine the public key sizes that offer comparable work factors for each of the three AES key sizes. We use the relative strengths proposed by Hillary Orman [ORMA00] and NIST [FIPS1862]. Most researchers agree that the commonly used 1024-bit RSA, DSA, and Diffie-Hellman keys are not sufficient. Similarly, the commonly used 161-bit elliptic curve keys are also insufficient. Many products also support 2048-bit RSA and Diffie-Hellman keys and 191-bits elliptic curve keys.[1] Even at these larger key sizes, these algorithms are significantly weaker than AES with a 128-bit key.

The current signature algorithms (RSA, DSA, and ECDSA) can achieve commensurate levels of security. However, this requires much larger keys than are commonplace today. Table 17.2 provides a rough comparison of the key sizes needed.[2] Comparing public key algorithms with symmetric algorithms is a mix of science and art, and several researchers will vigorously disagree with this data. However, without consensus from the research community, implementers need guidance. This is the best available.

The key sizes in Table 17.2 represent a development challenge, particularly to cryptographic token developers. For example, the processor and memory limitation of a smartcard make these particularly difficult to implement. The hardest part will be RSA key generation. As a result, we may see more DSA and ECDSA tokens deployed. We may also see more products where the keys are generated on a secure device at the RA and downloaded onto the smart card.

---

[1]DSA is currently undefined for key sizes larger than 1024 bits. NIST is expected to enhance the algorithm to support larger keys in the near future. See http://csrc.nist.gov for the latest information.

[2] The table lists only the public key size. The size of the private key is also important. As a rule of thumb, the private key must be at least twice the size of the symmetric key. These details are not usually visible to the user, since most cryptographic modules hide the private key.

Multi-Prime RSA [PKCS00] also offers hope for cryptographic token developers. By using more than two prime factors, the RSA private key operations become less processor intensive. The ANSI X9F1 working group is studying this technique for possible inclusion in an update to ANSI X9.31.

PKI Architectures

Chapter 6, "PKI Architectures," described seven PKI architectures: a single CA, trust lists, hierarchies, mesh PKIs, extended trust lists, cross-certified enterprise PKIs, and bridge-connected PKIs. We have a lot of experience with single CAs. We have significant experience with large and small hierarchical PKIs. One large hierarchical PKI includes over 400 CAs. We have vast experience with trust list architectures containing a large numbers of trust points. For example, the current version of Internet Explorer can support hundreds of trust points. The strengths and weaknesses of these architectures have already been discussed.

Our experience with operational large mesh PKIs, cross-certified Enterprise PKIs, and bridge-connected PKIs is less complete. The deployed PKIs using these architectures are relatively small (less than a dozen CAs). The discussion of these PKI architectures in Chapter 6 is based on theory, experience with pilot systems, and experience with small operational systems. There is no substitute for wide-scale deployment experience. As PKIs are developed using these architectures, operational experience will surely provide new lessons. This new information will help us build better PKIs, and it may lead to a new hybrid architecture.

Certificates

The X.509 public key certificate should remain relatively stable in the future. Since the certificate format allows for extensions, there is no compelling reason to modify the base certificate format. However, new standard extensions are likely to be specified. These extensions will be designed to meet challenges that are recognized as larger general-purpose PKIs are deployed. Other extensions may be necessary to facilitate world-wide consumer electronic commerce.

New developments in certificates are likely to focus on attribute certificates. These certificates do not contain a public key. Rather, attribute certificates bind a subject to various attributes, such as privileges, organizational role, or credit rating. Another possibility is development of alternative encoding formats for public key certificates.

Attribute Certificates

Public key certificates are focused on the binding between the subject and the public key. Establishing and maintaining this binding has been the focus of this entire book. However, the relationship between the subject and public key is expected to be a long-lived relationship. Most end entity certificates include a validity period of a year or two years.

Organizations seek improved access control. Public key certificates can be used to authenticate the identity of a user, and this identity can be used as an input to access control decision functions. However, in many contexts, the identity is not the criterion used for access control decisions. The access control decision may depend upon role, security clearance, group membership, or ability to pay.

Authorization information, such as membership in a group, often has a shorter lifetime than the binding of the identity and the public key. Authorization information could be placed in a public key certificate extension. However, this is not a good strategy for two reasons. First, the certificate is likely to be revoked because the authorization information needs to be updated. Revoking and reissuing the public key certificate with updated authorization information is quite expensive. Second, the CA that issues public key certificates is not likely to be authoritative for the authorization information. This results in additional steps for the CA to contact the authoritative authorization information source.

The X.509 attribute certificate (AC) binds attributes to an AC *holder* [X50997]. This definition is being profiled for use in Internet applications. The profile [FARR00] is likely to be published shortly after this book. Since the AC does not contain a public key, the AC is used in conjunction with a public key certificate. An access control function may make use of the attributes in an AC, but it is not a replacement for authentication. The public key certificate must first be used to perform authentication, then the AC is used to associate attributes with the authenticated identity.

ACs may also be used in the context of a data origin authentication service and a non-repudiation service. In these contexts, the attributes contained in the AC provide additional information about the signing entity. This information can be used to make sure that the entity is authorized to sign the data. This kind of checking depends either on the context in which the data is exchanged or on the data that has been digitally signed.

An X.509 AC resembles the X.509 public key certificate. The AC is an ASN.1 DER encoded object, and is signed by the issuer. An AC contains nine fields: version, holder, issuer, signature algorithm identifier, serial number, validity period, attributes, issuer unique identifier, and extensions. The AC holder is similar to the public key certificate subject, but the holder may be specified with a name, the issuer and serial number of a public key certificate, or the one-way hash of a certificate or public key. The attributes describe the authorization information associated with the AC holder. The extensions describe additional information about the certificate and how it may be used.

The contents of an AC are shown in Figure 17.1. This is a version 2 AC, and the AC holder is Alice. The AC was issued by the Hawk Data *Attribute Authority*, and was signed with DSA and SHA-1. The serial number is 4801, and the AC is valid from 8 A.M. precisely on January 2, 2001, until noon that same day. The attributes indicate that Alice is VPN Administrator. The AC extensions indicate that this certificate is targeted toward the Hawk VPN server, and that revocation information is not available for this certificate. ACs often have no revocation information.

ACs may be short-lived or long-lived. In Figure 17.1, the AC permits Alice to administer the VPN for four hours. As a result of the short validity period, the AC issuer does not need to maintain revocation information. By the time revocation information could be compiled and distributed, the AC would expire. So, with short-lived ACs, revocation information is not distributed. In this example, Hawk Data accepts the risk for that

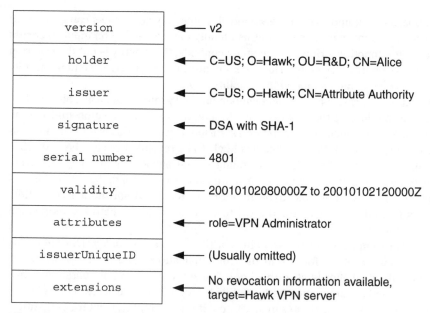

Figure 17.1   An attribute certificate for Alice.

four-hour window rather than maintain CRLs for attribute certificates. If an AC has a longer life span (for example, weeks or months), Hawk Data would need to maintain AC status information.

The Hawk Data VPN server can obtain Alice's AC in two different ways. Alice may provide the AC to the server when she initiates a connection. This is known as the *push* model. Alternatively, the Hawk VPN server can request the AC from the AC issuer or a repository when Alice initiates the connection. This is known as the *pull* model. A major benefit of the pull model is that it can be implemented without changes to the client or to the client-server protocol. The pull model is especially well suited for interdomain communication where the client's rights are assigned within the server's domain, rather than within the client's domain.

Returning to the AC in Figure 17.1, the AC specifies the Hawk VPN server as the target through an AC extension. The intent of this extension is to specify the servers or services that may use this AC. This means that a trustworthy server that is not listed as a target will reject the AC.

The X.509 specification supports a broader definition of authorization than the IETF attribute certificate profile. X.509 defines authorization as the "conveyance of privilege from one entity that holds such privilege, to another entity." The privilege could be further delegated by the AC holder if he or she chose to do so. X.509 allows for the construction and validation of an attribute certificate path that describes the delegation of authority.

Assume that all Hawk Data privileges derive from the CEO. The CEO could delegate authority for all network access decisions to the corporate security officer. The corporate security officer could delegate authority to manage VPN access to the VPN administrator,

Alice. The VPN administrator delegates the privilege to use the VPN to employees who are authorized to telecommute. In the extreme case, an AC represents each of these delegations of privilege.

The Hawk VPN server's access control function must construct a path of four attribute certificates to verify an employee VPN access. The Hawk server will also need to construct a path for the employee's public key certificate, so it can perform authentication. In fact, the Hawk VPN server must construct a certification path for each link in delegated privilege chain, so they can verify the signature on each AC!

This adds considerable complexity, and our experience with ACs is quite limited. As a result, the proposed Internet AC Profile does not recommend use of AC chains. This is good advice, at least for the near term. The simple case, where a single authority issues all of the ACs for a particular attribute, adds considerable functionality without adding considerable complexity. The Internet AC Profile authors envision scenarios in which more than one AC is required. For example, Alice might need an AC to demonstrate membership in the R&D group and another AC to assert a managerial role. Different authorities might issue each of these ACs. Implementations should be ready to support such a scenario.

Qualified Certificates

Certificates can bind many different identity forms to a public key. The certificate subject may be a person or a device. If the subject is a person, he or she may have many different identities. Different certificates may correspond to a different identity for the same person. The connection between the Internet user and a physical person can, at times, be tenuous. Certificates often bind an Internet identity, such as an electronic mail address, to a public key.

For example, consider the following certificates. The first certificate binds the names *C=US, O=Hawk Data, OU=R&D, CN=Alice Adams*, and *alice.adams@hawkdata.com* to a public key. The second certificate binds a public key to the electronic mail address *A.Adams@freemail.com*. Are these, in fact, the same physical person? The Hawk Data CA knows what physical person corresponds to the subject of the first certificate. In the second case, the issuer may not know the identity of the physical person associated with that address.

For many applications, the Internet identity is the only important identity. For example, many S/MIME implementations verify that the subject of the certificate identifies the e-mail address of the sender. There is no requirement that the certificate identify the physical person who sent the message. In some cases, the sender and recipient have met electronically and the physical people have never met.

On the other hand, there is a broad class of applications that depend upon the ability to determine the identity of the physical person linked to a public key. In particular, signature keys that will be used to generate legally binding signatures must be linked to a physical person. The difficulty is determining which certificates meet these legal requirements.

The term *Qualified Certificate* (QC) is used by the European Commission to describe certificates that meet the requirements in European legislation for legally recognized electronic signatures [EP99]. PKI practitioners often refer to this legislation as *the Directive*. The QC is one component of a framework for legally recognized signatures. The framework is discussed further later in this chapter. QCs are issued exclusively to physical persons, and their primary purpose is identifying a person with a high level of assurance. Support for public non-repudiation services is the goal.

The IETF and ETSI have coordinated the development of a QC Profile [SANT00, ETSI00a]. The IETF specification describes a format for certificates intended to support public non-repudiation services. A CA may include certificate information to explicitly specify this intent. There are two complementary ways to indicate that a certificate is a QC: through a certificate policy and through the QC Statement extension.

The goal of the IETF QC Profile is to define a general syntax that is independent from local legal requirements. The QC profile is, however, designed to allow further profiling in order to meet specific local needs. The QC Profile is based on the Internet Certificate and CRL Profile specified in RFC 2459 [HOUS99], but refines its provisions in several areas.

- Mandatory and optional naming components are defined with explicit semantics for both the issuer and the subject. The issuer name identifies the CA and the jurisdiction under which the CA was operating when issuing the certificate. The subject name may be a legal name or a pseudonym, but the issuer must know which physical person corresponds to the subject name.

- The key usage extension in a QC may assert only the non-repudiation usage flag.

- An extension is defined for storage of biometric information. Biometric information is stored in the form of a hash of a biometric template. The purpose of this extension is to provide means for authentication of biometric information. The biometric information that corresponds to the stored hash is not stored in the extension, but the extension may include a URI pointing to a location where this information can be obtained.

- The QC extension allows CAs to include relevant predefined statements. Each statement consists of an object identifier (OID) to identify the type of statement, followed by optional qualifying data. A typical statement might indicate the legal system associated with the QC or a maximum reliance limit for the certificate.

The ETSI QC Profile details the means by which an implementation of the IETF QC profile can meet the requirements of the Directive. Three standard QC statements are used. The first statement asserts that the certificate was issued as a QC according to the Directive. The second statement asserts a limitation on the transaction value for which this certificate can be used; this statement corresponds to another requirement in the Directive. The third statement indicates the retention period for information received from the subject at the time of registration. This statement indicates the number of years the information will be available after the certificate expires.

The IETF and ETSI QC specifications will be used in European PKIs to satisfy the requirements of the Directive. Outside of Europe, the legal framework is less prescriptive. Without this framework, it is unclear whether QCs are necessary.

Alternative Certificate Formats

The X.509 certificate format has many detractors. Some people are not comfortable with the ASN.1 syntax or the DER encoding rules. Others are not happy with the reliance on names during certification path construction. Every few years, there is a move to replace the X.509 certificate with something better. However, replacement now seems unlikely due to the momentum behind the many X.509 implementations. However, we will briefly mention a few possibilities.

Some PKI developers find the learning curve associated with ASN.1 encoding rules to be very steep. The DER encoding rules are a bit arcane, and it is very common for new vendors to discover flaws in their encoding or decoding software. The ASN.1 encoding rules have been enhanced over the years, and some of the newer constructs are quite difficult to understand. To cope with this situation, the IETF PKIX Working Group has standardized on the original 1988 ASN.1 syntax. Others would prefer to abandon ASN.1 altogether.

Some people want to replace ASN.1 encoding with XML encoding. Developers who are already familiar with XML would prefer to encode everything in XML. However, XML is probably not a good choice. In the first place, an XML certificate would be far larger than an ASN.1 encoded certificate. This is not crucial in some environments, but it is very important with handheld wireless devices. Such devices have limited storage capacity and limited bandwidth. Secondly, XML can be reformatted in a variety of ways without modifying the content. In fact, XML processors commonly reformat documents to suit their own requirements. Of course, digital signatures will not verify if the bit pattern is changed in the slightest detail. To verify an XML signature, the certificate must be processed by a canonicalization routine to ensure that the data processed by the CA and the certificate user is exactly the same. XML does have one significant advantage: ASCII text representation. This would aid PKI developers when they are debugging their implementations. However, most PKI users do not attempt to read their certificates. All in all, XML offers more problems than it solves.

Some researchers feel that the reliance on names for certification path construction is a mistake. In some cases, they reject the use of names at all. They prefer to chain based solely on public key values. In other cases, they declare that names have only a local context. Regardless, the basic premise is that names may be an attribute of a key holder, but that name is not of any security interest.

The IETF Simple Public Key Infrastructure (SPKI) Working Group developed the most complete specifications that implement this philosophy. The SPKI specifications describe a theoretical framework, certificate formats, and a path validation algorithm for public key certificates and authorization. The SPKI Requirements, in RFC 2692, describes general requirements for a simple public key infrastructure [ELLI99a]. The SPKI Certificate Theory, in RFC 2693, defines certificate formats for public key certificates as well as path validation rules [ELLI99b]. The SPKI documents are considered Experimental specifications, and so far they have not stimulated product development.

The X.509 certificate benefits from years of experience and incremental development. A competing standard must need to be clearly superior to change the course of the market. We should look to projects such as SPKI for new and useful concepts to extend or clarify X.509-based PKI. We should not expect them to replace it.

Certificate Status

In Chapter 3, "PKI Basics," we noted that there were two models for credit card status: the hot list and the real-time status check. The basic mechanism for certificate status is the CRL, which corresponds to the credit card hot list. Developments in the area of certificate status may be considered along two lines: development of real-time status checks and enhancing the performance of CRLs. The emerging standard for real-time status checking is the On-line Certificate Status Protocol. Other potential revocation developments are focused on the Delta CRL.

Online Certificate Status Protocol

RFC 2560 defines the Online Certificate Status Protocol (OCSP) [MYER99]. OCSP enables applications to determine the status of a particular certificate by querying an OCSP responder. An OCSP client issues a status request to the OCSP responder and suspends acceptance of the certificate in question until the OCSP responder provides a reply. The OCSP responder sends the certificate status information to the requester. Support for OCSP is included in a certificate using the authority information access extension. CAs may host this service locally or delegate this responsibility to an OCSP responder.

Figure 17.2 depicts a simple OCSP request. Bob sent the request. The four data items in the certID field describe the certificate in which Bob is interested: hash algorithm, issuer name hash, issuer key hash, and serial number. The issuer name hash is the result of hashing the certificate issuer name field. Similarly, the issuer key hash is the result of hashing the issuer public key, as obtained from the subject public key field in the issuer's certificate. The hash algorithm used for both these hashes is identified in the hash algorithm field. The serial number is the serial number of the certificate for which status is being requested. In Figure 17.2, the certificate of interest has serial number 2560. Bob has included a nonce in an extension field to guard against replay.

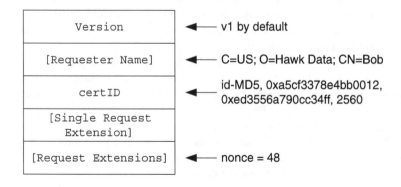

Legend:
[ ] Optional Field

Figure 17.2 An OCSP request message.

When using CRLs, the pair of issuer name and serial number identifies a certificate. OCSP uses the more complicated certificate identifier structure. In the absence of a global directory system, it is possible that two CAs could choose the same name. Since an OCSP responder may provide service for multiple CAs, the OCSP responder must be able to distinguish CAs with the same issuer name. Two CAs will not have the same public key. By using the hash of the issuer public key in addition to the hash of the issuer name to identify the issuer, the possibility of collisions is removed.

In Figure 17.2, Bob has requested status information for one certificate. The OCSP request format supports requesting status for multiple certificates in a single request. In that case, the CertID and the optional single request extension fields appear for each certificate. Bob may optionally sign his OCSP request message. By omitting the signature, lightweight clients may reduce the number of expensive signature operations they perform. However, an OCSP responder may insist on signed requests for billing or access control purposes.

An OCSP response message includes the version, the responder identifier, the time the message was produced, the certificate identifier, the certificate status, the time that the status was last updated, and the time when the next status update for this certificate is expected. In the single extensions, the OCSP responder includes additional information about that particular certificate. If the response conveys information about more than one certificate, the certificate identifier, status, update information, and single extension appear for each certificate. The response extensions include additional information for the entire response. Every OCSP response is digitally signed by the OCSP responder.

Figure 17.3 depicts the data in the OCSP response to Bob's request. The response came from the Hawk Data's OCSP1 server. The message was produced at 2:12 P.M. Greenwich

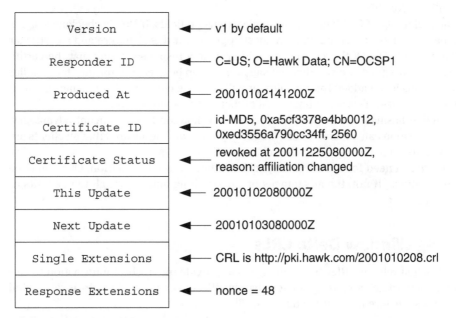

Figure 17.3 An OCSP response message.

Mean Time on January 2, 2001. The certificate was revoked on December 25, 2000, at 8 A.M. Greenwich Mean Time. The last update for this certificate's status was 8 A.M. this morning. The next update is expected at 8 A.M. the following morning.

The IETF PKIX Working Group is considering enhancements to OCSP. Additional methods to specify a certificate in an OCSP request or response are one likely enhancement. The draft specification for *Online Certificate Status Protocol, Version 2*, permits a certificate to be identified using the issuer and serial number of a certificate, by including the certificate in the request, or simply the subject name [MYER00b]. If the CA is the OCSP responder, or if the responder serves a community with a well-managed name space, these attributes are sufficient to identify the certificate of interest.

OCSP is often described as providing revocation information in a more timely fashion than CRLs. An OCSP responder can provide the most up-to-date information it possesses without repository latency. If the OCSP responder is also the CA, the most up-to-date information will be provided. With CRLs, the CA may have additional information that it cannot provide to certificate users. However, in practice, there has been little difference in freshness of the certificate status information provided by an OCSP responder and a CRL.

Most OCSP responders are not CAs. Rather, they are single-purpose machines that handle certificate status requests for a large number of CAs. Typically, these servers obtain their revocation information *periodically in the form of CRLs*. The information obtained by the requester is no fresher than if they obtained the same CRLs themselves.

When the OCSP response is returned to the requestor, it is digitally signed. The requestor must validate the signature on the response. How can the requestor determine if the OCSP responder has been revoked? It cannot. To do so, the requestor would have to ask the OCSP responder for status information on itself. The actions needed to revoke an OCSP responder is similar to the actions needed to remove a trust point from a certificate trust list.

The real utility of OCSP lies in the single extension fields. If Bob is checking a signature on a purchase order, he could request approval for this signature and a particular dollar amount. The OCSP responder could provide a response stating that the certificate status was good and whether the signature could be accepted for the stated dollar amount. This is the added functionality provided to the credit card companies through the online request. This is the functionality that CRLs cannot deliver.

Coupling business decisions with certificate validation has significant advantages. The organization can administer one OCSP responder and be assured that all clients are applying the same business rules for all transactions.

If there is a need for transaction-specific authorization information, OCSP may be the best choice. If not, the advantages of CRL caching may outweigh the benefits of online checking.

Sliding Window Delta CRLs

For PKIs that rely on CRLs, the challenge is to provide the freshest information to certificate users while minimizing network bandwidth consumption. When PKIs rely on full CRLs, these requirements are in direct conflict.

To maximize the freshness, CRLs must be updated frequently. As the delta between updates shrinks, the probability that a client will find a useful CRL in its cache goes to zero. This results in certificate users downloading a new CRL for each certificate validation. Most of the information on the CRL is the same, so the identical information is transmitted repeatedly, consuming bandwidth without providing any benefit. To minimize the consumption of network bandwidth, CRLs should have reasonably long lifetimes. As the delta between updates grows, the greater the probability that relying parties will have the appropriate CRL in their cache.

Current PKI products rely on CRL distribution points to segment CRLs into reasonably sized data objects. Segmented CRLs cover a smaller portion of the certificates issued by a CA. If a relying party retrieves a segmented CRL, substantially less network bandwidth is consumed (compared to a full CRL for the same issuer). The segmented CRLs carry less information, so they further reduce the probability that a certificate user has the correct CRL.

There is insufficient experience with CRLs and segmented CRLs to determine the utility of these solutions. However, extensive modeling has been performed comparing these certificate revocation mechanisms. Most notably, David Cooper analyzed the performance of CRLs and segmented CRLs in [COOP99] and delta CRLs in [COOP00]. He suggests that the ideal performance metrics for delta CRLs could be achieved using *sliding window delta-CRLs*.

In the simple case, delta CRLs and full CRLs are issued together and the delta CRL lists all the certificates revoked since the last full CRL was issued.[3] The current full CRL is denoted as CRL_X. A certificate user, who has the previous full CRL, denoted CRL_{X-1}, may obtain complete information by obtaining the delta CRL and combining it with the full CRL. The certificate user obtains the freshest information available, but consumes a fraction of the bandwidth required to download CRL_X. However, a relying party that holds CRL_{X-2} must instead obtain CRL_X.

A sliding window delta CRL lists all the certificates revoked since an earlier full CRL, CRL_{X-n}. This delta CRL may be combined with any of the CRLs from CRL_{X-n} through CRL_{X-1} and provide complete information. Figure 17.4 depicts a timeline for generation of full and delta CRLs by a CA using the sliding window scheme. In this case, a full CRL is issued every four hours. A delta CRL is issued simultaneously covering all revocations that occurred in the last 36 hours.

Assume that the CA in Figure 17.4 issued Bob's certificate. Alice arrives at work at 7 A.M. on Monday and validates the signature on an S/MIME message from Bob. Alice will obtain full CRL number 22, which was issued at 4 A.M. Alice sends a reply to Bob, and heads off to a meeting. Alice returns to the office at 1 P.M. Bob has sent another message. The CRL in Alice's cache has expired. Alice retrieves the noon delta CRL. This CRL covers all revocations since midnight Sunday, so Alice can combine this with full CRL number 22 and validate Bob's certificate. Obtaining the delta CRL is very fast, so Alice does not notice the time taken to fetch the delta CRL from the repository.

---

[3] This example was devised to be consistent with IETF requirements that full CRLs be issued with every delta CRL. This guarantees that the most current information is available to certificate users that can't process delta CRLs. The sliding window technique can also be employed with less frequent publication of full CRLs, as described in [COOP00].

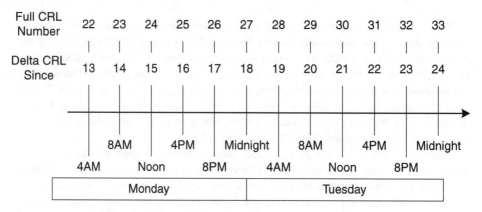

Figure 17.4   Timeline for full and sliding window delta CRLs.

Under this scheme, a certificate user will only obtain a full CRL if it has not checked this CA's CRL in a day and a half. If the relying party has a full CRL that is less than one-and-a-half days old, it will only require a delta CRL with 36 hours of revocation. A relying party that uses certificates frequently will only download the very small deltas, consuming little bandwidth. Yet, the information is quite current. On average, the information available to a certificate user is just two hours old. In extreme cases, [COOP00] projects a 99% reduction in peak network bandwidth by using the sliding window technique while providing status information no more than ten minutes old.

Today's PKIs do not exceed the limitations of full and segmented CRLs. As a result, delta CRLs are not widely deployed. Few commercial PKI client implementations process delta CRLs. Fewer CA products can generate sliding window deltas. However, as PKIs grow, the incentive to deploy innovative certificate status may grow.

Repositories

Before a certificate user can validate a certification path, it must gather a sequence of certificates to form a certificate chain and obtain revocation data for each certificate in the sequence. Certificates and CRLs are distributed using diverse mechanisms. Commonly used technologies for retrieving certificates and CRLs include X.500, LDAP, HTTP, and FTP, as well as proprietary methods.

If X.500 is the sole means for distributing certificates and CRLs, a certificate user needs to support only one protocol, and all queries are directed to the same server. If a combination of technologies is used, including mixing LDAP and X.500 directories, the certificate user may need to support multiple protocols. The certificate user must also be able to identify an appropriate repository for each query.

The authority information access and subject information access certificate extensions enhance the ability of CAs to provide the necessary information to the certificate users. If these extensions appear in every certificate, and the relying party supports the appropriate protocols, they will be able to construct the certification path, if one exists.

However, these extensions are only useful if the certificate user possesses the appropriate end entity certificate. This is often true, but there are situations in which the relying party wishes to discover an end entity certificate before the application begins. Without a global directory, the certificate user has no information to help it locate the end entity certificate.

A *DNS Repository Locator Service* has been proposed to solve this problem. The proposal describes a technique that uses the Domain Name System (DNS) to locate a repository [BOEY00]. Certificate users obtain a PKIXREP SRV record from the DNS. The PKIXREP SRV record specifies a protocol, such as LDAP or HTTP, and the host address of the repository. In combination with the authority information access and subject information access certificate extensions, the DNS Repository Locator Service could provide a comprehensive solution. However, the utility of this solution will depend upon widespread acceptance and implementation.

As new PKI-enabled applications attempt to leverage PKIs across different enterprises, the problem of disjointed directories will become more pressing. This should motivate PKIs to include the authority information access and subject information access certificate extensions. If a standard approach to location of foreign repositories emerges, disjointed directories will cease to be a problem.

Certification Path Construction and Validation

Current PKI products offer inconsistent functionality and performance in certification path construction and validation. Different PKI products may return different results when validating the same certification path. In other cases, one product may be able to develop a certification path while the other claims that no path exists. Achieving consistent results while experiencing an acceptable delay is critical to customer acceptance. Recent developments in certification path construction and validation offer a variety of mechanisms addressing different aspects of this problem.

Certification Path Validation Testing

Certification path validation is critical, but implementations are inconsistent. Unfortunately, different implementations return different results for the same sequence of certificates. This presents a very dangerous situation for both the CA and the relying party. The CA cannot depend on implementations to correctly interpret the information they include in certificates. Application owners may find service denied to authorized users, or even worse, service offered to inappropriate users.

Certification path validation was relatively straightforward in X.509 v1 and X.509 v2. Each certificate in the sequence had to be within its validity period and a CRL checked for each certificate. The names and signatures needed to chain for each subsequent certificate in the path. If these checks passed, the chain started at a trusted point, and the client could determine that each issuer was a CA, then the certification path was valid.

X.509 v3 added both functionality and complexity to certification path validation. Now, certificates identify CAs explicitly. They also include limitations on subject names, the appropriate use of public keys, and certificate policies. The concept of criticality added additional processing requirements. Initially, different vendors supported different sets of standard extensions. This led to inconsistent results, as valid certification paths were rejected when unrecognized critical extensions were encountered. The Internet Certificate and CRL Profile [HOUS99] has generated greater consensus, but inconsistent results persist because implementers have interpreted non-critical extensions differently. If one implementation ignores a constraint in a non-critical extension and another implementation honors the constraint, the two implementations can return different results.

One mechanism to increase consistency and enhance quality of certification path validation software would be a comprehensive set of conformance tests. A set of test certification paths that exercise the nuances of the certification path validation algorithm would assist vendors and consumers alike.

NIST, the National Security Agency (NSA), Cygnacom Solutions, and Getronics Government Services recently completed a suite of 76 conformance tests for relying parties that validate X.509 certification paths. These tests are available at http://csrc.nist.gov/pki/testing/x509paths.html. The tests cover X.509 v3 certificates and X.509 v2 CRLs.

Each test consists of a set of X.509 certificates and CRLs. Each test verifies one or more of the X.509 features used in the U.S. Department of Defense (DoD) Class 3 PKI. Additional features will be added in the future. The tests cover only commonly used fields and extensions: base certificate fields, basic constraints, key usage, certificate policies, and policy constraints. Expected test results assume that the implementation requires certificate status information and processes CRLs.

Hopefully, these tests will result in consistent processing of common extensions by all PKI implementations. Additional tests examining more advanced features, such as name constraints and policy mapping, are required as well. These organizations intend to continue the development of the test suite to cover additional extensions. The goal is to test every facet of the certification path validation.

Delegated Certification Path Construction Services

Certification path construction is straightforward in small PKIs or hierarchical PKIs. However, many factors promote the acceptance of more complex PKI architectures. Regardless of the architecture, there is a strong incentive for PKIs to grow. As with the Internet itself, the value of a PKI to a relying party increases as the number of certificate holders grows. PKI vendors are enhancing their certification path construction software to meet the challenges of complex PKI topologies, but more complex PKIs will constantly be emerging.

When a relying party obtains an end entity certificate that it wishes to validate, two challenges in constructing a path are faced. First, as noted earlier, disjointed repositories complicate retrieval of appropriate certificates and CRLs. A relying party may need to locate the appropriate repository for each certificate in the chain. Second, without additional knowledge, a relying party may pursue dead-end or cyclic paths. As PKIs grow, users may become impatient and abort processing before all the possibilities have been exhausted.

Relying parties must be able to construct certification paths efficiently. Most relying parties will communicate with the same certificate holders repeatedly. Effective use of caching can minimize delays incurred by repository requests. In addition, a wealth of network routing algorithms have been developed. By adapting and applying these routing techniques to the PKI path construction problem, PKI clients will certainly improve in efficiency and reliability.

However, some PKI vendors are pursuing an entirely different solution: *path construction servers* [MYER00c]. In their eyes, the delays incurred waiting for repositories to return certificates and CRLs are unmanageable. As the number of dead-end paths explored increases, the situation becomes even more unmanageable. Instead, they prefer to offload the entire certification path construction problem to a server. A path construction server is designed to return a complete certification path to the relying party upon request.

The path construction server (PCS) is essentially a smart repository. It contains a database of CA certificates and perhaps CRLs. The PCS maintains information regarding the possible certification paths that are formed using these certificates. Given an end entity certificate and one or more trust points, the path construction server can quickly form chains that connect the end entity and a trust point. The client receives the certification path and validates it locally. If the certification path is not valid for this application, the relying party could request a different path from the PCS. Alternatively, the PCS could return several paths from which the relying party could choose. This process is depicted in Figure 17.5.

The PCS can take full advantage of both complex networking routing algorithms and caching. The PCS should only be forced to obtain objects from a repository when a CRL expires or a new CA is encountered.[4] A repository crawler could accumulate new CA certificates. This would work in similar fashion to the Web search engines building and maintaining their database of links. Relying parties do not need to trust the server for certificate status since it only supplies data that is signed by CAs. As an untrusted system, the PCS can be designed for performance and availability. The security relevant operations—certification path validation—are all performed on the local system.

This is a very attractive model. Certification path validation may be complex, but it requires a fixed number of iterations through an algorithm. The algorithm can always be performed in some finite time. Certification path construction, on the other hand, may not be deterministic. The number of certificate retrievals before a relying party can declare that no certification path is available is highly variable. The PCS assumes it has all available CA certificates; if a certification path cannot be constructed from the cache, then it does not exist.

However, a PCS does not guarantee deterministic processing. The relying party cannot be sure that the certification path returned by the PCS will be acceptable. As shown in Figure 17.5, the relying party may need to iteratively request certification paths until

---

[4] Each time a CA certificate is obtained it would be cached by the PCS. The PCS could obtain new CRLs automatically when those in the cache expire. Unless the end entity certificate was issued by a previously unknown CA, path construction would not require retrieval of any certificates or CRLs.

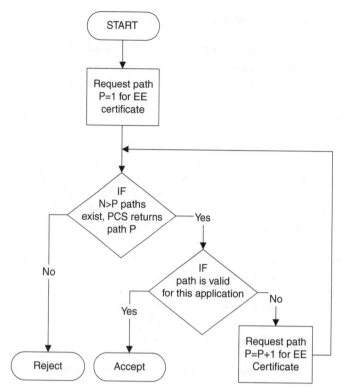

Figure 17.5 A relying party uses a path construction server.

an acceptable path is returned. The PCS can use various heuristics, such as the number of certificates, to select the most likely paths. However, the PCS cannot be sure that the path is acceptable unless it understands all of the relying party requirements. To date, PCS proposals do not permit the transfer of sufficient context for the PCS to know all relying party requirements.

Certification Path Validation Services

The advances in certification path construction and validation do not satisfy some PKI implementers. Their goal is to offload the entire process of certification path construction and validation to a server [HOFF00]. A relying party would provide a validation server with an end entity certificate, one or more trust points, and the initial values for certification path validation. The *path validation server* (PVS) would respond with a message informing the relying party whether the certificate was acceptable. Standard protocols for these services have not been standardized, but work is currently underway in the IETF PKIX Working Group to provide these services [MALP00, MYER00d].

Delegating the certificate validation process to a trusted server has a number of advantages. The certificate user achieves path construction and validation in a single round-trip, and then the certificate user verifies a single digital signature on the response. The single round-trip is especially important in bandwidth-limited environments. If the certificate user has limited processing power, the reduction in signature verifications may be significant. Also, the reduction in client code may accelerate deployment of PKI-enabled applications.

Delegating the certificate validation process to a trusted server may also provide performance advantages. If the PVS has cached the necessary certificates and CRLs, and verified them, the PVS may be able to construct and validate a certification path very quickly.

These benefits are not free; there are several disadvantages. All of the security-relevant operations are performed by the PVS. The PVS must be as secure as a CA; it is, in effect, the sole trust point for the relying party. It will also be more complex to determine from the database if the certification path is valid for the relying party provided context. It may be necessary for the PVS to construct certification paths and validate them iteratively before responding. In that case, the internal process will mirror the overall flow with the PCS in Figure 17.5.

In addition, the performance enhancements are based on the ability of the server to obtain and cache information. PKIs that rely on online status services are counterproductive to this model. In such a case, the PVS is unlikely to hold the required status information. The server will have to retrieve information from the OCSP responder, mitigating much of the performance gain.

However, performance is not the only reason to centralize certification path validation services. If path validation is performed locally, the application owner must manage the set of trust points and acceptable policies. This scenario permits an organization to design different policy enforcement mechanisms. When policy decisions are delegated to application owners, this is appropriate. Other organizations impose a centralized management discipline and want consistent policy enforcement across all clients for each class of applications. Allowing a client to manage its own trust points and acceptable policies does not satisfy this requirement. If applications use the same trusted PVS, consistent results are assured.

In summary, certification path validation services may be required to serve light-weight application systems as the Internet absorbs wireless application protocol (WAP) telephones and personal computing devices. These services are not required to serve systems with average network connectivity and processing power, but they could achieve superior performance in some PKI implementations. An organization may also implement such a service to ensure consistent application of organizational policy. To achieve these gains, the relying party must relinquish responsibility for security decisions to a single highly trusted server.

Management Protocols

The most pressing problems in PKI management protocols are interoperability and availability of clients that support advanced management protocols, such as CMP and CMC. Since PKI products are not interoperable, current PKIs generally rely on CAs and RAs from a single vendor. If the management protocol is PKCS #10 with SSL or PKCS #7, the clients may be a mixture of Microsoft and Netscape applications. For more advanced protocols, such as CMP and CMC, the client software is usually obtained from the vendor that provided the CA and RAs. Future developments are expected to bring interoperable products implementing advanced protocols to the marketplace.

As these problems are resolved, PKI deployments will begin to incorporate more advanced management operations. In-person authentication, central public/private key pair generation, and private key recovery will become requirements rather than frills. Central key generation and private key recovery services were not discussed in detail in Chapter 11, "PKI Management Protocols," but are addressed briefly here.

Interoperability of Heterogeneous Products

Without interoperability, PKI deployments cannot mix products obtained from different vendors. Even where vendors have selected the same protocols, interoperability has been difficult to achieve. The new protocols are significantly more complex than PKCS #7 and #10. Developers do not have the experience with these protocols, and they cannot rely on an available code base.

Bob Moskowitz has been organizing PKI product interoperability testing since May 1999. His work continues under the auspices of the PKI Forum, which was formed early in 2000. To date, this testing has focused on interoperability of CMP-based PKI products. A number of different companies have participated, including Entrust Technologies, IBM, Certicom, and Baltimore Technologies. The PKI Forum intends to facilitate interoperability testing for CMC-based PKI products as well. Microsoft has already announced support for CMC in the next release of Cert Server.

Interoperability testing has two benefits. First, testing highlights ambiguities in the specifications. This drives clarifications to the specifications, and improved specifications ease the burden on future PKI developers. Second, PKI products become more interoperable. This provides PKI consumers the ability to select the best PKI products for each platform.

For current results of this interoperability testing, check the PKI Forum Web site at http://pkiforum.org.

In-Person Authentication

As noted in the discussion of qualified certificates, the ability to bind a key to a physical person is often an important policy requirement. There are multiple techniques to achieve this requirement, but the most powerful is in-person appearance at the RA. As organizations seek to extend the range of applications beyond secure e-mail and Web browsing, the need for such transaction models will clearly grow.

One of the major drivers will be legally binding signatures. Organizations have a strong incentive to replace paper documents with handwritten signatures. Organizations need to reduce cost and increase efficiency to remain competitive. Replacing paper-based transactions with electronic documents offers these benefits. However, replacing paper demands that the digital signatures stand up in court. The digital signature must link the signer to the document at least as strongly as a handwritten signature. This is easier to achieve if the signer appeared in-person at the RA when obtaining the certificate for that signature key.

Many PKIs do not currently require in-person appearance to obtain certificates. Some PKI implementations do not support appropriate transaction models for in-person appearance at an RA. In the future, in-person appearance will become a common policy requirement, and support for these transaction models will become ubiquitous.

Private Key Recovery

The business case for recovery of private keys needed to decrypt data is compelling. An employee may encrypt data to protect the confidentiality of critical information. While it may be critical to protect this information from competitors or adversaries, the organization itself must be able to access the data in the future.

The organization can access the data as long as it has access to the private key. In general, this access is achieved directly by the employee. However, the employee's cryptographic module could fail or be lost. Even if the module functions, employees leave, die, and take vacations. In any of these cases, the organization cannot access the encrypted data. This is unacceptable.

An organization must be able to access its own encrypted data, even when the employee or the employee's cryptographic module is unavailable. Obtaining a backup copy of the key management private key for emergency access is called *key recovery*. Key recovery services may be offered through a variety of avenues, including as an added-value PKI service.

There are several reasons to implement key recovery in conjunction with a PKI. First, PKIs readily distinguish between signature public keys and key management public keys. Key recovery should *never* ever be applied to signature private keys. The mere existence of a centrally managed backup for a signature private key undermines non-repudiation. This is likely to adversely impact the legal standing of any signature generated with this private key. Second, the protection of these private keys is critical to acceptance of the system. If the key recovery system is weak, an adversary will simply obtain the private key from the key recovery system and decrypt the data. If the CA manages the storage of the private keys, many of the same security features used to protect the CA may be applied to the key recovery system. This can provide an economy of scale.

Several PKI products support private key recovery today. PKI products based on CMP may use standard transactions to implement it. Other products perform private key backup with nonstandard transactions. As organizations seek to leverage the PKI to protect confidential data, the business requirement to support key recovery will become more apparent. PKI products will increasingly offer support for private key recovery. Standard transactions may also be defined in other protocols in the future. For example, Microsoft has developed an approach using CMC.

Centrally Generated Keys

In general, it is preferable for each certificate user to generate his or her own public/private key pairs. If a certificate holder generates a key pair, he or she can control the dissemination of those keys to other parties. In theory, this provides the best security. However, there are pragmatic reasons to accept central generation of key management public/private key pairs.

First, many cryptographic modules do not have sufficient processing power or memory to rapidly generate RSA public/private key pairs. This is compounded by AES, which will require larger RSA keys. As discussed earlier, key management RSA keys must be large enough to provide commensurate strength to the symmetric operations. Cryptographic devices with limited processing power may be able to perform the AES encryption and decryption. However, these devices may not be able to generate RSA key pairs of an appropriate size. Delegating key generation to a more powerful cryptographic module will increase efficiency and allow less powerful cryptographic modules, such as smartcards, to employ larger RSA keys.

Second, central generation of key management keys can simplify the implementation of key recovery systems. If the key recovery and key generation services are colocated, then the CA and key recovery service may coordinate their efforts. This permits the CA to ensure that critical private keys are backed up before issuing a certificate. The private key can be encrypted and transmitted to the certificate holder. If the CA allows the certificate holder to generate the key pair, then the CA must confirm that the public key and private key provided by the certificate holder belong together. The CA must perform some cryptographic operations to ensure the correct private key correspondence.

Legal and Policy

The future developments in the legal and policy areas are most difficult to predict, but there will certainly be changes. The base documents for certificate policies and certification practice statements will certainly be revised. In fact, the American Bar Association Information Security Committee is working on an update to RFC 2527 [CHOK99]. Accreditation procedures, such as WebTrust and tScheme, will be enhanced or replaced. An installed base of certificate policies will both simplify and complicate the task of the CP author. It will become easier to develop a new CP, as text and concepts are easily borrowed from existing CPs. On the other hand, CP authors will be forced to compare their CP with the CPs of other similar organizations. Due diligence will require comparison to ensure that the CP provides a similar or higher level of assurance.

New legislation is also impacting policies. Legislatures and regulators make key decisions that have far-reaching implications on PKI and PKI-enabled applications. For example, digital signature initiatives impact the types of services that may be offered, who may offer them, and the procedures they must follow. Digital signature initiatives have been passed in many nations and states. These laws and proposed laws vary widely in specificity.

There are several Web sites devoted to legal information affecting electronic commerce and PKI, such as the McBride, Baker, and Coles Web site at http://www.mbc.com. Much of the legislation (passed or pending) is available online as well. For U.S. federal legislation, the Government Printing Office maintains congressional publications online at http://www.access.gpo.gov/su_docs/legislative.html.

In the following sections, we briefly examine three U.S. federal initiatives: the Electronic Signatures in Global and National Commerce Act (E-Sign), the Health Insurance Portability and Accountability Act (HIPAA), and the Government Paperwork Elimination Act (GPEA). We also discuss the European Directive 1999/93/EC.

E-Sign

The Electronic Signatures in Global and National Commerce Act (E-Sign) was signed into law on June 30, 2000. McBride, Baker, and Coles say: "E-Sign grants electronic signatures and documents equivalent legal status with traditional handwritten signatures" [MBC00a]. This removes a major legal barrier to the use of electronic signatures in electronic commerce.

The E-Sign bill is technology neutral. Digital signatures and PKI are just one method for implementing its requirements. If the two parties agree that PINs and passwords are sufficient, then they may constitute electronic signatures for this application. Pen-based technologies or biometrics could also be used.

Note that E-Sign is actually broader than electronic signatures. E-Sign covers electronic delivery of documents as well. In industries where documents must be provided by law, this provides an opportunity to deliver the required documents more efficiently. For example, brokerage companies can deliver account statements and fund prospectus electronically, rather than paper form. If two parties wish to transact business electronically, the transactions have the same basis in law as if they were performed on paper. However, if either party does not agree to use electronic records, the transaction has to be performed on paper.

E-Sign does not obligate any party to accept electronic signatures or documents; the law requires consumers to consent to receiving the document electronically.

Health Insurance Portability and Accountability Act (HIPAA)

The Health Insurance Portability and Accountability Act (HIPAA) was passed in 1996. One part of this legislation was designed to improve efficiency through the use of uniform electronic data exchange mechanisms for health information. To achieve this, the legislation required electronic processing and transmission of administrative and financial health care information (HIPAA transactions). Final Rules were published in the *Federal Register* on August 17, 2000, adopting industry standards and requiring that the health industry use them for HIPAA transactions [MBC00b].

FAs with E-Sign, and security concerns, HIPAA also mandates national security and national privacy standards to protect this health information. HIPAA called on Congress to draft the privacy standards. If Congress did not act in a timely fashion, this requirement was to be delegated to the Department of Health and Human Services (HHS). Congress did not act, so HHS published Proposed Regulations late in 1999. Final regulations are expected sometime in 2001.

Clearly, the requirements of HIPAA are in tension. Institutions are required to transmit administrative and financial information electronically. This requirement does not relieve the institution of its obligations to protect the security and confidentiality of personal health information. In addition, individual rights over control of the uses and disclosures of their protected health information are not modified.

As with E-Sign, HIPAA does not mandate the use of specific technologies. Instead, it describes minimum requirements for technical protection and access to the data. For example, HIPAA requires that transmitted patient information and transactions are only accessible by the appropriate person. There is no explicit requirement for encryption or digital signature. However, the broad range of HIPAA requirements certainly promotes the use of a comprehensive security infrastructure such as PKI.

The health care industry has two years to comply with the new standards that implement HIPAA. HIPAA is a two-edged sword. Compliance will not be achieved without cost. However, the act provides an opportunity to improve efficiency of current regulatory paperwork requirements.

Government Paperwork Elimination Act (GPEA)

The Government Paperwork Elimination Act (GPEA) requires federal agencies to offer services electronically. GPEA requires federal agencies, by October 21, 2003, to provide an option to submit information or perform transactions electronically and to maintain records electronically. As with E-Sign and HIPAA, the law specifically establishes the legal standing of electronic records and their related electronic signatures.

Agencies are required to use electronic authentication (electronic signature) methods to verify the identity of the sender and the integrity of electronic content. As with E-Sign, the act was technology neutral. GPEA defines *electronic signature* as any method of signing an electronic message that identifies and authenticates the person who is the source of the message and indicates his or her approval of the contents. Digital signatures and PKI offer a very strong mechanism to implement these requirements.

European Directive 1999/93/EC

The European Directive 1999/93/EC of December 13, 1999, on a Community framework for electronic signatures, established a new legal framework guaranteeing European Union-wide recognition of electronic signatures. As with the U.S. legislation, it specifically states that an electronic signature cannot be legally discriminated against solely on the grounds that it is in electronic form.

However, the Directive goes much farther than E-Sign or GPEA. It says: "If a certificate and the service provider as well as the signature product used meet a set of specific requirements, there will be an automatic assumption that any resulting electronic signatures are as legally valid as a hand-written signature. Moreover, they can be used as evidence in legal proceedings." While E-Sign and GPEA established only the broadest of requirements, the Directive establishes requirements for the CA, the certificate, and the cryptographic device used to generate a signature.

The certificate requirements, such as qualified certificates (QCs), specify the mandatory and optional certificate information. CA requirements address how the system is operated and accredited. Each member state is required to implement an accreditation process for CAs that will issue QCs. The legislation also establishes that CAs are liable for the validity of the certificate content. The legislation places requirements upon the user as well. It requires an approved signature creation device (a cryptographic module). The cryptographic module requirements address key generation, key management, and the signature creation process.

Applications

PKI exists to support the digital signature and key management needs of applications. The utility of a PKI rests in its promise to provide security services to a broad range of applications. Secure Web browsing and secure e-mail are important, but they are not the only applications that require security.

In this section, we attempt to identify some of the applications that are reaching maturity and could be widely available in the next few years. Application areas discussed include signed document formats, PKI-enabled servers, and security for wireless devices.

Signed Document Formats

Signature formats for signed documents are one core area for application development. Replacing paper documents with their electronic equivalents provides opportunities for efficiency and convenience. However, the format of the electronic signatures continues to be problematic. Many applications for signed documents are based on proprietary formats. Others are very limited in the types of signatures that can be expressed.

Two ongoing projects may relieve this situation. The first is the development of the ETSI Electronic Signature Format. The second is the development of an XML signed document format.

ETSI Electronic Signature Format

The ETSI Electronic Signature Format specification defines an electronic signature that remains valid over long periods. To achieve this goal, the signature format includes evidence of its validity that can be used even if the signer or verifying party later attempts to deny the validity of the signature. The document also specifies the use of Time Stamping Authorities (TSAs) to provide verifiable and traceable time. An electronic signature meeting the ETSI electronic signature format can be used for arbitration in case of a dispute between the signer and verifier, which may occur at some later time, even years later. The format includes a signature policy, referenced by the signer, as the basis for establishing the semantics and validity of the electronic signature.

The ETSI format is depicted conceptually in Figure 17.6. The ESTI format defines three levels of signatures. The basic signature, denoted as ES, contains a signature policy identifier, additional signed attributes, and the digital signature. The signature policy identifier specifies the signature semantics. There is a great deal of difference between "I have seen this document and am aware of its contents" and "I agree with the contents of this document." The ES-T format adds a timestamp over the digital signature. The ES-C format adds references to all the certificates and status information that apply to this signature.

The signature policy identifier clarifies the signer's intent. The ES-T timestamp demonstrates that the signature itself was applied on or before a stated time. The certificate and status information (usually CRLs) may be used to establish the validity of the signature public key and its binding to the signer. Note that the certificate and status references

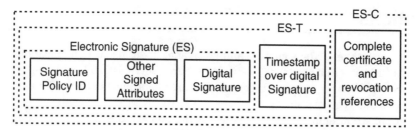

Figure 17.6 ETSI electronic signature format.

could be constructed after signing. This permits the signer to include a reference to a CRL that is issued *after* the document is signed.

The ETSI format is designed as an abstraction, and can be implemented in many underlying technologies. However, a concrete implementation of the ETSI format has been defined in terms of the Cryptographic Message Syntax [HOUS99a], the same syntax that provides the foundation for S/MIME.

XML Signatures

XML is one of the hot buzzwords. Many people predict that XML will replace HTML. Digital signatures of XML content were not supported in the original specification. The W3C and the IETF formed a joint working group to develop a specification for digitally signed XML documents. In this context, a document is any Web resource addressable by a URI. The working group defined a highly extensible solution [EAST00].

Signatures are related to data objects via URIs. Within an XML document, signatures can be related to local data objects. In this case, the signature can be included within an *enveloping signature* or can enclose an *enveloped signature*. A *detached signature* is computed over external network resources or local data objects that reside within disjointed elements of the same XML document as sibling elements. In either case, the signature is neither the parent nor the child of the signed data object.

The XML signature process requires a canonicalization step to prepare the document for signature generation. XML documents may be extensively reformatted without modifying their meaning, and XML processors commonly take advantage of this feature to simplify local processing. However, the digital signature must be generated and verified using precisely the same input. The canonicalization process reformats the document into a unique format so that the input to the generation and verification process is the same.

The canonicalization step is not robust, but the working group is not finished with its work yet. XML signatures will not be widely interoperable until this thorny problem is solved. Once this problem is solved, XML signatures will provide the foundation for exciting new Internet applications.

Wireless Application Protocol (WAP)

The Wireless Application Protocol (WAP) is an open, global specification for providing Internet communications and advanced service to mobile users with wireless devices.

WAP is designed for handheld wireless devices such as mobile telephones, pagers, two-way radios, smart phones and communicators—from low-end to high-end. WAP runs on top of the existing protocols, such as CDMA or GSM for cellular transports. The WAP Forum wrote the WAP specification; it has become a de facto standard. More information on WAP Forum activities can be obtained at http://www.wapforum.org/.

WAP is intended to support a broad range of applications, including e-mail, interactive gaming, shopping, traffic reports, stock trading, and funds transfer. Providing security services to support these diverse applications is a major challenge, especially in light of the limited processing power, memory, and network bandwidth available to these devices.

Current WAP products operate as shown in Figure 17.7. The device is authenticated by the gateway using the basic protocols (for example, CDMA or GSM). The gateway establishes the network connection to a service provider through standard Internet protocols. For example, the connection may use HTTP or SSL. The gateway is able to identify the handset through its normal operations. The Web server identifies the user through passwords or information provided by the gateway. Depending upon the protocol, the information obtained on the user's behalf may be protected in transit between the Internet server and the gateway. The handset depends upon the native protocols for security between the gateway and handset.

This may provide adequate security for many applications, but not for others. The server and handset cannot authenticate each other. This is unacceptable for some of the applications identified earlier, such as funds transfer. To establish end-to-end security, WAP intends to use a PKI. The PKI features will be available in a future release of WAP. The WAP Forum PKI strategy is defined by the *WAP Certificate and CRL Profile* and the *WAP Public Key Infrastructure Definition* [WAP-211, WAP-217].

The WAP Certificate and CRL Profile is based on RFC 2459 [HOUS99]. It specifies three types of certificates: user certificates for authentication, user certificates for digital signatures, and authority certificates for WAP CAs. Future versions will also specify profiles for wireless TLS (WTLS) servers and role (authorization) certificates.

The *WAP Public Key Infrastructure Definition* describes the WAP PKI model and the PKI operations to be supported by each component. The WAP PKI model defines two classes of WAP PKI service: *WAP Class 2* and *WAP Class 3*.

Currently, WAP components implementing WAP Class 2 operate as shown in Figure 17.8. The client is configured with the public key of the root CA. The gateway has generated a key pair and obtained a certificate from a WAP CA. When the handset user wishes to communicate with the server, he or she establishes a WTLS session with the gateway. The gateway establishes an SSL/TLS session with the server. Note that all information is in the clear within the gateway. This is known as the WAP Class 2 Two-Phase Security model.

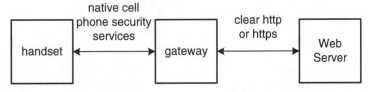

Figure 17.7   Basic WAP client model.

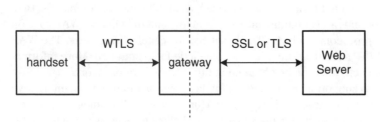

Figure 17.8 WAP Class 2 Two-Phase Security model.

Future versions of WAP will support the WAP Class 2 End-to-End Security model. In this model, the server has also obtained a certificate from a WAP CA. The handset and server are able to establish a WTLS session. The gateway routes the traffic, but it remains encrypted. Figure 17.9 illustrates this architecture.

In WTLS Class 3, the handset will have its own public/private key pair and certificate. The handset private key is used to sign a challenge from the WTLS server. This establishes mutual authentication. As before, WTLS provides confidentiality, but WTLS Class 3 authentication may be applied to either the Two-Phase or End-to-End model.

WTLS Class 3 will also provide for digitally signed data transfer. This mechanism, called *signText*, permits a client device to create a digital signature. This supports some useful application models, including buying stock. In this case, the server responds with the reformatted order and requests confirmation. The client signs the confirmation message to complete the transaction.

PKI-Enabled Trusted Third-Party Services

PKI can enable new services between clients and trusted third parties (TTPs) by supporting confidentiality and mutual authentication. In particular, services where a trusted third party provides some proof or attestation can be implemented. In the discussion of ETSI electronic signature format, we have already referred to one: the timestamp server. We will discuss the timestamp server as one particularly important example of PKI-enabled TTP services.

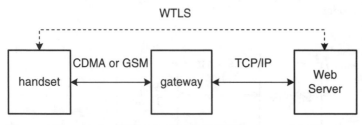

Figure 17.9 End-to-End Security for WAP client.

Timestamping Servers

A timestamping service allows a client to prove at a later date that some datum existed before a particular time. In the ETSI electronic signature, the client can prove that the digital signature was generated before a particular time. A protocol to support these services on the Internet was recently completed by the IETF PKIX Working Group, and it should become an RFC in 2001. The *Internet X.509 Public Key Infrastructure Time Stamp Protocol (TSP)* [ADAM00] describes the format of a request sent to a Time Stamping Authority (TSA) and the response that is returned.

Alice has a document, and she wishes to obtain a timestamp so that she can prove that it exists at this point in time. Alice digitally signs the document, and then she sends the document hash and the signature value to the TSA in a TSP request. Alice sends the hash, not the document. This allows the contents of the document to remain secret. Alice may not be willing to trust the TSA with the document. Also, the document is probably much larger than the hash value, so sending the hash value keeps the network bandwidth requirements small.

The TSA may insist on authenticating Alice. This may be necessary for billing purposes. However, there is no security requirement for the TSA to perform authentication. The TSA generates a signed response and returns it to Alice. Then, Alice validates the digital signature on the signed response, and she stores it for later use.

If a dispute arises, the Alice produces the signed object and the TSA response. The signature on the document is verified in the usual way. After constructing and validating Alice's certification path with respect to the claimed signature time, her public key is used to verify the document signature. This establishes that Alice signed the document with her private key and that it was valid at the claimed signature time.

Next, confirm that the signed response was generated using the hash of the document. The certification path for the TSA must also be validated. If that succeeds, verify the signature on the signed response using the TSA public key.

If Alice's signature and the TSA signature are both valid, including their certification paths, then we have proof that Alice possessed the document in question at that point in time. Note that this does not prove sole possession or origination.

Conclusion

PKI is still a young field. We have made a few predictions about the new features that will appear in products over the next few years. Some will emerge sooner than others. We hope that our crystal ball is not too cloudy. We are looking forward to using many of these new features ourselves.

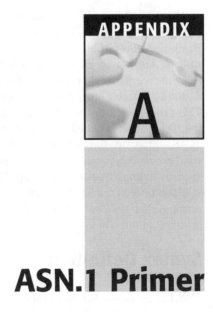

APPENDIX
A

ASN.1 Primer

The reader must have a fundamental understanding of ASN.1 to fully understand the data structures presented in this book, including X.509 certificates and certificate revocation lists (CRLs). For this reason, we include this primer as an appendix. We do not attempt to cover ASN.1 completely; rather, we present just enough material to understand the data structures presented in this book. For a more complete coverage of ASN.1, we suggest [KALI93a], [STEE90], and [LARM00]. Kaliski provides a tutorial of ASN.1-1988 aimed at programmers and standards developers. [KALI93a] is available as a Microsoft Word document on the Web at ftp://ftp.rsasecurity.com/pub/pkcs/doc/layman.doc. Steedman provides a complete discussion of ASN.1-1988. Larmouth provides a complete discussion of ASN.1-1997, and he covers ASN.1-1988 as well.

Much of the discussion in this appendix is adapted with permission from [KALI93a].

Open Systems Interconnection (OSI, defined in [IS7498]) describes a widely accepted architecture for the interconnection of computers. It defines seven protocol layers, from the physical layer up to the application layer. Abstract Syntax Notation One (ASN.1, defined in [X20888]) is a tool for specifying the syntax of data objects used in the application layer. The semantics of the data elements within the data structures is not covered by ASN.1. Generally, prose is used to specify the semantics. ASN.1 is a flexible notation, permitting the definition of a variety of data types. Simple types, such as integers and bit strings, are provided as primitive types. Structured types, such as sets and sequences, can be constructed from a collection of these primitive types.

ASN.1 encoding is the set of rules for representing data structures as a stream of bits. The output for each type consists of a type identifier, a length, and a value. The Basic Encoding Rules (BER, defined in [X20988]) describe how to represent values of each ASN.1 type as a string of octets. Unfortunately, there is almost always more than one way to BER-encode any given value. BER-encoded objects are not suitable for digital signatures, since the signature will only be valid for one of the legal encodings. This property led to the creation of a subset of BER that only permits a single encoding. This subset is called the Distinguished Encoding Rules (DER).

ASN.1 has two flavors: ASN.1-1988 [X20888] and ASN.1-1997 [X68097]. ASN.1-1988 is used exclusively in this book. More programming tools are available that support ASN.1-1988, including a freeware compiler. Also, we find ASN.1-1988 much more intuitive to the unindoctrinated reader. Fortunately, experts can define a data structure in ASN.1-1988 and in ASN.1-1997, such that the resulting DER-encoded output is identical.

Syntax Definition

ASN.1 is a notation for describing abstract types and values. Some types permit a finite number of values; others permit an infinite number of values. ASN.1 has four type classes: simple, structured, tagged, and other. Simple types are primitive; they have no additional components. Structured types have components; they are sets or sequences of other types. Tagged types are derived from any of the other types. Other types are special ones that do not fit in the first three categories; CHOICE and ANY are other types. Types are given names with the ASN.1 assignment operator (::=), and then those names can be used in defining other types.

ASN.1 types, except CHOICE and ANY, have a tag. There are four tag classes: universal, application, private, and context-specific. Universal tags are associated with types whose meaning is the same in all applications; these types are only defined in the ASN.1 specification. Application tags are associated with types whose meaning is specific to one application. For example, application tags are used in the specification of directory names. Care must be exercised with these tags; two different applications may have the same application-specific tag but with completely different meanings. Private tags are associated with types whose meaning is specific to a given enterprise. No private tags are used in this book. Context-specific tags are associated with types whose meaning is specific to a given structured type. Context-specific tags are used to distinguish components within a set or sequence that would otherwise be indistinguishable. For example, if a sequence includes two optional integer types, a context-specific tag is used to remove ambiguity when an instance only includes one of the optional integers.

Types with universal tags are assigned universal tag numbers. Types with other tags are always obtained by either implicit or explicit tagging.

ASN.1 uses a notation that is very similar to a programming language. Comments start with a pair of hyphens (--). Comments end with another pair of hyphens or at the end of the line. Identifiers must begin with a lowercase letter, and type references must begin with uppercase letters.

Simple Types

Simple types are primitive; they have no additional components. Next, the simple types used in this book are briefly described.

BIT STRING. A string of bits. The length in bits does not have to be a multiple of eight.

BMPString. A multilingual string. BMPString is a subtype of UniversalString that models the Basic Multilingual Plane of ISO/IEC 10646-1. This universal type is not part of ASN.1-1988, but most tools allow it to be easily added.

BOOLEAN. A single bit value, either TRUE or FALSE.

GeneralizedTime. A coordinated universal time value, including the date and the time of day. The year is represented with four digits.

IA5String. A string of ASCII characters.

INTEGER. An integer. The value may be positive, zero, or negative.

NULL. A null (or empty) value.

NumericString. A string of digits.

OBJECT IDENTIFIER. A sequence of integer components that identify an object. Object identifiers are often used to name cryptographic algorithms, attributes, name components, and extensions.

OCTET STRING. A string of octets. The length in bits must be a multiple of eight.

PrintableString. A string of printable characters.

TeletexString. A string of teletext characters.

T61String. A string of T.61 characters. Each character is 8 bits long.

UniversalString. A multilingual string. This universal type is not part of ASN.1-1988, but most tools allow it to be easily added.

UTCTime. A coordinated universal time value, including the date and the time of day. The year is represented with two digits; the century digits are omitted.

UTF8String. A multilingual string. The content of this type conforms to RFC 2279. This universal type is not part of ASN.1-1988, but most tools allow it to be easily added.

Structured Types

Structured types are those consisting of components. Next, the structured types used in this book are briefly described.

SEQUENCE. An ordered collection of one or more types. Some or all of the types may be optional.

SEQUENCE OF. An ordered collection of zero or more instances of the same type.

SET.   An unordered collection of one or more types. Some or all of the types may be optional.

SET OF.   An unordered collection of zero or more instances of the same type.

Implicit and Explicit Tagging

Tagging is commonly used to distinguish component types within a structured type. Often, optional components within a set or sequence are given distinct context-specific tags to avoid ambiguity. There are two ways to tag a type: implicitly and explicitly. Implicitly tagged types are derived from other types by changing the tag of the underlying type. Implicit tags are denoted by [*number*] IMPLICIT. Explicitly tagged types are derived from other types by adding an additional tag (or prefix tag) to the underlying type. Think of explicitly tagged types as structured types with a single component of the underlying type. Explicit tags are denoted by [*number*] EXPLICIT.

Explicit tags may be required to avoid ambiguity if the tag of the underlying type is indeterminate. That is, explicit tags may be required if the underlying type is CHOICE or ANY.

Other Types

Other types in ASN.1 include CHOICE and ANY. The CHOICE type provides a list of alternative types. Only one of the alternative types may be selected for a particular instance. The ANY type denotes an arbitrary value of an arbitrary type. An object identifier or an integer value is often used to define the syntax within the arbitrary type.

Basic Encoding Rules

The ASN.1 Basic Encoding Rules (BER) provide one or more unambiguous ways to represent any ASN.1 value as a stream of octets. BER provides three ways to encode an ASN.1 value, depending on the type and whether the length of the value is known. Simple string types employ any of the methods, but structured types employ either of the constructed methods. The three methods are as follows:

Primitive, definite-length method.   This method applies to simple types and implicitly tagged types that are derived from simple types. This method requires that the length of the value be known in advance. Simple nonstring types employ this method.

Constructed, definite-length method.   This method applies to simple string types, structured types, implicitly tagged types that are derived from simple string types and structured types, and any explicitly tagged types. This method requires that the length of the value be known in advance.

Constructed, indefinite-length method.   This method applies to simple string types, structured types, implicitly tagged types that are derived from simple string types and structured types, and any explicitly tagged types. It does not require that the length of the value be known in advance.

In each method, the BER encoding has three or four parts:

Identifier.   These octets identify the class (universal, application, context-specific, or private), indicate whether the type is primitive or constructed, and include the tag number of the ASN.1 value. If the tag number is between 0 and 30, then the identifier is a single octet.

Length.   For definite-length methods, these octets contain the number of octets within the contents. If the length is between 0 and 127, then the length is a single octet. For the constructed, indefinite-length method, these octets contain a flag (a value of '80' hexadecimal) that indicates that the length is indefinite.

Contents.   For the primitive, definite-length method, these octets contain a representation of the value. For the constructed methods, these octets contain the concatenation of the BER-encoded components.

End-of-contents.   For the constructed, indefinite-length method, these two octets denote the end of the contents. The two octets contain a value of '00 00' hexadecimal. For the other methods, these octets are absent.

Distinguished Encoding Rules

The ASN.1 Distinguished Encoding Rules (DER) are a subset of BER, providing exactly one way to represent any ASN.1 value. DER is intended for applications in which a unique (or distinguished) octet stream encoding is needed. For example, a distinguished octet stream is needed when a digital signature is computed on an ASN.1 value, such as the contents of an X.509 certificate. DER is defined in Section 8.7 of [X50988].

DER requires that definite-length encoding always be used. When the length is between 0 and 127, the length must be encoded as a single octet. When the length is 128 or greater, the length must be encoded in the minimum number of octets. For simple string types and implicitly tagged types that are derived from simple string types, the primitive, definite-length method must be employed. For structured types, implicitly tagged types that are derived from structured types, and any explicitly tagged types, the constructed, definite-length method must be employed.

Other restrictions are defined for particular types. These rules ensure that there is only one way to encode any ASN.1 value. In general, the fewest possible number of octets is used to represent the value using definite-length encoding.

Object Identifiers

Object Identifiers (OIDs) are one of the sinple data types defined by ASN.1. An OID is a sequence of integer components (for example, 1.3.6.1) that uniquely identifies an object or an *arc*. Authorities are assigned OIDs in a hierarchical manner. Each authority is responsible for assigning semantics to all subordinate OIDs. An authority may delegate that responsibility to a subordinate authority.

OIDs appear frequently in X.509 certificates. They are used to indicate cryptographic algorithms (for example, RSA or DSA), specify a naming attribute in a distinguished name (for example, organizational unit or common name), identify certificate policies, identify extended key usage (for example, IPsec key management), and identify certificate and CRL extensions.

The OIDs for cryptographic algorithms, naming attributes, and standard extensions have already been defined. A PKI should always use the well-defined OIDs for these functions. PKI products will recognize these OIDs and automatically process the information.

However, almost every PKI deployment will require at least one new OID. Each PKI will need an OID for each supported certificate policy. A typical enterprise PKI might include four or five different policies. Some PKIs will require OIDs to specify locally important application information. For example, a private extended key usage OID might be assigned to indicate that signatures validated with the certified public key are used to approve travel requests for Fox Consulting employees. A smaller number of PKIs will require OIDs for private certificate or CRL extensions. OIDs defined to meet these local PKI requirements are often referred to as *private OIDs*, as they belong to a particular company or organization.

Obtaining Private OIDs

It is critical that private OIDs are obtained from legitimate authorities! Making up an OID will result in collisions, and the system that processes the certificate may misinterpret the information. There are two basic strategies for obtaining legitimate OIDs. The first is to register the objects with an authority. This strategy is very convenient if the PKI uses a small number of relatively stable OIDs to represent certificate policies. The second strategy is to obtain an arc from an authority and assign OIDs as needed. This strategy may be preferred if policies are less stable or many OIDs are needed.

Legitimate OIDs can be obtained from a variety of sources. Any of these sources may be used. The important point is that the OID be legitimate, so it is unique. A few of the more common sources are discussed next.

American National Standards Institute

ANSI is the registration authority for the United States for organization names under the global registration process established by ISO and ITU. A fact sheet with links to an application form is located at the ANSI Web site (http://web.ansi.org/public/services/reg_org.html). The ANSI OID arc for organizations is 2.16.840.1.

ANSI maintains a database that is searched with every new registration request to ensure that duplicate OIDs are never registered. ANSI has developed formal procedures to administer this process. These procedures specify the syntax of names, describe the way in which applications for organization names are handled, including mechanisms for assuring the assignment of unique names at this level in the hierarchy, and provide for the assignment of organization names.

Under these procedures, the client may choose to register an *alphanumeric name*, a *numeric name*, or both. At the time of publication, the fees are $1,500, $1,000, and $2,500, respectively. Contact ANSI or visit the Web page to verify the current fee structure.

It takes approximately two weeks to receive the assigned numeric name from ANSI. ANSI will assign a number (NEWNUM), creating a new OID arc: 2.16.840.1.NEWNUM. To register an alphanumeric name, ANSI conducts a three-month public review to ensure that there are no challenges to the requested name.

ANSI has already assigned arcs to each state government (for example, Maryland and Virginia) in the United States. The states have been assigned arcs of the form 2.16.840.3.(STATENUM), where (STATENUM) is the FIPS state code, as defined by FIPS 5-2. FIPS 5-2 may be obtained at http://www.itl.nist.gov/fipspubs/. To identify the naming authority for a particular state, contact ANSI.

Other National Standards Bodies

In most countries, the national standards association maintains an OID registry. As with the ANSI arc, these are generally arcs assigned under the OID 2.16.

It may take some investigation to find the OID authority for a particular country. The addresses for ISO national member bodies can be found at http://www.iso.ch/addresse/

membodies.html. The information includes postal address and electronic mail address. In many cases, a Web site is specified as well. It may take a few iterations to find the right contact.

Another possible starting point is the International Register of ISO DCC NSAP schemes. NSAP stands for Network Service Access Point, and is used in various international standards. The registry for schemes may be obtained at http://www.fei.org.uk/fei/dcc-nsap.htm. The Web site currently lists contact information for 13 naming authorities, some of which will also assign OIDs.

Internet Assigned Numbers Authority

The Internet Assigned Numbers Authority (IANA) assigns private enterprise numbers, which are OIDs, in the arc 1.3.6.1.4.1. For example, SPYRUS has been assigned the private enterprise number 1.3.6.1.4.1.1152. IANA has assigned arcs to over 7500 companies to date.

The application page is located at http://www.iana.org/forms.html, under Private Enterprise Numbers. The IANA usually takes about one week to assign a private enterprise number. An OID from IANA is free. IANA will assign a number (NEWNUM) so that the new OID arc will be 1.3.6.1.4.1.NEWNUM.

Computer Security Objects Registry

The U.S. federal government maintains the Computer Security Objects Registry (CSOR). The CSOR is the naming authority for the arc 2.16.840.1.101.3, and is currently registering objects for security labels, cryptographic algorithms, and certificate policies. The certificate policy OIDs are defined in the arc 2.16.840.1.101.3.2.1.

The CSOR provides policy OIDs to agencies of the U.S. federal government. For more information about the CSOR, go to http://csrc.nist.gov/csor/. For more information on OIDs for certificate policies, go to http://csrc.nist.gov/csor/pkireg.htm.

Researching OIDs

As PKIs grow and cross-certify with other enterprise PKIs, unrecognized OIDs may be encountered. In many cases, unrecognized information may simply be ignored. For example, non-critical private extensions can be readily ignored. In other cases, such as certificate policies, one may need to track down the OID and determine its meaning. Several useful resources are available when an unrecognized OID is encountered.

Harald Alvestrand maintains an Object Identifier Registry, which can be accessed at http://www.alvestrand.no/objectid/. This registry shows the OID value, provides a description, and includes links to superior references. If the OID identifier is an arc, it also includes links to its immediate subordinates. This registry is not an official database, and it depends upon voluntary submissions.

Another resource is the configuration file that is provided with the dumpasn1 utility program written by Peter Gutmann. The DumpASN1 utility can be obtained from a variety of Web sites, including Peter's home page, http://www.cs.auckland.ac.nz/~pgut001/index.html. The configuration file includes over 1100 security-related OIDs, with very brief comments and the common textual name for each OID.

To identify the company and the authority contact information for OIDs in the IANA private enterprise number arc, go to ftp://ftp.isi.edu/in-notes/iana/assignments/enterprise-numbers. The Web site lists over 7500 arcs, most of which list the electronic mail address for the authority as well.

To determine the name and semantics of OIDs assigned by the CSOR arc, go to http://csrc.nist.gov/csor/. If the OID is associated with a certificate policy, the CP will be available at that site.

Bibliography

[ADAM99]   Adams, C., and S. Farrell, *Internet X.509 Public Key Infrastructure Certificate Management Protocols*, RFC 2510, 1999.

[ADAM00]   Adams, C., P. Cain, D. Pinkas, and R. Zuccherato, *Internet X.509 Public Key Infrastructure Time Stamp Protocol (TSP)*, work in progress, 2000.

[ATKI96]   Atkins, D., W. Stallings, and P. Zimmermann, *PGP Message Exchange Formats*, RFC 1991, 1996.

[BALE93]   Balenson, D., *Privacy Enhancement for Internet Electronic Mail: Part III: Algorithms, Modes, and Identifiers*, RFC 1423, 1993.

[BERN94]   Berners-Lee, T., L. Masinter, and M. McCahill, *Uniform Resource Locators (URL)*, RFC 1738, 1994.

[BAUE82]   Bauer, R., and T. Berson, "Local Network Cryptosystem Architecture," *Proceedings of IEEE COMPCON*, February 1982.

[BAUE83]   Bauer, R., T. Berson, and R. Feiertag, "A Key Distribution Protocol Using Event Markers," *ACM Transactions on Computer Systems*, vol. 1, no. 3, 1983, pp. 249–255.

[BOEY99]   Boeyen, S., T. Howes, and P. Richard, *Internet X.509 Public Key Infrastructure LDAPv2 Schema*, RFC 2587, 1999.

[BOE400]   Boeyen, S., and P. Hallam-Baker, *Internet X.509 Public Key Infrastructure Repository Locator Service*, work in progress, 2000.

[BURR98]   Burr, W., and W. Polk, "A Federal PKI With Multiple Digital Signature Algorithms," *PKS98 Conference*, April 1998.

[CAISO99a] California Independent System Operator, *Certificate Policies For The California Independent System Operator Public Key Infrastructure*, Version 1.1, June 1999.

[CAISO99b] California Independent System Operator, *California Independent System Operator—Certification Practice Statement—Generator Communications Certification Authority*, Version 1.07, July 1999.

[CAISO99c] California Independent System Operator, *California Independent System Operator—Certification Practice Statement—Medium Assurance Certification Authority*, Version 1.04, July 1999.

[CAISO99d] California Independent System Operator, *California Independent System Operator—Certification Practice Statement—Basic Certification Authority*, Version 1.08, June 1999.

[CAISO99e] California Independent System Operator, *CA ISO Certification Practice Statement—User Security Considerations*, 1999.

[CALL98] Callas, J., L., Donnerhacke, H. Finney, and R. Thayer, *OpenPGP Message Format*, RFC 2440, 1998.

[CHOK99] Chokhani, S., and W. Ford, *Internet X.509 Public Key Infrastructure Certificate Policy and Certification Practices Framework*, RFC 2527, 1999.

[COOP99] Cooper, D., "A Model of Certificate Revocation," *Proceedings of the Fifteenth Annual Computer Security Applications Conference*, December 1999, pp. 256–264.

[COOP00] Cooper, D., "An Efficient Use of Delta CRLs," *Proceedings of the 2000 IEEE Symposium on Security and Privacy*, May 2000, pp. 190–202.

[CROC95] Crocker, S., N. Freed, J. Galvin, and S. Murphy, *MIME Object Security Services*, RFC 1848, 1995.

[DENN81] Denning, D., and G. Sacco, "Timestamps in Key Distribution Protocols," *Communications of the ACM*, vol. 24, no. 8, 1981, pp. 533–536.

[DIER99] Dierks, T., and C. Allen, *The TLS Protocol Version 1.0*, RFC 2246, 1999.

[DIFF76] Diffie, W., and M. Hellman,. "New Directions in Cryptography," *IEEE Transactions on Information Theory*, vol. IT-22, no. 6, 1976, pp. 644–654.

[DUSS98a] Dusse, S., P. Hoffman, B. Ramsdell, L. Lundblade, and L. Repka, *S/MIME Version 2 Message Specification*, RFC 2311, 1998.

[DUSS98b] Dusse, S., P. Hoffman, B. Ramsdell, and J. Weinstein, *S/MIME Version 2 Certificate Handling*, RFC 2312, 1998.

[EFF98] Electronic Frontier Foundation, *Cracking DES*, Sebastopol: O'Reilly & Associates, Inc., 1998.

[ELKI96] Elkins, M., *MIME Security with Pretty Good Privacy (PGP)*, RFC 2015, 1996.

[EP99] Directive 1999/93/EC of the European Parliament and of the Council of 13 December 1999 on a Community framework for electronic signatures.

[ETSI00a] European Telecommunications Standards Institute, *Electronic Signature Formats*, ETSI TS 101 733 v1.2.2 (2000-10).

[ETSI00b] European Telecommunications Standards Institute, *Time Stamping Profile*, draft ETSI TS 101 861 v1.1.4 (2000-10).

[ETSI00c] European Telecommunications Standards Institute, *Qualified Certificate Profile*, draft ETSI TS 101 862 v0.0.2 (2000-10).

[FARR00]   Farrell, S., and R. Housley, *An Internet Attribute Certificate Profile for Authorization*, work in progress, 2000.

[FIEL97]   Fielding, R., J. Gettys, J. Mogul, H. Frystyk, and T. Berners-Lee, *Hypertext Transfer Protocol—HTTP/1.1*, RFC 2068, 1997.

[FIPS5]   U.S. Department of Commerce, *Codes for the Identification of the States, The District of Columbia and the Outlying Areas of the United States, and Associated Areas*, Federal Information Processing Standards Publication 5-2, 1987. [Supersedes FIPS 5-1 published in 1970.]

[FIPS46]   U.S. Department of Commerce, *Data Encryption Standard*, Federal Information Processing Standards Publication 46, 1977.

[FIPS81]   U.S. Department of Commerce, *DES Modes of Operation*, Federal Information Processing Standards Publication 81, 1980.

[FIPS113]   U.S. Department of Commerce, *Computer Data Authentication*, Federal Information Processing Standards Publication 113, 1985.

[FIPS140]   U.S. Department of Commerce, *Security Requirements for Cryptographic Modules*, Federal Information Processing Standards Publication 140-1, 1994. [Supersedes FIPS 140 General Security Requirements for Equipment Using the Data Encryption Standard.]

[FIPS180]   U.S. Department of Commerce, *Secure Hash Standard*, Federal Information Processing Standards Publication 180-1, 1995. [Supersedes FIPS PUB 180 published in 1993.]

[FIPS186]   U.S. Department of Commerce, *Digital Signature Standard (DSS)*, Federal Information Processing Standards Publication 186, 1994.

[FIPS196]   U.S. Department of Commerce, *Standard for Entity Authentication Using Public Key Cryptography*, Federal Information Processing Standards Publication 196, 1997.

[FORD94]   Ford, W., *Computer Communications Security: Principles Standard Protocols and Techniques*, Englewood Cliffs, NJ: Prentice Hall, 1994.

[FREI96]   Freier, A., P. Karlton, and P. Kocher, *The SSL Protocol, Version 3.0*, Netscape Communications, 1996. [http://home.netscape.com/eng/ssl3/draft302.txt]

[GALV95]   Galvin, J., S. Murphy, S. Crocker, and N. Freed, *Security Multiparts for MIME: Multipart/Signed and Multipart/Encrypted*, RFC 1847, 1995.

[GUTM00]   Gutmann, P, *X.509 Style Guide*, August 2000. [http://www.cs.auckland.ac.nz/~pgut001/pubs/x509guide.txt]

[HALL95]   Haller, N., *The S/KEY One-Time Password System*, RFC 1760, 1995.

[HARK98]   Harkins, D., and D. Carrel, *The Internet Key Exchange (IKE)*, RFC 2409, 1998.

[HOFF99]   Hoffman, P., *Enhanced Security Services for S/MIME*, RFC 2634, 1999.

[HOFF00]   Hoffman, P., private correspondence, Electronic mail on path validation.

[HORO97]   Horowitz, M., and S. J. Lunt, *FTP Security Extensions*, RFC 2228, 1997.

[HOUS95]   Housley, R., "Message Security Protocol," *InSight*, May 1995, p. 12.

[HOUS99]   Housley, R., W. Ford, W. Polk, and D. Solo, *Internet X.509 Public Key Infrastructure Certificate and CRL Profile*, RFC 2459, 1999.

[HOUS99a]   Housley, R., *Cryptographic Message Syntax*, RFC 2630, 1999.

[HOUS99b]   Housley, R., and W. Polk, *Representation of Key Exchange Algorithm (KEA) Keys in Internet X.509 Public Key Infrastructure Certificates*, RFC 2528, 1999.

[HOUS99c]   Housley, R., and P. Hoffman, *Internet X.509 Public Key Infrastructure Operational Protocols: FTP and HTTP*, RFC 2585, 1999.

[HOWE95]   Howes, T., S. Kille, W. Yeong, and C. Robbins, *The String Representation of Standard Attribute Syntaxes*, RFC 1778, 1995.

[IS7498a]   ISO/IEC, *Information technology—Information Processing Systems—Open Systems Interconnection—Basic Reference Model—The Basic Model*, ISO/IEC 7498-1:1994.

[IS7498b]   ISO/IEC, *Information technology—Information Processing Systems—Open Systems Interconnection—Basic Reference Model—Part 2: Security Architecture*, ISO/IEC 7498-2:1989.

[IS8372]   ISO/IEC, *Information Processing—Modes of operation for a 64-bit block cipher algorithm*, International Standard 8372, 1987.

[ISRA82]   Israel, J., and T. Linden, *Authentication in Star and Network Systems*, Xerox Corporation, Office Systems Division, OSD-T8201, 1982.

[KAHN67]   Kahn, D., *The Codebreakers: The Story of Secret Writing*, New York: Macmillan, 1967.

[KALI93a]   Kaliski, B., *A Layman's Guide to a Subset of ASN.1, BER, and DER*, An RSA Laboratories Technical Note, 1993. [ftp://ftp.rsasecurity.com/pub/pkcs/doc/layman.doc]

[KALI93b]   Kaliski, B., *Privacy Enhancement for Internet Electronic Mail: Part IV: Key Certification and Related Services*, RFC 1424, 1993.

[KALI98a]   Kaliski, B., *PKCS #10: Certification Request Syntax, Version 1.5*, RFC 2314, 1998.

[KALI98b]   Kaliski, B., *PKCS #7: Cryptographic Message Syntax, Version 1.5*, RFC 2315, 1998.

[KAUF95]   Kaufman, C., R. Perlman, and M Speciner, *Network Security: Private Communication in a Public World*, Englewood Cliffs, NJ: Prentice Hall, 1995.

[KAUF99]   Kaufman, E., and A. Newman, *Implementing IPsec: Making Security Work on VPNs, Intranets, and Extranets*, New York: John Wiley, 1999.

[KENT89]   Kent, S., *Privacy Enhancement for Internet Electronic Mail: Part II: Certificate-Based Key Management*, RFC 1114, 1989.

[KENT93]   Kent, S., *Privacy Enhancement for Internet Electronic Mail: Part II: Certificate-Based Key Management*, RFC 1422, 1993.

[KENT98a]   Kent, S., and R. Atkinson, *Security Architecture for the Internet Protocol*, RFC 2401, 1998.

[KENT98b]   Kent, S., and R. Atkinson, *IP Authentication Header*, RFC 2402, 1998.

[KENT98c]   Kent, S., and R. Atkinson, *IP Encapsulating Security Payload (ESP)*, RFC 2406, 1998.

[KOHL93]   Kohl, J., and C. Neuman, *The Kerberos Network Authentication Service (V5)*, RFC 1510, 1993.

[KRAW97]   Krawczyk, H., M. Bellare, and R. Canetti, *HMAC: Keyed-Hashing for Message Authentication*, RFC 2104, 1997.

[LAMP81]   Lamport, L., "Password Authentication with Insecure Communication," *Communications of the ACM*, vol. 24, no. 11, 1981, pp. 770–772.

[LARM00]   Larmouth, J., *ASN.1 Complete*, San Diego: Morgan Kaufmann Academic Press, 2000.

[LINN87]   Linn, J., *Privacy Enhancement for Internet Electronic Mail: Part I: Message Encryption and Authentication Procedures*, RFC 989, 1987.

[LINN88]   Linn, J., *Privacy Enhancement for Internet Electronic Mail: Part I: Message Encryption and Authentication Procedures*, RFC 1040, 1988.

[LINN89a]   Linn, J., *Privacy Enhancement for Internet Electronic Mail: Part I: Message Encryption and Authentication Procedures*, RFC 1113, 1989.

[LINN89b]   Linn, J., *Privacy Enhancement for Internet Electronic Mail: Part III: Algorithms, Modes, and Identifiers*, RFC 1115, 1989.

[LINN93]   Linn, J., *Privacy Enhancement for Internet Electronic Mail: Part I: Message Encryption and Authentication Procedures*, RFC 1421, 1993.

[MADS98a]   Madson, C., and R. Glenn, *The Use of HMAC-MD5-96 within ESP and AH*, RFC 2403, 1998.

[MADS98b]   Madson, C., and R. Glenn, *The Use of HMAC-SHA-1-96 within ESP and AH*, RFC 2404, 1998.

[MADS98c]   Madson, C., and N. Doraswamy, *The ESP DES-CBC Cipher Algorithm With Explicit IV*, RFC 2405, 1998.

[MALP00]   Malpani, A., P. Hoffman, and R. Housley, *Simple Certificate Validation Protocol (SCVP)*, work in progress, December 2000.

[MAUG98]   Maughan, D., M. Schertler, M. Schneider, and J. Turner, *Internet Security Association and Key Management Protocol (ISAKMP)*, RFC 2408, 1998.

[MBC00a]   McBride Baker & Coles, *The Federal E-Sign Law—Why Was It Passed, What Does It Mean?*, 2000. [http://www.mbc.com/news]

[MBC00b]   McBride Baker & Coles, *HIPAA Mandates Privacy and Security Regulations for Electronic Health Information*, 2000. [http://www.mbc.com/news]

[MENE97]   Memezes, A., P. vanOorschot, and S. Vanstone, *Handbook of Applied Cryptography*, New York: CRC Press LLP, 1997.

[MILL96]   Mills, D., *Simple Network Time Protocol (SNTP) Version 4 for IPv4, IPv6 and OSI*, RFC 2030, 1996.

[MYER99]   Myers, M., C. Adams, D. Solo, and D. Kemp, *Internet X.509 Certificate Request Message Format*, RFC 2511, 1999.

[MYER00a]   Myers, M., X. Liu, J. Schaad, and J. Weinstein, *Certificate Management Messages over CMS*, RFC 2797, 2000.

[MYER00b]   Myers, M., R. Ankey, and C. Adams, *Online Certificate Status Protocol, Version 2*, work in progress, September 2000.

[MYER00c]   Myers, M., S. Farrell, and C. Adams, *Delegated Path Discovery with OCSP*, work in progress, September 2000.

[MYER00d]   Myers, M., C. Adams, and S. Farrell, *Delegated Path Validation*, work in progress, September 2000.

[NEED78]   Needham, R., and M. Schroeder, "Using Encryption for Authenticating in Large Networks of Computers," *Communications of the ACM*, vol. 21, no. 12, 1978, pp. 995–999.

[NEUM94]   Neuman, C., and T. Ts'o, "Kerberos: An Authentication Service for Computer Networks," *IEEE Communications*, vol. 32, no. 9, 1994, pp. 33–38.

[NIST98]   SKIPJACK and KEA Algorithm Specifications, Version 2.0, 1998. [http://csrc.nist.gov/encryption/skipjack-kea.htm]

[ORMA98]   Orman, H., *The OAKLEY Key Determination Protocol*, RFC 2412, 1998.

[ORMA00]   Orman, H., and P. Hoffman, *Determining Strengths For Public Keys Used For Exchanging Symmetric Keys*, work in progress, August 2000.

[PIPE98]   Piper, D., *The Internet IP Security Domain of Interpretation for ISAKMP*, RFC 2407, 1998.

[POLK00]   Polk, T., and N. Hastings, "Bridge Certification Authorities: Connecting B2B Public Key Infrastructures," *PKI Forum Meeting Proceedings*, June 27–29, 2000.

[PKCS00]   RSA Laboratories, *PKCS #1 v2.0 Amendment 1: Multi-Prime RSA*, RSA Security, 2000.

[POST80]   Postel, J., *User Datagram Protocol*, RFC 768, 1980.

[POST81]   Postel, J., *Transport Control Protocol*, RFC 793, 1981.

[RAMS99a]   Ramsdell, B., *S/MIME Version 3 Certificate Handling*, RFC 2632, 1999.

[RAMS99b]   Ramsdell, B., *S/MIME Version 3 Message Specification*, RFC 2633, 1999.

[RESC99]   Rescorla, E., *Diffie-Hellman Key Agreement Method*, RFC 2631, 1999.

[RIVE78]   Rivest, R., A. Shamir, and L. Adleman, "A Method for Obtaining Digital Signatures and Public-Key Cryptosystems," *Communications of the ACM*, vol. 21, no. 2, 1978, pp. 120–126.

[RIVE92]   Rivest, R., *The MD5 Message Digest Algorithm*, RFC 1321, 1992.

[SANT01]   Santesson, S., W. Polk, P. Barzin, and M. Nystrom, *Internet X.509 Public Key Infrastructure Qualified Certificates Profile*, RFC 3039, 2001.

[SCHN96]   Schneier, B., *Applied Cryptography: Protocols, Algorithms, and Source Code in C*, 2nd ed., New York: John Wiley, 1996.

[SDN701a]   Secure Data Network System, *Message Security Protocol*, Specification SDN.701, Revision 1.5, 1989.

Dinkel, C., *Secure Data Network System (SDNS) Network, Transport, and Message Security Protocols, Standard for Entity Authentication Using Public Key Cryptography*, U.S. Department of Commerce, National Institute of Standards and Technology, NISTIR 90-4250.

[SDN701b]   Secure Data Network System, *Message Security Protocol*, Specification SDN.701, Revision 3.0, 1994.

[SDN701c]   Secure Data Network System, *Message Security Protocol 4.0*, Specification SDN.701, Revision B, 1998.

[SDN702]   Secure Data Network System, *Directory Specifications for Utilization with SDNS Message Security Protocol*, Specification SDN.702, Revision 2.6, 1994.

[SDN703]   Secure Data Network System, *X.400 Rekey Agent Protocol*, Specification SDN.703, Revision 0.9, 1991.

[SDN908]   Secure Data Network System, *MISSI Management Protocol (MMP)*, Specification SDN.908, 1999.

[STEE90]   Steedman, D., *Abstract Syntax Notation One (ASN.1): The Tutorial and Reference*, Twickenham: Technology Appraisals Ltd., 1990.

[STEI88]   Steiner, J., C. Neuman, and J. Schiller, "Kerberos: An Authentication Service for Open Network Systems," *Proceedings of the Winter 1988 Usenix Conference*, 1988.

[SWAN98]   Swanson, M., et al., *Guide for Developing Security Plans for Information Technology Systems*, NIST Special Publication 800-18, December 1998.

[TEBB95]   Tebbut, J., *Guidelines for the Evaluation of X.500 Directory Products*, NIST Special Publication 500-228, May 1995.

[TUCH79]   Tuchman, W., "Hellman Presents No Shortcut Solutions to DES," *IEEE Spectrum*, vol. 6, no. 7, July 1979, pp. 40–41.

[TUNG00]   Tung, B., C. Neuman, M. Hur, A. Medvinsky, S. Medvinsky, J. Wray, and J. Trostle, *Public Key Cryptography for Initial Authentication in Kerberos*, work in progress, June 2000.

[W21100]   Wireless Application Forum, *Wireless Application Protocol—WAP Certificate and CRL Profiles*, Proposed Version 9, March 2000.

[W21700]   Wireless Application Forum, *Wireless Application Protocol—Public Key Infrastructure Definition*, Proposed Version 3, March 2000.

[X20888]   CCITT, *Specification of Abstract Syntax Notation One (ASN.1)*, Recommendation X.208, 1988.

[X20988]   CCITT, *Specification of Basic Encoding Rules for Abstract Syntax Notation One* (ASN.1), Recommendation X.209, 1988.

[X392]   American National Standards Institute, *Data Encryption Algorithm*, ANSI X3.92, 1981. [Most recently reaffirmed in 1998.]

[X50988]   CCITT, *The Directory—Authentication Framework*, Recommendation X.509, 1988.

[X50997]   ITU-T, *The Directory—Authentication Framework*, Recommendation X.509, 1997.

[X50900]   ITU-T, *The Directory-Authentication Framework*, Recommendation X.509, 2000.

[X68097]   ITU-T, *Information Technology—Abstract Syntax Notation One (ASN.1): Specification of Basic Notation*, Recommendation X.680, 1997.

[X68197]   ITU-T, *Information Technology—Abstract Syntax Notation One (ASN.1): Information Object Specification*, Recommendation X.681, 1997.

[X68297]   ITU-T, *Information Technology—Abstract Syntax Notation One (ASN.1): Constraint Specification*, Recommendation X.682, 1997.

[X68397]   ITU-T, *Information Technology—Abstract Syntax Notation One (ASN.1): Parameterization of ASN.1 Specifications*, Recommendation X.683, 1997.

[X69097]   ITU-T, *Information Technology—ASN.1 Encoding Rules: Specification of Basic Encoding Rules (BER), Canonical Encoding Rules (CER) and Distinguished Encoding Rules (DER)*, Recommendation X.690, 1997.

[X69197]   ITU-T, *Information Technology—ASN.1 Encoding Rules: Specification of Packed Encoding Rules (PER)*, Recommendation X.691, 1997.

[X9301]   American National Standards Institute, *Public Key Cryptography for the Financial Services Industry—Part 1: The Digital Signature Algorithm (DSA)*, X9.30-1, 1997.

[X9302]   American National Standards Institute, *Public Key Cryptography Using Irreversible Algorithms for the Financial Services Industry, Part 2:*

The Secure Hash Algorithm (SHA-1), ANSI X9.30-2, 1997. (Originally published in 1993.)

[X952]   American National Standards Institute, *Triple Data Encryption Algorithm Modes of Operation*, ANSI X9.52, 1998.

[X955]   American National Standards Institute, *Public Key Cryptography For The Financial Services Industry: Extensions To Public Key Certificates And Certificate Revocation Lists*, ANSI X9.55, 1995.

[X957]   American National Standards Institute, *Public Key Cryptography for the Financial Services Industry: Certificate Management*, ANSI X9.57, 1997.

[XNS82]   Xerox Corporation, *Authentication Protocol*, XSIS 098210, October 1982.

[XNS84]   Xerox Corporation, *Authentication Protocol*, XSIS 098404, April 1984.

[YEON95]   Yeong, Y., T. Howes, and S. Kille, *Lightweight Directory Access Protocol*, RFC 1777, 1995.

Index